OUT
OF THE
PAST

ALEXANDRA TOLSTOY

translated by various hands
edited by
Katharine Strelsky and Catherine Wolkonsky

NEW YORK   COLUMBIA UNIVERSITY PRESS   1981

Library of Congress Cataloging in Publication Data

Tolstoy, Alexandra, 1884–1979.
Out of the past.

Includes material reprinted from: I worked
for the soviet. New Haven : Yale University
Press, 1934.
"Publications of Alexandra Tolstoy:" p.
Includes index.
1. Tolstoy, Alexandra, 1884–1979.   2. Soviet
Union—Biography.   3. United States—Biography.
4. Tolstoy family.   5. Tolstoy, Leo, graf,
1828–1910—Biography—Descendants.
I. Strelsky, Katharine.   II. Wolkonsky,
Catherine.   III. Tolstoy, Alexandra, 1884–
1979.   I worked for the soviet.   1934.
IV. Title.
CT1218.T63A35   947.084′092′4   [B]   81-7714
ISBN 0-231-05100-X   AACR2

Columbia University Press
New York and Guildford, Surrey

*Clothbound editions of Columbia University Press books are
Smyth-sewn and printed on permanent and durable acid-free paper.*

Contents

Entrance to Yasnaya Polyana, the Tolstoy estate. Photograph taken about 1908.

One of the villages within Yasnaya Polyana.

Houses in Yasnaya Polyana. The roofs of the log cabins were either
thatched or made of shingles or sheet iron.

Peasants at Yasnaya Polyana drinking tea on Sunday after mass.
About 1905.

Girls in homespun clothes. In summer they wore sandals made of birch, in winter felt boots. About 1905.

The Tolstoy residence at Yasnaya Polyana. In the foreground is the "tree of the poor," so named because people asking for help came here to wait for Tolstoy to give them money.

The Tolstoy family on their porch. From left to right: unknown visitor; Andrei; Tolstoy; Alexandra; Leo junior; Maria; and Tolstoy's wife Sophia holding little Ivan. About 1892.

The Tolstoy family at table in the garden. From left to right: Mikhail; Tolstoy; Ivan; Leo junior; Alexandra; Andrei; Tatiana; Sophia; and Maria.

The Tolstoy family with some of their tutors. Counterclockwise from the left: Mikhail (at the head of the table); his friend Diakov; the French tutor; the Russian tutor; Maria; Miss Walsh (Alexandra's governess); Alexandra (nine years old at this time); Sophia; the composer Taneyev; Tolstoy; Tatiana; Nadia Ivanov (a neighbor from Tula); Andrei; and an unknown Tolstoyan.

After tennis. Alexandra is on the left holding a racket; her brother Mikhail is lying on the grass; Tolstoy is in the center with Sophia on his right. Standing behind Tolstoy is Count Leo Bobrinsky, great grandson of the empress Catherine the Great.

Tolstoy (in the foreground) playing tennis. Opposite him, on the other side of the net, is Alexandra, in a white dress. Tatiana is sitting on the grass with her mother Sophia standing next to her.

On the far left is Dr. Makovitsky, sitting next to Alexandra. To her left is Tolstoy's niece, Princess Obolensky; then Vladimir Chertkov, a Tolstoyan and editor of Tolstoy's works, who is sitting next to Tolstoy. Sophia is at the head of the table. Secretaries and guests sit at the right side of the table, and two waiters—Vanya Shuraev and Ilya Vasilievich Sidarkov—are standing.

Alexandra riding sidesaddle on her Arabian horse at Yasnaya Polyana. About 1905.

Tolstoy; Alexandra (near window); and typist Barbara Feokritova. About
1905.

From left to right: Maria Nikolaevna (Tolstoy's sister, who became a nun after her second husband died); Tolstoy; Alexandra (standing); Tatiana; Sophia; and Ivan. Mikhail, Alexandra's brother, is the father of the two children. About 1908.

Tolstoy with Alexandra. About 1908.

Tolstoy drinking tea with guests at Yasnaya Polyana. This is one from a set of stereopticon views of the Tolstoy family and Yasnaya Polyana. About 1908.

15. Яснополянскій паркъ. На переднемъ планѣ дочь Л. Н. Толстого, графиня А. Л. Толстая.

1907

Alexandra about 1905. Another stereopticon view.

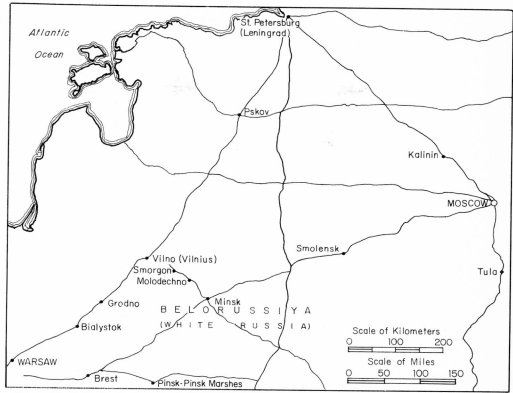

The northwestern front, 1914–1917.

Alexandra in her nursing uniform on the Caucasus front in 1915.

Alexandra in her Caucasian cloak (*shuba*) while working on
the Caucasus front in the mountains in 1915.

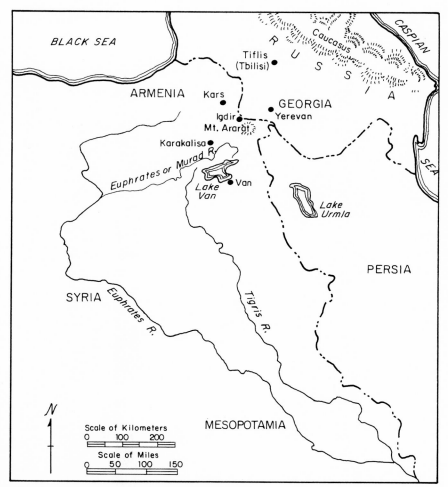

The Russian Caucasian front, spring 1915.

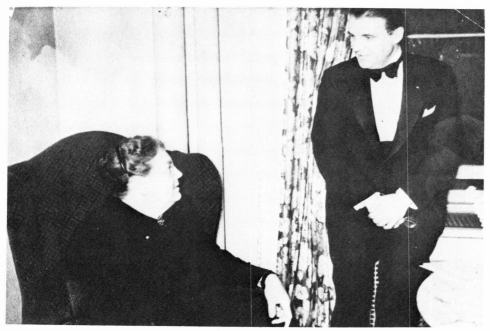

Professor Nikander Strelsky, founder and chairman of the Russian Department at Vassar College and later director of the Tolstoy Foundation, with Alexandra the first time she lectured at Vassar, about 1940.

COUNTESS ALEXANDRA TOLSTOY

YOUNGEST DAUGHTER OF THE FAMOUS WRITER AND PHILOSOPHER, LEO TOLSTOY

President of THE TOLSTOY FOUNDATION which is dedicated to protecting the rights and liberties of non-Communistic Russians in this country, and from whose refuge the school teacher, Oksana Kasenkina, was kidnapped by the Russian Consul General. Author of "L E O T O L S T O Y, M Y F A T H E R"

Be sure to hear the Countess' revealing and factual lecture on:

"Christianity Can Conquer Communism"

Exclusive Management: LEE KEEDICK, 475 Fifth Avenue, New York 17, Phone MU 3-5627

Poster announcing one of Alexandra's American lectures.

Former weaving shop at Yasnaya Polyana, built by Tolstoy's maternal grandfather, Prince Volkonsky. Alexandra later renovated this building and, after her mother's death in 1919, moved here from the main house and lived on the upper floor. She set up other apartments in the building for the staff of the museum at Yasnaya Polyana.

The school at Yasnaya Polyana, built by Alexandra. It was damaged by the Germans in World War II and is now completely restored. This photograph was taken in the late twenties.

Alexandra in 1932 in the United States.

The farmhouse near Newtown Square, Pennsylvania.

Alexandra with her cow in Pennsylvania.

Alexandra working in her kitchen garden.

Alexandra's older brother Ilya, shortly before
his death in 1933.

Ilya's cottage at Churaevka, a Russian village near Southbury, Connecticut.

Alexandra in 1976.

Foreword

Can I have lived only one lifetime? For there seem to have been many lives, no one like another.

The first and best period of my life was with my father. It lasted twenty-six years—perhaps only six or eight conscious years, and perhaps then not fully conscious, for it was not an easy period. When my father died, everything stood still for a time. Life seemed over. There was no longer anyone to live for; I had no purpose. There was an emptiness I did not know how to fill. Then World War I broke out, and I turned all my energies to working first as a nurse and then as a representative of the All-Union Zemstvo Medical Service.

In 1917 the Revolution erupted. Everything was suddenly upside down. Nothing remained of the traditions or the faith in which I had been brought up. I had to seek quite a new path in life.

For twelve years I struggled to find some possibility for creative work. Finally I succeeded in organizing a cultural center at Yasnaya Polyana.* The house where my father had lived became a museum. A second museum there was filled with his things, with portraits and photographs from his former school for chil-

---

*Yasnaya Polyana was the family estate of 2500 acres in the province of Tula, a hundred and thirty miles south of Moscow. The Tolstoy Museum, which remains a national shrine, was damaged by the Germans in World War II and restored in 1946.

dren. In Moscow a Tolstoy Society was created with the coopera-
tion of a group of scholars to study the works of Leo Tolstoy.

The State Publishing House took advantage of this research,
which lasted many years, to print the first and only complete collection of my father's writings. These filled some ninety volumes.
The Soviet government put out this edition under its own name
and editorship. So far as I know, it was limited to a thousand
copies. Thus it could be purchased only by the very rich or by
large foreign university libraries.*

This edition included a wide range of variations of *War and
Peace* which had nearly been lost. They had been lying in a special wooden box, and, because of their "worthlessness," were
thrown into a ditch at Yasnaya Polyana, where fortunately my
mother found them. Later she donated them to the Rumyan-
tsevsky Museum, along with other manuscripts of his.

It was hard for me to work in the Tolstoy Museum at Yasnaya
Polyana, where everything had been created in the spirit of
Christ's teachings and faith in God. Now it was impregnated with
Marxist ideology—one which denies the presence of a divine
spirit in thought and creativity, bans the idea in museums and
schools, and spreads the colossal propaganda apparatus of atheis-
tic materialism. I decided to drop everything and depart. I tore
myself away from my native land, where I had passed forty-five
years of my life, from friends and relatives, from all that was dear
to me, from my father's home, from his grave.

Then came twenty months in Japan, where I knew neither the
language nor the customs of the people. From there I went to the
United States.

Now I have been in America for almost forty-six years. The
following pages cover the years from 1914 to the outbreak of the
Second World War. They relate what I experienced during the
First World War, and later during the Revolution and the following decade. They tell of my twenty months in Japan and how I
came to America, how I gradually became accustomed to this new

*This was done deliberately by the Soviet government because of its opposition to
Tolstoy's Christian teachings, which were thus prevented from being disseminated among
citizens of the USSR.

country, the wonderful people I met, what I learned. Little by little I fell in love with this land, which I now think of as my second fatherland.

But I shall never forget the land of my birth.

A.L.T.
Valley Cottage, New York, 1977

A Note on the Author

Countess Alexandra Tolstoy, youngest and last surviving child of Leo Tolstoy, was fully as remarkable in her way as her father was in his. Here she has recorded her early years, her distinguished service in World War I on the German and Turkish fronts (for which she was awarded several decorations), her persecution under the Bolsheviks, the months in Japan lecturing on her father, her initial struggles in America, always under difficult, sometimes dangerous conditions, and finally the organization of the Tolstoy Foundation, which has rescued tens of thousands of refugees all over the world. These pages reflect three cultures from a unique position. She has written repeatedly of her father, but this is the first time she has set down her personal experience in so inclusive a way.

K.S.

Editor's Note

It may interest the reader to learn of the conditions surrounding preparation of this book. Alexandra Tolstoy wrote the bulk of her memoirs, in Russian, between 1929 and 1939. After establishing the Tolstoy Foundation, she devoted herself entirely to its work and did not look at her manuscript again. Various parts, in English translation, began coming to me from Professor Catherine Wolkonsky, Alexandra's secretary and companion, in March 1977. Alexandra had discarded her original script, from which portions had been printed in the New York newspaper, *Novoye Russkoye Slovo*. It was two years later that we gained access to the complete Russian version.

Difficulties with the English translations were immediately apparent. There were errors of vocabulary; chapters without titles; first names of many persons were missing; other names were incorrect or unverified. Only two or three footnotes appeared.

Professor Wolkonsky and I worked closely together, she checking every page I altered. All questions of detail we could not answer ourselves were put to the author. By that time Alexandra had lost the use of her eyes, though not her remarkable memory. Suddenly, however, we were deprived of any chance to ask further questions. Already in her nineties, Alexandra Tolstoy suffered a crippling heart attack. From then on we had to make do; a few inconsistencies and errors no doubt remain.

We have been aided immeasurably by the devoted assistance of

Spencer Barnes, who translated Parts I and IV of *Out of the Past*, as well as certain pages that turned up at the last moment. In assembling the illustrations, we have had the signal contributions of Helen Nicoolicheff, who supplied the photographs of Ilya Tolstoy and his cottage. The staff of Widener Library and other members of the Harvard community have been generous with their help. To all who gave assistance we extend our grateful appreciation.

K.S.

The Tolstoy Family

Leo Nikolaevich Tolstoy (1828–1910)
married Sophia Andreevna Behrs (1844–1919) in 1862.

Their children:

Sergei	1863–1947
Tatiana	1864–1950
Ilya	1866–1933
Leo	1869–1945
Maria	1871–1906
Pyotr	1872–1873
Nikolai	1874–1875
Varvara	1875–1875
Andrei	1877–1916
Mikhail	1879–1944
Alexei	1881–1886
Alexandra	1884–1979
Ivan	1888–1895

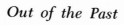

Out of the Past

PART ONE

Russia: 1884-1917

CHAPTER ONE

Growing Up

Only now as I near the end do I remember my childhood without any bitterness. Not until many long years had passed did a reconciliation come about between me and my mother. On her deathbed she thanked me with tears in her eyes for my care of her, deeply contrite for not having loved me. She had given all her affection to my little brother Vanechka, beautiful as an angel, and this had been a decisive fact in my developing personality.

It never occurred to me that the good Lord had given me any talent. When I was seventeen I sent my first story about a dog to *Niva*, a literary review, which accepted it. Then suddenly I was so apprehensive about its being published that I asked the editor to return it. Probably I destroyed it, for I never found it again.

The reason for such dread lay with my brother Leo. A. S. Suvorin, the publisher of *Novoye Vremya*, the leading Russian daily newspaper, was always very sarcastic about Leo's writings and called him "Tigr Tigrovich," a play on words on his name, Leo Lvovich, meaning "Lion son of Lion," Russian fashion.

I adored my little brother Vanechka. To me he was an unusually gifted child. His death from diphtheria at the age of seven in 1895 was the first heartbreak of my life.

I was educated at home by governesses. Some of them beat my hands with a ruler, and for a long time I was scarred, but I never complained. I was afraid to, so none of the family knew of this—they were all taken up with their own lives. No one paid any attention to a plain little girl.

I was rather wild and had managed to acquire something of a

reputation in the placement bureaus of Moscow: "O, la petite Sasha Tolstoy—non, merci!" My mother therefore had great trouble in finding me a teacher. The only one I remember with gratitude was an Englishwoman, Miss Walsh, who was wise, kind, and gentle. Unfortunately she could come only in the summer, for she had a music school in Moscow the rest of the year. We got along marvelously with never the least misunderstanding, and she came to us every summer for ten years. We became very attached to each other; every time she left I wept bitterly. Even after I was grown she continued to come to Yasnaya Polyana, and we always corresponded.

All the other governesses tormented me. They chided me for being a tomboy, for my passion for sports, my love of nature. How I cried when I was punished for falling down and soiling my dress! They would pull me about by the hair and give me all sorts of harsh penalties. I was in such despair that I once ran away to drown myself in the Moscow River.

My eldest sister Tanya, twenty years my senior, was the only one to care for me. Whenever she showed me some kindness or gave me a loving word, how happy, how grateful I was! A vivacious, attractive girl, she had lots of admirers. Many years later I heard her and a friend—Sophia Alexandrovna Stakhovich, a former lady-in-waiting to the Dowager Empress Maria Fyodorovna—reminiscing about their suitors. Tanya had had twenty proposals and Sophia twenty-three.

Tanya could not devote much time to me. She attended the Moscow School of Art and Architecture. Leonid Pasternak, the painter and father of Boris, the Nobel laureate, was the director. He was a great friend of my family. He did a study of the family, and illustrated my father's novel *Resurrection*, as well as other works of his.

By the time I was eighteen both my sisters, Tanya and Masha, had married and left home. It was then that I began to work for my father, copying his manuscripts and typing his correspondence. This gave me the sense of having a goal in life and became my joy.

My father was very lonely. Many a time I longed to help him, but how? He would sigh, "Why are you too young for me to share everything with you?" Once when he was dictating some very complicated philosophical thought I asked him what he meant. "Well, are you trying to understand everything I am saying?" And he added half involuntarily, "Now I shan't be able to dictate freely." Gradually he became accustomed to dictating to me from his diary, in which he expressed his inmost thoughts, but it was hard for him. I tried not to ask any questions but to struggle by myself to grasp his meaning. Such hours were really lessons, which in later years were a guide to my life.

Life was never easy in our family, for we always had to choose between two styles: either the life of an aristocrat, or the life of a peasant, a toiler on the land, as my father advocated. How, amid twelve servants, in a large if modestly furnished home, with food that was excellently prepared, varied, and all too nourishing— how could we follow my father's precepts? How much easier it would have been had our surroundings been otherwise. Each of us would have worked as hard as his strength allowed and then would have picked up after himself. At the time, however, that seemed difficult, even impossible, especially for my mother, who would have been deeply unhappy in such reduced circumstances.

Yet even she, poor dear, was destined to suffer privation when, toward the end of her life, the Revolution was a constant threat and she had to eat, day after day, boiled beets grown for cattle fodder and bread made with chaff. Then we all learned to toil, to practice patience, and even to derive satisfaction from ordinary physical labor.

Only my sister Masha (before her marriage) had had the moral strength to live according to my father's teachings in an environment he considered luxurious. She was then a strict vegetarian, as he was. Always modestly dressed, her unruly hair tied in a knot, she would go out every morning to work with one or another peasant family, helping rake in the hay, heap up the winnowed grain, or tend the sick. During a village fire she ruined her health standing in water up to her knees filling buckets to fight the flames. She slept on boards covered with a thin felt mattress and denied herself all youthful diversions. Father adored her, and she was ready to tax herself to the utmost for his sake.

Eventually youth had its way, and she fell in love. She married Prince Nikolai Leonidovich Obolensky,* who was a lazy sybarite. Having not the least understanding of work of any kind, he little by little squandered the dowry Masha had received. Then she fell ill, and all her failing energy was concentrated on her husband. It was her poor health, I believe, that prevented her from giving any more time to copying Father's manuscripts. Gradually I took her place.

No, it was not easy for us, his children. I did not have the spiritual force of my sister Masha. In those times we knew very well what was good and what was bad; for example, I knew that smoking was forbidden, therefore bad. Yet I smoked—though not inhaling. It seemed very dashing when, riding sidesaddle at a fast trot on my good Anglo-Kabardin, I lit a cigarette, like my brothers, and sent up smoke rings. Later, in tears, I would confess such peccadilloes to my father. I also used to flirt a bit. When I was staying at the house of my married brother Sergei in Moscow, I would slip out through a little window to visit the gypsies with a girl companion and my other brothers. All this was harmless enough, and Father treated my lapses with benign tolerance. He understood everything.

Nothing, however, kept me from the work I loved, transcribing my father's manuscripts. Into this, too, the zest of youth entered, to work without faltering, quickly and well, to deserve his thanks and a few encouraging words. His ideas, in spite of my frivolities, took root in me for all my life. Wonderfully expressed, for example, in "Kornei Vasiliev," *The Forged Coupon*, or "The Divine and the Human," which I copied, they made a deep and lasting impression on me. "There are no hopeless persons, in the sense of a [possible] spiritual awakening. God's spirit lives in every human being."

Throughout my life I have remembered how my father opposed the conventional attitude that one should behave like everyone

---

*Prince Nikolai Obolensky was the husband of Alexandra's sister Maria. He died in Russia, but little is known of his latter years. His family was held to be descended from Rurik, the legendary founder of the Russian state.

else. "Stop and verify," he would say, "then do what your reason and your conscience dictate, not simply as others do."

I remember his words about the joy and necessity of physical labor. At the time I knew nothing of such work, but later I learned to love it when the need arose. The longer I live, the more I understand him, the greater riches I find in his thoughts.

There was much, however, that I did not then understand. I was not fond of the Tolstoyans,* with the exception of a few who deeply and genuinely accepted my father's teachings. The others adapted only superficially, concealing their shallowness with their dark Russian blouses, their long unkempt hair, their unwashed beards.

Once one of the Tolstoyans asked me and my niece Annochka,** "What is that song called? May I write down the words?"

"The words? Why do you want them?"

"Well, I want to know. . . ."

Annochka and I were in a quandary. How could a "dark person," as my mother used to call them, someone who had renounced all earthly passions, be concerned with the poetry of moonlit nights, the song of nightingales, the throbbing of love?

Finally we discovered the reason. He wanted to write, in his memoirs, of the destructive surroundings in which Tolstoy, the great teacher, was obliged to live and work.

On some evenings I would pick up a guitar, the young people would gather around me and joyously we would sing the gypsy songs we all (my father more than anyone) adored, so carried away that we did not notice when Father came in. Quietly he would stand by the door, his hands as usual hooked in his belt. When we ended, he would remark, "It's odd, the words are silly, yet in the song they seem to come out so well." Annochka and I would be enchanted.

Father always protected his daughters. Just let some young man appear and, God forbid, begin to court us, and Father would watch like a hawk. "Whom did you go riding with? Why were

---

* Followers of Leo Tolstoy who claimed to believe in his philosophy and live by it.
** Annochka, or Anna (1888–1954), was the daughter of Alexandra's brother Ilya.

you late home yesterday?" At the same time, the last thing he wanted was frustration for his daughters.

One event made a strong impression on me. My brother Andrei was an enthusiastic hunter. One day he asked me to go hunting with him and some neighbors. We would be taking along our Russian wolfhounds—borzoi. I gladly agreed. To ride a horse for a whole day of hunting—the height of joy for me. I was then eighteen. It was 1902, when young girls were always chaperoned at a hunt—at least by their brothers. Everything was simple, delightful. No cares, no thoughts of tomorrow, of human cruelty, no worries of how to survive, or why. The damp woods smelled of mushrooms. Already the trees were thinning their boughs, and the ruts in the country roads were deep in gold and red leaves.

My pleasure in the hunt was soon spoiled, though, because one neighbor, the young Count K., had joined us. Instantly I disliked him. First, he called me countess, which I could not bear, and then he spoke Russian with an affected foreign accent.

We all rode out of the woods. The vast plain opened up before us. In the fields the stubble had already turned gold in the chill autumn dew. Here and there we saw patches of silver-gray wormwood and blue cornflowers. Andrei had brought our pack, as our neighbors had theirs. They were all proud of the hounds, and boasted of their skills.

The first hare got away; I didn't care, I was even a little glad. When we were at full gallop, my Jairan, to my brother's great annoyance (he was an avid horseman) passed all the rest. For a long while we rode over the fields. Finally Andrei hoisted his whip: "Tally-ho!"

It was a fox we were chasing. My Jairan went like the wind far ahead of the rest. Suddenly a ravine, and below it a stream. The slope was steep. Impossible to rein in my horse. I could feel Jairan's muscles tense—and before I knew it we were at the bottom of the ravine. Waving his tail, the fox disappeared, the hounds after him.

Where was I? The fields were unfamiliar. I must be a good twenty kilometers from home. No one of our party was in sight but Count K., occupied with picking a shallow place to walk his horse across.

We both forded the stream and began to search for the others, but they had vanished. On and on we rode until the sun began to sink. Fields and yet more fields. What direction should we take? Not a house, not a person anywhere. I began to be alarmed. What would Father say? It was not so much that he would worry but that he would know I had been alone with a strange young man, until evening.

Finally we came to a dirt road. I told the count, "I'm going to let the reins go loose." Jairan would take us to the right track. The clever horse snorted, sniffed the road, turned abruptly in the other direction, then with a decisive air took off at a brisk trot.

When we first spied a light, it was already pitch dark. I knew this must be the cottage of our forester, who cared for the Yasnaya Polyana woods. But we were still five kilometers from home. When we finally approached the main house, I told the count, "Please don't go in with me." I dreaded my father's encountering him, but the count insisted on escorting me in.

Dinner, it appeared, was already over. A group of Tolstoyans was sitting around the table in the living-dining room, where they often gathered to question my father and note down his replies. As we entered, they all fell silent, staring. Embarrassed, I stood before my father in my black riding habit made by an English tailor, my bowler hat and my crop in my hand, beside the rascally, dandified Count K. "Where have you been? Why so late?" asked my father.

My companion answered: "We got lost, Count, but here I have brought your daughter back safe and sound. I have the honor to pay my respects."

With that he disappeared. The Tolstoyans looked reproachful, my father, inquiring. I was ready to sink through the floor. The next day I told my father how it all happened, and he was reassured. In the evening I read him some humorous verses in which I described my adventures with Count K. Father laughed until the tears came. He always understood everything.

Gypsy songs were popular among many aristocratic families. There were various kinds of gypsies. Some remained nomads like their ancestors, but others spent the winter in poor, cramped quarters on the outskirts of towns, while in summer they camped in tents on landowners' large estates. They themselves sang their songs unmusically in a primitive style, but they performed their dances magnificently to those tunes, shaking their shoulders and stamping out the rhythms. Some aristocrats married gypsy girls, but only rarely lived with them out of wedlock. The girls were very chaste; their parents brought them up strictly.

My father's brother, Sergei Nikolaevich Tolstoy, had married a gypsy. I loved Maria Mikhailovna. She had always been small of stature, but when I knew her she was no longer young and seemed even shorter, with graying hair. She always went about in soft slippers that made hardly a sound, her head wrapped in a kerchief. I called her Aunt Masha, yet she never called me Sasha, but always very courteously said Alexandra Lvovna, and only occasionally, when she had a reason, "my wonderful little one."

"My wonderful little one, please sing for me, 'I traveled a hundred versts.' "

Then I would take my guitar, made by the famous master Kresnoshchekov in 1833, and softly sing her beloved songs for her. She would beat the time with her little foot, and her lips would move soundlessly. Sometimes my uncle, tall and handsome, would come to listen at the door. I felt he loved me and enjoyed my visits, and this made me very happy.

After a boring journey of more than thirty-five kilometers over the plain, their home at Pirogovo seemed an oasis to me. It lay on the Upa River, and above the steep banks there stood an ancient church in the park of the estate, where all the paths were decorated with the skulls of wolves, for Uncle Sergei had been a great hunter in his youth. There was a mysterious charm to the scene, something inimitable, in later years destroyed for all time. On the opposite bank of the Upa was the small estate of my father's sister, Maria Nikolaevna Tolstoy. She had married twice, and both husbands had died. One of them was a Tolstoy, a distant relative. My father visited her on his last journey in the convent of Shamardino, where she had become a nun. Her estate then passed to my sister Masha.

My father greatly dreaded depriving me of a family life of my own. Once he brought up the subject of my marrying. He called me into his study and with a grave countenance tried to persuade me to marry Alyosha D., the son of a friend. I felt affronted. Alyosha, as we all agreed, was an idler, reared only for pleasure; he didn't know how to do anything, he had no profession, but for some reason he had fallen in love with me and in the old-fashioned way had asked my father for his daughter's hand.

"You want me to trade you for that worthless thing?" I cried angrily. At this response Father embraced me tenderly. I vowed I would never put anyone in his place, that I would never marry. He kissed me, assuring me how happy he was that I did not want to part from him. Then we laughed, but with tears in our eyes. So I went on copying his manuscripts and taking his dictation in shorthand, which I was gradually mastering.

Some time earlier I had gone to the Crimea, for there were signs of tuberculosis in both my lungs, particularly the right one. Our family physician was a Slovak, Dushan Petrovich Makovitsky. On his diagnosis, I went to Yalta and entered a sanatorium. There I told our friend Dr. Altschuler why I had come. He did not believe me, and burst into laughter. "What nonsense! When you look so healthy!"

After he examined me, however, his verdict was different. "Well, all right. I'll tell you one thing; it's true both your lungs are affected, but it won't finish you, you'll finish the tuberculosis, and very soon."

He put me on a heavily protein diet of ten eggs a day and also meat, which I had not eaten for a long time. He forbade me the seashore and ordered me to avoid the slightest atmospheric dampness. With that hearty diet (and several subsequent visits to the Crimea) the infection was eventually healed.

On my first trip to the Crimea—in the spring of 1910—a stenographer accompanied me, for I had resolved to learn shorthand as a present for my father. By the time I came home I had achieved considerable speed. United with my father again, we

both wept with joy. From that day on I never left him until the
end of his life. I myself closed his eyes.

CHAPTER TWO

On the Eve

It is probably only natural for the masses of any country to pay
little attention to major political events, whether these are on
a national or an international scale. People are involved in
their personal interests, looking no further ahead than their own
well-being, their own worries or misfortunes. Why bother with
matters of importance to governments? Let the presidents, the
kings or tsars take care of all that. Only when adversity touches
our fortunes directly do we wake up.

For many Russians, therefore, World War I broke out unexpectedly. Those who thought and read, however, were aware of
the warlike mood in Germany, Germany's fear of a great and then
powerful Russia, Austria's enmity to Hungary and Serbia, the
hatred of the Serbs for Austria, unable to forgive the latter for her
domination of the provinces of Bosnia and Herzegovina. Everyone knew of the attitude of the Austrian imperial dynasty of the
Hapsburgs, who considered themselves, in their pride and
power, a chosen people.

Most Russians knew these things, but no one wanted to believe
in the danger that menaced them. Every people has a comforting
phrase to which it turns when it prefers not to think, not to be
disturbed or upset. "Never mind," they say, "it will all work out."
So said the Russians, just as the Americans have said at times,
"Everything will be all right."

Even when the young Serbian Gavrilo Princip assassinated the

Austrian Archduke Franz Ferdinand in Sarajevo, and the rattle of arms could be heard in Austria and Germany, searching for an excuse for war with Russia, even when the attaché in the British embassy in Berlin was vainly trying everything to achieve a satisfactory settlement, the Russian people did not believe there was any real chance of war. "It will all turn out for the best, it will work out."

My reason for writing these pages, however, is not to describe political events. The historians will attend to that. I am not a person who ever delved deep into political affairs. I had heard a little, I had read the newspapers, but political attitudes had gone over my head. And so I was thunderstruck when war was declared on August 1, 1914.

The years between the death in 1910 of my father, Leo Tolstoy, and the declaration of war were the hardest in my life. While he was with me, I had no life or interests purely my own. All that was serious and genuine in me was bound up with him. When he died, there remained a yawning void, an emptiness, which I did not know how to fill.

My father's will had left me in charge of all his literary rights and of the posthumous three-volume edition of his unpublished work. I also had to buy most of the land of our country estate, Yasnaya Polyana, from the family and transfer it to the peasants, as he asked.* It would seem that all this should have filled my life.

Yet in fact this was not the case. My relations with my family had become embittered. My favorite older brother and sister, Sergei and Tatiana, who had been very close to my father (especially my sister Tanya), my mother, and my other brothers, who had not received author's rights—all were offended. This was hard for me to bear.

Very soon there were difficulties with the followers of my father, the Tolstoyans. Vladimir Grigorievich Chertkov, with whom it was my lot to work closely, depressed me with his frequently

---

* Leo Tolstoy's will specified that the land should be given to the peasants, freely and without recompense, except for two hundred acres reserved for the museum at Yasnaya Polyana.

senseless stubbornness and stupid dictatorial ways. It was hard for me, only twenty-six and with little experience, to struggle with him when I thought him in the wrong. He had been considered a devoted friend of my father's since my early youth. He had given up the promise of a glittering career at court, had become a strict vegetarian, and had taken up the simple life and given himself entirely to distributing my father's philosophical works. With Ivan Ivanovich Gorbunov-Posadov, he had founded a publishing house, Posrednik (Mediator), which distributed my father's popular tales for a price of one to three kopecks per booklet, and this activity constituted the main interest of his life.

An essential quality in my father was his gratitude for anything anyone did for him. In relation to Chertkov he felt this to an unusual degree. "No one else has done for me what Vladimir Grigorievich has done," he would say. It was hard, however, to find two people more different in character, though it is not easy to define this difference.

There was no flexibility in Chertkov. He was heavy-handed in his singleness of purpose, in his complete inability to adapt to circumstances. His conduct, his actions, his mind, all were focused in one direction and permitted no compromise. Chertkov had no sensitivity, there was no warmth in him. His approach to people was from a standpoint of rigid analysis: if a person ate meat and was rich, that person was immediately uninteresting. To Tolstoy, on the other hand, every human being was interesting. He loved people. Just here perhaps lay the difference between him and his faithful follower. Tolstoy was happy whenever he was communicating with people, for he found them absorbing. No matter who came to him, he always saw something special, individual, in that person.

For Chertkov a lady of society was a zero. For Tolstoy, she was something, from one point of view or another. Chertkov did not notice the half-wit standing by the door with a silly smile, begging for a kopeck. For Tolstoy that man was a human being. He was kind and loving toward everyone. To me, Chertkov was tedious, and he weighed me down.

Yes, with rare exceptions, I did not greatly love the Tolstoyans.

I felt in them a lack of sincerity, a constraint, an unnaturalness. I remember once my little six-year-old nephew reading a notice in Chertkov's house: "Today at eight o'clock in the evening there will be a lecture on spiritual marriage." The child asked our cook, "Annushka, what is spiritual marriage?" Annushka, a healthy, hard-working woman who every day cooked food for these idlers, waved her hand. "They haven't anything to do. They invent foolishness. Today spiritual marriage—tomorrow we shall have spiritual children."

All too often the Tolstoyans were dirty, smelling of unwashed clothes, killing all joy of life. They wore Russian blouses, high boots, and some grew beards. Their teacher, on the contrary, understood perfectly the joy of life—it showed in his facial expression, his smile, his jokes, his laughter. His followers, though, preserved their gloomy Lenten faces, fearing to spoil their state of perfection by an unnecessary smile or a happy song. My father liked not only classical music, but also popular pieces, gypsy songs. The Tolstoyans shunned all cheerful, catchy airs.

Once Wanda Landowska was my guest on the estate next to Chertkov's house. Famous for her harpsichord renditions of old familiar classical music, she played for his visitors. The next day reports reached us that the young people had slept badly. Her playing had disturbed them and awakened sinful thoughts. When she heard this, she laughed heartily. The next evening, when she was again playing at Chertkov's, I said to her, "Wanda, what are you doing? You play so brilliantly, I'm afraid none of the Tolstoyans will close an eye tonight."

There were some who were different, however, like Maria Alexandrovna Schmidt, a great friend of my father's. She had made a sharp break with her early life, and now devoted herself entirely to helping the peasants among whom she lived. There was no shadow of insincerity in her. She influenced others through love, not through moralizing words. She was a great help to me in that difficult, insipid, and unhappy period of my life.

I found some diversions—I worked with the peasants on the transfer of the land to them, according to my father's will, and with the cooperative organizations. With the aid of an agronomist, I was trying to help them improve their field work. Gradually, the peasants took up crop rotation and began to plant clover to restore the soil. In the winter I lived in our Moscow house, in the summer at our place in the country.* I kept a herd of pedigreed cattle, sent milk daily to the hospital in Tula, and acquired some purebred Orlov horses.** My mother's former secretary, who was a great lover of dogs, lived with me. We had two black poodles in the house (one my faithful Marquis, named by my father, the other his friend Nitouche) and two white Eskimos, large, powerful beauties, Belyak and Belko. I accomplished some things, kept busy somehow or other, but it was all rather futile, and my soul felt empty.

Suddenly, unexpectedly—war.

Now I began to read the newspapers avidly. On July 26, 1914 the tsar addressed a joint meeting of the Council of State and the Duma. "We will not only defend our honor and dignity within the confines of our own territory," he said in conclusion, "we will also fight for our Slav blood brothers."***

The response was a loud, enthusiastic hurrah. Then V. V. Golubev, chairman of the Council of State, spoke, and then M. V. Rodzyanko, president of the Duma, delivered a magnificent address. The fatherland was in danger, and Russians of different parties, different schools of thought, united in a fiery outburst of love for their native land and devotion to the monarchy.

To sit with folded hands was unthinkable. One after another workers and relatives departed. My thoroughbreds were taken for war service. Our country estate was desolate. Everything that had filled my life—agriculture, the organization and direction of the cooperatives—all faded away. I could not sit at home.

---

* Alexandra's own house at Novaya Polyana, three miles from the Tolstoy estate at Yasnaya Polyana.

** Alexis Orlov developed this famous breed as carriage horses, not to be ridden. During the Revolution, however, they were forced to work on the land; they were also used as work horses during World War I.

*** See A. I. Spiridovich, *Velikaya voinai Fevralskaya Revolutsiya*, *1914–1917* (New York: Vsevlavienskoe Izd., 1960–1962), 3 vols.

CHAPTER THREE

On the Northwestern Front

I decided to go to the front as a nurse, and went to Yasnaya Polyana to say goodbye to my mother. It was hard to recognize in this quiet, timid old woman the mother I had once known. Where were her limitless energy, her combativeness, her domineering ways? She now would sit the entire day in an armchair, dozing.

Not much else, however, had changed at home. Now only my elder sister Tanya lived in one wing of the house with her daughter Tanichka. The same cook as before, Semyon Nikolaevich, my mother's godchild, prepared a meal at twelve noon and a dinner of four courses at six in the evening. Our old servant Ilya Vasilievich waited on table. It was quiet in the house, empty and boring.

"Why go to the war?" asked my mother. "There's no point to it. Your father was against war, and now you want to take part in it."

"I don't think he would have been against my helping the sick and wounded."

But my mother was not satisfied. "Well, I've given you my opinion, but I know it's useless. You always go your own way."

Chertkov and the Tolstoyans also criticized me, but to no effect. I could not stay home.

When my father was alive I had formed an interest in medicine, and I had studied anatomy and physiology. Dr. D. V. Nikitin—whom my mother had engaged to look after my father's health—and I organized a dispensary in the village. We admitted not only sick peasants of Yasnaya Polyana but also those from the rest of the county. Dr. Nikitin taught me a great deal. While we were examining patients, he would give me whole lectures on this or that illness. He taught me to dress wounds, make bandages, prepare ointments, give injections. At the Zvenigorod Hospital near Moscow, where Dr. Nikitin was head physician, I took short nursing courses and did practical work. This experience helped me pass the examination for war nursing without any trouble.

In the hospital they appointed me nursing assistant to a surgeon. It was difficult to get used to this work. The first time I saw a naked man, I was embarrassed.

"Sister, what's wrong with you? Wake up, the scalpel, the tampons," cried the doctor.

I was ashamed, but my awkwardness vanished, a man in pain was before me, needing help. Another time I felt faint when the doctor pierced a sick man's skull. But one gets used to everything.

Work behind the lines, however, did not satisfy me. I determined to request a transfer to the front. I wanted to forget myself, see great deeds, heroic acts. Political events were passing over me, leaving me untouched. The destruction of the German embassy in Petersburg, everywhere the flaring hatred of everything German, our military offensive in Galicia, our defeat in East Prussia during August—all this, to my shame, interested me but little. Only my own problem stirred me: would I get to the front?

The chairman of the All-Union Zemstvo Medical Service* was

---

*Vserossisky Zemsky Soyuz. The zemstvo system was instituted by Alexander II in 1864. It set up in each rural district or province a self-governing organization whose board was elected every three years, and which was financed by taxes levied on everyone who owned land. Each zemstvo was responsible for community medical care, the running of the schools, the delivery of mail, and the upkeep of the roads and highways. In addition, it administered agronomy centers with a staff to teach the peasants how to grow better crops and how to maintain the fertility of the soil. Also, on each staff were feldschers, who, while not accredited doctors, had had two or three years of medical training, much like American paramedics.

When war broke out in 1914, the zemstvo boards organized the All-Union Zemstvo Medical Service, comprising field hospitals with doctors, nurses, orderlies, and drivers of horse-drawn vehicles. The personnel were supplied with forty horses and stablemen on the average. One field hospital could usually handle four hundred wounded men, and its staff served directly behind the firing line. These units were separate from the regular army medical corps, and were attached to specific companies of infantry, cavalry, and other branches. The Red Cross was a separate institution.

The zemstvo was the sole organ of self-government in autocratic Russia. It was abol-

Prince Georgi Yevgenyevich Lvov.* I approached him to ask for a place, no matter where, if only it was close to the front lines. He smiled—ironically, I thought. "You at the front? If you want responsible work, let me speak plainly: you are not fit for it. You are too impractical, too inexperienced."

I grew angry at his mocking face. "What right have you to think I don't know how to work?"

"Don't be offended. I observed once in Tula how you leased your apple orchard, and how the tenant cheated you. You have no business sense."

Yes, I remembered that occasion in a lawyer's office. I was not then acquainted with Prince Lvov, but I was struck with his practicality, his clever way of talking to a tenant, squeezing every kopeck out of him. He was right. I did not know how to do that.

"But what has that to do with work at the front?"

In any event, he did not give me a responsible position then. Only several months later was I appointed representative of the All-Union Zemstvo Medical Service. Finally I found myself a nurse on a hospital train serving the northwestern front. The train was bringing the sick and wounded to a dispensary at Bialystok,** where they were bandaged and evacuated farther behind the lines.

The appearance of our senior doctor, Maria Alexandrovna Abakumov-Savinykh, did not at all fit my notion of how a woman physician should look. She was very beautiful with regular features, black brows, dark lively eyes, a youthful face, and completely white hair. We all loved and respected her.*** She was a wonderful companion, gay and sociable, but she was incompetent and inexperienced. Serious wounds frightened her, and she lost her head when extreme measures had to be taken, such as an operation to save the life of a sick or wounded man.

---

ished by the Bolsheviks during the Revolution and replaced by their own system.
*Prince Georgi Yevgenyevich Lvov (1861–1925) was to head the first provisional government, from March to July 1917, and played a prominent part in the development of the zemstvo system. He was succeeded by Alexander Feodorovich Kerensky.
**A city in the province of Grodno on the northwestern front, in what is now northeastern Poland.
***After the Revolution she worked at Yasnaya Polyana as the school physician.

The wounded were brought to us straight from the battlefield, many with critical injuries to abdomen or head. Sometimes a man died just as he was being bandaged. I shall never forget a terribly wounded man. Both buttocks had been virtually torn off by shell-fire. Evidently he had not been carried promptly from the field. A fearful stench rose from his gaping wounds, dirty gray holes. There was movement in them. Leaning over to look, I saw maggots, fat white maggots. To clean the wounds and kill the maggots, it was necessary to wash the flesh with a strong solution of mercuric bichloride.

The injured man lay on his stomach until I had done this. He did not groan or complain, he only ground his teeth from the terrific pain. It was no easy thing to dress such wounds so that the bandage would stay in place and the anal orifice remain free. I do not know whether I handled this problem very well. I know only that I was inexperienced, and needed much more training in order not to get upset but to put such hideous injuries, and the maggots, out of my mind so that I could eat and sleep normally.

I remember another case. At the first-aid station at Bialystok I was bandaging a soldier wounded in the leg. He was a merry fellow, and, although his leg hurt badly, he rejoiced at being evacuated. "I am going home to my wife and boys, they must certainly have been missing me."

A German was sitting on a chair opposite this cheerful soldier. His arm was bandaged, and blood was oozing through the gauze in a darkening brown spot.

"Hey, Fritzie," the happy soldier suddenly shouted, "no goot, no goot, why did you shoot me in the leg, you German snout? Eh?" He showed his wound.

"Ja wohl," agreed the German, showing his arm, "you shot me through the arm."

"Well, all right, Fritzie, it's war, it can't be helped," said the soldier as if excusing himself. Then the two smiled benevolently at each other.

Once our train stopped at a small German town. It was a clean little place, for the army had not yet made a mess of it. The Germans had retreated, leaving all their belongings. It was depressing to see how our men went from house to house collecting sacks full of various articles, clothing, wall clocks, bed linen. Furniture was not carried off but simply broken. Crack, crash. Chairs, tables, bureaus flew out of the upper window of a clean, comfortable little house, and after those a piano crashed on the pavement with a mournful sound from its hundreds of strings. The soldiers roared with laughter.

The doctor assigned me to an officers' car. I accepted, but without enthusiasm. It was easier to work with the soldiers. They were simpler, and consequently more considerate than the officers, and they did their best not to embarrass a nurse. Some of the men in the officers' car had only light wounds. While we were bandaging them, they would crack off-color jokes and make quips with double meanings. One could not enter or leave these cars except at station stops. When our work was over, we had to sit and wait until the very long train would pull into a station and only then would it be possible to go to the personnel car. It was particularly unpleasant and also boring to listen to the officers' banal conversation. At one point the train was barely crawling up a high embankment, probably only recently constructed. With my eyes I measured the distance to the ground—not very high. Without further thought, I jumped out onto the bank. But horror! Just then the train began to pick up steam. Faster and faster, one after another, the cars slipped by, our personnel car too. It was winter, there was a heavy frost, and I was clad only in a nurse's smock. What to do? It was impossible to leap back onto a train traveling at such a rate. I was terrified. What if the train disappeared, leaving me on the track? Not a single house was in sight. In every direction, the snowy forest. Then the wheels began to clank, the bumpers knocked against one another, and the train pulled to a stop.

"Knowing you, and what you can do," said Maria Alexandrovna reproachfully, "I looked out of the window and saw your forlorn figure standing on the bank in your white smock. I stopped the train. Next time please don't do such things." She shook her head reprovingly.

CHAPTER FOUR

The Caucasian Front, Spring 1915

On October 16, 1914, without any declaration of war, the Turkish fleet bombarded Odessa, Novorossiysk, and Sevastopol. Russia immediately accepted the challenge. Our army, after winning a number of victories, penetrated well into Turkey without meeting much resistance.

Commander T. N. Polner, our administrative officer, was a man long active in rural government. He and Sergei V. Glebov, an energetic and loyal young man whose family we had known since childhood (his sister married my brother Mikhail), were then organizing the seventh medical detachment of the Russian Red Cross under the All-Union Zemstvo Medical Service, under orders to operate on the Turkish front. It was solely through the influence of Polner and Glebov that I was taken into this unit, since only qualified Red Cross nurses were in general being accepted. I was the single exception, having only a war-time appointment.

Our echelon spent over a week traveling from Moscow to Tiflis. There we had to await further orders for about a month. Everyone's spirits fell. The wonderful mountain walks, the famous sulphur baths, the abundant leisure—all that was for tourists. We were spoiling for battle.

Finally a general meeting was called. Polner, shaking his graying beard, his clever brown eyes piercing, took the floor.

"We must go in two directions, one toward Erzurum-Kars, the other toward Yerevan-Igdir and beyond, to Karakalisa-Alashkertskaya, deep in Turkey. The second is the dangerous one. Bands of Kurds are attacking the highways. Typhus, typhoid, malaria have broken out everywhere. There will be long hard horseback rides over passes without roads. You yourselves must decide who goes in which direction. I will give no orders."

Before he had finished nearly half the detachment had formed a group and voted for going to the Yerevan-Igdir area in Turkish Armenia. At last, we thought, real work is beginning!

"Thank you," said Polner. "I will lead your group myself."

Igdir was a small settlement inhabited by Armenians and Kurds. It lay at the foot of Mount Ararat* on the banks of a rushing river, headwaters of the Euphrates. In the spring the valley was flooded for many miles—and this was spring. It was a dismal, marshy place, with unbelievable swarms of mosquitoes carrying the worst kind of tropical malaria. Here we organized the first dressing station for the seventh advance detachment of the All-Union Zemstvo Medical Service.

Soon we were in full swing. The woman doctor there was swarthy and malicious, with a cigarette always dangling from her mouth. A socialist, she took a strong dislike to me. "See what a worker they've sent us," she complained to the young male doctor. "Without pull she wouldn't be here. What does she know, a countess, an aristocrat?"

"Sister," she ordered me, "wash all the floors, the windows, and the doors into the wards; it must all be perfectly clean."

There were no brushes. Silently, gritting my teeth, I scrubbed the floors with a cloth. I was so afraid of being laughed at for my ineptness, sneered at as a lady in white gloves. In truth, I had had no experience whatever in washing floors. Thanks to a male nurse, Emilio Ferraris, an Italian volunteer who for some reason was serving in our detachment, I was rescued.

"Impossible, signorina," exclaimed Emilio fervently. "This doctor she love all the men, and the handsome commander, and she jealous. You are very tired, I will help you."

---

*Mount Ararat, of volcanic origin, rises to 17,000 feet. Called Egri Dagh by the Turks, its summit is the supposed site of Noah's landing.

We scrubbed the floors, washed the windows, made the beds and put them in place. Meanwhile, the woman doctor prowled around the premises, while the goat she had tamed and often treated to tobacco crept behind her like a dog. When they brought in thirty men suffering from rheumatism, this doctor ordered me to massage them. So for hours I rubbed their feet and hands and backs, the perspiration pouring off me. I did not then know that scrubbing floors and massaging dozens of the sick were not included in the duties of a nurse. Naturally, she did not order regular nurses to do such work.

"Now, sister, call it quits, slow down," the sick soldiers told me. They were sorry for me; but I kept on massaging them for hours and paid no attention. Was I performing such a feat? My notion of a feat was something quite different.

For several months we remained in Igdir. The warm days set in, the streams began to murmur, the rivers swelled and spread over the valley. The heat became unbearable. There was little work to do and life was boring. Some students serving as male nurses in the detachment brought grape juice back from the village. It had a pleasant bittersweet taste and quenched one's thirst wonderfully. We poured it into large enameled jars and drank glass after glass.

"Why, Katy, what's the matter with you?" Katy was a very nice, unassuming Red Cross nurse and a good friend. She broke into laughter, unable to stop. Taking a few steps, she stumbled, held on to the balcony with both arms, still laughing, unable to move. The entire detachment of nurses and attendants, all were tipsy. Only then did we discover that fermented grape juice is almost more intoxicating than wine. We were expecting the commander. Luckily, the ill-tempered doctor had already gone to her room. Though we were fond of Polner, we were afraid of him, for he was very strict. What if he saw his personnel in this state? Out of the whole group only the administrative officer and I were sober. Quickly we gathered our comrades and put them to bed. We had barely finished when Polner arrived. "Where is everybody?" he asked, staring at the empty dining room and terrace, where the young crew usually sat until late evening.

"They've gone to sleep, the heat tired them out."

The old zemstvo surgeon sent me to the operating room to help an experienced assistant surgeon. I was glad to escape the domineering woman doctor. She was finally deprived of the satisfaction of harassing me.

The wounds we were then treating were severe. The Turks were using dum-dum bullets, and it was hard to get used to the terrible amputations. You might be holding a leg or an arm, and suddenly you felt a dead weight. A part of that person remained in your hands. "Sister," one handsome young Cossack asked me as he came out of the anaesthetic, hopefully but fearfully, "have they left my leg on? They haven't cut it off, have they? My heel itches." What could one reply? His dark eyes beseeched me.

Learning the truth, he covered his face and sobbed like a child. "Sister, of what use am I now? Dunya—she won't love a cripple— she will leave me—and the youngsters—how shall I earn anything?"

"But don't you have some skill, some trade?"

"Only one, I'm a shoemaker; I could earn a little money somehow. But what do you think? Won't she stop loving me? Will she still want to live with me?"

"If your Dunya is worth anything, she will love and care for you even more."

Within a week he was cheering up the whole ward, singing his Cossack songs at the top of his voice in his rich tenor.

We stayed only a little longer in Igdir. Then our detachment was ordered to move on to Karakalisa-Alashkertskaya, a little over a hundred versts* away. To transport us a herd of camels was assembled—to deliver provisions, food, medical supplies, and kerosene to heat the mosquito sprayers for the tents.

Within a few days our marching orders came. Everyone was

---

*A verst is slightly over one kilometer, or five-eighths of a mile.

glad. Feverishly we prepared for departure. I resolved to acquire a horse of my own. The Kurds and Armenians brought up several mounts, but none of them suited me.

Then I saw one I fell in love with, but he was too young, only three years old; he could not have withstood the forced marches over the rocky mountain passes. He was a white Arab stallion with a dark mane, and I could not take my eyes off him. I had never seen a white horse before. As it appeared, here only Arabs were white, and even those only rarely.

An old, swarthy, white-bearded Kurd in a striped silk robe and white turban sat calmly astride him, the reins tight in his hand. For a saddle he had only a bright-colored rug. Nervously, the horse pawed the ground.

Oh, how I wanted him! I would have bought him at once, only I was afraid he could not have held out during the long marches over mountain trails. This creature with a swan's neck, his nostrils flaring, dancing nervously, was not made for harsh work. I had to buy another beast, sturdy but unpretentious. Later I exchanged him for a splendid Kabardin* with a gray coat, on whom I subsequently made all our journeys throughout Turkish Armenia. His name was Alagez.

Our caravan was a long and strange one. The camels were loaded. All the personnel, nurses and doctors, were mounted; many did not know how to ride their horses, sitting like dogs on a fence, as the cavalry say. When we camped in the evenings, it was almost impossible for them to walk or sit down, they were so lame. It made me laugh, though. Not for nothing had my father taught me to ride at the age of six. Now it was spring, and the mountains were still deep in snow, so there could be no thought of wagons for anyone.

Even Commander Polner looked highly uncomfortable sitting on a horse. Turning out his toes, bending forward on his saddle, he ambled along on his lop-eared mare with its hanging lip. An old member of the zemstvo, he was an indoor person accustomed

*A Cossack horse of great stamina from the Kabardino province in the Caucasus.

to administrative life. Notwithstanding his poor horsemanship, however, he never let anyone see that he was tired or that his legs and back were aching cruelly. His stamina was impressive.

It was rather terrifying when we had to make our way across a rushing river. The Euphrates and its tributaries had overflowed their banks. Whenever we had to cross one, the strong current carried us far to the other side. No matter how much I drew up my feet, I was soaked above the knees.

Behind us the snowy crest of Mount Ararat shone in the distance. Beyond, a range of mountains swam in a haze. We climbed higher and higher. The slopes were already blue with forget-me-nots. These, unlike the flowers we knew in the Tula province, were large and heavy, and we also saw wild narcissus and tulips. We reached the Chingil pass, yet went on ascending. The cold increased. Snow surrounded us—in places the horses sank into it up to their bellies. When I slid off to lighten my animal's burden, I would tumble into drifts. Ascent followed descent, again and again. In that wilderness there was no sight of a house, not a living thing.

Suddenly, a voice. "Hello, sister." On my right, under a cliff, there was a group of Cossacks in white-topped fur hats and Circassian coats, with their horses. Dressed like them was a tall dark general with regular features. It was he who had called. I reined in my horse and stared in inquiry. "I am General Abatsiev, married to your second cousin.* Well, aren't you a Tolstoy?"

Though I had heard much about him, we had never met. He was one of our bravest generals, an Ossetian, and a Knight of St. George with all the crosses and arms of that order.** It was said of him that he never feared anyone or anything. In battle he commanded his troops from a hill in full view of the enemy, all the more visible because of his great height. He was bound for Igdir, but his staff headquarters were in Karakalisa, where we were going.

* Related through Alexandra's mother's family, the Behrs.
** Ossetia is a region on the southern slopes of the Caucasus; its people were renowned for their bravery. The cross of St. George was the highest award for courage in battle.

At length the Chingil pass was behind us. Again we encountered heat. The valley floor was thick with grass. A multitude of flowers everywhere. There were rushing streams and little bridges with stone handrails. Occasionally we saw the ruins of gigantic buildings of granite or marble. Were these perhaps temples? Whose temples? Who had once lived here?*

Here and there from deep in the earth hot and cold springs forced their way up. The water bubbled, steam issued from some. In one, there sat an apparently blissful Armenian, his naked back bronzed. What a wealth of nature, what a beautiful region, what a wilderness!

There were but few houses, and only occasionally, as if from beneath the earth, there rose a wisp of smoke. This meant an underground home, such as the Kurds and Armenians construct. On the ground floor were the stalls for cows and sheep, while the family lived beneath in the cellar. It was warmer in winter down there, so there was less need for firewood.

CHAPTER FIVE

Karakalisa

Karakalisa-Alashkertskaya was a dirty, unpaved little village. The soldiers' barracks were in several miserable shacks. The general and his staff occupied the largest, with two stories. We set up tents for the sick and wounded and for the personnel. There were not enough nurses; we could hardly cope with the situation. There were few wounded, but every kind of fever was raging; typhus, typhoid, and relapsing fever. If for some

*These were undoubtedly the ruins of the earliest Christian churches, despoiled by successive Turkish attacks.

reason a camel caravan was delayed, we had insufficient food. The only means of transporting provisions, kerosene, and mail was by camel. We awaited these impatiently, and when the long line of a caravan was to be seen rounding the mountain, a shout went up. "They are coming, the camels are coming!"

Slowly, slowly, the camels approached, their cargo lashed to their sides. Their loads had to be weighed accurately: exactly four poods* on each side. After they were unloaded, the camels lay down in rows and devoured their food with their small mouths.

We had a number of young men with us, mostly half-trained wartime doctors. One of them was always immaculate in his new uniform. His round red face, freshly shaved, glowed with youthful vigor and love of life. When preparing for an operation, he would blush like a school girl. In spite of his clean appearance, without washing his hands he would urge us to hurry up and remove bandages. The assistant and I had to train him: we just stood there, holding up our freshly washed hands, not obeying him.

"Take off the bandage. Didn't you hear me?"

"Excuse me, doctor," the assistant would answer. "We are waiting for you to wash your hands."

Finally he learned.

Once, when the camels were lying down in a row, this doctor took it into his head to surprise the nurses by walking on the animals' backs. The camels leaped up like lightning, throwing our doctor off as if from a springboard. He flew through the air for a good twenty feet. We gasped, but luckily he fell on a pile of soft hay. When we saw that he was unhurt, we all laughed heartily. For a moment we quieted down, but then, remembering how he flew, and looking at his red disconcerted face and his new uniform covered with hay, we again burst into loud laughter.

General Abatsiev was very kind to me, always helpful. "Sister, what can I do for you?"

"It's hard to take care of my men, Your Excellency. There's not enough to eat. If we could get a few chickens, we could have eggs, but as it is, the food is pretty bad."

*A pood is thirty-six pounds avoirdupois.

"All right, sister, I will do what I can."

In a few days I saw some Cossacks galloping up. "See, His Excellency has sent you some hens."

I looked at the hens, tied to the saddles with their heads down. When untied, they could not stand on their feet, and their legs were swollen. I found a large iron basin and gave them a hot foot bath. The young people made fun of me, but gradually my patients' legs recovered, and within a few days they began to lay. I was glad my boys could get eggs, but the other nurses envied us, and in fact stole eggs for their own patients.

On another visit, General Abatsiev asked, "What else can I do for you, sister?"

"There is no milk, Your Excellency. Perhaps we could find some cows?"

He thought. "I'll try, sister," he said. Several days later we saw a cloud of dust down the road. Some Cossacks were driving up seven cows. There was food enough for the cattle, much grass, and plenty of wheat, too, only one had to find it. The Cossacks went around the Armenians' houses, stabbing the ground with their spears. Wherever the spear sank in easily, they began to dig for the hidden grain.

Now I had a new task, milking the cows. They were thin and small; they gave little milk, but somebody had to milk them. There was nobody else, so I sat on a bench and milked, my hands aching from lack of practice. "What are you doing, sister?" I had not noticed General Abatsiev approach.

"I am milking, Your Excellency."

He stood for a moment, shaking his head. In the evening he sent a Mennonite* over to do the milking.

The nurses took turns on the night shifts. There were four wards with forty or fifty patients in each. One orderly was on duty in each ward, and one nurse for all the wards.

---

*The Mennonites are a Protestant sect with very strict ascetic rules. The Amish people in the United States belong to this sect. They came into Russia from the Tyrol in 1784 and settled in the province of Tauris near the Dnieper River. They were prosperous farmers.

Almost all the sick were suffering from typhus. The whole night long you would be running from one tent to another. The men groaned, hallucinated, were delirious. You felt completely unable to ease them or help them in any way. There were terrible moments, when the groans turned into a rattle. You hurried over. The sick man was quiet, his breathing had stopped, there was no pulse. You barely had time to cross yourself, say a prayer, then close his eyes—he was dead.

Once while making my rounds, I stopped in at a typhus ward only to see a very weak convalescent standing by the washstand. In the back of the tent an Armenian was screaming and swearing in delirium. Before I had time to reach him, he sprang up like a cat, leaped over two or three beds, threw himself at the wash basin, seized a bottle of mercuric bichloride, and aimed it at the head of the convalescent, whom he would have killed had I not managed to grab his arm. The bottle just grazed the patient's skull. At that the Armenian knocked me to the floor, seized me by the throat, and began to strangle me. We rolled across the floor, fighting, and blocked the door. The man's hands squeezed like pincers. The orderly on duty was trying to force open the door but could not. Somehow I managed to push the Armenian away from the door. Two orderlies burst into the room, captured him, and put him in a straitjacket.

Trembling all over, I went off duty and into the dining room.

Several days later, when the Armenian was himself again, he smiled at me as I entered the ward. "What made you want to strangle me?" I asked jokingly. He was embarrassed. "Excuse me, sister, God knows, I don't remember a thing. If I had been in my right mind, I would never have done such a thing."

The surgeon's assistants did not like the wounded men and did not know how to care for them. I had to take over from one assistant a Cossack foot soldier, wounded in the head. From his shaven skull wisps of gray matter protruded. He had bed sores the size of saucers. His mattress was soaked and stinking. He was

---

Because they were pacifists, the Mennonites were sent to work in the Russian hospitals during the war.

quite out of his mind, remembering only his wife Marusya and calling her by name. "Marusya, give me something to drink, rub my legs, they hurt."

We had to evacuate him, and he died on the road.

A brave Tersky Cossack, a *sotnik*,* often dropped in to see us. He was short, with a high-bridged nose and a dark wedge-shaped beard. His swarthy face was almost obscured by his huge, shaggy, white-crested turban. His black Circassian coat with its Caucasian insignia seemed too long for him. He came often, for it was natural that young men deprived of feminine company for months on end should attach themselves to us. But Commander Polner did not encourage officers to visit the nurses. He would mutter something hardly courteous to our guests.

One day this sotnik cantered up on a beautiful horse and, dismounting, asked me: "Do you like my new horse? I've just bought him, he's a half-breed Arab."

"He's splendid. How does he ride?"

"Take a look." The captain leaped straight from the ground into the saddle, galloped a little way, and returned. "Well, what do you say, sister?"

"Fine. I didn't know there were so many Arab horses in Turkey."

Several days passed. As we were coming out of the dining tent, the administrative officer cried, "What's this? Look, the captain has ridden your horse away!" (I had not yet acquired my faithful Kabardin.)

In its place stood the captain's dark bay stallion. Without thinking, I had praised his animal; therefore, according to Caucasian custom, the captain had given him to me. Our men leaped into their saddles, the administrative officer on the Arab, our boys on their own mounts, and galloped off in pursuit of the captain. With some difficulty, they persuaded him to return my sorrel gelding and take back the Arab. He was both sorry and offended. That evening when we were having tea, the captain's orderly ap-

* *Sotnik* means captain of a hundred Cossacks. These people came from the Terek river region of the northern Caucasus.

peared. "The captain begs the sister to be so kind as to be present at the Naursky dancing and singing."*

Commander Polner jumped up angrily, shaking his head. "Tell your captain that the nurses are not here to entertain officers but to work. Get out."

On learning this, the captain went on a regular spree. Cossack songs rang out far into the night, his hundred men joining in. They danced and sang right under General Abatsiev's window. In the morning the general summoned the captain. The Cossacks were reprimanded, and the captain was sent to the front. Several days later he came to see me.

"I am going to the front. One of two things will happen: either I will be promoted again, or I'll be killed. I make one last request of you: give me one hour of your time."

We saddled our horses and rode into the hills. What he said to me, I cannot remember, but I do remember that he was quiet and sad. For some reason I felt guilty. I never saw him again, but fifty years later he sent me a very nice letter from France. He was then in an old people's home.

CHAPTER SIX

From Karakalisa to Van

One day Commander Polner brought me a new assignment. I was to go to the city of Van. "The situation is critical there. Many are sick, typhus is raging, also typhoid and relapsing fever. The American mission there is in terrible straits, there is no medical attention, and we have to open a kitchen for the hundreds of Turkish prisoners."

*The Naursky Cossacks were from the northern Caucasus.

Van was an Armenian city a hundred and eighty miles from the Russian border. Our route would take us back to Igdir and then south over very difficult and dangerous terrain. I would be accompanied by two male student nurses and an orderly. (Commander Polner was coming as far as Igdir). In Van we would work with the American mission run by two couples, the Yarrows and the Ushers. Onisim I. Denisenko and Kolya Krasovsky would be the nurses. Onisim was the son of my cousin Elena Denisenko and the grandson of my father's sister, Maria Nikolaevna Tolstoy. Kolya was his close friend.

"When must I go?"

"As soon as possible. Send for your student nurses."

So there we were heading back to Igdir. By now I had my Kabardin, Alagez, and we all moved along briskly, walking a verst, trotting a verst, sometimes gathering speed. We were cheerful, for the sick and wounded were behind us, and we did not think of what awaited us. We felt at one with nature, filling our lungs with pure mountain air. All our surroundings, the infinite mountain ranges, the rushing streams, the valleys covered with tall grass—all this in its heavenly beauty was far from human malice, murder, and suffering.

We felt no fatigue. At midday we halted for an hour or so, unsaddled the horses, ate something, rested, and again moved on. Toward evening we camped at a military post, and early in the morning we were again on the road. All that day we traveled. That evening, as it was getting dark, we were descending a steep mountainside when suddenly a bullet whistled by us, then another.

"Kurds!" shouted the Ossetian orderly at the top of his lungs. We female nurses feared the Kurds, for there had been incidents of killing and raping women. We always carried cyanide capsules in case we were taken prisoner.

We gave our horses their heads and raced down the mountain slope, but it was steep, darkness had fallen, and nothing was visible. Stones were thick on the road; at any moment a horse might stumble and fall—then one was lost. I leaned back as far as I could to lighten the weight on Alagez's forefeet and kept repeating, "Bring us through safely, my sweet darling, only don't stumble." We galloped on and on, and we escaped.

Approaching Igdir, we found ourselves among salt marshes. It was pitch dark. The horses did not hesitate, they chose dry spots, straining, jumping from one hillock to another, avoiding the swamp. Never did I appreciate my Alagez as much as on that arduous ride. We went on like this for four or five versts. Finally we reached dry ground.

We spent several days in Igdir, going to Yerevan* to buy necessary equipment. We were very glad to get back to the civilized world of automobiles, electricity, good restaurants. Perhaps we lingered a little longer than necessary. "Why haven't you started for Van yet?" growled Commander Polner. "You are far overdue. Be kind enough to get going right away. Your help is badly needed there." He turned to another officer. "Accompany Alexandra Lvovna to the half-way mark."

Again we were on the road; the two student nurses, the orderly, and I. My cousin Onisim** was a handsome young fellow with blond wavy hair, slow in his movements. When his elders spoke to him, he would be confused, murmuring from embarrassment, his large dark blue eyes inquiring, as if he wanted to understand something as yet unsaid. He always seemed to me like a being from some other world, and I feared for him. I had no such feeling about his comrade, though. Kolya Krasovsky was sure of himself. Hardier and physically stronger, he lorded it over Onisim, whom he kept under his thumb. Whenever he saw camels, horses, turbaned Kurds, his dark eyes would flash. He wanted action, adventure.

Once more we had to cross the Chingil and the even higher Toporisky passes on horseback. By evening we would be nodding, half asleep in the saddle. Long ago Alagez and I had fused into one being, and I was aware of his every movement. At the half-way point, the officer assigned to us by Commander Polner left, to return to Karakalisa.

---

*Today Yerevan is the capital of Soviet Armenia.
**Onisim later joined the White Russians and was killed by the Red Army.

We arrived at an overnight stop. At such places half of the wide
Caucasian fur cloak is laid on the ground, the other half folded
over one's body as a cover; a Cossack saddle serves as a pillow.
In the clear, transparent air, gazing at the cloudless sky, with
thousands of stars twinkling overhead in the divine silence, one
lost oneself.

Alagez, not being tethered, moved about sampling the juicy
grass. I knew he would never run away, and that he would never
step on me. Blissfully, I fell asleep. In the early morning, a bright
sun awoke me. Before me lay a lake, its shores invisible, water
melting into sky on the horizon. There was hardly any movement
on the azure surface as it lapped against the rocky banks. How
wonderful it was, how beautiful!

The students were not to be seen. Probably they had gone to
wash. I went down to the shore. Suddenly, involuntarily, I
jumped aside. Something huge in front of me stopped in its
tracks. An immense tortoise, its head and feet withdrawn, lay on
a stone. I had intended to swim, but, having seen this monster,
I only washed on shore.

I joined the students and we rode on along the path by the
lake. At the last stop before reaching Van, we unsaddled the
horses and sat under shade trees to eat something and rest. We
had just stretched out on the grass when we saw a large, shining
automobile approaching. The people in the car seemed impossibly real in the midst of that wilderness, two ladies and a man who
seemed to have appeared by some mistake. The women were
Americans, beautiful in their bright dresses, gloves, and hats,
their hair dressed as if by a coiffeur. For the last few months I
had entirely lost contact with civilization. As to my appearance, I
had paid it no attention whatever. In fact, it was impossible during our forced marches. Probably I looked awful, my face peeling,
my rough gray coat of Caucasian cloth greasy and soaked with
horse sweat, with my loose Turkish trousers, boots, and the black
fur hat with the white crest, worn in this region as protection
against sunstroke. I do not know what the American women took
me for. They asked, "Where is the countess?"

The embarrassed countess answered, "Here."

Exclamations and greetings. The Americans from the mission had come to meet us. They took me into their shining automobile, and I rolled into Van* with the Americans, regretting the necessity of having to leave my comrades and my Alagez, who had been given into the care of our orderly.

CHAPTER SEVEN

The City of Van

The city had been devastated. Before our arrival there had been fierce fighting between the Turks and Armenians. The Turks had besieged the citadel on its high hill. There the Armenians had dug in, fighting like tigers. Day and night the women filled bombs with gunpowder and threw them down on the Turks. In the end they could not hold out. Their food was exhausted, their powder and shells were used up. If our Cossack infantry had not rushed to the rescue, the Armenians would have had to surrender. A bloody battle took place, with tremendous losses on both sides. Corpses were thrown into the lake, where they rotted, poisoning the water, so that we could not drink it or eat its fish.

At length the Turks retreated, leaving about a thousand prisoners in the town, the sick, the elderly, and the women. In revenge, the Armenians burned down the Turkish quarter. The houses were made of clay, and since clay houses do not easily burn, they set fire to each individually.

In the three former school buildings that housed the American mission, some fifteen hundred Kurds and Turks were dying of

*The city of Van is on Lake Van, a salt water lake of 1500 square miles, lying 5600 feet above sea level.

typhus and dysentery. Groans, cries for help, with filth and excrement all over the floor, no water either hot or cold. On the floors lay dirty bodies in rags, men and women, old and young, children, huddled together. Some of the children had suspicious spots on their faces—what could they be? Smallpox? Their emaciated arms stretched out to us. The women wept, beseeching us, trying to explain, repeating "Khanum, khanum!"*

The old men, however, were silent. Sullenly, malevolently, they kept their eyes lowered, their gaunt dark bodies bared; busily, they looked for lice, crunching them with a crack of their nails.

I turned to one woman sitting in a corner, her sleeves hanging in a strange, lifeless manner. Barely audibly, she was groaning. To my questioning look, my companion, Sam Yarrow, responded, "Her arms have been torn out of joint."

"Who did that, why?"

"The Armenians in the fighting."

"The Armenians? But why mutilate a woman like that?" I was astounded. "I've read in the papers that it was the Turks who acted like beasts and slaughtered the Armenians. I don't understand."

"Everything has happened here—slaughter on both sides."

In war it is only natural that such things should happen. For centuries the ancient enmity between Turk and Armenian had gone on, producing cruelty on each side. Here in Van we were in a position to observe the inhuman savagery of the Armenians. They had cut off women's breasts, it was said, they had pulled limbs from their sockets, they had broken arms and legs. I myself saw the victims of such beastliness.

Before we found our own living quarters, we put up for several days with the Yarrows. Theirs was a large house with every comfort, a bathroom, fresh, clean bedrooms, soft beds, a large living room, and a dining room. All this seemed unbelievably luxurious to me.

* Madame, madame.

During the night I began to itch. Something was biting me. However, the fact that I could undress, take off my filthy, sweaty coat and Turkish trousers was such a luxury that I paid no attention and fell asleep instantly.

In the morning I took a hot bath, put on a freshly starched dress—but again something bit me. A number of disgusting insects were crawling over the sheets. Lice. I could not understand this in an American house. Our host explained: "All the grounds, all the buildings are lice-ridden. Nothing to be done."

Sam and Jane Yarrow and their three children (two boys and a girl) were most pleasant, and I liked them very much. They had been impatiently awaiting us. I got to know Dr. Russell, the mission physician, less well. He and his wife fell ill soon after our arrival. That left only Dr. Russell's sister as nurse.

The problem we faced was immense, and I saw at once how little we could do. Many of the prisoners had already died, leaving about eight hundred. There was not a stick of furniture where they lay. No beds, no chairs, no tables, nothing. We managed to get food rations from the military, though there was not much to be had. We heated water to wash our patients and their clothes. Soap—impossible to get. Instead we used a salt-soda from the lake; this would do in a pinch. We set up a primitive laundry.

It was inconvenient to stay in the Yarrow's house, so we moved into a small Armenian one. I lived in one room; the orderly and male nurses had their quarters below.

Then the Americans came down with typhus, first Dr. Usher, then Jane Yarrow, next her husband. By now the only medical personnel remaining in Van were the military doctor and myself. My two nurses had also fallen ill. We could have no thought of rest, working on and on, with never a moment free, without sleep and almost without food. I do not know how I ever lived through those days, feeding and caring for the hundreds of prisoners, looking after the Americans and my nurses. By now Sam Yarrow was cyanotic, with hardly any pulse. "He will die, of course," said the doctor, waving his arms hopelessly. "Well, pour on the saline solution." This was to prevent dehydration. We nurses were not supposed to do this.

"But doctor, I have to attend to another patient."

"Give him some coffee and cognac and camphor injections three times daily."

The doctor turned away and left. Incredibly, Sam survived. All the Americans recovered. Now my orderly fell ill. I was very afraid for my student nurses, especially Onisim. He was an only son, the apple of his parents' eyes. If he fell ill, I thought, how could I ever face his family? He had come on my responsibility. I decided to send him to the rear. A few days after his departure I heard that he had caught typhus and had been transferred to the hospital in Yerevan.

Kolya Krasovsky was also ill, but improved. He remained in Van to convalesce, and our orderly stayed with him while he too was recovering.

In what had been the American schools, however, there were still several hundred Kurdish and Turkish women, sick or wounded, almost without any care. They had only meager rations, mainly corn, which they themselves cooked. Every day some twenty died, usually from typhus.

Everywhere lice, thick in our bedding and our clothes as well. Our closets were heavily infested with these vermin. Impossible to get rid of them. Even our underwear was impregnated with their whitish slime. Even if we washed every morning, by evening one's whole body itched madly from their bites. It was unbearable.

And all sorts of other things required attention. For instance, one day before he got ill Onisim had come running to me.

"Aunt Sasha, come quickly."

"What has happened?"

"They are going to bury a live Turk."

Behind the building a group of Turkish boys were running off with corpses on stretchers. Every day they threw from fifteen to twenty corpses into trenches and covered them with earth.

"Look."

We stopped two boys with a stretcher. It bore an old man, his eyes closed, not breathing, as it seemed. One arm dangled. I took it, to feel whether there was a pulse. Suddenly the eyes opened, the hand was withdrawn, to lie on his chest. He was alive! We sent him back to the barracks; but from that day on, when the boys carried off the dead, we went to see whether there were any still living. Kolya and the medical assistant were assigned to this task.

Onisim had to be relieved from such work. He felt faint at the sight of those terrible, livid bodies with their glassy eyes, piled one on another, at the odor of death rising from the trenches.

We insisted that the dead should always be well covered with earth, and we made the healthy adult Turks help the boys do this. There were no doctors. Only our Russian military physician remained, for all the others in Van had come down with typhus, and some of them had died.

The situation was growing increasingly desperate. With our lack of personnel, medical supplies, and adequate provisions, it was hopeless. I went to the commanding general. He did not receive me. Instead, he spoke to me from his window. "What do you need, sister?" Probably he was afraid of infection.

"Your Excellency, I need thirty carts, a full supply of corn and flour, a flock of sheep, and . . ."

"What are you saying? What's it all about?" The general looked at me in horror. "Why, what for?"

I explained. "The school buildings where the sick Turkish women are housed are on a hill. From there a stream flows down to your military barracks. All the filth from the sick people is carried by this stream. Each and every person must be taken out of the schoolhouses and sent back to their villages. Only in this way will you save your army as well as the Moslem women and their old men, for they are now infecting everyone with the dirt and the crowding and the lice."

"All right, I'll think about it, sister."

Within a few days some carts appeared. A flock of sheep arrived, and then some provisions. The Turkish women were in ecstasy as they departed. As they took their leave, they murmured, "Khanum, khanum," trying to express their thanks. They took off their necklaces and bracelets, set with some sort of semi-precious stones, and pressed them on me, and it was hard to refuse them. Somehow, they felt, they had to show their gratitude.

I waited on the general. A Cossack announced me, but the general did not come out to meet me. No doubt he was still afraid of infection. Again he spoke to me through the window. "What's the matter, sister?"

"I've come to tell Your Excellency that, if you do not resettle the other Turkish and Kurdish prisoners still held in the old American schools, your whole division is going to be sick. Typhus and typhoid are raging, as well as dysentery and smallpox."

"What can I do, sister? Where can I resettle them?"

I explained again. The schools were located on a hill, and all the filth from them was borne downwards by a stream. The army was camped on low ground, and the soldiers were drinking the infected water and washing their clothes in it.

"I tell you, Your Excellency, resettle these Turks in their villages, give them some wheat and some sheep, let them live in the only way they know how. What else can one do?"

For a moment the general pondered. "Let me think."

After two days a Cossack came to tell me my plan was accepted. More bullock carts appeared. Another flock of sheep was driven in. The sick and elderly and the children were loaded on the carts. I bade them goodbye, and my Turkish wards went off to their villages. My business was over. There was no reason for me to stay any longer in the city of Van.

When I left Van, Kolya Krasovsky remained with the orderly. He was recovering, but was still very weak. The general gave me his car and driver to take me to the pass in the mountains. It was as far as he could go. Farther would have meant only a two-wheeled cart or horseback.

Our route went through the village to which I had sent the Turkish women. As we progressed, I looked ahead, and there on the road was a beautiful Turkish woman, one of those who had wanted to give me their jewelry. On her head was a pitcher of water. Seeing me, she smiled. "Khanum, khanum!" she cried, waving her hand. A lovely girl, cheerful and spirited.

We reached the pass and began to ascend. The automobile got stuck. With the driver's help we managed to push it into a hollow, where it could not be seen from the road, for we feared a night attack from the Kurds. There we had to spend the night, no help for it.

One grows extremely drowsy after three weeks without a decent night's sleep. One's eyes close of themselves. I was sitting on the rear seat and was already falling asleep when the driver suddenly began to clamber in beside me. Without knowing why, I was frightened. "Go sit in front!" I said severely.

"But why?"

"You hear what I tell you? Sit in the front seat."

"Why? I don't understand; if the Kurds attack, I will protect you. I am a military man; give me your revolver!"

"Do you hear what I say? Do what I order you." Unwillingly he moved away. Indecent expressions, dirty words, followed. I took my revolver out of its holster and cocked it. If he moves, I will shoot, I thought.

I sat like this until dawn. I watched every movement of this half-mad man. A long night. Hard to keep my eyes open. My brain was foggy. My whole head ached. To sleep, only to sleep, to close my eyes for a second . . . but I knew I would be lost. He would take the revolver—and then I would be no match for him. At moments fright banished my drowsiness, but only for a moment. I pinched myself to drive away sleep. But the least movement of the driver steadied my finger on the trigger. Where shall I shoot him, the arm or the leg? I thought. I didn't want to kill him. Repulsive though he was, I did not want a man's death on my conscience.

Finally the faint light of dawn appeared. Slowly the sun rose from behind the hills. I looked around. Everywhere mountains. We were in a hollow, a narrow road above us. Suddenly I heard the sounds of cartwheels. I bolted out of the car, and looking up saw soldiers in a two-wheeled cart hauling a wagon wheel to be repaired. "Brothers, brothers," I cried, "take me with you."

"What's the matter, sister, where do you come from?"

I told them the whole story, as if I were talking to close relatives. I could not help breaking down, crying.

"Oh, my poor girl, what a vulgar dog, to scare you so. Have a seat, sister."

One soldier carried my things out of the car, and settled me on top of the wagon wheel. I never looked at the driver. As soon as we started, I fell into a dead sleep. When I awakened, I saw that the soldier had his arm around me, holding me by my leather strap so that I would not fall out. He slid down, took off his cap, and filled it with water from a puddle. "Here, sister, have a drink."

How I arrived, I do not remember, for I slept the whole way. The next morning I went to visit Onisim. Happily, he was already better.

If I had put in a complaint about the driver, they would probably have handed him over to a court martial or perhaps shot him. I didn't want that. The main thing was that nothing serious had happened. Let him be.

On reaching the rear lines, I learned that the All-Union Zemstvo detachment of nurses and doctors had been sitting in Tiflis for about two months, wasting away from lack of work, waiting for an assignment. What might they have done in the city of Van! Evidently, Commander Polner, who had retired from Karakalisa with our detachment, had not found time to send reinforcements to Van. Not having heard from me, he had not realized our desperate situation. Under our divisional commander, our detachment had retreated from Karakalisa in good order.

"Too bad we had to lose our chickens and cows," I said. "Oh, no," he laughed, "I didn't leave anything for the Turks. We took everything, and I herded the cows along with us."

Thank God, my student nurses entirely recovered, and I had them sent back to their parents in Novocherkask, near Rostov. But for a long time I could not rid myself of tropical malaria, and it went on being painful for many years. You feel quite well, then suddenly, without warning, you begin to tremble. The paroxysm lasts about one day. You have chills in bed, your teeth chatter, you cover yourself with blankets—nothing helps. Your temperature climbs to forty-one, forty-two degrees Celsius. In a few hours you begin to perspire, then the temperature falls. Once more you are perfectly well, only very weak.

Nevertheless, malaria did not prevent me from spending some happy days on leave of absence in Tiflis. I stayed in a magnificent hotel, and reveled in civilization. I dashed from store to store, buying new clothes, since all my dresses hung on me as a coat hanger—I had lost about forty pounds. My former secretary had come from Moscow to be with me, and every evening we would sit in a restaurant until late, eating shashlik and listening to a good orchestra. At last, however, we had to go home to Yasnaya Polyana, and then on to the Western front.

CHAPTER EIGHT

Again the Northwestern Front

I did not stay long in the country. It was dull without my favorite thoroughbreds. The agronomy jogged along slowly under the direction of an honest and reliable man who had already worked for me for several years. My mother, my sister Tanya, and her daughter lived quietly in Yasnaya Polyana. Mama would sit in an armchair and doze for days on end. Her sight was already poor, she could neither read nor write, and there was little that interested her. I spent a few days with them, then went to Moscow.

When you are working at the front, occupied with routine chores, caring for the sick and wounded, to tell the truth, you hardly think of political and military matters. Once back from the lines, however, I immediately found myself in a web of gossip—

talk of what was going on at court, reverses at the front, the destructive activities of the socialists, who were undermining the authorities wherever they could. All thoughtful people—the best elements in the aristocracy and the intelligentsia—were terrified as they observed the increasingly blatant propaganda on the one hand, and on the other the decline of imperial prestige, already visible in the early days of the war.

A particular concern was the tsarina, Rasputin's influence on her, and her interference in government affairs. Silly scandals were spread abroad, and much was blamed on a close friend of the tsarina, Anna Vyrubova. In the Duma intrigues were rife. The members accused the military of espionage. They blamed Minister of War V. A. Sukhomlinov for our retreat on the southwestern front. They said that the minister of war had sent the army into battle armed with staves instead of rifles. In Moscow the people destroyed German stores.

Everywhere ferment, beginning with the capital: dissatisfaction and confusion at the top and in the staff. Endless talk in the Duma, leading nowhere. Everything was unclear, mixed up, focused on selfish, personal interests. People did not consider that thousands were dying at the front owing to lack of organization, to intrigues, to careerism. They did not want to imagine (or perhaps they could not) the distress suffered by those in the front lines. The front and the rear were entirely separate worlds with no connection.

It was repulsive to hear the conversations that went on behind the lines. I tried not to get involved in them. I was anxious to get to the field again, and was glad when I received a new assignment to the western front as representative of the All-Union Zemstvo Medical Service charged with the task of organizing work with children.

Many of the families who lived on a strip of land near the front lines did not wish to be evacuated to the rear. Despite the danger threatening them every minute, they remained in their homes. The children were left without schools. My job was to organize school dining halls along the entire western front.

The report I presented was approved by the All-Union Zemstvo, and I went to Moscow to hire personnel. About two hundred teachers responded to my advertisement in the papers. I explained briefly to them what their duties would be, the dangers and difficulties of the work. When I finished, I called in each teacher individually, talked with her a while, and asked her a few questions. They had all taken teaching courses or had just finished their higher education. What interested me most was their motivation.

"Why do you want to work at the front?" I asked a pretty young girl with light curly hair.

"Oh, it's so interesting, so exciting." Not suitable, I thought to myself, writing down her name and putting a minus sign next to it.

"I want adventure, change," answered another. Again a minus.

"No one should sit idly behind the lines during such difficult times," responded a graduate of a normal school, a girl with smoothly combed hair, not very pretty. "Please take me." A plus sign.

"I love children. To think that they are not studying, living in these miserable conditions! I would like to work for them." A plus sign.

In this way I picked out about sixty teacher-nurses and, as it turned out, I was not mistaken in a single one of them. They worked magnificently. I used the same system with the housekeepers. The young people were wonderful, idealistic, willing to work.

In Minsk they furnished me with an apartment of two rooms, a bath, and a kitchen, requisitioned from a distinctly mediocre artist. I gasped when I entered. The walls were covered with erotic pictures of naked women in all possible poses, painted without talent. I went into Minsk but rarely, however, only to meetings of our representatives. I was not at all fond of my apartment and its pictures.

I spent nearly all my time going from place to place. It was necessary to find premises for the children's dining rooms, arrange for supplying them, get equipment and accessories for the schools. We had to build some of the halls underground in *blin-*

*dages.** The young people worked tirelessly, with enthusiasm, and within a few days the meals were organized. Now the children in this area near the front not only had a chance to study but got hot food as well. The work was not easy. Both children and personnel were in constant danger.

"We had all gone to sleep," a housekeeper related about one bombardment. "A terrific explosion woke us up, very close: one bomb, then another. Scared, we ran into the dining hall just as we were, in our night dress. We fell on the floor and lay there. One nurse crawled under a table in panic. We got up off the floor, but Valentina Pavlovna kept on lying down, covering her head with the hem of her nightgown, like a new-born child. We got a good laugh out of that."

I inspected one dining room after another. One school in the Pinsk marshes was entirely inaccessible either by car or on foot. They sent me over on a boat. As I entered, the lads were writing at their desks in a large room. One of my favorite teachers, a healthy, round-faced girl with a turned-up nose, Zina Ivanovna, was moving about the class holding something in her arms, swinging it as she dictated to the boys.

"What's this, Zina, a baby?"

"Why, yes, a baby. A few days ago his father and mother were killed by a shell. Where could we put him? I picked him up. What to do now, I don't know. He wears me out. We have to teach the boys, and here I have to take care of a little baby besides. What shall I do with him?"

And there I was, going back to Minsk with a baby in my arms. I didn't know how to hold him, I was afraid I might drop him. He cried. My dress was dirtied from his belching. Zina had given me a bottle, and I put it in his mouth so he would not cry. By evening I reached home and handed the child over to the orphan asylum. My friends, our representatives, were waiting for me in front of my own home.

"Why so late? We've been waiting for you. Where have you been?"

---

*Armored shelters to protect from enemy fire.

"Taking a child to the orphanage."

They laughed. "Oh? What child? Where is he from?"

"From the Pinsk marshes."

I could see that they were in a cheerful mood and had something up their sleeves, but I did not feel like laughing. It was a shame to give up the baby, but I was tired and wanted a rest. I was still oppressed by the impassable marshes of Pinsk, by the children's dog-like affection, taking in every word, every movement, of their self-sacrificing teacher, by the child left without father or mother, and by the dangers to which all the children and the teachers were constantly exposed. So I could not share this light-hearted, jolly frame of mind.

When I went into my apartment, however, I gasped. It seems they had spent the whole evening in it. No more nude women. They were all tastefully clothed. Ladies in fashionable dresses, ballerinas, peasant women in red, yellow, blue, green—little cotton dresses, full skirts, blouses—all carefully pasted onto the canvas.

"Barbarians!" shouted the artist next day. "And they call you cultivated people! This is a profanation of art!"

When I left again for the front, he undressed all his women.

After the school dining halls were all organized, I handed them over to my sister-in-law, Sophia Nikolaevna Tolstoy, the wife of my brother Ilya, and their daughter Annochka. I myself was ordered by the All-Union Zemstvo to organize immediately a medical unit with a base and three mobile detachments, one of only two women appointed to do this in the field. We had to stock up on provisions, arrange for medical transportation, recruit doctors, nurses, the housekeeping and administrative personnel. All this had to be done within ten days on order of the chief representative. Luckily, a part of the personnel who had worked with me both in Turkey and in the children's dining halls was now allotted to me. My friend Dr. Nikitin was assigned to us as senior physician. The woman doctor was one with whom I had worked as nurse in the hospital train, and there were several nurses from the Turkish detachment.

My team of about two hundred and fifty persons joined me without delay. The most difficult thing turned out to be procuring horses. I went to the director of transport. "I must have three hundred horses at once," I told him. "On order of our chief representative, the unit must start for the front within the week."

The director of transport was S. V. Petlyura. His red, rather unpleasant face flushed and his mouth twisted angrily. "There are no horses, I've already told you so." Not a likeable fellow. Not for nothing did we in the zemstvo call him "Podlura."*

"There must be horses!"

"But there are no horses! How many times do I have to repeat it?" He began to write something, paying no further attention to me.

"I command you, by order of our chief representative, to furnish me with horses at once!"

In a fury, I hit the table hard with my fist, not noticing from near-sightedness a spindle with some papers. I struck the spindle with such force that it pierced my hand. I pulled it out; blood ran all over the desk. Petlyura was then frightened. "What shall we do? How can I help you? Shall we call a doctor?"

"Not necessary. Give me the horses!"

I got those horses. But they were half wild, from the Kirghiz steppes in Siberia, and our team had to break them in.

Here I was again on horseback. Under me was a small, fiery Kirghiz roan, not a bad horse, but not as good as my Caucasian Kabardin, Alagez. As was customary, I rode ahead of the unit. The air was warm, for it was spring, but I was chilled and shivering. A short while before reaching Molodechno,** we stopped at a pine wood. By the time our team had put up the tents, I was almost unconscious. I was trembling, my head ached, my whole body ached. Finally, they put me on a cot. The nurses covered me with several blankets, put a thermometer in my mouth. Over

---

* Simon V. Petlyura (1879–1926) was a famous Ukrainian nationalist politician. In January 1919 he became leader of an independent Ukrainian republic. In 1926 he was assassinated while in exile in Paris for his role in pogroms. "Podlura" had an unflattering connotation—vile, base.
**Then a town in the province of Vilno.

forty-one degrees Celsius.* It was tropical malaria again. The next morning I was still terribly weak, but we had to go on. Again I was on horseback.

The unit was in three sections, which went in three different directions. Our base was not far from Molodechno. Our work began. The sick and wounded were brought from forward positions, bandaged, and sent behind the lines. The section commanders were ordered to arrange for night alarms. However, the personnel was dissatisfied, for they had never been bothered at night, and the nurses growled. Nevertheless, after a few alarms, we finally achieved the point at which, within twenty minutes of a command, each detachment was ready to move. Horse collars hung beside each pair of horses. Each orderly, each nurse, knew how to pack up the tents, equipment, and medicines.

Things remained calm until another order came from the divisional commander. This time we had to set up a hospital of four hundred beds in Zalesie, near Smorgon within only three days. "Impossible," I told V. V. Vyrubov, our chief representative. "How can I get the big tents for the hospital, and the beds, all the equipment, in such a short time?"

Vyrubov laughed. "*You're* telling *me*, Alexandra Lvovna! But if there's an offensive—"

"I understand. It shall be done."

For three whole days I hardly left the automobile. I worked our two drivers to the bone: Cherenko, a fine Russian lad, and our old Polish driver, Pan Kowalski, took turns. Molodechno—then Minsk. I had trouble requisitioning the equipment. Again unpleasant conversations with Petlyura. I demanded additional horses. On the fourth day, I advised Vyrubov that a hospital of four hundred beds had been set up and that we were prepared to take in the sick and wounded.

It was quiet then at the front. Our regular work went on, the sick and wounded were brought in. German planes flew over us and occasionally dropped bombs not far from our unit. One night

*Approximately 106 degrees Fahrenheit.

I was just about to turn in, when suddenly there came the familiar sound of planes, closer and closer. A bomb exploded somewhere near, then another. In their underclothes, without shoes,
the orderlies were leaving the sick, running into the blindages.
Our dog Ryabchik flew ahead of the rest. Whenever we were
under fire, he panicked. At the first sound of a plane overhead,
he would dash into a blindage.

"Where are you going?" I screamed in a voice not my own.
"Abandoning the sick? Come back! Get your guns, you scoundrels!"

The orderlies obeyed. First one, then another, then a third
plane flew over us. Everyone hid in the blindages or the tents. It
was a clear moonlight night, without a cloud. The shadows of the
stately old pines fell on the ground covered with needles. I wandered alone among the tents, for it was so terrifying that I was
ready to run anywhere to escape the noise of the planes, the
bombs bursting nearby. It was a wild animal fear, and I could not
overcome it.

"How brave you are! I've come so you wouldn't feel so frightened alone." The thin, little, not very attractive woman doctor
with the wavy hair was standing beside me.

"I'm not brave, doctor, I'm afraid of being underground, I'm a
coward. When I think a bomb might fall on a blindage and cover
it with earth, I'm terrified."

But she would not accept my explanation. When people believe a thing, it is impossible to convince them otherwise, and so
an undeserved reputation establishes itself.

It was hard for me, especially in the beginning to get along
with the orderlies, but three things helped me. First, my knowledge of horses. Nothing seemed to command the respect of our
team more than when I would lift the hoof of a lame horse, press
it between my knees, and show the blacksmith how he should
attach the shoes in such a way that the forefeet would not be cut
by the hind hooves. Second, it pleased the team that I did not
usually eat the food set aside for the officers but would have the
cook bring me every day a sample from the soldiers' mess. Last,
I earned the team's complete confidence after I removed a ser-

geant-major for having struck a soldier in the face. Discipline was essential. To maintain it, I had to discharge one of the nurses, who had allowed herself, with the collusion of an artillery officer who was being attentive to her, to fire a gun at the Germans. It is not a nurse's business to kill people, not even enemies.

I shall never believe that people are not afraid of being under fire, of bombs or infantry charges. Everyone is afraid. It is all a matter of stamina, the ability to control oneself, and not showing fear.

The station of Zalesie where we had stopped was six versts from Smorgon in a strip of land near the front lines. I was sleeping when the Germans began to bombard us one night. It seemed as if the shells were exploding right beside me. I slid out of my bed in terror. "Are you alive?" I called to the woman doctor through the wall. "Where are you?"

"Under the bed."

"Me too."

Another crash. I jumped and got dressed, but as each shell exploded, my head would sink between my shoulders and jerk forward. What to do? I could not show myself a coward in front of the orderlies. Stepping outdoors, I saw that they were breaking their necks to get into the blindages.

"Where are you going? Come back!"

When I had settled the orderlies in their places, I went toward the main tent. I noticed that I was walking upright, not bending over, not jerking my neck. Where had the fear gone?

"Where is the director of transport?" I asked.

"He's gone," cried Dr. Nikitin. "He shouted to the orderlies at the top of his voice, 'Save yourselves, whoever can!' Then he jumped on his horse and cantered off."

One more to discharge, I thought.

Within an hour the bombardment had ceased. The station of Zalesie was in ruins. Yet we had to bring in the wounded.

I seldom went into Minsk. My niece Annochka had taken over the children's dining rooms and she came twice to see me there. Some of our staff lived in Minsk, while others like myself worked at the front and came to town only on business. I had known many of these people since my early youth and in the evening sometimes we would gather in one of the apartments on Zakharevskaya Street.

Annochka had a lovely voice, a low contralto, while I had a fairly weak but true soprano. All of us would sing gypsy songs, I would accompany on the guitar, and sometimes we danced. The gaiety might go on until early dawn, then we would go straight to work without any sleep at all.

Once Vyrubov kept me late, and I returned to my unit only by evening. As I was approaching Zalesie a black cat ran across the road. Suddenly I felt uneasy, depressed. Why? I thought, a cat is hardly a reason.

On approaching the tent, however, I realized something had happened. I saw it in the faces of the personnel, in the whole gloomy, agitated atmosphere. Seven orderlies had been killed by a bomb dropped from a plane. Two doctors were wounded, and the blond woman doctor with the wavy hair was seriously injured in the hip. My tiny plywood hut had been shot through and through. Bomb splinters had broken the enameled pitcher, which still stood by the window, and had riddled my briefcase. These last German bombs had exploded with dreadful force, not from above but horizontally, along the ground. If our chief representative had not detained me, I too would have been killed. Fate.

CHAPTER NINE

Smorgon

I had to visit all three detachments, but the second and third were a good distance from the front line positions. There was less work to be done there, and it was less dangerous. I spent most of my time in the first section.

There were rumors, connected with the order to expand the hospital so as to accommodate many more men, that our troops were preparing for an offensive. I received this order: immediately, with no time to be lost, to move a detachment with doctors, nurses, and orderlies into Smorgon and deploy it in blindages along the communication routes. Within twenty minutes we moved out.

We came to an old pine forest; behind it, a hollow and a hill. Our new position was on this side of the hill. On the other, the Germans. Our blindage lay at the foot of the hill. We took our places, and waited. No offensive. Two German sausages* were hanging there. From time to time German six-inch shells broke around us. When the shells fell in the river Vilya, spray flew in all directions. This pleased the soldiers.

"Look, the Germans are turning on the fountains!"

When the shells did not explode: "A mere peck," the soldiers would call out, laughing. "The Germans seem to have got their shells wet."

"Your Excellency," a young officer said to me, "His Excellency requests your presence. I will accompany you."

We reached the deep blindage through a narrow passage. One could enter only by bending down. Behind a table covered with papers sat the general. He advised me confidentially that our army was preparing an offensive before dawn. He questioned me as to the medical personnel, the number of military vehicles, and the hospital. "By the way," he said smiling, "Do you know where we are now? Under the Germans."

That startled me. "What, there are Germans above us? Are we that far underground?"

"Yes, we are underneath the Germans."

We waited, tense. At two in the morning we observed that the German shells as they exploded gave out yellow smoke. It spread along the hollow and it smelled like chlorine. "Masks! Put on your masks!"

A half hour passed. The shells filled with gas went on bursting, and the hollow was gradually covered with a thick yellow fog.

*Observation balloons shaped like sausages.

"It smells to high heaven, brothers!"

Chlorine gas.

Again that terrible animal fear, jaws trembling, teeth chattering.

All at once I remembered that three orderlies were still in the courtyard with the horses, and that they had no masks. I grabbed three, but did not have time to go out before a nurse snatched them away.

"Leave them alone, sister, that's not a nurse's work." Two orderlies took the masks from her and ran out to the horses. Again, just as during the bombardment, fear quite unexpectedly died away.

Now they began to bring in the wounded. The artillery duel was in full swing. On both sides heavy shells were landing. To issue orders from behind a Zelinsky mask (recently issued in place of the simpler muzzle masks, as our soldiers called them) was impossible. I tore off my mask in order to give the orders. Nothing could be heard over the crackling roar of the heavy artillery. One had to scream at the top of one's voice.

"Krivaya Mashka is gone!" One of the orderlies yelled in my ear. "Can I go and look for her?"

Krivaya Mashka was the lop-eared mare that hauled our drug supplies. Somehow she had got loose and gone home. As we learned later, by some miracle she remained alive as she successfully hauled an empty cart into Zalesie.

"What are you doing? You're crazy, they will kill you like a partridge. Are the drugs unloaded?"

"All done."

"Well, don't go anywhere."

No doubt it's like this in hell, I thought.

By now you could no longer hear individual shells bursting. Everything fused into one roar, the earth seemed to tremble, everything around us was shaking. The blindages were filled with the wounded. Groans, cries. The doctors and nurses worked feverishly, binding up the injuries. One of the male nurses panicked. Unable to work, he was incessantly running up and down the passages.

The battle went on for several hours. Orderlies brought in the wounded on stretchers. To give an order, one regimental commander took off his mask, and died of gas poisoning. Some of the rest of us suffered from the gas too.

Dawn was breaking. Suddenly we saw a solitary horseman on the road. Shells were bursting all round him, but he came on at full gallop. What was he holding in his right hand? "That's my orderly," a young officer said. "The idiot, he could be killed any second."

"Sir," cried the soldier, cantering up to the blindage, smiling tenderly. "Don't be angry, your honor, I know you have not eaten for three days, so I've brought you some hot cabbage soup."

"Oh, you nitwit," the young officer's voice trembled, "Why, you've been risking your life, silly."

The German sausage was still hanging, but things were beginning to quiet down. We had to return to our base.

The senior driver, Pan Kowalski, drove me to Zalesie. The low ground we traveled on was still being shelled. When we started, the firing increased. Apparently the Germans thought that some important general was in the automobile. Suddenly, the car swerved to one side, gave a jerk, and stopped. Pan Kowalski lay face downward on the steering wheel. I could see that his neck and ears were turning pale and that his hand hung down lifelessly.

"Pan Kowalski," I cried in a voice not my own, "control yourself!" But Pan Kowalski did not hear. He was unconscious. It had never been my lot to have to beat a man, but our situation was critical. At that time I did not know how to drive a car. A shell could kill us both at any minute. So I shook and beat Kowalski on the neck and cheeks with all my strength until he recovered consciousness and began to drive. We reached our hospital without further mishap.

There people were working strenuously. The wards were filling with the wounded, particularly the gassed. The personnel and the orderlies did not suffer since there were enough masks for everyone there. But the trees and grass, from Smorgon to Molodechno, about thirty-five versts in all, had turned yellow as if from fire. At night, during the gas attack, the director of transport had driven the horses back of the lines, so that they had not suffered either. A spotted bitch, who had just had puppies, dragged her offspring onto a little island in the Vilya marshes and so saved herself and her family. Our faithful dog Ryabchik was also saved.

The ambulances worked from morning to night. Next day the corps commander called me in. "Arrange to transport the gassed back here to Zalesie."

"But Your Excellency, I have no more ambulances, they are all in operation now."

"What do you have?"

"Freight wagons and a few vehicles for the personnel."

"Send everything you have."

"But Your Excellency, there is nothing, all the male personnel have gone with the wagons."

"But can't you really?"

"Yes, Your Excellency, the transport will move out immediately."

And there I was astride my Pegasus, leading the strange miscellaneous collection of vehicles.

"Your pass!" cried the officer at the gate.

What pass? Good God! I had forgotten my pass at the general's.

"Telephone the division commander," I said. "I am going on order of His Excellency for the men suffering from gas poisoning."

They let me through.

Impossible to forget what I saw and felt during those awful days. A field of rye. You see a place where the rye has been trampled down. A man lies there. His face is maroon, he is breathing heavily. We lift him up and put him in the wagon. He can still speak. We take him to the camp—but he is already dead.

The first group was brought in. We went out again. The unit worked day and night. The hospital was overcrowded, the gassed men lying on the floor in the courtyard.

"Sister, put on your smock," Dr. Nikitin suddenly called, in a peremptory tone. "We need help."

Once in my white nurse's smock, I administered drops for the heart—oxygen. Twelve hundred men now lay in a mass grave.

Many more were evacuated. On the fifth day work began to slacken off. I was near dropping from fatigue. Back in my little hut I undressed, my feet so swollen that my shoes would not come off—they had to be cut loose.

A few days later, when things had quieted, an aide-de-camp of the tsar, Prince Yusupov (formerly Count Sumarokov-Ellston)* arrived. In the name of the tsar, he awarded six crosses of St. George to our unit, and a St. George's medal, third class, to me. I had already received a medal of the fourth class for my work on the Turkish front.

Many years have passed since then, but I still cannot forget horrors I witnessed during those terrible days. In that era, when so-called civilization had not yet invented even more efficient ways of destroying human beings, nothing was so cruel, so frightful, so despicable as poison gas. At no danger to themselves, people poisoned thousands of their fellow humans who had no chance of protecting themselves or fleeing. Mass murder. The evil shroud of gas drifted for over ten versts, spreading the most terrible of poisons, chlorine, destroying every living thing, people, animals, trees, grass. Men were swaying helplessly, their faces purple, gasping, falling, and dying. Why?

As I often did, both then and now, I remembered my father. In 1910 he had planned to attend a peace conference in Stockholm, but at the last minute changed his mind—and was glad he had not gone. Nothing but meaningless words. What was the sense of all those conferences, those endless discussions of peace, if Christ's teaching and the commandment, "Thou shalt not kill," are not accepted as fundamental law? Either the complete disarmament of all nations must be achieved—or we can only continue on our present course of allowing instruments of destruction for defense. But where is the boundary line? One country has fifty thousand troops, another mobilizes a hundred thousand to defend its frontiers, and so on, indefinitely. Until people understand the

---

* By imperial decree, Count Felix Nikolaevich Sumarokov-Ellston was given the title of Prince Felix Yusupov when he married Princess Zinaïde Yusupov, the last of that name. Their son, Prince Felix, organized the conspiracy by which Rasputin was killed.

crime of murdering one another, wars will continue. What are
the results of war? Moral disintegration. Revolution.

In 1916 a strained atmosphere was already noticeable. In the
larger cities strikes began to take place. The normal Russian kindliness was disappearing. An unpleasant contentious spirit hung
in the air. People shoved one another, answered questions unwillingly, rudely. Respect for the tsar's family was disappearing.
People sang limericks about "Sasha" and "Nikolasha."* Filthy,
unfounded gossip was spread about the tsarina, Alexandra Fyodorovna. Workers became slovenly. The newspapers carried articles
about railroad accidents. Somewhere, something was coming to a
head, something huge, unknown, terrible, even more terrible
than war. Behind the lines, however, people lived as always,
making profits, avidly pursuing the extra ruble, heedlessly making merry even while reading the papers.

Victories. Defeats. "No change on the western front." Sukhomlinov, the minister of war, was hauled into court because of the
defeats. In the rear the situation was accepted lightly, superficially. It was as if the people were hypnotized, unhearing, un-
seeing, not understanding what was happening, oblivious of the
threatening clouds slowly covering the land.

In our unit too we lived from day to day, occupied with our
small personal interests. It was quiet. Occasionally, planes flew
over us. Twice the Germans laid down a shrapnel bombardment,
but no one was wounded. Such a bomb would burst, sounding an
unpleasant whistle, and its splinters would bounce off our tents as
if on springs. I remember as if it were today how a Polish tailor
was sewing on his machine near the tents. When the shrapnel
splinters began to fall round him, he carried his machine to another spot, calmly, methodically, and continued his work.

In each of our sections people did their duty, healing the sick,
bandaging the wounded. In the second section, however, conditions were not satisfactory. The doctor made fun of the imperial
family, he criticized the regime, and whenever I approached him,
he would look at me obliquely and unpleasantly. He was friendly

* Impertinent diminutives for Alexandra and Nicholas.

with one of the nurses. They were constantly talking about something in secret. Later, after the first revolutionary coup, this doctor stirred up a whole Bolshevik revolution in the second section. I had to reconstitute it.

Probably everywhere, in all the units and detachments, there were secret revolutionary agents whose existence no one suspected. One such, posing as an assistant to a representative of our All-Union Zemstvo Medical Service, was comrade Mikhail Frunze. Later on, after Trotsky's downfall, Frunze was named military commissar by the triumvirate of Stalin, Zinoviev, and Kamenev. To the end of his life he was prominent in the Communist party. No one has ever known how he perished at last. Did he die a natural death? Or, as was rumored in Moscow, was he killed on Stalin's order?*

In the Zemstvo Union he conducted himself modestly, but he was not accepted in the society of our representatives in Minsk. He was not one of us, though he acted with exaggerated politeness toward us all. Saying nothing, simply bowing, he took orders. "Yes, sir, certainly." In fact, he did carry out, carefully and accurately, the tasks assigned to him. He was considered of no importance. I do not even remember his face. The faces of insignificant persons are not remembered. In his there was neither character nor strength.

CHAPTER TEN

The Russian People

In the last chapter of *War and Peace,* Tolstoy poses the question: what is the force that moves a people? And he answers, "The only conception which can explain the movement of

---

*In October 1925 he was called by Stalin to Moscow and ordered to undergo a surgical operation, during which he died.

peoples is that of some force commensurate with the whole movement of peoples.

"If the source of power lies neither in the physical nor the moral qualities of the individual wielding it, then naturally the source of this power must lie outside the individual—in the relation to the people of the man who wields the power.

"Power lies in the collective will of the masses, transferred by express or tacit consent to the leaders chosen by those masses."

Why did the people choose Communist power? I think there is one answer. Tolstoy answered that question, too. It lies in the absence of faith.

Faith had ceased to burn bright in the Russian people. Its spiritual strength, which might have been able to cope with the rough, cruel, and unprincipled power of the Third International, faded.

As M. A. Voloshin* has written about the Russian Revolution,

> And the ragged pauper went along, of all
> slaves, the lowest.

* Maximilian A. Voloshin (1877–1931) was a gifted symbolist poet known for great erudition and a deep love of country.

PART TWO

I Worked for the Soviet: 1917-1929

Abridged from the book of that title (New Haven: Yale University Press, 1934), except for "A Tale of Potatoes, a Pig, and Beautiful Sukhum."

CHAPTER ONE

The 1917 Revolution

A plump face with rosy cheeks and a small birdlike nose bent over me. This nurse with her shiny face and perpetual smile irritated me. She had been sent from the detachment to the hospital at Minsk to take care of me. I was sick with pyemia, I had been operated on, my temperature was high, and my head giddy.

But the Revolution had just broken out, and the uncertainty of the political situation worried me much more than the pain of the wound. Why was the nurse so happy? Her white teeth sparkled. Her small merry gray eyes almost disappeared in the creases of her fat cheeks.

The surgeon, an elderly Jew, came and sat by my bed and counted my pulse.

"Well, Doctor, how are things?"

"The infection is all right, but the malaria gives you a high temperature."

"No, I don't mean that. Has the Revolution gone any further?"

"Yes, the Grand Duke Mikhail Alexandrovich has refused the throne."

"Oh! That means . . . it looks as if. . . . Now Russia is lost."

"Yes, Russia is lost," the doctor repeated sadly as he left the room. The nurse smiled stupidly.

I left the hospital before my wound was healed. The doctor said I was crazy but he let me go. In March 1917, when the snow was melting and the roads were very bad, I went back to the front.

Nothing had changed with the Revolution. The soldiers stayed on in the trenches, lazily exchanging bullets now and then with the Germans. In the rear, life went on as usual. The men cut wood, heated their mud huts, and stood duty. Only, instead of calling the officers "Your Honor" and "Your Excellency," they began using the absurd and not less bourgeois "Mr. Colonel," and "Mr. General." In some regiments the officers themselves took off their epaulettes; in others, the soldiers tore them off. As before, the hospital detachments, having little to do, were bored and listless; and the officers continued to flirt with the nurses.

Yet officers, doctors, nurses, the zemstvo workers—everybody—pretended that with the change in government we had a group of intelligent people at the head of our country instead of Nicholas II, and that everything was utterly changed. Officers and men forsook the tsar. There were no monarchists left in the army. The officers were suddenly very polite to the soldiers, adding "please" to their orders.

And I who had awaited a more liberal government for many years, one without militarism, and with religious and political freedom, and with land for the peasants, watched these changes with mixed feelings. Like other Russian liberals, I had considered an overthrow of the monarchy essential, but felt that it should not come until after the war. With the Grand Duke Mikhail's refusal of the throne, and the war going on, anything might happen.

"The soldiers are waiting for you," the commander said. "When do you wish to speak to them?" The soldiers had never asked me to speak to them before. I realized that I, too, must behave differently.

"I'll do it now. Call the men together."

"Good morning, men," I said as I entered the barracks, packed with soldiers.

"Good morning, Madam Representative," they answered. They said it just like that: "Madam Representative."

"Citizens!" I began, "in this short time, Russia has passed

through great events. The Russian people have torn off the chains of the old tsarist tyranny . . ."

For some reason I was ashamed of myself, though the words I was saying seemed to be the right ones and I went on talking. When I had nothing more to say:

"Hurrah!" I shouted. "Hurrah! Long live free Russia!"

"Hurrah!" shouted the soldiers. They surrounded me and wanted to toss me in the air. I could already feel the pain of my wound. The chief of the detachment hurried to my rescue, and the soldiers tossed him.

"Will you allow us to ask you, Madam Representative," the chairman of the soldiers' committee said, "why the detachment is going to be moved?"

"It is the order of the chief of the division."

"Will you allow me to suggest that it would have been a good idea to let the committee of the detachment see the place and consult us on the matter?"

The idea of collectivism was being instilled. We could no longer ignore it.

The new location was examined by five persons. We rode about on horseback, looking for something better. We argued and discussed and lost five days, but we could not find anything more suitable than the place the commander had chosen. It was safe and quiet.

No sooner were we settled in the valley between two steep hills than the Germans opened fire. About two o'clock in the morning a familiar sound wakened me. Cannon were rolling. One after another heavy shells screamed over our heads. The men awoke, their excited voices echoed in the stillness of the night, horses clanked the chains of their tethers, and our big spotted dog began to howl. A few shells plunked into the opposite bank, splashing a fountain of dirt around. The men ran in scattered groups toward the blindage.

"What? Abandoning the sick and wounded, you scoundrels!" the commandant shouted, forgetting the new politeness.

It was impossible to stop them. Neither anger nor reason had any effect.

Down the hill, from neighboring regiments, soldiers in white shirts and shorts were running to our hollow.

"Brothers!" one of them shouted. "Brothers! save yourselves!"

In the red-yellow glow of the coming dawn, over the foggy dimness of the woods, a large black spot surrounded by smaller spots appeared and drew nearer. Looking like swallows, they flew over us toward the German front—a big Sikorsky * surrounded by small Farmans.

Open-mouthed and slowly turning their heads, the soldiers watched the planes till they disappeared. Suddenly the cannonade stopped. One by one the men returned to their regiments. There was something infinitely weak and miserable in those white, barefooted figures slowly climbing the hill.

In July, on the western front near Krevo, an enormous army was concentrated against the Germans. Troops and batteries were hidden in every thicket. Never in my life had I experienced such fire. Cannon roared day and night. We could not speak or hear each other. Guns burst from the terrific heat. New ones were brought and ammunition caissons traveled at all hours.

We had but few wounded, and most of these were invalids and officers. The soldiers were leaving the front in large numbers.

"Will you take care of me? And be quick about it." A soldier poked his wounded finger into the nurse's face.

"Please wait, comrade, we've got some that are wounded much more seriously than you are."

"But I tell you you must take care of me."

"I cannot, I have orders."

"You bitches! Bandage my finger, I say, or I'll . . ."

"What's the matter? What's the noise about?" the surgeon inquired, coming out of the ambulance tent, his clean hands in the

---

*The plane's designer, Igor Sikorsky (1889–1972), built the first successful four-engined plane in 1913. In 1919 he emigrated to the U.S., where he became the leading designer of helicopters. He was later to become one of the founders of the Tolstoy Foundation.

air. "The worst cases first—head, stomach, chest!" He disappeared into the tent. The soldier cursed.

It was said that seven lines of German barbed wire and trenches had been swept away by the shelling. The Germans retreated. But the Bolshevik propaganda kept on.

"Germans, comrades! Look out! German cavalry!" men shouted as the Germans were seen wheeling off with their limbers. The soldiers ran. By evening the Russian troops which had moved forward easily earlier in the day had retreated to their former positions.

A boy officer sat in the dining room of our detachment. He covered his face with his hands and wept. "Oh, the beasts, the beasts!"

"Who?"

"The soldiers. What swine! I never knew they were such swine! My best friend was shot down. Every one of the officers . . . and my best friend. Oh! but it's not that. I wish I'd been killed! Do you know how he died? Those devils! They left the machine gun and ran. He was wounded in the foot. He crawled up to the gun, pressed the button and kept on firing. The second shell killed him. What do you think of a death like that? And do you know what they said? I heard them. 'The war must be profitable to the officers. Even when they get wounded, those servants of the bourgeoisie still go on fighting!' The devils!" And the boy officer started weeping again.

A stream of curses. Everybody started up. One of the nurses shrieked. "You bastards!!! You're . . ." A heavy fist hit the table with enormous strength. The dishes clattered and one of the cups belonging to the woman doctor bounced off and fell to the floor, and again the frightened medical staff started.

The steward, a Pole, jumped up and approached the soldier with an amiable smile. In prerevolutionary days he might have smacked his face, but he was polite now:

"What's the matter with you, comrade?" he asked. "Please calm yourself, I beg you . . ."

"By God! Sending me at night with the wounded! You're warm—drinking tea . . ."

A grayish face, spattered with clay as gray as his coat, trembling lips, a quivering chin, and running eyes.

"Stop. We'll talk about it tomorrow," I said, putting my hand on the cuff of the coarse coat and looking into his dark blue eyes. Suddenly he shriveled, and became confused, small and pitiful.

"The cart turned over. I couldn't get out, the horses dragged me in the mud, my foot got caught in the reins. . . . I'm dog tired. . . . How can you send us out so late at night?" He burst out again. "The wounded should be moved in the daytime!"

And banging the door, he went out, leaving clumps of mud on the floor. The neat little nurse-housekeeper picked up the broken pieces of the cup and wiped the floor with a mop.

"His brain isn't quite right," said the surgeon. "He's been hit on the head. The men said he had those fits once in a while. He nearly killed someone with an ax in a fight."

"This is just the beginning," the Pole grumbled. "If that fellow knew he'd be punished for abusing his superiors, he wouldn't have any brain trouble, believe me. There's no discipline."

"Anyhow," the woman doctor suggested, "we must get rid of the man. He is dangerous not only for us, but for the sick."

"We'll try and send him to the front," said the Pole. "We can't have such behavior."

"I was frightened to death. I thought he'd kill us all," said the pretty nurse with curly dark hair over her forehead, looking sideways at the surgeon, with whom she was usually flirting. "Why didn't you stop him, Nikolai Petrovich? Were you afraid, too?"

"Oh, no! But you must never irritate a person who is mentally ill. . . . Let's have a game of chess."

The air was close and suffocating. Our talk, too, was flat and dull. Outdoors the wind was blowing, gusts of rain were beating against the windows. And in the dark, crowded barracks a new power that had been checked for ages was growing. It was rising with dreadful force, sometimes exploding in ugly fantastic forms; it had been suppressed so long that nothing could hold it down now.

I talked with the soldier the next day. "What the devil did we have the Revolution for?" he asked. "Instead of Nicholas II, we've got Lvovs and Kerenskys. Nothing's changed. We're still feeding lice in the trenches."

He spoke rapidly, swallowing his words, breathing heavily, as if afraid he would not have time to say all he wanted to. "It's all just the same. Your little Pole is drinking tea, maybe wine, in a warm room, and I. . . . Am I worse than he is? I haven't seen my wife and children for more than a year. . ."

The man wept like a child, rubbing his eyes with his dirty fist and smearing the dirt all over his face.

"Where's the truth, where is it? The surgeon's assistant says: 'You've fought enough with the Germans. Now you fellows go home and fight with the bourgeois. Take the land from the land-owners and the factories from the capitalists!' And our commander says: 'Cowards! Why do you swallow all that nonsense? Can't you understand you're betraying your country? The duty of every soldier is to stand up for Russia till his last breath, till the victorious end.' Oh, where's the truth, where is it? I don't know."

CHAPTER TWO

Talk

The barracks were crowded. Two dim kerosene lamps were burning at each end. The fumes of cheap tobacco mingled with the smell of cabbage soup and onions.

At the detachment base about fifteen miles from the front, the first election of the delegates for the Constituent Assembly was taking place. The chief of the base, a curly-haired, freckled young man, smoked nervously, his knotted fingers trembling slightly.

He was popular among the soldiers and we all thought that he would be chosen, but we were mistaken. A soldier who took care of the warehouse, Bormin,* was elected. The soldiers couldn't have done better. Bormin was an honest, serious man. The other candidate was as good.

The whole atmosphere of the assembly was businesslike and serious, as if the soldiers were entirely used to voting.

"Comrades!" Bormin said in his calm, gentle voice. "Forgive me, but I can't, really I can't. It's no joke to be a delegate . . . you have to be educated and smart, and what am I? Just a peasant who only went to primary school. No education, no experience! I can't, comrades, excuse me."

The soldiers urged him, but he would not change his mind. "It's no joke to be a delegate. I can't."

"Well, then, Bolotov will be our delegate. He's next."

"Oh, no comrades. I thank you heartily, comrades. If a man like Bormin refuses, how can I accept? I'm nearly illiterate! I can't!"

Dismay, confusion, almost horror were in the man's face, in his very figure, as he stood there tense and strained, at attention. His wide round face with light whiskers and eyebrows was scarlet.

"You've got to, Comrade Bolotov," one of the soldiers shouted. "We trust you. If everybody refuses, what will we do?"

"You're foolish, Bolotov!" another soldier cried. "If you fellows had chosen me, I wouldn't have refused!"

But Bolotov would not consent. "I can't upon my word of honor, I can't. I haven't got . . . I can't talk. . . . Well, I don't known how to explain it, but I haven't got the courage to try. I just can't—and that's all."

There was an uproar in the barracks. For a few minutes no one could make himself heard. The curly-headed young man tried to bring the assembly to order.

"Sukman! Let's have Sukman, the clerk," a loud voice cried.

Somebody laughed. Sukman sat motionless, as if the matter did

---

*I have thought it best to give fictitious names to many of the people who appear in these pages (ALT).

not concern him in the least. He was busy writing down the proceedings of the assembly. He was always like that, paying no attention to what was going on around him, bent over his desk,
writing in his clear round hand.

"But he's got only three votes."

"But if everybody else refuses?"

"He's a Jew. We want a Russian delegate."

"Shame on you, comrades. We've got freedom and equality
nowadays," the same voice insisted. "Sukman! We want Sukman
to be our delegate!"

The soldiers were silent. Suddenly and unexpectedly, putting
his pen behind his right ear, Sukman rose.

"Comrades, I will be your delegate! Thank you for the honor,
comrades!" He was silent for a moment, took the pen from behind his ear, started to sit down, then all at once straightened up,
his black eyes shining, and cried out, raising his voice strangely:
"Com-rades! I shall defend the interests of the proletariat to the
last drop of my bloooood!"

Then he became calm and silent again. His small dark head,
his body in a neat, clean suit tightened with a new yellow belt,
bent over the minutes of the proceedings.

The assembly was closed. The next day, a new clerk was doing
the work in the office, and delegate Sukman started for Minsk.

Everybody was making speeches. Platforms sprouted like
mushrooms. There were meetings everywhere. Strangers—all
sorts of extraordinary people—appeared and urged the soldiers
not to submit to the officers but to leave the front. Officers, soldiers, nurses, everybody made speeches. I went to a detachment
and found myself taking part in a meeting. A Bolshevik agitator
was on the tribune. He had scarcely finished before my chauffeur
jumped on the platform.

"Comrades," he cried, as if he had done nothing but deliver
speeches all his life, "comrades, I am a Pole, but I am a Russian
patriot. I am for the continuation of the war until the victorious
end with no annexations or indemnities." He ejaculated short
loud sentences and struck his chest. When he had finished, the

soldiers shouted "Hurrah!" They were going to toss him in the air, but a new speaker sprang to the platform.

"Down with the spongers of capital!" he shouted at the top of his voice. "Down with the bloodsuckers who are drinking the blood of the working class! While you soldiers are feeding lice in the trenches, while you are damp, hungry, cold, and miserable, the tsar's spies, avoiding military service for their own selfish ends, are trying to . . ."

He spoke for about half an hour. "Long live the Council of the Soldiers' and Workers' Deputies!" he concluded.

"Hurrah!" the soldiers roared, and, seizing the speaker awkwardly by his hands and feet, they flung him into the air.

I felt something boiling in my breast. I could bear it no longer. I, too, was standing on the platform delivering a patriotic speech.

It was madness.

I shall never forget one division commander, an old Bulgarian general. It was said that his body was covered with scars; that he had once been flogged in his native country for his revolutionary activities. He spoke very calmly but wholeheartedly of the necessity for holding the front, of our duty to the new revolutionary government. When he finished, there were tears in his eyes and the soldiers, too, were moved. But at the first sounds of a new shrill-voiced speaker, the impression of his quiet words disappeared.

Anger, hatred, vengeance were beating on strained nerves, awaking powerful, long-suppressed waves of independence and rage.

"Down with the tsar's generals! United into one peaceful front, the proletariat of the whole world will repulse all the capitalists and hangmen of the world! Comrades! Down with the war against our brothers! Let us begin building a peaceful socialist life. Peace to the huts! War to the palaces!"

Those were new, not quite understandable, words, but they burned like fire. They were a call to something unknown, unexperienced, and certainly something better than tsarism.

The general bent his white head as if he had suddenly become very old and weak, and making strange short sounds through his nose, walked slowly away.

Once, as I drove up to the quarters of the first detachment, the doctors and the commander rushed excitedly out of the tent to meet me.

"Please let us take your automobile! They're having a meeting three miles from here and Kerensky* is going to speak!"

I wanted to hear him, too, and we all jumped into the car.

We were late. A crowd of soldiers had collected. On a high tribune a slender man in a soldier's khaki coat was shouting words that were scarcely distinguishable. He was very hoarse. But I thought I detected an artificial emotion in the words I caught.

As we drove home and the doctors exchanged enthusiastic banal talk about the speech, I was bored and anxious.

Can people seriously believe, I thought, that this hoarse man can save Russia with his speeches?

An inspection team consisting of the division veterinary, a general, and representatives from the zemstvo came to the first detachment to examine the horses. At that time, because of lack of discipline and care, many of the horses in the army were infected with mange. But in all our three detachments we had succeeded in avoiding the disease. I gave an order to the commander of the detachment, who passed it on to the sergeant major, as military procedure required, for the horses to be brought to the front door by the soldiers. Five, ten, twenty minutes passed. The inspectors were waiting. I had begun to feel a little nervous, when the commander came in and asked to see me privately. The sergeant major reported that the soldiers refused to bring up the horses.

"What! Send the sergeant to me."

"What's the matter? Why don't you bring the horses?" I asked him.

*Alexander Feodorovich Kerensky (1881–1970). After the February Revolution of 1917 he became minister of justice, then war minister under Prince Lvov, and in July succeeded Lvov as premier. In November his government was overthrown by the Bolsheviks and he escaped to Paris. He came to the U.S. in 1940.

"The soldiers say that if the general wants to see the horses, he can come to the line and look at them."

Pretending not to hear or quite understand the sergeant major, I said sternly, "I don't like this at all. You are keeping the inspectors waiting. You know that our horses are in good shape and that there is nothing to be worried about. Tell the men that everything will be all right. The other horses have mange but ours are in fine condition. Four gallons of wine if the inspectors are pleased."

"But, Madam Representative . . ."

"Don't you understand me? Now hurry. The horses must be here in five minutes, and don't forget to give the order about the wine for the men."

"Yes, Madam Representative."

In five minutes the men came up in fine order, each leading his well-fed healthy team. The general was pleased.

"Very good, men!"

"Glad to carry out your orders, Mr. General!"

Everybody cheered up. The soldiers began to smile good-naturedly.

But on the whole the situation became more complicated every day. Discipline was breaking up. It was especially bad in the second detachment. The commander could not do anything with the soldiers. They insolently refused to work. They would not move to a new location ordered by the commander of the division. Part of the reason for this was that the surgeon of the unit happened to be a Bolshevik, and the woman doctor of the second detachment was infatuated not only with the doctor's ideas but with the doctor himself. There was also a Bolshevik nurse in the detachment who was spreading Communist propaganda among the soldiers.

During an inspection of the troops, the commander of the division visited a military detachment. Nobody met him. He walked into the barracks; the men were lying on their boards and barely answered his greeting. The old general was astonished when he found that in our detachment, which was not a military organization, the soldiers stood at attention and were polite, but he never knew how we had worked for that.

Communist propaganda spread through the second detachment like a plague. The soldiers stopped working, stopped grooming the horses; everything was dirty and in disorder. Unable to bear it any longer I disbanded the detachment. There was little more to do at the front and, in fact, the war was really over. The soldiers were either fraternizing with the enemy or deserting. I decided to give up the whole unit, and turned it over to a naive man who thought that work could still be accomplished, and I left for Moscow.

The committee of all the detachments decided to have a farewell meeting in my honor. The chairman delivered a weighty speech.

"Comrades!" he said. "Today, we are seeing off our highly honored representative, who has been working so hard for our native, I mean our revolutionary, country! Comrades! Our detachment is really the best one. Comrades! Why is that so? I'll explain it, comrades. In all the other detachments they haven't got enough food for the men and for the horses. We've got plenty. The people and the animals are all satisfied. And why is that, comrades? It is because our representative . . ." and so on and on.

At last he concluded:

"Comrades! I wish our representative good luck and a happy journey, and I ask you to stand up in memory of our representative."

Everyone rose, as they do in Russia when someone has died.

Later I learned that this same committee which thanked me so politely and solemnly decided to arrest me as a bourgeois and counterrevolutionary. But it was too late. I had started for Moscow.

"Vaska, you devil, come on, I tell you!"

Raising one shoulder, a soldier slung his bag on the plush seat of the train with exaggerated jauntiness. A timid, freckled face appeared from behind the door.

"But this is the first-class compartment, isn't it? Won't they turn us out?"

"They won't, I tell you, you fool! Come on! That's all over. Now it's our turn to throw the bourgeois out. . . ." And the soldier looked at me.

"Grand!" said Vaska, bouncing up and down on the springs. "The bourgeois certainly knew how to travel!"

"They're through now! You, lady, move! We want to make ourselves comfortable."

There was no place to move to. I was sitting in the very corner. The soldier stretched out on the seat and pushed me with his dirty boots. I was going to get out when he jumped up and rushed into the corridor. The train had just left Minsk. There was a terrible racket in the aisle—yelling, swearing, the sound of breaking glass.

"Oho, ho, ho! Fine! That's the way to do it!" the soldier shouted. "They've sucked enough of our blood."

I looked out into the corridor. It was full of soldiers. Vaska stood with his mouth open, watching attentively.

"What's the matter?" I asked.

"Well, they've thrown an officer's luggage out the window. And I shouldn't be surprised if the officer followed. The boys look pretty mad."

I went back to my place in the corner, wishing I could throw out the whole carload, with their dirty boots and their insolence—especially the first loutish soldier. I was to have the pleasure of his company for two days.

The train sped on. Gathering his blouse in his hand, Vaska came in, scratching his chest.

Well, that fellow is lucky," he said. "They left him alone, but I don't know how he did it. I'd have bet they'd throw him out, too!"

"Why are you standing?" I asked. "Sit down. Will you have a cigarette?"

With dirty, rough fingers, Vaska awkwardly pulled a cigarette from my case and sat down.

"What province are you from?"

"Tula."

"Oh! Then, we're fellow countrymen. I'm from Tula province, too."

"What district?"

Vaska was going home. He wanted to tell me everything about himself, his family, his young wife. In about twenty minutes I knew his whole story. We were so absorbed that we did not notice the other soldier come in.

"Vaska, have you got any tobacco?"

"No."

I handed him my cigarette case. Silently, without thanking me, he took a cigarette.

"Now, look here!" I said. "We have a long journey ahead of us. There's no use being disagreeable to each other. I have a kettle, tea, sugar, and food. One of you can fetch hot water from the next station and we'll have tea. Stop swearing, and we'll try to make things pleasant."

"Sure!" Vaska said. His friend was silent, but when the train stopped, he took the kettle and brought boiling water from the station.

At every station more soldiers got into the train. The compartments were jammed. Men sat, stood, lay in the corridor, so that if you wanted to get out, you had to climb through the window. My kettle was handed from one to another. The soldiers got out their tin mugs, and, blowing on their fingers, sipped hot tea. No one tried to insult me. It seemed to be understood that I was one of the party. They tried not to curse, but they smoked all the time and spat on the floor.

"Oh, the devil! Isn't she fat?" a soldier shouted, leaning out of the window of the compartment and pulling me up by the hands with all his strength. "Climb in, I tell you! Now then! Ugh!"

"Wait, wait a moment!" Vaska shrieked in his high tenor. "I'll boost her, there's plenty to push."

"Be careful, you fool! She'll break your back, she will!"

When we arrived at Moscow, the soldiers helped me carry my baggage to a cab.

"Goodbye, sister!" they shouted as I drove away, "good luck, good health to you!"

CHAPTER THREE

Homeless

I reached Moscow in November 1917. The fighting had just stopped, and the Whites had been beaten. But, strange to say, although everyone I met sympathized with the Whites, no one seemed depressed. On the contrary, everyone was animated. The people of Moscow, who during the war had been well in the rear of the armies, were excited by gunfire. They were more concerned about someone's running out in the street during a battle, or about having to break into a store and eat caviar with large spoons to keep from starving, than about the issue of the battle or the future of Russia. The Bolsheviks and the Council of the Soldiers' and Workers' Deputies seemed so insignificant that it was absurd to be worried over Russia. It never occurred to anybody that they would hold power for long. Events followed each other with astonishing rapidity, and we felt sure that Bolshevism would be a transient thing, gone in a few weeks or perhaps months. Everyone I met was of the same opinion.

None of us knew what was going to happen or what we were going to do. Some were still trying to save their money, others to save themselves. The Bolsheviks were arresting and shooting people, but with a certain discretion. They were not at all sure themselves that they would be able to keep in power. Radicalism seemed to mean something in those days. A person involved in one way or another in revolutionary activity under the old regime could be saved from persecution.

Opposite my home in Moscow were the ruins of what had been a large stone house. There were signs of recent fighting—battered houses and tumbled walls—on every side. The house where I had lived was still standing, but my room was empty of personal belongings: everything was gone except a few pieces of furniture. The White and the Red staffs had lodged there alternately.

I tried to save the money I had in the bank, but that was a waste of time. The banks were nationalized and I lost nearly everything I owned. In the excitement I felt neither terror nor disappointment, but only relief, as though I had taken off a shuba* which had been warm but had weighed heavily on my shoulders. Loss of property meant very little in comparison with one's loss of inner balance. How were we going to live? Why should we live? The Bolsheviks proclaimed the destruction of the old life. The Revolution was sweeping everything before it, declaring proudly that a new world was to be built. What was to become of the old world in the process?

I could find no place for myself. Life was empty and weary, and any kind of creative work was choked. I waited as everybody waited. But meanwhile I had to think of earning my living. I had received a month's salary from the zemstvo when I left the front, and on this I got along for a few months. Rooms were to be had free or for a very low rent immediately after the nationalization of houses; railroad passes were free to workers; and clothes were simply not to be found. Food was my greatest need. People said that it was easy to get a job as a bookkeeper. I loathe figures and bookkeeping, but what did that matter? For a while I studied debit and credit conscientiously. But that did not last long. I soon threw the books away. Friends tried to get me into political activity; that was not my metier, either. Politics had always seemed to me among the worst inventions of mankind.

At about ten one night, as I was thinking of going to bed, someone knocked at the door.

"Come in!"

---

* A Caucasian coat usually lined with long-haired goatskin.

A tall, very dark man in a black cassock entered. I noticed at once his large bright eyes and his pallid face, which seemed paler because of his black beard.

"I am Bishop——," he said.

I looked at him in amazement—what could I do for him?

His name was well known. I had heard of his remarkable work in the far north. I got up, but did not ask for a blessing and did not kiss his hand as Orthodox custom required. I simply shook hands with him. He smiled as if to say, "I did not expect anything else."

"No one will hear us?" he asked, looking around.

"No. I am alone in the attic. Don't worry."

He sat down and again looked around, still hesitating. I did not break the silence. I watched him. There was nothing holy about him. He looked strong and ardent, and he was handsome, too. Women must be crazy about him, I thought.

He began speaking in a solemn whisper, looking me in the eyes, trying to impress me as one does who is used to being admired. He spoke of the salvation of Russia, of our duty to unite no matter what our ideas or religion, for the sake of Russia.

His eyes sparkled, his speech was brilliant and convincing.

"Wouldn't you make a sacrifice for your country? Even risk your life?" he whispered.

"Perhaps, if it were not against my conscience," I answered. "What do you want me to do?"

"Would you help us even if it were very dangerous?"

"Tell me, Father, what this is all about, and I will answer you frankly."

"You see," he began hesitatingly, "our anti-Bolshevist group has decided that the only thing we can do now to save Russia is to restore the monarchy. It is certain that if the family of the tsar remains in the hands of the Bolsheviks, they will all be massacred. We have made up our minds to kidnap the tsarevich. We will keep him abroad, say in England. And at the right moment, we will declare to the people that the Grand Duke Alexis is alive and will be proclaimed tsar. The people will follow us. Can you help us plan the kidnapping of the Grand Duke Alexis?"

I had expected anything, yet I was so thunderstruck that for some time I could not say a word. For a moment his contagious madness got hold of me and I really considered the idea. I always liked adventure, and this was one such as I had never dreamed of. But that was only for a few seconds. My thoughts returned to the rut of common sense. Without taking his black eyes off my face, the bishop waited for me to speak.

"I cannot, Father, I cannot. . . ."

What help would there be in a sick, delicate boy, even if he were on the Russian throne? The Russians had suffered too much these last years. They did not need the reestablishment of the old regime. The mistakes of tsarism and the Orthodox church had prepared the soil for the Bolshevik Revolution, and it was absurd to think of restoring that same government.

The bishop went, leaving me an enormous package of proclamations. I looked them over. They were appeals to the people, written in a bad monarchic-orthodox style. I burned them and stopped thinking about politics.

It was not easy to give up my country home, which was declared government property. The members of the village Soviet had come and laid claim to what they wanted—horses, cows, machinery, and tools. I could not realize that my house and the horses and dogs I had raised and trained myself no longer belonged to me.

I went through the cold empty rooms. Long before I returned from the front, thieves had gotten in and stolen furniture and clothes and dishes. I could not bear the sight of the place. I visited the servants' quarters and the barn, and talked with the workers. Nothing interested me; nothing was mine. I went into the garden and sat on a bench. Two large white Eskimo dogs that I had raised from puppies ran to me, looking in my face, licking my hands.

"What shall I do with them?" I thought. "Take them with me? Where?"

For the first time it was borne in upon me that I did not have a home any more.

I had to get it over with, and the sooner the better—give up my house, but not the animals. I called the estate manager. He had been platoon commander in my detachment at the front—a silent, businesslike Ukrainian. His small brown eyes squinted, and his drooping mustache could not hide his cunning half-smile.

"Harness all the horses to the carts."

He stood before me as silent and stubborn as only a Ukrainian can be.

"Harness the horses," I repeated, getting angry.

"But may we?"

"May we what?"

"The village Soviet forbade anyone's taking anything away."

"It's not your business to argue about it!" I said. "Harness up. I'll be responsible for whatever happens."

He was used to obeying my orders. "All right."

With the help of the workers who were still on the estate, we loaded the carts with machinery, tools, beehives, and furniture, and drove to the old Tolstoy home at Yasnaya Polyana. As soon as the carts were unloaded, we went back for more. We worked all day. The workers shook their heads and laughed, but did not object.

I slept in the empty house on a pile of hay, and next morning about three o'clock, in the darkness, we took the horses to market and sold them for half what they were worth. But I was happy at not having left them for the village Soviet.

Then I went to the department of agriculture. A section had just been established to protect thoroughbred animals. Peasants were taking over great properties and farms with purebred cattle, and, not knowing what to do with them, they simply killed stallions and bulls that had cost thousands of rubles. A peasant would try to harness a thoroughbred trotter to his cart. The harness wouldn't fit, the horse would be nervous, and the cart would get smashed and the horse hurt. One peasant got a stallion which had won a number of prizes at the races; but his stable was too small for the huge animal. Not knowing what else to do with it, he killed it.

The chief of the section, whom I had known before, came and marked my cows and bull as thoroughbred cattle belonging to the Agricultural Department of Tula, so that no one had the right to kill them or dispose of them.

There was nothing more to be done. I whistled to the dogs and drove off to Yasnaya Polyana with the last horse that was left, the dogs joyfully following.

My mother, my sister Tanya with her little daughter Tanichka, and, later, my aunt lived at Yasnaya Polyana. All the neighboring estates were in ashes and nearly every house in our district had been robbed and burned. There had been rumors that Yasnaya Polyana, too, was going to be destroyed, not by our own peasants but by others.

Tanya told me afterward how they had packed everything and awaited the pogrom from hour to hour. It probably would have come, but the Yasnaya Polyana peasants had told the rioters that they would meet them with pitchforks and axes. And Tanya had telegraphed to Kerensky, who immediately sent a hundred soldiers to protect the estate. Now everything was quiet.

The three ladies lived simply enough. The cook, Semyon Nikolaevich, had been dismissed. I met him in the village and hardly recognized him. He was farming now. His once plump red cheeks were unshaved and thin, his clothes rough, his big round stomach was gone.

"I couldn't keep him any longer," Mother said. "It was too expensive."

But Father's old valet, Ilya Vasilievich, was still serving dinner in his quiet way, though the food was scanty and his white gloves were darned.

My mother was an old woman now. She sat dozing in a rocking chair all day.

"My eyes are very weak," she would say. "I can't write or read any more."

She had some gold saved. She lived on that. I was astonished to see how cool she was about everything that was going on around her. Now that everything was lost, she did not worry at all about her own welfare or the welfare of her children and grandchildren.

In the village, the peasants boasted that they had not even touched Yasnaya Polyana, but had defended the estate from their neighbors.

"It would have been a shame if you had," I said, sensing some regret under their words. "Didn't you get all the land of the estate free in 1911? What else do you want?"

"Sure," they agreed, "that's right. But in other places people got lots of things: furniture, clothes, cattle, machinery."

"And we never got anything," interrupted a woman nicknamed Queen Helen because she was the tallest woman in the village. "They got plenty from the landlords and what did we get? Absolutely nothing. It's not fair."

There wasn't much more to be done at Yasnaya Polyana, and I decided to divide my time between it and Moscow until I could find an occupation somewhere.

CHAPTER FOUR

A Tale of Potatoes, a Pig, and Beautiful Sukhum

In Russia about this time there was a famine. Senseless, utterly unnecessary. Throughout the country plundered by the Reds there was neither fat, nor meal, nor salt, nor sugar, nor bread. What had become of all the agricultural wealth of this land—the wheat from the Ukraine and the Volga provinces, the rye from the central districts, the potatoes and fruit from the south?

People who lived in the cities were emaciated. Hoarding their last bits of value, their last rags of clothing, they streamed into the provinces of Tula, Kursk, Kharkov, where they hoped to trade warm garments for flour and other staples. In the markets of Moscow and other cities they could exchange their old dresses, overcoats, watches, earrings, or bracelets for potatoes and other farm produce.

You would be sitting on a crate somewhere, chilled to the bone. A fat woman in a sheepskin coat and felt boots, her head wrapped in a kerchief, would approach you. "What are you selling, little lady?"

She would paw over your things, scattering them on the wet, filthy pavement.

"What are you looking for? What do you want? Stop throwing my things in the puddles!" you'd cry, furiously.

"I want a thick woolen coat, little lady, a warm one. This trash of yours doesn't suit me. Haven't you a newer one of cheviot or velveteen?"

"Well, how about this quilted one? Don't you want it? It's very warm and it has hardly been worn."

Sometimes I would sit like this for half a day and go home without having traded a thing, my feet numb with cold. Inside me hunger had produced a shuddering. I dreamed of baked potatoes with salt, hot tea—a tea made from dried carrots or linden blossoms, for there was no real tea in those days. But this was out of the question. These things were not to be found anywhere.

When I stayed at Yasnaya Polyana there was nothing to eat either. Ilya Vasilievich Sidarkov would bring us—not roast beef, steak, or grouse—simply boiled beets, sometimes even without any oil and, rarely, porridge. During the last years of her life my mother's main dish was beets.

Our old man-servant was very faithful. He remembered, no doubt, that Father had never let him do the dirty jobs, but always carried out the garbage into the forest himself. There, too, he would open the traps set for various creatures and let the mice free if any had fallen into them.

In this period I was living in Moscow and went to Yasnaya Pol-yana only in the summer. Detachments of the Red Army were constantly going about the country requisitioning, blocking all roads to the cities, searching people at railroad stations and high-way gates, seizing any provisions they found. Sometimes, though, I managed to climb into a freight car with a sack hidden under my skirt; or perhaps I could only get up onto the steps, holding onto the railing with both hands. When the train picked up speed, I had to grip with all my strength so as not to slide off with my precious load. The heavy sack would sway and drag at me, threatening at any moment to throw me off. Praying, I clung and finally squeezed inside the car.

When I got home and the flour turned into fragrant black bread—what a joy! Now I could feed beloved friends weak from hunger. What didn't we do in those days to get food? In Moscow everybody's chief concern was the hunt for something to eat. Gradually, even in the villages, potatoes disappeared.

How to describe the feeling of nausea in one's stomach from hunger? For days on end your head would spin. It was hard to fall asleep at night.

Once in the spring I came to Yasnaya Polyana. I no longer re-member where or how, but Ilya Vasilievich and I found two whole bags of potatoes. One part we ate at once. We decided to plant the other part. By chance I had read several pamphlets about how to grow rye by the Demchinsky system, oats by the Ovinsky system, and potatoes in pits. By this time I had already appointed Ilya Vasilievich superintendent of the house and the museum at Yasnaya Polyana. Together he and I decided to try growing potatoes in pits.

We each dug forty holes about three-fourths of a cubic yard in size. On the bottom of each hole we sprinkled wood ashes mixed with a little good earth and manure. Then we laid down potatoes, covered them with soil, and waited. We were far from certain that our experiment would succeed, and so we worried. Within a few days Ilya Vasilievich came to me in great excitement. "They've sprouted! They're beginning to grow! Come, I'll show you!"

They had indeed sprouted. We covered the shoots with sifted soil and again waited. Several weeks passed. The shoots kept climbing out of the ground. The rain watered them. Stubbornly, we went on covering them with soil. Wet by rain and warmed by the sun, they kept rising into the light of day.

Now we each had forty little potato hills in the garden. They looked like ants' nests with their long runners. At last, to our immense joy, the runners flowered and began to dry up. A main runner was a yard long. On it—according to how well we had covered the mounds—potatoes were growing! The earliest shoots produced the largest, the last to be covered with soil, the smallest. Finally the moment to harvest arrived. We began to dig up our crop. Ilya Vasilievich and I each collected two full cartloads from our twice-forty pits. Success! A brilliant success!

Even now, after so many years in luxurious America, all that seems like a miracle, a fairy tale. At the time we could hardly believe our eyes. Ilya Vasilievich and his family lived for a whole winter on potatoes, and so they experienced no extreme hunger. Some of my portion I exchanged for a tiny piglet, which I fed with a share of my potatoes. It grew up, turned into a three-hundred-pound sow, and produced twelve piglets. Yet that was not the end of the tale. I sold the huge mother and all her children. On the proceeds I took a trip to the Caucasus.

What a marvelous journey! The lofty, mysterious, inaccessible peaks covered with snow, the rushing streams, the Georgian Military Highway, the pass to Sukhum and Lake Tiberda just where the glaciers begin. I couldn't resist, despite the protests of my comrades, and went for a dip. The water was icy, it burned like fire, and I scrambled out like a shot, my feet slipping on the ice.

The pass to Sukhum was far from easy walking, but what beauty! Underfoot glittered the blinding ice. Above and beyond towered the mountains with their springing waterfalls. One night we spent on a glacier, wrapped in furs, lulled by the sound of the stream.

Toward evening the next day, having left the glacier far behind, we trod on the soft mosses of an immense forest of beeches. Suddenly we emerged. There on a distant horizon were tiny houses and the Black Sea, deep blue in the sunlight.

Our small mountain packhorses with their thick manes were sure-footed. They crossed the rushing streams on narrow log bridges. We humans were aware of the precipices, the swift currents, but the horses cared only for what was underfoot. They walked with assurance, clever beasts.

In Sukhum I stayed with our friends the Smetskys, a well-known botanist and his wife. Some miles outside the town he had cultivated a famous garden of tropical plants, hundreds of kinds of palms, cactuses, acacias—all the result of a lifetime of exquisite care. The Reds, however, had seized everything, above all, the orange, mandarin, and lemon groves, leaving him only the little watchman's cottage to live in for the rest of his days.

Now the old couple were very poor, supported only by the sale of the wife's pastries, which she carried daily four miles to sell in the town. These were exceptionally educated people, finely bred, gentle and considerate. Never did I hear a single word of complaint from them, they were always thankful for the least aid or sympathy.

Higher up on the slope of the mountain was the large villa they had built. It had been expropriated by the government. For a time Trotsky lived there surrounded by his followers. At night the jackals would run about it howling. I longed to creep up there to steal the roses Smetsky had planted, but I was too afraid. I don't know which I feared most—Trotsky, or the jackals.

It was the potatoes to which I owed that journey to the Caucasus and my encounter with such exceptional persons as the Smetskys. Nevertheless, no matter how I tried, I could never repeat the pit experiment. Later, on my American farm, the pits filled up with rain water and the potatoes rotted.

CHAPTER FIVE

Tolstoy's Sister

I received a letter from Aunt Tanya. She had been to see her sons in Petersburg and was going back to Yasnaya Polyana. She would stay with me a few hours in Moscow and wanted me to put her on the night train.

At that time, transportation had gone to pieces. Trains were irregular and very scarce. But crowds of people in the cities wanted to go on to the southern grain provinces, where flour and bread could be got in exchange for clothes, shoes, tobacco, and soap. The railroads had been nationalized and certificates were being used instead of tickets. These were given to all workers and their families and were easy to get. But to put someone on the train was a different matter. Stations and platforms were packed with people who sat or lay on the ground, keeping an eye on their bags and boxes for fear of thieves. They would wait sometimes for days to get on a train, and when the train came in, it was rushed. The crowd stampeded, yelling and cursing. People were crushed and baggage smashed. Several times I saw the bodies of those who had been killed in the jam.

Once in such a melee someone seized my box and tried to get it away from me. I held on, but the crowd drove me along and nearly tore me in two. I fell on my back, still holding on to my luggage. Somebody's heel grazed my face. I shouted, and they picked me up.

People climbed through the windows and onto the roofs of the coaches, hung on the steps, or stood on the couplings. The police tried to drive them off, menacing them with the butts of their guns, but they kept pushing forward. Boxes and baskets burst open, women shrieked, windowpanes were broken.

I imagined my gentle old aunt in this scene. . . .

A cab took us to the station. The place was packed. The only train that was leaving that night for the south was "The Maxim Gorky," a real proletarian train with nothing but fourth-class accommodations.

I singled out a porter with broad shoulders and told him to take the luggage. Leaving Aunt Tanya seated in a corner of the station on one of her boxes, and, telling the porter to protect her from the crowd, I hurried to the station master.

"Comrade!" I said, "Tolstoy's sister is taking the next train and she's an old woman. She was Natasha Rostov in *War and Peace*. Please give her a seat in the train. She's going to Yasnaya Polyana."

The comrade blinked at me and gave no sign of understanding. If I had been talking of Karl Marx's sister, the result would have been exactly the same.

From all sides people were attacking him. "Comrade! Here is my certificate!"

"An urgent commission from the Commissariat!"

"Comrade, I insist on getting a seat in the train. I have government documents."

"I am a member of the party, comrade, from the Women's Department," shrieked a young girl. "I shall complain to the Central Committee, you are obliged . . ."

The station master jumped up, crossed the room, took down the telephone receiver, put it back again.

"Comrade, please, I beg you, the sister of Tolstoy . . ."

He drew in his head, hunched his shoulders, and walked out.

"He's gone out on the platform," one of the employees said. "No use waiting for him. He won't come back."

There was nothing to be done. We moved with the crowd toward the platform. I led the way and the huge porter guarded Auntie from behind.

We were stopped in the passage.

"Is this your luggage? Open it."

"O Sasha, Sasha!" Auntie cried. "They will mix up my manuscripts."

"Stop blocking the way! Move on!" There were shouts from the crowd behind us.

"Bourgeois! The devil take them! Don't you see the grandmother has just dropped down from the other world. . . ."

Auntie's hands were trembling. She could not find the keys in her handbag.

"What have you got here? Flour, bread?"

"Certainly not! Nothing of the kind!"

"Gold, that's what to look for. She's got gold and diamonds!"

"O Sasha, Sasha! How dreadful! They look like robbers!"

"Sh,sh, Auntie! For goodness' sake . . ."

The comrade shook out a few of Auntie's dresses and blouses.

"All right. You can close your boxes."

We went out on the platform. The train had not yet come, but people were standing in a solid wall, pressing forward to get nearer the edge. At the end of the platform where the crowd was not so dense I seated Auntie on a box, telling the porter to protect her. It was impossible to rush the train as everybody did, and even if we succeeded in pushing Auntie in, she could not possibly stand with the mob in the train.

The train rumbled in, and before it stopped, the crowd surged forward and up the steps. Soldiers drove them off. There were curses, cries for help. Auntie sat on her box in her old-fasioned cloak and her little black fur hat, frightened and pitiful. The porter stood in front of her like a statue.

The scramble lasted a few minutes. Nearly everyone succeeded in squeezing on board, and only a few were left, hopelessly trying to force their way in. I hunted up the chief conductor, whom I discovered I knew.

"Please help me," I begged. "My aunt, Tolstoy's sister, must get on your train. Please give her a seat."

The old man shook his head.

"I'd do it willingly," he said. "I've traveled with the late count many times. But what can I do? There's no room."

"How about the employees' car?"

He waved his hand. "Full!"

The cars were buzzing like beehives. People were still trying to climb in.

I dashed along the train. All at once I saw a Pullman.

"Who is in this car?" I asked the porter.

"Commissars."

"Let me in. I want to speak to them."

"Impossible."

I went to the windows.

"Comrades! Comrades!"

No one answered.

"Comrades! Please come to the window. It's something urgent."

A disheveled head appeared.

"What's the matter, comrade?"

"The sister of Tolstoy, an old woman of seventy, simply must go to Yasnaya Polyana today. The crowd has nearly killed her—she is sick—please take her."

"And who are you?"

"Tolstoy's daughter."

"Wait a moment!"

The head disappeared and in a moment popped out again.

"We'll take your old lady."

I rushed to the other end of the platform where Aunt Tanya was waiting.

"Auntie, Auntie! Come quickly!"

We ran to the Pullman. Auntie was gasping, and I was afraid she would have a heart attack. I pushed her into the car from below; the porter pulled her up.

Third bell. Whistle. The train started. Auntie was knocking at the window, smiling, and saying something that I could not hear.

In a few days, I got a letter from her. She had traveled very comfortably, the car had been warm and clean, and the comrades most cordial. "They even treated me to roast chicken," she wrote, "but they were disappointed that I was not Tolstoy's sister, but only his sister-in-law. Now," she concluded, "I won't go anywhere, except to the other world."

CHAPTER SIX

The Benefactor

There was hardly any life in the old Tolstoy home now. My mother and aunt—both old ladies—lived in the big house at Yasnaya Polyana, while my sister Tanya and her little girl occupied the wing. Instead of the coming and going of visitors, instead of music, conversation, and the varied interests we had known, life was thoroughly dull. Sometimes Auntie would try to break the tedium of the days by asking mother or Tanya to accompany her singing, but it was not altogether pleasant to hear her sweet broken voice echoing in the old hall. There were too many memories for all of us.

I felt happier in the wing, where the shadows of the past did not torment me and where little Tanichka was growing up—the joy and consolation of her mother and grandmother.

One night a troika stopped at the door. It was Prince Nikolai Obolensky,* who, with his wife and three children, was fleeing from his estate, which the peasants had been about to destroy. They had hardly had time to take the most necessary things with them. In one village through which they had passed, the peasants had stopped their horses and surrounded them. Anything might have happened if the coachman had not suddenly whipped up the team, so that the spirited animals bolted, knocking aside the men who were trying to hold them.

The Obolenskys stayed. Tanya moved to the second floor, and later to the big house, leaving them the whole wing.

---

*The former husband of my sister Maria, who had died in 1906 (ALT).

After a few months, Obolensky came to see me in Moscow. He told me that many people at Yasnaya Polyana, including my mother and sister, had suggested having the estate nationalized, first, because it would be safer to have it protected by the government; and second, because my mother and Tanya had no money to keep it going. The prince asked me if I had anything against his being manager. I said frankly that I did not believe in his capacities as a businessman; but my opinion had no influence upon events, and he was so appointed by the Commissariat of Agriculture.

In 1918 the Yasnaya Polyana Society was organized in Tula. It was composed of the intellectuals who were left in the city, and its aim was to protect the Tolstoy estate and to organize educational work for the peasants. It was just as well for the peasants, the local Communists and the Tula citizens to know that a society legally registered by the government was taking care of Yasnaya Polyana; and the mere fact of its existence at a time when the wave of peasant raids on estates was not yet over was very important. As for its educational work, that was mostly discussion.

One of the subjects most fervently debated in 1919 by the society was the offensive of the White army. Denikin* was in the provinces of Orel and South Tula, about seventy miles from Yasnaya Polyana. A battle might easily take place at Yasnaya Polyana, which was situated on the highway between Tula and Orel. So it was decided to petition the staffs of both the Red and the White armies to avoid battle on Tolstoy's estate. The chairman of the society** assured us that a telegram on the subject was sent to Denikin by the staff of the Red army.

The chairman played an important role at Yasnaya Polyana. He was a writer and had been acquainted with my father. He was tall and dark, with long arms and fingers, and he stooped as if he were too tall to stand erect. His voice was soft and his talk syrupy, he never spoke simply or intelligibly, and everything he did was

---

*Anton Ivanovich Denikin (1872–1947) was commander of the anti-Bolshevik forces in south Russia. When the Whites were defeated at Moscow he escaped to France and emigrated to the U.S. in 1946. He was the author of several books on the Revolution.
**The chairman was never named by Alexandra Tolstoy in her manuscript.

mysterious. I seldom noticed his noiseless entrance into a room, but I often felt the uneasy weight of his presence before I saw him. Chekhov once said that he reminded him of a funeral hearse stood on end.

This man used to come to visit my father, always bringing some new invention. When automobiles were introduced into Russia he took my father for his first ride. Upon another occasion he brought as a present a gramophone, and asked in return that Father make records for it in four languages from his *Readings for Every Day*.

Now, as chairman of the Yasnaya Polyana Society, he occupied the library downstairs, which had been my father's study in the seventies. To the inhabitants of Yasnaya Polyana, he appeared as a savior. He was always distributing something: little pieces of soap, chocolate, buttons. He bestowed these trifles on people as if he were anointing them. With a shrewdness peculiar to him, he wheedled out of the government in the name of Tolstoy food, clothes, and other necessities for Yasnaya Polyana. But instead of storing them in the warehouse for fair distribution, he kept them, and from time to time made presents. Once, while I was at home, he distributed thirty pairs of boots among the employees of the farm and the household. I tried to find out where the boots came from and to whom they were really supposed to go. But the chairman was so vague and honeyed that I discovered nothing and only lost my temper. The next day a gang of men who were working on the road came to the house for the boots which the government had promised them. The chairman spoke to them suavely, reassured them, and promised that they should have their boots. A team of horses drove up to the front door early next morning, and in the afternoon a fresh supply of boots was distributed to the workers.

The idea of building a school in Tolstoy's memory first occurred to the members of the Yasnaya Polyana Society. They also planned to build a stone road between the estate and the highway, to repair the house, and to reorganize the farm. The foundations of the school were laid, and lumber appeared in great quantities. Then one day the work stopped and the lumber disappeared. After a while another quantity of lumber was delivered, to be used for the repair of the house, I was told. Again nothing was done and the lumber disappeared; the chairman turned his attention to building the road. The prince, who had become interested in bees, began building out of fresh lumber a shed which he intended to use as an apiary.

Although the chairman no longer consulted anyone and acted independently, he still used the authority of the Tolstoy Society. Several times members of the society protested against such conduct on the part of the chairman of a collective organization. But he disarmed them with his torrent of words which confused the respectable gentlemen and made them feel as though they had intruded.

Never was the chairman's prestige among the inhabitants of Yasnaya Polyana greater than when, after having secured various certificates from the estate and the Society of Yasnaya Polyana, he started for the Ukraine to get food. There was a drought in our district in 1919, and the government requisitioned all the grain, so that the peasants had nothing left to eat but potatoes. They baked bread out of acorns, green apples, and sorrel. There were great quantities of acorns that year, as if nature herself had taken care to save people from starvation. Men, women, children carried bags full from the woods. They were ground into flour and baked into bread that was tasteless and black but nourishing. The peasants had discolored teeth from eating it. It was always a little startling to see a handsome young girl or a child smile and show black teeth.

The chairman came back from the Ukraine with several carloads of flour, grain, and sugar, which were distributed to the workers on the estate and to the peasants roundabout.

"O dear Father!" the women exclaimed. "God send health and happiness to you and your children and grandchildren. You have saved us from death!"

A few days later the chairman said, "Tell the peasants that I need a hundred eggs. I am going to Moscow."

"For our benefactor!" said the women. "It's easy enough to get a hundred eggs for him! One egg from each house will make more than that!" And they brought him eggs and butter and homespun cloth.

"I don't know what we should do without him," the prince said. "I never saw a man like him. He can get anything he wants."

One day the chairman and the prince drove to Tula in two sleighs, taking food with them for their friends and relatives. A detachment of soldiers was stationed on the road. They stopped Obolensky's sleigh.

"What have you got there?"

"Flour."

"You can't take it to town." And two men loaded the sacks on their backs and marched off with them.

"What have you got?" a soldier asked, looking into the sleigh in which the chairman was riding.

"Comrade!" the chairman interposed. "Comrade! Don't you realize that your life is precious to our government, our free country?"

The comrade opened his mouth.

"Dear comrade! You will catch cold. You shouldn't be so careless about your health. Come now, let me button your coat for you, like this!" And he began fastening the soldier's coat. "That's it! Thank you! You must not forget that the life of every soldier nowadays is precious to our revolutionary government!"

Bewildered, perhaps flattered, the soldier stood, while the "benefactor," patting the coachman on the back, said, "Go on, go on, we have lost sight of the first sleigh."

The chairman became the sovereign of Yasnaya Polyana; he began to find fault with things and to be rude to my mother and sister.

"Why are you meddling in my business?" he would shout at my sister when she asked, for example, what he had bought. "Don't you know that your specific gravity is zero?"

My sister was hurt, but I was furious. I could not bear to go to Yasnaya Polyana often. Everything seemed too strange and hopeless, and there was little I could do to improve matters. My mother, sister, and aunt were not taken care of. Mother could get no one to help her wash the windows and put the winter frames in when it was getting cold. I remember her standing on the sill, cleaning the panes herself, with the windows open and the cold November wind blowing hard.

There were about a hundred and fifty people at Yasnaya Polyana receiving shares of food from the government, and hardly any work was being done. If an inspector had been sent there, he would undoubtedly have found a great deal wrong.

"The work in Yasnaya must go on like a splendid orchestra," the chairman said. "Everyone knows his own instrument and plays it, no false notes, no delays . . ."

My sister listened with an ironic smile. She was used to such speeches. The prince smoked thoughtfully, elegantly holding a cigarette between his white fingers with their long polished nails.

My eldest brother, Sergei, who always took people very seriously, said, with that shyness that was strange in such a respectable-looking, bald-headed man:

"I should like to play one of the instruments in the orchestra."

"Pff!" sniffed the chairman. "Didn't I tell you that there was to be absolute harmony? You would undoubtedly bring in false notes. You might try the last violin."

I went to Moscow in the early part of 1919 and obtained an interview with Lunacharsky,* Commissar of Education. He was very polite, rose as I entered, and shook hands with me.

"Sit down, I'm glad to see you. What can I do for you?"

At the first sound of his deep-toned, agreeable voice, I thought: This man is kind, and, he is an actor. Those first impressions never disappeared.

Two painters and a sculptor were working on portraits and a bust, and the commissar was posing. It seemed to me that everyone in the room, the commissar, the artists, the pale young secretary, the typists, the stenographers, every one of them was acting a part.

It was hard to talk casually in this atmosphere. I made my speech and concluded:

*Anatoly Lunacharsky (1875–1933) was a dramatist and literary critic who tried as Commissar of Education (1917–29) to induce Lenin to spare artistic works of the past.

"I think that the Tolstoy estate ought to be not a Soviet farm but a museum, something like Goethe's home."

Before I had finished, the commissar jumped up and, never for a minute forgetting his role, began pacing the room and dictating to a stenographer. I watched him. Certainly this man with the pointed beard, gold spectacles, round stomach, and melodious voice was admiring himself and his power, and the boldness and quickness of his decisions. My amazement only added to his pleasure.

In a few minutes I was holding in my hands a paper which appointed me commissar of Yasnaya Polyana, with all possible authority. At the bottom of the page was the signature of A. Lunacharsky in red ink, and the seal of the People's Commissariat of Education.

My victory was so easy that I did not even rejoice.

"Today I am a commissar, tomorrow I may be in prison," I thought to myself.

I dismissed the chairman. It was a hard and disagreeable job.

Later on I heard of him again. He evidently had not wanted to abandon a business somehow or other connected with the name of Tolstoy. He had procured certificates and started for the Ukraine. This time he had the brilliant idea of organizing a sanatorium for Ukrainian scientists in Gaspra, the former estate of Countess Panin in Crimea, where my father had been ill in 1901. He got hold of several wagons of food and bedding to start the sanatorium, but, on his way to Crimea, he changed his mind, and when he reached Sevastopol, sold everything and sailed off to Turkey. He told someone that he wanted to buy English clothes there. When the scientists came to the sanatorium in Gaspra, they found a cold, empty house and of course they had to go back.

Bulgakov, my father's former secretary, told me that when he was in Crimea he met the writer there, accompanied by an inspector of the Ukrainian Food Commissariat, the "Narkomprod." This inspector had been sent to investigate the matter of the sanatorium. The writer had already returned from Constantinople and must have done something with the English suits. He was now carried away by a new project: the organization of a Tolstoy Museum in Sevastopol. Instead of giving an account of his activities to the young official, he instructed him in the philosophy of Tolstoy. He spoke of his close relations with Tolstoy and the great meaning of Tolstoy's personality in his life.

I do not know how long this comedy lasted. I know that the writer avoided any kind of prosecution and that the Tolstoy family and the Tolstoyan organizations and societies were unanimous in disclaiming publicly all responsibility for his activities.

CHAPTER SEVEN

In Moscow

Midnight. The room was very cold. The furnace had not run for more than a year and the "Lilliputian," as we called the small iron stove, had filled the room with smoke so that I had to put it out. It took courage to wash oneself for the night; the temperature in the bathroom was not more than one or two degrees above freezing.

In bed at last under a pile of woolen and cotton blankets and a fur coat. A blessed warmth crept through my body. But my feet were as cold as ice. I drew my hand out from under the covers, put out the light and fell asleep.

Bang! Bang!

I woke up in a panic. The door was shaking with blows. The bell, of course, was out of order, like every other apartment bell in Moscow.

"Hey, there! Are you deaf? Open the door."

The blessed warmth left me quickly. I began to shiver, perhaps with cold, perhaps with fright.

"Well, are you going to let us in? It is the president of the house committee."*

"Wait a moment."

My bare feet found my felt boots. I tried to pull on my dressing gown. One of the sleeves had turned inside out and would not go on.

"Damn you!" I did not know what I was cursing—the cold, the sleeve, or the man who was knocking at the door.

"What do you want? It's midnight."

"We must search you."

The president of the house committee, with turned-up collar, stepped in, shrugging his shoulders. Then the small antechamber filled with "leather coats."**

"Have you a search warrant?" I asked.

"Yes," answered the president, avoiding my eyes. He had an order not only for a thorough search but for my arrest.***

In a few minutes I was standing in a dark, lonely street with my hastily packed bag. There was silence all around—no one was in sight. The "leather coats" were busy with their motor car. And suddenly the machine began to roar, resounding between the walls.

"Get in quickly."

A mad idea flashed through my head. What if I try to run away? A feeling of terror came over me, the feeling I had in the war during a cannonade. I could hear my teeth chattering. But running away was as impossible now as it had been at the front.

As the machine rushed through the empty streets of Moscow toward the prison of the Secret Police, I began to grow calmer. I do not know what quieted me—the speed of the machine or that nameless feeling that protects one from fear of hunger, imprisonment, or death. But there was no longer any fear in me when we reached the prison.

They put me in a cell. The lock clicked. I found a pallet in the

---

* A managing committee chosen by the residents of the apartment house.
** The nickname for the secret police.
*** Alexandra was arrested five times. She spent two months in Lubyanka prison and several months in the prison camp of the Novospasky Monastery.

dark, lay down, and fell asleep. It seemed to me that I had slept but a short while when a guard called:

"Hello, citizens! Get up. Tea is ready."

I opened my eyes. It was dark in the cell. The wall of the neighboring house shut off the light. A fat elderly woman was sitting on the pallet next to me and hunting for something in a large basket. Her efforts seemed to get her quite out of breath. In another corner three fair-haired, blue-eyed girls, all very alike, were talking gaily together.

"Latvians," the fat woman whispered. "They're in prison for speculating in jewelry."

"Why are you here?" I asked.

She looked at me suspiciously.

"I? Well—I really don't know. It's a long story."

I saw that she was afraid of me. But she was also talkative and bursting to tell her troubles to somebody. In a short time I heard her whole history. At first she kept looking at the Latvian girls and tried to speak in a whisper, but as they paid no attention to her she went on with her story and forgot them.

Her husband had been a colonel in the old Russian army. Then he had fled with the White army to the south. She lived with her stepdaughter and her son, a boy of fifteen, in Moscow. They were very poor. She had had to sell anything she could to get food.

For a long time she had not known whether her husband was alive or dead. But a month ago a soldier had come from the White army and brought her a message from him. He was well; he had not forgotten his family; he hoped that things would change for the better, and that he would soon be with them.

"Oh, I nearly went mad I was so happy," she told me. "I could not do enough to entertain him. I heated the samovar and lighted the stove. I had some white flour and fresh butter. I baked him cakes. I got some lump sugar that I had saved in my trunk. I gave him jam for tea. Oh, I treated him as well as I could. And he— he told me all about my husband—how he looked, how he lived, and how he spoke about us. You cannot imagine how upset I was! And I said:

" 'O God! When shall we be able to live together? When will all our sufferings be over?'

" 'Very soon,' the soldier said, 'very soon. The White army will come to Moscow and then all your troubles will be finished.'

"And I sighed and said, 'O God be merciful to us sinful creatures. Put an end to our sufferings.' Believe me, that's all I said, nothing else. Nicholas and Anna were sitting there, listening. Nicholas is such a sensitive boy he began crying.

"Well, about six in the evening we saw the man off, and we didn't bother with supper; only Nicholas ate some porridge. We were too excited. Nicholas couldn't learn his lessons. He kept talking about his father. About eleven I put the children to bed and lay down myself. But I couldn't sleep. I was so happy and so restless.

"Then I heard the noise of a car under the windows. We live on the other side of the Moscow River, in a very quiet little street. Automobiles don't come there much. But—I heard distinctly, there could be no mistake—the car stopped right in front of our house. I held my breath, my heart sank.

"Officers rushed in. Three of them. They searched the house. Of course they didn't find anything. They took Nicholas and me; they put us in the car and brought us here. Nicholas was as pale as death, but he tried to soothe me. 'Don't be afraid, Mother,' he said, 'it's a misunderstanding. They'll let us out soon.' But I knew right away that the soldier was a spy. Nicholas is in a cell above us."

And covering her face with her puffy hands, the woman cried bitterly.

"I'm not afraid for myself," she went on. "I'm afraid for Nicholas. He's just a child, just a child." And again her fat body shook with sobs. "Oh, why did they take us, even if this man was a spy? I didn't say anything, nothing at all." Then leaning toward me, she whispered in my ear: "They'll shoot me. I know it. I feel they will. O Nicholas! My boy! What will become of him? He'll be lost without me."

And she cried again. I tried my best to comfort her.

The next morning the guard brought her some sugar wrapped in a piece of newspaper.

"The young citizen in the upper cell sent that to you," he said.

"Nicholas, my darling!" exclaimed the woman. "No, no, I don't want it. He shan't give up his sugar. He's sent me all his day's ration. For heaven's sake, take the sugar back; tell him I have plenty."

She got her legs off the pallet; but when she reached the door the guard was gone, and she was left standing there, reaching out her hand with the sugar.

In the morning the Latvian girls were set free, and I was called for questioning. When I came back the colonel's wife wanted to know what the examining magistrate had asked me. I did not care to speak about myself; and the woman was so eager to discuss her own affairs that she soon stopped questioning me, and talked about Nicholas and his kind heart, and said over and over that the Reds would kill her.

The next day the guard came in again with a broad smile and brought the mother a day's ration of sugar and a piece of herring from her son.

"I never saw such a boy in my life!" she sighed. "Never! And what if he is . . . if they . . . Tell me—they can't kill a child, can they? He is only fifteen, just a boy, a child."

She talked so wildly that I had no time to think about myself. I did everything I could to calm her, but she cried all day long and did not sleep at night.

On the fifth day of my arrest the guard came to the cell.

"Citizen Tolstoy," he said, "get your things ready."

"Where are you taking me?"

"Home."

I began to pack as fast as I could. The colonel's wife bustled around me and seemed much more excited than I was. When I was ready to go, the guard moved to the door. At this moment the woman slipped something hard into my hand.

"Give that to Nicholas, to the children, when I am dead," she whispered. "That is all I have. Here is the address," and she stuck a piece of paper in my pocket.

"Hurry up," the guard cried. Picking up my bag, I followed him.

"Leave the bag here," he said when we reached the office.

"Where are you taking me?"

"To the magistrate."

I took out my pocket handkerchief, wrapped the hard objects that the colonel's wife had given me in it, and held them tightly in my hand.

"If they find them, I'll be executed," I thought.

The magistrate's questioning was a mere formality. He had no proofs whatever that I'd been involved in counterrevolutionary work, and an order was given to set me free. I was taken back to the office. The agents of the Secret Police had opened my bag, and were searching it. They led me into a small room where a Latvian girl met me.

"Undress. I must search you."

I took off my dress.

"Don't you understand?" she cried. "Take off everything."

Now only my shirt, stockings, and shoes were left.

"Damn you!" she shrieked. "Don't you hear what I say? Take off everything."

I stood naked in front of the girl, gritting my teeth and clenching my fists with rage, and wiping the perspiration from my forehead with the handkerchief in which the hard objects were wrapped.

"What does this mean?" exclaimed the girl in a piercing voice, as she drew out of my pocket the scrap of paper with the address of the fat woman.

I dressed, and, as if scalded, rushed out of the prison and ran until I got home. Only then did I unfold the handkerchief. It was full of precious stones—a ring with nine diamonds, earrings with seven big diamonds. The things were old fashioned and showy, but they were certainly valuable.

What was to be done? The address was gone. It was dangerous to keep precious things. Jewels had been declared nationalized by the government, and people were put in prison or executed for keeping them.

A dying plant stood on the window sill. I dumped the earth out of the pot, wrapped the jewels in an old oilcloth, put them in the bottom, and again planted the flower.

"When the colonel's wife gets out of prison she will come for them," I thought.

But she did not come. The pot with the dead flower stood on the shelf in the kitchen. Every time I looked at it I thought of the round, naive face of the woman.

"Where is she?" I wondered. "Why doesn't she come for her jewelry?"

Thinking of her made me depressed and I tried to put her out of my mind. I had other things to think about, too. One had to struggle desperately to live, to get food, wood, clothes, for there was nothing to be had at the stores. Rumors spread through Moscow: "The Bolsheviks are searching for arms." And the people of Moscow tried to get rid of old hunting guns, Finnish knives, and anything that might be looked on as a dangerous weapon. They were afraid to give them up to the Soviet, as they were ordered to do. There would be questions: "Where did you get this gun? Why did you keep it so long?"

"The Bolsheviks are searching for gold and jewelry." And again there was panic. I was terribly worried about the jewels entrusted to me by the colonel's wife. What if the Secret Police should take them away? What should I tell her?

Then for a while I forgot all about her.

It was not until two years later, in another prison, that I learned what had happened to her. I had caught cold and went to the dispensary to get some aspirin. In the corridor the nurse stopped me.

"Your name is Tolstoy?"

"Yes."

"Were you kept in the prison of the Secret Police?"

"Yes. But it doesn't concern you, does it?" I said tartly.

We all knew that spies were set to watch the political prisoners in the camp, so we tried to avoid speaking to people we did not know.

"Have you forgotten the officer's wife?"

"The officer's wife? Do you know her? Where is she? How can I find her?"

"She was shot."

"Shot?"

"Yes."

"And Nicholas? Where is he? Is he alive?"

"Yes, he lives with his sister."

"Do you know his address? For mercy's sake, give it to me."

"They live in the same place, on the other side of the Moscow River."

She tore off a scrap of paper and wrote the address.

Several months later I was freed. At home once more, I thought of the diamonds. The clay pot was still standing on the shelf in the kitchen. I wrote to Nicholas and Anna, and they came—a girl of twenty and a tall bony lad of seventeen. Anna was poorly dressed, but her clothes were neat and clean. Nicholas was haggard, dirty, and very pale. He either did not know how or did not want to hide his misery. His trousers were in tatters, his shoes split, and while we talked he kept trying to draw down his sleeves which were too short.

"Are you Nicholas and Anna?"

"Yes."

"Have you any papers to prove it?"

I asked the stupid formal question, afraid to show my emotion. Anna opened her shabby old handbag.

I did not even glance at the papers, but hurried to the kitchen, blew the dust off the flowerpot, and emptied out the earth around the dead plant. The oilcloth was dry and stuck together. I unwrapped it.

"Here, Nicholas, your mother gave me these for you."

But this is to get ahead of my story.

CHAPTER EIGHT

"I Repented Bitterly"

In November 1919, I had spent a few days in Yasnaya Polyana and was to start for Moscow at midnight. I packed my things and went upstairs. Auntie was sitting at a table playing a game of solitaire.

"Auntie dearest, tell me my fortune."

She finished her game, made me cut the cards with my left hand, and spread them out.

"That's bad!" she said, "very bad." And with a quick movement she swept the cards together.

"What was it, Auntie? Tell me, I'm not afraid."

"No, no. It was bad, I tell you. You can't always believe cards!"

But I kept at her: "Please, Auntie, I insist; tell me."

"All right, if I must, I'll tell you. Illness and death of a close relative. You won't go away tonight . . ."

For some reason I could not laugh and turn it into a joke. I felt sick at heart with the gloomy prophecy. The wind rattled the windowpanes, and the cold and darkness of out-of-doors seemed to enter the room.

"Auntie," I said, "if I cut the seven of spades,* you've really told me the truth."

The trees were rustling in the old park, the big-bellied samovar puffed and boiled on the tea table.

We were scarcely astonished when I turned up the seven of spades. A shudder ran down my back.

"And the ace of spades."**

*The seven of spades is a sign of illness in fortune telling.
**Death.

And again we expected it. Now I was trembling from head to foot and Auntie was pale.

"Nonsense! Are you mad?" Auntie cried angrily, not knowing herself what she was blaming me for. "Forget it and let's have tea. Go and call your mother."

With quick, light steps, she went to the table and began preparing the tea. I went to mother's room. A small kerosene lamp was burning dimly on her desk. Mother lay on the bed with her face turned toward the wall. She was crumpled in a heap and trembling from head to foot.

"What is the matter, Mama!"

"I am very cold, cover me up, will you?"

I covered her. Her head and neck were burning hot—I took her temperature. It was high. I undressed her and gave her some tea with wine. She was still shivering. Auntie and Tanya came.

The doctors diagnosed pneumonia. Tanya and I took care of her. She suffered a good deal. Her breathing was heavy and the cough suffocated her.

She did not complain, did not moan, was very patient and gentle.

One day she called Tanya and me.

"I want to tell you, before I die," she said, "I was the cause of your father's death. He might have lived longer if I had not tormented him. I repented bitterly. But I never stopped loving him, and I was always a true wife to him."

Her large, dark, nearsighted eyes looked at us. They were very beautiful. Tanya and I were both crying—she seemed so wonderfully calm, and I felt ashamed of the animosity I had once had for her.

The next day she was very much worse. She could not speak but her wide open eyes looked as though they knew us. I could not watch her suffering, and left the room.

She was buried with Greek Orthodox rites in the cemetery beside my sister Masha.

CHAPTER NINE

The Arrest

One day toward the end of March 1920, I was returning to Moscow from Yasnaya Polyana. Again I had to travel in a cattle car and stand for more than twenty hours. My feet ached dreadfully, my eyes were swollen, and I felt lice creeping all over my body. I longed for a bath, a cup of hot tea, and a warm bed, and I wondered whether I had the strength to get home and carry my things upstairs. How frequent that feeling was: I have no strength left, I am utterly exhausted, my feet will not hold me; but I must go on, one more effort, another. . . . There is a limit to patience and strength, but it seems to advance with difficulties. One gets used to suffering and learns how to bear it.

There was the seal of the Secret Police on my door. What could that mean?

I left my things at a neighbor's and ran to the telephone.

"Kremlin . . . The Secretary of the Central Executive Committee! The commissar of Yasnaya Polyana is speaking."

I knew the secretary and as soon as I got hold of him, began telling him indignantly that I had just come from Yasnaya Polyana, that I was very tired, and that I wanted him to order the police to let me into my room. I was certain that there was a misunderstanding. I had not meddled in politics. I had no arms, no gold, or anything prohibited at that time by the government.

In about ten minutes the secretary called me back: "The agents of the Secret Police will be there in a few minutes. They say that the matter is serious."

The curt tone of the secretary, who was usually very polite, surprised me.

Two uniformed agents of the Cheka* came. I did not quite understand the role of a very slender young man dressed in a velvet blouse, with a pale, unhealthy face, languid eyes, and long, curly chestnut hair, who accompanied them. There was something abnormal and strange in his whole appearance.

"You . . . ?"

"I am with them," he nodded at the agents. "I am an artist, a futurist."

"And a Chekist?"

"Yes, I am an agent of the Cheka."

They did not search long, and they found nothing.

"Pack up," one of the agents said.

"Why?"

"You are arrested!"

"Arrested? What for? You didn't find anything."

"There is an order to arrest you."

"Impossible!" I cried. "Absolutely impossible! Why? I am the commissar of Yasnaya Polyana! I have had nothing to do with politics! This is a misunderstanding!"

"Please get your things."

"Indeed I won't, I tell you! This is absurd!"

My indignation and protests were so earnest that the police, leaving me in the care of the artist, went to the neighboring house to telephone to the Cheka.

Yes, they had an order to arrest me immediately.

"But I have money and accounts belonging to the government. I must put them in order. Give me three hours or I won't go."

And again the Chekists went to the telephone.

"All right," they said when they came back, "but be quick about it."

My niece and some friends who had come to welcome me had the samovar ready in a moment. The artist helped himself to tea and the provisions I had just brought: white bread, honey, butter, jam.

I took a bath, changed my clothes, packed, and gave my ac-

---

*The Soviet political police, who were later the GPU, and then the KGB.

counts and money to my niece. We got to the Lubyanka prison about nine o'clock in the evening. I was kept in the office of the commandant until one. The commandant, a big man with sandy hair and a perpetual malignant smile, took away my scissors, penknife, and needles. Sitting on a chair I fell asleep.

At one o'clock I was questioned by the examining magistrate.

"Do you remember having meetings in your rooms?" he asked.

"No, I don't," I answered, suddenly understanding why I had been arrested.

More than a year before, some friends had asked me to lend them the office of the society* for meetings. I consented. I had known that the meetings were political, but at that time I had never suspected that this group was the so-called Tactical Center that was planning the Whites' advance on Moscow under General Denikin. I did not take part in the meetings, although once or twice I heated the samovar and served tea. Sometimes there was a telephone call for me, but when I entered the room to answer it, everyone fell silent. I had forgotten all about those meetings. Now, for the first time, I realized that my situation was serious.

"Comrade," I said to the guard who led me to a cell, "won't you give me a mug of water?"

"No, there's no rule for giving water to prisoners at night. . . ."

He shut the door, and the lock clicked in the stillness.

I looked about me. The cell was very small. Along one wall was a wooden pallet made of three boards very badly stuck together. There was a plain chair, and nothing else in the room. I hardly had time to spread my plaid over the boards of my cot and get a pillow from my bag before the light was turned off and I was left in the dark.

When I was younger I had a happy gift. After strong emotion, suffering, strain of mind and will, there was always a beneficent reaction. I could fall asleep wherever I was, in any position, lying or sitting. During the war I even succeeded in sleeping on horseback. Now I thought I should fall asleep immediately. I closed

*The Tolstoy Society, created to study Tolstoy's works and copy and edit manuscripts for a complete edition of his writings. See pp. xxxiv and 161.

my eyes, but instantly opened them and began listening. There was a rustle in the heating pipes. It grew louder and louder; I sat up and listened. There seemed to be living creatures in the cell. Something fell softly on the floor. Once, twice, three times. Now I could hear distinctly. The room was full of rats, lots of them running about the floor, scraping against the walls. I knocked at the edge of the bed to frighten them. For a moment the noise ceased but then it began again. The room was alive. I could hear rats scratching and squeaking in every corner. I knocked again. Now they paid no attention. I was the intruder, they were the masters here, and they became more and more impudent as time went on.

"I hope they won't creep into my bed," I thought. And at that very moment I could feel them climbing up onto my plaid, onto my legs.

Wet with perspiration, I shook the edge of the plaid. Two or three animals fell to the ground with a plop. I tucked the cover up, so that they could not reach me. That did not help. They crawled up the wall, up the legs of the pallet, onto the window sill, I could feel them. . . .

I seized the chair, and began hitting about in the darkness. Again I heard the animals squeaking and scampering.

"Hello, citizen! Do you want to be thrown into solitary?" cried the guard, looking into the cell. "What are you making all this noise for?"

"Please turn the light on," I begged. "The cell is full of rats."

"It's against the rules," he said and walked away.

There was silence for a few moments. My eyes closed. I was so tired. Then I heard the rustling again near the heating pipes. And in a few moments the creatures filled the room. They swarmed on me from every side. Nearly crazy with horror, I rushed to the door and shook it with all my strength. It did not move.

Suddenly it came over me that I was locked in with these terrible creatures. I could not get out. I could not do anything. Tears of helplessness came to my eyes. I jumped on my pallet, threw myself on my knees, and beat the wall with my head. The noise kept the animals from crawling on to my bed. As time passed the strokes of my head against the wall became slower. My eyes closed.

"Our Father, which art in Heaven," I said, knocking at the wall, "hallowed be Thy name," knock, "Thy kingdom come . . ." There was something mechanical in the words and movement; they were soothing. I remembered the prayer, though years had passed since I had said it on my knees. Perhaps kneeling had made me think of it.

"Forgive us our trespasses . . ."

When I had finished I began again.

The rats were quarreling, squeaking, and scurrying in the room. I paid no attention. I forgot everything in the world.

I awoke feeling something soft on my breast, on my cheek. I threw it away with force. A rat thudded to the ground.

Through the barred window and the opaque glass, I saw the blue light of the coming dawn.

CHAPTER TEN

The Brooder Hen

A soldier took me to the washroom in the morning. I had only begun washing when he knocked at the door.

"Hurry up, citizen, give the others a chance."

I had a small basin with me which I filled with water so that I could finish washing in my cell.

It was dark in the cell, the windows were opaque and barred. My paper, pencils, and pens had all been taken away. There was nothing to do. Rats were scratching in the walls. I was not afraid of them now, but I dreaded the night.

At noon the superintendent came.

"Get your things!" And in answer to my questioning look, he added, "You're moving to another cell."

I carried my things in one hand, the basin of water in the other. The superintendent unlocked the last cell in the corridor. There was a group of women at the table. They looked at my basin and laughed.

"Is your name Tolstoy?" an elderly lady with small piercing eyes and a nervous face asked.

"Yes"—but how did she know?

"We are making playing cards out of cigarette boxes. This is your bed," she said, pointing to an empty pallet near the door.

The room was long and of irregular shape, wide at the entrance and narrowing toward the other end. The windows on each side were barred. There was a close-set row of pallets, a table, two chairs. That was all.

"I am a doctor. Petrovsky is my name," the elderly woman went on. "I was arrested for the Petersburg plot. We were waiting for General Yudenich. . . ."*

"*Madame parle français, n'est ce pas?*" my neighbor asked me. Her accent, her make-up, and that chic peculiar to the Parisienne showed her nationality.

"*Mademoiselle la princesse parle français aussi,*" she nodded toward a girl of about eighteen with a fine aristocratic face.

"What is the basin for?" a girl with big black eyes asked me. "It looks so funny!"

"It's for washing. Have you got rats here?"

"Not many. The guard brings us a cat once in a while."

I was very sleepy. I made my bed. The pallet consisted of three boards with spaces between them through which the thin mattress of shavings kept slipping. The edges of the boards cut into one's body. I had to put my pillow under my side and use my coat for a pillow. I covered myself with my plaid and fell asleep.

*Nikolai Yudenich (1862–1933) was commander of the Russian forces in the Caucasus in 1914–15, and again in 1917. After the Revolution he commanded the White forces in the Baltic area.

I soon got acquainted with my companions, and got tired of them, as you tire of everybody and everything when you are locked up.

"Enough smoking, Doctor! The cell is full of smoke. There's no air to breathe!" the handsome, phlegmatic typist would grumble, lazily turning on her bed. "And why are you going back and forth like a pendulum?"

"Don't be angry, dear, I can't bear this! My soul aches . . . I have no peace day or night!"

"Well, what's the use worrying? You can't help things. See how quiet I am!"

"Oh! But there's no comparison. You have no family! I have a son and a daughter. I got my husband, who is a professor, mixed up in this business, and he's been arrested, too. Now think! How can I be calm knowing they may all be shot! And it's my fault. I'm responsible."

"You told us they had forgiven your son."

"Oh, well! Do you think anyone can be trusted? I don't. Today they have granted him his life. Tomorrow they may shoot him." And Doctor Petrovsky tore a piece of cigarette paper, rolled some tobacco and smoked it rapidly.

The typist did not argue.

"You know," said the Frenchwoman in her funny broken Russian, "when you speak to the examining magistrate, you must, well, *enfin, soyez un peu coquette*. A little *rouge* and a little *blanc* on your face, you smile and he begins smiling. . . ."

"Did you smile the night they told you to pack up?"

"*O mon Dieu!* No! I did not smile. I wept. I thought they were going to kill me!"

"It was dreadful," Doctor Petrovsky went on. "When they came and told you to pack up your things, it nearly always meant execution. So once they came and told her to take her things with her. She was frightened to death, and began laughing and crying. Then she threw herself on her knees. 'Doctor,' she said, 'pray for my sinful soul!' I nearly went crazy with her. And in the morning they brought her back."

"Where did they take her?"

"Just to be questioned."

"They try to terrorize the prisoners on purpose," the girl with the large eyes said, "so as to get everything out of them."

"*O mon pauvre Henri! ma pauvre mère! Ils ne sauront jamais ce que j'ai souffert!*"

"She has a fiancé in France," the doctor continued. "She is accused of being a spy. She got intimate with a dishonest man. . . ."

"*Mais non, docteur! Pas du tout!* They took me for a spy, and *ce monsieur* saved me. I did not love him, *ce monsieur*, but, oh, *Henri comprendra ça*, I became his . . . *enfin son amante*, out of gratitude. Oh, that was only for a few days. . . ."

"It's impossible to understand them," the typist said, shaking up her pillow and making herself comfortable. "I've been listening to them for a whole month and I can't make it out. Why were they arrested and what were the relations between them all?"

"I'll tell you all about it," whispered the doctor in my ear, leaning toward me with the smell of bad tobacco. "Yudenich was approaching Petersburg. There was an Englishman in our organization . . . I lost my head, I was mad. . . ."

The doctor spoke quietly, without pausing, as if she had repeated her story many times. I do not know why, but I wanted her to stop and leave me alone. She spoke nervously. Her story was involved and I did not follow her.

"My stepson was shot, perhaps they will spare my son, my daughter is in prison. And I, I alone am to blame. O God!"

She sobbed hysterically. I was ashamed of myself, but I could find no words of consolation. I did not want to listen to her. She made me uneasy. But she spoke, spoke for hours. You could see that everybody in the cell knew her story and was tired of it. They all avoided her, but, once in a while, she would get hold of someone and begin talking again about the Englishman she was in love with and her family. All day long, moistening the tips of her fingers, she would play one game of patience after another, and smoke. She seldom took part in our occupations.

I introduced gymnastics. Every morning, we opened the window as far as the iron bars would allow, stood in a row, and, following Müller's system, made all kinds of movements with our hands, bodies, and feet. I told the French woman that it was good for her health and looks, and she tried hard.

"*Un, deux, trrrois! Un, deux, trrrois!*" she gasped, breathing heavily, the curl papers tossing on her head. Her weak muscles were not used to exercise and every time she had to squat slowly, her feet would not hold her and she would sit down on the floor. It was so funny that we all stopped our exercises and laughed until the guard knocked at the door.

Sometimes the doctor joined us. Her flabby yellow flesh which you could see through the shirt, her false pigtail, all her person was distasteful and pitiful. And when she collapsed on the floor, just as the Frenchwoman did, no one laughed.

Once the doctor got very excited. Either she or somebody else noticed that the plaster was loose around the heating pipes which ran from our cell to the neighboring one. I tried to pick it off with a hairpin, and suddenly I heard a rustle from the other side, as if a mouse was scratching.

"Watch the door, will you?" I whispered to my companions.

Doctor Petrovsky sprang to her feet and took the post of observation, urging me on. "Try with this," she said, handing me a knitting needle.

I pushed the needle through, and suddenly it was pulled out of my hand from the other side of the wall. All my companions, except the doctor, were kneeling beside the heating pipes. Even the typist was aroused from her usual apathy. The needle reappeared with a small scrap of paper at the end: "Who are you? We are . . . (five names)." We knew nearly all of them. One of them had participated in the meetings at my lodgings. We answered at once. A correspondence between the two cells started. I wanted to know how I was to behave at the interrogation, for, so far, I had not answered the questions of the police. "Everything is known. There is nothing to be concealed," was the answer.

Naively thrusting the knitting needle into the hole, I never suspected that we were following a program that had been worked out by the administration of the prison; never guessed that Doctor Petrovsky was a spy, a "brooder hen,"* who was reporting everything that was going on in our cell. That was why she was often questioned. It was said that she had bought the life of her son in this way. Later we were to learn all this—and that in the other cell, there was also a traitor, Vinogradsky, a childhood friend of two of the members of the Tactical Center. It was Vinogradsky who, overhearing the conversation of my friends about the meetings in my rooms, reported it to the Secret Police and brought about my arrest.

After two months in prison I was set free quite unexpectedly. I packed up my things and said goodbye. As I was about to leave the cell I suddenly had an idea, and wrote in big black letters on the white wall opposite the door: "The Holy Spirit in every one of us is free. No bars, no guards, no prison walls can deprive us of our Freedom!"

CHAPTER ELEVEN

The Trial

Several of those who were less deeply involved in the plot were let out of prison at the same time. The leaders were held with a number of others—about twenty in all—most of them professors or literary men.

My feeling on leaving prison was like the sensation one has on landing after a long sea voyage. I was unsteady, undecided; and I could not settle down to my everyday work at the museum and Yasnaya Polyana. I could think of nothing but the approaching

*In Soviet prisons this nickname was given to those who gave information to the examining magistrates.

trial. Would my friends, the five men who were chiefly impli-
cated, be executed or not?

The trial took place in the Polytechnical Museum where I used
to attend lectures and concerts. There were many familiar faces
in the crowd. The accused were seated on the front benches, the
judges at a big table, covered with a blood red cloth, and the
private and government lawyers on the left. Many of the private
lawyers had been men of reputation, some of them had once been
revolutionists; now they were considered enemies of the people
and they made a pitiful impression—especially one of them, who
lifted his hands to his face as if begging to be understood. The
judges rudely interrupted his eloquence, the government lawyers
smiled.

The government lawyers, ignorant, ungifted people who were
acquainted with the judges and familiar with the new methods of
jurisprudence, now played the main role. The brilliant pleaders
of the old days, who could stir their listeners to pity or indignation and soften the hearts of the judges, were powerless. And
skill, knowledge, and logic were dispensed with.

At a small separate table to the right sat the prosecutor, Krylenko,* with his smooth head and massive jaw, reminding one of
a savage dog that needed to be kept muzzled. He looked blood-
thirsty, hungry for victims. His voice was like metal; he chopped
his words and they resounded splendidly, carrying into every corner of the great hall.

There was no use in pleading not guilty. A few of the accused,
such as Vinogradsky and Professor Kotlyarevsky, had turned
state's evidence and confessed everything. Krylenko did not con-
ceal his contempt for the fawning, flattering way they answered

*Nikolai Vasilyevich Krylenko (1885–1938) organized Bolshevik propaganda in the army
after the February Revolution, but was arrested by Kerensky. In November 1917 Trotsky
made him commander-in-chief of the armed forces. In 1918 Krylenko organized the revolutionary tribunals. In 1922 he became chief public prosecutor of the supreme court and,
in 1936, he became commissar of justice of the USSR. Alexandra therefore had to face one
of the most dreaded of Bolshevik leaders. Krylenko was tried in 1938 in Stalin's party
purge and was executed.

the judges. Their activities would very likely earn them pardons and even promotion. Khiryakov, who composed a poem about the trial, described them creeping on all fours and singing to the judges: "You are ours, we are yours, and we love you so much . . ."

My attention was so concentrated on the group who were on trial for their lives that I almost forgot that I was one of the accused. I was still free. I had come from home, I walked freely about the hall, and talked with friends. It came as a surprise to me when an agent of the police ordered me to sit on the front bench under guard with the other accused. That evening when the court adjourned all of us were taken to the Lubyanka prison.

We had with us not so much as a comb. But Nikolai Mikhailovich Kishkin, a well-known doctor, had a knapsack on his back. They put us all in a big dirty cell with a lot of bare wooden cots. Everybody was excitedly discussing the trial. Nikolai Mikhailovich opened his bag and took out tea, sugar, and black rusks.

"What does this mean?" I asked. "How did you know we would be arrested today?"

"Well, there's nothing surprising in that, Alexandra Lvovna. How many times have you been arrested?"

"Three."

"That is not much. I have had much more experience. I have lost count of the times I've been in prison. I went to prison during the old regime, and I keep it up now. I've been taking this bag to the court for several days."

The guard brought hot water, bread, and sugar. We all had tea. In a far corner sat the bent figure of Vinogradsky. No one offered him tea.

"It's awkward, though," one of the professors said. "We ought to ask him . . ."

No one answered. The professor got up and went over to Vinogradsky.

I stretched out on my cot and put my hand under my head for a pillow, but no sooner did I close my eyes than I felt a sharp bite. The boards were full of bugs. Right and left professors were tossing about and groaning.

"Oh, the devil take them! It's no use trying to sleep," someone sighed, turning from one side to the other.

But Kishkin made his bed comfortably, spreading his pillow and blanket on the cot, and fell asleep as if he were at home. And the mutterings of the professors did not prevent me from sleeping, too.

We awoke in the morning tired and pale, with lined faces. My white dress looked like a dirty rag. We washed our hands and faces without soap, dried them with our pocket handkerchiefs, combed our hair with our fingers, and, surrounded by guards, walked to the Polytechnical Museum.

Pardon or death for those five men? Probably the verdict had already been dictated by the government; the questions of the lawyers seemed stereotyped. In contrast every word of the accused rang out with emphasis.

"I never worked for any government. But I have worked all my life for the entire people," Kishkin concluded. His brilliant defense was received with applause. The audience seemed to have forgotten where they were, and the judge roughly reminded them:

"Anyone who causes a disturbance will be expelled from the hall."

The excitement became most intense when the five were to be questioned: five good-looking young men, all of them talented, honest, energetic, and each in his own way learned.

Suddenly there was a stir in the hall. Everyone began moving about and conversing in whispers, even the judges. A number of people came in and scattered among the audience, and the peaked helmets of the Secret Police appeared in the corridors and doorways. A man with a pointed black beard and a shock of hair, protruding ears, and glasses on his nose, entered the hall, and began to speak calmly and self-confidently. It was Leon Trotsky, Commissar of War. He spoke about one of the five, a young scientist. People like this young man were necessary to the Republic, he said. His work was known. It was brilliant. When Trotsky had finished and left the hall, there was confusion for a few minutes. The guards at the doors vanished, together with the civilians who had come in just before the speech.

It now became evident that the chances of saving the five from death were better. I could never understand why the man who at this time possessed such unlimited power, by whose orders thousands were executed in Crimea, wanted to save the young scientist.

The trial went on.

"Citizen Tolstoy," Krylenko asked me, "what was your role in the Tactical Center?"

"My role," I answered in a loud voice, "my role consisted in heating the samovar for the members of the Tactical Center."

"And serving tea?"

"Yes, and serving tea."

"That was the only part you had in the business?"

"Yes."

The audience laughed and the prosecutor was ruffled. This dialogue evoked the following verses from Khiryakov:

> O citizens! Move with care
> In a country where a bold maiden
> Is put into a narrow cell
> For heating a samovar!

> Let a hundred tortures threaten me!
> I do not fear disaster.
> In defiance of Soviet power
> I'll always heat my samovar!

The five were only nominally sentenced to death; in actual fact they got ten years' imprisonment. All the others were sentenced to prisons and camps for different periods. Vinogradsky and several others were released. I was given three years in a prison camp. It did not matter to me. I was happy not to be with those who were set free.

CHAPTER TWELVE

You Can Be Happy Anywhere

Soldiers led us out—a pretty girl with thick fair hair and dark blue eyes and me. It was sultry and hot; we had to wait in the yard. Other prisoners who had been condemned to various prisons and camps as a result of the trial were being led out by the guards. We exchanged greetings, and said goodbye. Then two armed soldiers led us away.

A heavy bag weighed on my shoulders. It was hard to walk in the middle of the cobblestone streets, and after several miles our feet were blistered. The heat became more and more unbearable, and we had to go to the other end of the city.

"Comrades," said the pretty girl to the soldiers, "please let us walk on the sidewalk, our feet are so sore."

"Not allowed."

The clouds thickened, the sky grew dark. We went very slowly, though the "comrades" hastened us. The air became heavier and heavier. A drop of rain fell on my face and then another. At first the drops were large and infrequent. Then the sky was torn by a sharp flash of lightning, thunder reverberated between the stone walls, and the rain began to pour. It cleared and purified the air, and washed the dust off the dirty streets and houses. Streams flowed in the gutters. People hurried past us.

"Stop a moment," one of the soldiers said. "We'll wait till it's over." And he made for a sheltered archway.

I got out my cigarette case, and held it out to the men.

"Have a smoke?"

They smiled and I felt as if for a moment they had become more human.

I took off my shoes and stockings, washed my swollen feet under the drain pipe, and felt much better.

The rain was over. The sun, breaking through a blue-black cloud, shone on the wet pavements, the roofs of the houses, the leaves of the few trees.

"Citizens!" our guard said. "You can go on the sidewalk. Your feet look as if they were scalded."

We were much more comfortable walking barefoot on the smooth asphalt.

At last we reached the ancient, high-walled Novospasky Monastery, now a prison camp. Two soldiers guarded the entrance.

"Two more!" cried our guards. "Here they are!"

One of the soldiers got up lazily from a bench. A bunch of keys clanked, the big lock grated as the key turned. We were let in and the old gate closed after us slowly and silently.

As we walked, I looked around. On the left was a cemetery with battered monuments and blistered iron crosses. On the other side were the low white monastery buildings and old shade trees. The air was full of the bitter-sweet fragrance of poplar leaves.

I felt as if I knew this place. Its quiet and solemnity took hold of me as they always had when my mother had taken me to ancient monasteries in my childhood.

"You slut!"

Two women came running around the corner of a building. Their faces were flushed with anger, their hair was disheveled. The older woman had seized her companion by the hair, while the younger one cursed and tried to bite her.

A guard ran past us, pushing us aside.

"Stop fighting, you bitches!" he cried, tearing the women apart.

Scolding and cursing and smoothing their hair, the women disappeared.

We entered the office. Perhaps because of the fatigue of the journey, perhaps because of the scene I had just witnessed, my knees trembled.

"And I shall have to stay here for three years with such women," I thought to myself.

A handsome Jewish girl with short curly hair was writing at a table. A middle-aged woman, wearing a plain cotton blouse, rough homemade skirt, and felt slippers on her bare feet, got up from another table and beckoned to us, smiling.

"Please come here. I must register you. Your family name? Age? Your family name is Tolstoy? What is your first name? Father's name?"

"Alexandra—Lvovna," I answered.

For a second she raised her eyes; then she went on with her questions.

Lighting a cigarette and swinging her hips, the handsome Jewish girl left the room.

Immediately the face of the other woman changed. She seized my hand and shook it warmly.

"Are you the daughter of Leo Nikolaevich? Oh!"

I was hardly listening. The violent scene outside had thoroughly upset me, and I was in no mood to answer banal questions about my father.

"Are these all criminals?" I asked. "How beastly it all is!"

"Dear Alexandra Lvovna," she said, "don't be distressed, please don't. We can live anywhere—it all depends on ourselves. And this place is not so dreadful as it seems at first. Believe me, you can be happy anywhere. Come, I'll show you to your cell. Let me help you carry your things."

She had a soft, deep voice.

"Will you tell me your name?" I asked.

It was familiar to me.

"Are you related to——, the governor?"

"Yes."

"That is why you are in prison?"

"Yes," and she smiled wistfully.

A little woman with bobbed hair, carrying an armful of linen, met us.

"Anna Fyodorovna," said the governor's daughter, "have we

got a spare cot in our room? This is the daughter of Tolstoy. Let's take her in our cell."

The little woman smiled and nodded.

"Come."

Again to our left the ancient graves and to our right the old white buildings of the monastery.

"Here we are. Upstairs, on the second floor. Keep to your right."

I pushed the door open and entered a little room with a low ceiling, unpainted floor, small windows and a stove of ancient blue-rimmed tiles—the cell of a monk in bygone days. And again I felt the peace of the monastery.

A tall dark old woman in a neat black cotton dress with white dots and a white shawl tied under her chin got up from her bed and bowed.

"Aunt Liza," said Anna Fyodorovna, "did you ever hear of Leo Tolstoy?"

"Yes, certainly," she said, "I always had great respect for him."

"Well, this is his daughter."

"A strange place to meet her," sighed the old woman. "But God knows what He is doing!" And again she bowed and sat down.

She had a noble face and a clear happy smile. More the face of a saint than of a criminal, I thought. Why can she be in prison?

"Put your things here," said Anna Fyodorovna, who I learned had been chosen by the prisoners as a sort of leader, and she showed me an empty cot beside Aunt Liza's.

Suddenly the door opened, and a tall very prim lady came in with light quick steps. Her hair was smooth and gray, and she wore an old-fashioned tight-waisted dress. One could see that she had been very beautiful in her youth.

"Let me introduce myself," she said. "I am——"

"Are you Baroness——?" I asked.

"*Chut! Plus de baronnes maintenant! C'est à cause de cela que je souffre,*" she whispered. "But why are you in prison? Your father was known to the world as a radical—an anar-chist." She pronounced it with some difficulty and distaste.

"I am accused of counterrevolution," I said.

"*Affreux!*"

Anna Fyodorovna went to get hot water for tea.

I watched my cellmates with the greatest interest. Aunt Liza drank her tea from the saucer, as if she were performing a very important rite, slowly and in a business-like way, as the Russian peasants do. The baroness brought a pretty cup from her room and drank hers daintily, crooking her little finger. The governor's daughter took boiled water and a crust of bread.

"Why don't you drink tea?" I asked.

"You don't know her," Anna Fyodorovna said. "She is beginning to swell from hunger, and she hasn't a drop of blood in her, yet she gives all her food away—her butter, sugar, oil—everything she gets from the Red Cross."*

"Dear Anna Fyodorovna, please don't talk about me," said the governor's daughter. The blood rushed to her pale face and she frowned. "Please don't pay any attention to me."

When I went to bed the thought which had haunted me all these last days came to me again. "I am sentenced to prison for three years!" To my surprise it did not make me wretched as it had before. I began thinking about my cellmates—Aunt Liza with her grave, saintly face, the beautiful golden hair and gentle eyes of the governor's daughter. I heard her soothing voice: "You can be happy anywhere."

She is right, I thought to myself. There was no fear or loneliness in my heart as I closed my eyes.

Two men came from the Transportation Department of the Commissariat of Food Supplies. A few of us were summoned to the office and inquiries were made about our occupations. It had never occurred to me before that I really had no profession at all. What were my occupations? Editorial work? Farming?

"Say something!" one man whispered. "They'll take us out of here!"

"Typist!" I exclaimed.

*The Political Red Cross was a social institution organized by the Russian intelligentsia under the control of the Soviet government to help political prisoners.

The men made notes and went away, and we forgot all about them, as we forgot many other visits. But in about a week or two, some of us were again called into the office.

"Pack your things!"

I was ready in ten minutes and said embarrassed goodbyes to my companions, feeling both sorry to leave them and glad to go. A big green truck was standing by the gate of the monastery, and a pleasant-looking young man invited us to climb in. As the truck bumped through the streets of Moscow, I could not help smiling stupidly to myself. Four months in the camp, and now—freedom!

I was taken to a dirty little office full of tobacco smoke, and given an old Underwood typewriter, and a number of papers to copy. I had never typed anything but father's manuscripts before. These official forms were strange to me and nobody bothered to explain them.

"What are you doing?" one of the men exclaimed, when I brought him a copy of a paper written by the boss. I had corrected the spelling but had left the text, which was barely intelligible, as it was. "You can't do it that way! You've got to catch his drift and write it your own way. He'll sign it."

In a few days I learned how to do it. The director was pleased. But I hated my work, especially the accounts. Figures bored me and I never could type them in straight columns. Soon papers were given to me for typing, not only from our department, but from others, too. One paper followed another. The faster I typed, the more work was given to me. They did not even bother to write out the contents, but simply shouted to me across the room:

"Comrade Tolstoy! Department of Supplies: a reprimand for delaying . . ."

"All right!"

I could not understand why the other typists worked quietly till four o'clock, calmly put away their work and went home, while I worked every day until seven and was always tormented by the thought that I had not finished everything that was given me.

"Did you ever have a job before?" someone asked me.

"No, never."

"I thought so. You don't know how to do it. When they bring you something to copy, you must say that you have no time for it, that you have several urgent papers to copy and so on. But if you just accept all the typing that is given you, they'll work you to death!"

We did not receive wages for our work, but we did get dinner and food shares.

After work, I could go home, and see relatives and friends. Only theatres, concerts, and meetings were forbidden. But I could not resist going to a meeting held in my father's honor, at which Valerian Bulgakov, his last secretary, spoke against capital punishment. Bulgakov was not afraid to voice his thoughts publicly. His best speech was on November 20, 1920. The Communists tried to shout him down, and he told them sternly: "You have lost the habit of listening to free speech!" His immediate arrest was desired, but it was not carried out. In March 1923, he was exiled.

I do not remember who reported that I had attended a meeting; but the news got into the papers. A few days later I was again arrested and taken back to camp.

The prosecutor, Krylenko, was said to be furious. In any case, an order was given to keep me under strict surveillance.

CHAPTER THIRTEEN

Kalinin

In the two months I had been free everything seemed to have changed in the camp. The governor's daughter and the baroness had been taken to another prison, and there were a lot of new prisoners. I was put in a different cell with Anna Fyodorovna and some others. Now everybody was fascinated by the famous Baroness Von Stein—"Sonka of the Golden Hand," as she was nicknamed—a clever swindler and thief. As soon as I arrived all the prisoners began praising her and her remarkable fortune telling. Even political prisoners went to the baroness to have their fortunes told.

"She doesn't look like a dishonest person," they said. "She is so gracious and well dressed, she speaks several languages—and she tells your fortune wonderfully!"

"*Mademoiselle la comtesse! Charmée de vous voir!*"

A tall gray-headed lady in a black silk dress stood in the doorway.

I was silent.

"I am so happy to meet you, Countess," she went on in English, and, as I said nothing, she changed to German:

"*Ich habe Ihres Vaters Bücher gelesen!*"

She talked for at least three minutes, skipping from one language to another, smiling pleasantly.

"Will you allow me to tell your fortune?"

"No, thank you," I said at last. "I do not make acquaintances in prison."

She muttered something in French and, seeing that there was no use wasting time with such a rude person, she turned to my companions.

Very little happened during my second stay at the camp. I was depressed. Life was dull, and days and persons were all alike.

Meanwhile, friends were trying to get me out of prison. The peasants, too, were pleading my cause. Three representatives from Yasnaya Polyana and the two neighboring villages went to the president of the Central Executive Committee, Kalinin.* He was good-natured, this new commander, who wore glasses and tried to look like an intellectual. I saw him a number of times, until finally he called me in and said:

"Well, here you are! Free and ready to start counterrevolutionary work again?" I understood that I was now free.

---

* Mikhail Ivanovich Kalinin (1875–1946) was for many years titular head of the Soviet state. At this time he was chairman of the Central Executive Committee of the Soviets. He also became a member of the Politburo (1925–46).

"You are mistaken, Mikhail Ivanovich! I hate your politics and will have nothing to do with them!"

Kalinin looked at me searchingly.

"Tell me, how did you find our prisons? More like convalescent homes?"

"No, Mikhail Ivanovich."

"You are spoiled—accustomed to luxury. But imagine what it's like for a workman, a real proletarian!"

"It is hideous! The prisoners are starving, the buildings are filthy, cold in winter . . ."

"But, as I understand, you yourself have been doing educational work, organizing schools and lectures. There was nothing of the kind in the old prisons. Our government is concerned with making the prisoners conscientious, literate citizens."

I tried to argue, to tell the "Elder of All Russia," as Kalinin was called, about the conditions in prison, but it was useless.

"You are prejudiced, Alexandra Lvovna! Of course, there may be defects, but, as a whole, our prisons are good and cannot be compared with any other prisons in the world!"

My objections were disagreeable to Kalinin.

Just like the old regime, I thought to myself, deceiving himself and others.

It seemed strange that this half-literate man who had belonged to the working class, who was neither stupid nor ill-intentioned, had so soon lost touch with his own people, without even realizing it. He no longer felt their misery, their oppression and misfortunes.

"Everything is exaggerated," he said. "They keep saying that people are starving, that there is no food. I wanted to find out the truth for myself. I went to a restaurant, right here on the Mokhovaya. Incognito, of course. Do you know what they served me? Caviar, sturgeon, and wonderful pies. . . . And it was not expensive!"

I laughed.

"Do you seriously think, Mikhail Ivanovich, that you were not recognized? Your portraits are hanging everywhere."

"I don't think that I was," he said. "Now what food do you have. What did you have for dinner today?"

"Potatoes, fried with castor oil."

"Hm . . . What else?"

"Nothing else today. Sometimes I have cabbage soup, without meat of course, millet cereal . . ."

"That's not so good! Well, what can I do for you?"

Once Kalinin had been especially cordial. I was in the reception room, talking to his secretary—a stylishly dressed, dark, handsome young woman with a magnificent coiffure, polished nails and fine manners—when he saw me.

"Come in, come in!" he called, "I have representatives from Siberia, grand people!"

His visitors were three peasants and they were certainly splendid: big fellows with long beards, peasant fur coats and felt boots. There was a calm dignity about them very different from Kalinin's nervousness and fussiness. In a businesslike manner they stated their case: a Soviet farm had taken meadows belonging to their village. It was a common story. Local Communists, intoxicated by their unaccustomed power, interpreted the laws in their own way and "curved the line," as they used to say in Moscow. Kalinin listened, nodding his head, and asked questions, trying to talk as the peasants did.

Of course there were a great many such complaints against the local Communists, and Kalinin had no time to hear them all; but sometimes when the offended party succeeded in seeing him, the "line" was straightened.

Usually the "Elder of All Russia" received the petitioners in the general reception room. There was always a crowd of them. Kalinin went from one to another, trying to get each story as quickly as possible and hurrying on to the next, while his secretary followed, writing down the petitions and the decisions. Then, in the same hurried way, he walked out, and the crowd continued sometimes for hours to await his next entrance.

"If your father were alive, how happy he would be to see what we have done for the working classes," Kalinin said to me once.

"I do not think so!"

"What do you mean? Didn't he himself struggle against the old government for the welfare of the masses?"

"Oh, yes, but terror, exile, capital punishment, no freedom— all that would have been unbearable to him!"

"Oh, those are only temporary measures. But how about land for the working class? the eight-hour day? And . . ."

"Shall I tell you the truth?" I interrupted. "If my father were alive, he would have written another "I Cannot Be Silent." And who knows, perhaps you would have put him in prison for counterrrevolution!"

The handsome secretary came in several times and reminded the "Elder" about business and the crowd of petitioners waiting for him, but he paid no attention. He was excited, paced the room, smoked nervously, and argued with me for more than an hour.

Kalinin had visited Yasnaya Polyana while I was in prison. My sister had shown him Father's home, told him about Father's ideas, and described his fight against the old government and against capital punishment.

"Oh! Tatiana Lvovna," Kalinin had said, in a low voice, "you know, I have to sign death sentences sometimes . . ."

In 1922 I pleaded with Kalinin in behalf of seven old clergymen who had been sentenced to death. The government had ordered church treasure confiscated, and the measure was not accepted passively everywhere. In some places the population met the soldiers and the Komsomols* with stones. The government replied with a reign of terror. Clergymen suffered most of all. Many of the best of them were shot.

One of my friends, imprisoned with the seven clergymen who were condemned to death, told me about their last days. Knowing that no one would bury them with Orthodox rites, and suffering from the thought of having no religious ceremony, they re-

*The Young Communist League.

ceived extreme unction from each other, and performed the burial service over one another.

I do not remember what I said to Kalinin, I only know that I spoke fervently, and he, as he always did when excited, smoked and strode up and down the room. All at once he stopped.

"Why are you tormenting me like this?" he exclaimed. "I can't do anything! How do you know? Perhaps I was the only one in the Central Executive Committee who was against their execution. *I cannot do anything!*"

CHAPTER FOURTEEN

Yasnaya Polyana Again

I do not remember when it first occurred to me to start educational work at Yasnaya Polyana. The first incentive may have been the poor administration of Prince Obolensky and the "benefactor," * who took no interest in the estate or in the welfare of the peasants. It is true that they made "gifts" to the peasants but these gifts had a somewhat demoralizing influence, making the people think that without the slightest effort on their part they had a right to certain privileges.

On the other hand, imprisonment and lack of work that I cared for had had their effect on me. I thought a great deal about Yasnaya Polyana. I imagined the district provided with schools, hospitals, libraries and cooperatives; I pictured the peasants improving their farms and way of living, their children getting an education and all the advantages of the city without having to break away from the country. And I was concerned, too, about my father's house. It seemed to me that the only way the estate

---

* This is the chairman introduced in chapter 6, part 2.

could be made really safe was to have the house made into a museum and the rest of the estate attached to it as a kind of memorial.

With these ideas I went to Kalinin. He listened to me attentively.

"All right, give me your proposal, I'll support it!"

For several weeks Sergei Sukhotin* and I worked on the project, pondering over each word, trying to bring in Father's ideas and at the same time make it acceptable to the government.

At last it was ready. On the tenth of June, 1921, I was summoned to a meeting of the Praesidium of the Central Executive Committee.

It was a bright, sunny morning. I bicycled to the Kremlin, taking side streets and avoiding traffic. At the gate a soldier stopped me.

"Where are you going, comrade?"

"To the meeting of the Praesidium."

"Show me your papers!"

He took my pass and telephoned to the secretary. Permission was given for me to enter.

Leaving my bicycle near the gate, I hurried uphill, past the "Tsar Cannon" and the "Tsar Bell,"** and turned right into what had been the Court of Justice in prerevolutionary days. Again a soldier stopped me and I showed my pass. Here, in a small room, at a table covered with a red cloth, the meeting was being held. I took a chair by the wall and waited, nervously running over all the arguments I could use if the scheme met with opposition.

At last my turn came. The secretary explained the plan briefly. Three or four questions were asked. Someone suggested changing the word "commissar" to "curator" in paragraph three.

"Yes, that will fit the Tolstoy organization better," Kalinin said.

The project was adopted. All my worry was needless. A wide field of interesting and responsible work opened before me.

*Alexandra's sister Tanya's stepson, who took part in the murder of Rasputin with Prince Yusupov. He married Sophie Tolstoy, the daughter of Alexandra's brother Andrei.
**Relics of old Muscovite Russia, both dating from the end of the sixteenth century. The massive bell was recast in 1735.

There had been no good school in Yasnaya Polyana since my father gave up teaching. In the days before the Revolution, I sent a petition to the head of our zemstvo in the Krapivna district, asking him to open a zemstvo school in our village, but his answer was that the church parish school had to remain there *forever*, and that there could be no other in Yasnaya Polyana.

And so this old two-class school was the only one, and continued to be after the Revolution; but now it was a Soviet school, and belonged to the district Department of the People's Education. The same teachers were there—two daughters of the village priest—and I am sure that their methods of teaching never changed.

Besides this school building, we had at our disposal for the first year an old abandoned kitchen. The beams were rotten, and some of the ends hung from the ceiling. The teacher had his students prop them up so that the place could be used safely. In the morning, the boys learned carpentering; in the afternoon, one of the Tolstoyans taught them reading and writing and arithmetic. There were no teaching schedules then, and no textbooks. The Commissariat of Education had just been organized, and no one yet understood its functions. Old methods were abandoned, but no sooner were new methods adopted than they were changed to newer ones.

The sabotage on the part of the intelligentsia that characterized the first years of the Revolution was over. The intellectuals came back to work; many experienced teachers assisted the Commissariat of Education in trying to bring some system and order into the schools. Many of us believed that we could not only save the old treasures of Russian culture, but could build up new ones, and these hopes filled our lives.

To my great astonishment and disappointment, I got no sympathy for my work from the Tolstoyans. They declared bluntly that they despised education and culture, "just like Tolstoy," and they ridiculed all my plans. When I asked them to help with the educational work, they refused. They would not give us horses for the school workers or for bringing books from the city for our village library. At the same time, they had a hard time getting along. To help them out, I invited several young men to work in the schools and museum for wages and food.

The inhabitants of Yasnaya Polyana disliked the Tolstoyans, and hated one Gushchin especially. He was a dirty, illiterate young fellow with uncombed hair, filthy clothes, and great self-assurance. All day long he would strut about the yard, giving advice or orders to his companions, or he would harness my favorite stallion, Osman, and drive off, bringing the handsome horse back in a lather.

"The idea of bringing all those loafers to Yasnaya Polyana!" grumbled the cook, one-eyed Nikolaevna, when I went into the kitchen. "What did we need them for, the do-nothings, the God-forgive-me trash!"

"Stop it, Nikolaevna!" I interrupted sharply, feeling in the depths of my heart that the old woman was right. "They are good, idealistic people, they help everybody. . . . You should be ashamed to talk that way! They drive you to the city when you want to go. Who took you to Tula yesterday—Gushchin?"

"Gushchin, Gushchin, *nie tuda pushchen!* * He goes right into Tatiana Lvovna's room without even knocking, and sits down in an easy chair in front of her! A muzhik! Idealistic! Oh, God!"

Veniamin Bulgakov, the brother of Father's secretary, was elected representative. He was a young student who knew nothing about farming, and was afraid to contradict the Tolstoyans on questions of educational and museum work.

"I wanted to tell you, Sasha," Auntie said, "I think you did well to send the chairman and the others away. . . . But you were wrong to let those tramps in, and you will see that for yourself. They are lazy and impudent. Yesterday I passed the Remington room ** and saw someone lying on the couch. I went back to look twice, and raised my lorgnette. It was—oh! what's his name?—you know, he talked about Beethoven . . ."

"I don't know, Auntie."

---

* Gushchin, Gushchin
  Went where he shouldn't have been.
** So named for the typewriter used there.

"Of course you know—a big, good-looking fellow—he asked Lenochka to teach him French . . ."

"Valerian?"

"Yes, yes, Valerian! 'Are you sick, Valerian?' I asked, and kept on looking at him through the lorgnette. And he answered as calmly as possible: 'No, Tatiana Andreevna, thank you, I am quite well, but I am me-di-ta-ting!' And he continued lying there with his arms under his head. Well, I got angry and told him that if he wanted to visit a decent house, he had no right to lie on sofas! Just think of it: with an old lady standing and speaking to him, he lies there and meditates!"

The Tolstoyans did not know how to work. They had no discipline or system, they did everything carelessly. When they went to get water, they overturned the barrel. When they hauled manure to the fields, their carts stuck somewhere in the mud or snow. The peasants watched them and shook their heads.

"Volodya!" they would shout to a long, bony, red-haired fellow, "don't you see that your horse is unharnessed?"

I lost patience, and began to wonder what was the use of having all those people on the estate who did not help with the educational work, and could not even do their own jobs.

The "brothers" left. Only a few of them stayed as employees of the museum and the schools. After their departure a picture was found on the wall of the dormitory. It was a caricature of me, blowing soap bubbles. The bubbles—labeled museum, schools, hospital, library—flew in different directions and burst.

Later on, Gushchin and other Tolstoyans became Bolsheviks. I met Gushchin several times in the Tula Executive Committee. His hair was combed and greased, his suit was new and his shoes shiny. His attitude toward me was condescending. He was press correspondent of the Tula Executive Committee.

The red-haired Volodya also became a Communist.

Instead of a Tolstoyan community, we organized an agricultural cooperative for all the employees of Yasnaya Polyana.

We were glad to be working, but also, like all the members of the cooperative, we knew that farming was our only salvation from hunger, and we worked with triple energy. Everything went well during the summer of 1922, and one task followed another. From the vegetable garden, we moved into the fields and planted potatoes and beets. We had plenty of milk, since our own cows were well cared for, and the dairy was in good order.

There was plenty to do. Every little while, I had to run into the office, give the necessary orders, sign papers, or show tourists around the museum. The rest of the time I was farming.

Hay was plentiful. The rye, too, was excellent; but when the mowing machine cut it, it got tangled. Even the experienced workers had difficulty in binding it up.

I was so tired after the first morning's work in the rye fields that I could hardly get home. After lunch it was easier, but the next day all my body ached. I could hardly move. On the third day, I worked like the others.

Loading the sheaves on the carts was as easy as playing tennis. You speared a sheaf with a fork and tossed it up to someone on the load who caught it in his hands. Then you tied up the load and sat down on the sheaves to wait for the next cart. The field was clear and shone like gold; only here and there cornflowers and wormwood could be seen. The straw heated by the sun smelled like fresh-baked black bread. From far off came the sound of the empty carts hurrying back to the fields. I felt very warm, strong, and happy.

CHAPTER FIFTEEN

Cow Barns and Classrooms

I thought we were going to see the school . . ."

"Yes, don't be afraid, the bull is tied. Will you come in?"

We walked over straw mixed with cow dung, past the ruminating cows which watched us with large, indifferent eyes. A great dark-headed Swiss bull turned to look at us as we passed.

"But isn't this a cow barn?"

"Yes and no . . . it's not exactly a cow barn. Now please, the school is to the left."

We entered a large light room with wide windows on both sides, new wooden floors, and whitewashed walls.* There were twelve benches in the room and twenty boys were busy carpentering.

"A month ago this was a cow shed, too," I said. "The other side, where you saw the cows, we expect to make into lodgings for the teachers."

The old professor, an inspector for the Commissariat of Education, shook his fluffy white mane and smiled, showing a single yellow tusk.

The instructor met us—a carpenter, a big fair-haired man in a Russian shirt and high boots, with a jolly, laughing face. He loved his work and his students. He was eager to tell the inspector about his plans for the future organization of the workshops. He and his boys, with the simplest carpenter's tools, had just finished fixing over the room.

We continued to lack school buildings. In 1922 I had an estimate made on a school to be built in memory of my father, and presented it to the Commissariat of Education. The government had no money and the project was delayed; meanwhile new children wanted to come to school and we could only admit a small percentage of them. We rented a simple hut in the village and taught two sessions.

Our organization grew rapidly. As soon as we opened a school it was full of pupils. I was kept busy making trips to Moscow for textbooks and school equipment.

Once an official in the Commissariat of Education asked me what my position in the Yasnaya Polyana schools was.

---

*This building was built more than two hundred years ago by my father's grandfather, Prince Volkonsky, and was used for spinning and weaving in the times of serfdom. Later on most of it was made over into a stable. The building fell into decay but was rebuilt in 1928 for Tolstoy's jubilee. It was said to have been constructed by a famous Italian architect (ALT).

"Why, I don't know," I answered. "I am curator of Yasnaya Polyana."

"Yes, you are under the Museum Department as curator of the museum; but you are organizing schools, and you have to deal with the Department of Education in your school work."

It was true, although I had never thought about it.

"Do you get wages?"

"No."

"How do you live?"

"I sell honey."

The official laughed. He might not have laughed if he had known how hard it was to carry those heavy linden casks on my shoulders every time I went to Moscow. Selling honey was my only income. The Bolsheviks had nationalized all the Tolstoy property except the bees.

"All right. We will appoint you the director of the Yasnaya Polyana school and give you wages."

So it was arranged that I was to be paid forty-two rubles and fifty kopecks a month.

In the autumn of 1923 the Jewish American organization, "Agrojoint," through their representative, Mr. Rosen, gave us ten thousand rubles, and with this we put up a building that was used for the first four classes of the high school.* The oldest children still had to be taught in the village hut. At the same time, we received some money from the government for the memorial school. We did not want to change the appearance of the estate, so we asked the peasants to give us a few acres of land for the school. Several meetings were held while I was in Moscow. My assistants talked to the peasants about the necessity for a school and the benefit of instruction for their children, but to no avail. The peasants simply refused.

"You do not teach religion in your schools. Why do we need them?" they said.

---

*There were seven grades in the usual Russian high school and four grades in the primary school. By 1929 we had four primary schools and three high schools at Yasnaya Polyana. The high schools were a seven-year industrial school, a nine-year agricultural school, and the memorial school, which also had nine grades (ALT).

I called one more meeting when I got back from the city, and the peasants grudgingly consented to give us about three acres for the new school, but I felt that they gave it, not because they wanted the school, but because they did not want to displease me.

One enterprise led to another. The appearance of some ten orphans from I don't know where, who had to be taken care of, led to the opening of an orphan home. Also the American Relief Association presented us with medical supplies and a set of instruments, so we opened a dispensary.

It was a difficult task to get money for all these activities. I had to spend long hours waiting in the reception rooms of commissars, explaining, arguing. Sometimes the central authorities turned the matter over to the local authorities. Then I knew that my case was lost. The local Soviets had very little money, and would not bother with Yasnaya Polyana.

After the dispensary was opened in a small house in the village, we realized how much the population needed it. Later on, we organized a clinic for mothers and children, and several nurseries; and in 1928, the hundredth anniversary of my father's birth, a hospital was built.

By 1924 our small, poorly equipped school bore the name of "The Educational Experiment Station of Yasnaya Polyana," although hardly any experimental work was done. "We are giving you your title in advance," the Commissariat of Education told us.

Salaries were so low and conditions so hard that we had trouble finding teachers for our schools. We had no lodgings. A great number of our teachers had to live in peasant huts in the village. For more than a year, we could not find a teacher of physics and chemistry. At last we got a woman from Siberia. Although she had been told that life at Yasnaya Polyana was rough, she never expected to find it so bad. Living too close to the calves, cattle, and sheep, she was miserable, wept during most of the winter, and in the spring returned to Siberia.

The courses of study in the high schools worked out quite spontaneously. The nine-year school emphasized agricultural subjects, the seven-year school industrial ones.

We needed agricultural work. Farming was at a low level in our district as a whole. The three-field system of crop rotation was practiced in the old-fashioned way. The cows were few, poorly cared for, and gave little milk. The peasants could not make a living by farming, and had to work in town as cab drivers. Our nine-year school set out to teach agriculture to the students and help the peasants in their work. The farm belonging to the museum of Yasnaya Polyana was to be a model, where experimental work could be done. In 1924 the agricultural cooperative was abandoned, as the museum workers were too busy to farm, and the museum farm took its place. This was worked by hired hands and run for profit, to support the museum.

The industrial school trained smiths and carpenters so that they could mend machinery and make furniture in the winter months when outside work was impossible. Yasnaya Polyana is surrounded by forests and much of the timber is excellent for carpentering. We had ambitious plans, but their realization was difficult. The industrial school was closed several times, because the government would not give money for keeping it up; and again and again it was transferred from one department to another. We did not want to abandon the school because we felt that it was needed. It was always full of pupils. The peasants realized that here they could learn a trade which would enable them to earn a living; and the boys liked the work. In the daytime they studied; in the evening they returned to the workshops and made furniture—tables, chairs, chests, and trunks for their families.

The cow barn that we had made over into workshops was too small. We were flooded with applications for entrance to the industrial school, and there were hundreds of boys that we could not admit. I could not bear the sight of little chaps coming on foot for miles and begging to be admitted. They would stand watching the boys who had been admitted, and sometimes cry bitterly if we refused to let them in.

The houses in the village were full of students. They came from distant villages, went home each weekend and brought their food back with them. Sometimes they paid a ruble or two a month for their lodging.

Not until 1925, after many petitions, did we succeed in getting permission to use Telyatinky, the estate that had once belonged to Chertkov. It had become an orphan asylum after the Revolution.

It makes me shudder to think of this place. I had often heard about it before I saw it. One of the teachers came to me several times, asking for a position. She was a nervous girl, with a twitching face, and her black eyes seemed always frightened. She told me that the director—a Communist—violated the girls in the home, and that some of them, children of fourteen, were pregnant. I did not believe her, but later I met his successor (the orphanage was moved to another estate when we took over Telyatinky). She complained that the government did not give her money enough to run the home and feed the orphans, much less the babies that the girls had. "It's lucky," she added, "that the girls get alimony." *

When I visited Telyatinky I found a number of children roaming about the dark kitchen barefoot and in rags, but with fur caps on their heads. It was terribly cold in the house. The children were dirty, and their look of fear struck me. Behind a stove, in a filthy corner, a boy was hiding. One of the teachers went up to him and said something. The boy did not answer; I saw the blade of a kitchen knife sparkle in the shadow.

Chairs and windows were broken, the children paid no attention whatever to the teachers, and it was plain at once that they were out of all control. Vagrancy seemed no worse than such a seminary of dirt and corruption, and the children could not have been worse off in the streets, where the air at least was fresh.

Such was the Telyatinky place when we got it from the Provincial Board of Education. The walls were falling in, the roofs leaked, every window pane was broken, there was dirt everywhere. The plumbing was out of order, there was no running

---

* According to Soviet law, if a woman, married or unmarried, can prove the identity of the father of her child, she receives part of his wages for its support.

water and no toilet in the house, and the children, not wanting to go outside, had used the attic for a toilet.

We spent several months getting the money to repair the place: to rebuild and clean the house, put the plumbing in order, install electricity, and plant vegetable gardens. There were several houses on the estate. We moved the seven-year industrial school and the orphanage to Telyatinky.

CHAPTER SIXTEEN

Badgering

When the Yasnaya Polyana project was approved by the Central Executive Committee, one of the members said: "I think we can afford the luxury of having one Tolstoy nest in the Soviet Union."

I never forgot this sentence. I built my whole work on it. I repeated it to everyone who would listen. I tried to hammer it into the minds of all the local Communists, and when they spread the usual Soviet propaganda in Yasnaya Polyana, I said, "Do you know that even the Central Executive Committee has said that the Soviet government can afford the luxury of having one Tolstoy nest in the Soviet Union?" I repeated it to the Department of Education, to the members of the Central Executive Committee themselves, who had, no doubt, long ago forgotten this casual remark. My tone was so firm that it never occurred to the Communists to contradict me. We worked comparatively unmolested for more than three years.

Yasnaya Polyana was very independent. When an agent of the trade union came from Tula and tried to collect money for military purposes, we refused to give any. "Tolstoy was a pacifist," we said. "We do our work in his name and cannot support military organizations."

The Tula authorities were worried and held meetings to discuss Yasnaya Polyana. But these did not bother us.

The persecution began quite unexpectedly. In the newspaper *Pravda* an article appeared, asserting that a former countess and other members of the bourgeoisie were living in Yasnaya Polyana! "Secluding themselves on the estate, these bourgeois are holding to their old practices; they have orgies, they make the museum janitors serve them and keep the samovars lighted all night long; and as a reward for a night's work, they throw them the crumbs from their table. To disguise all this, Alexandra Tolstoy has organized an agricultural cooperative. She is president of the organization and gets most of the profit from the farm. The employees are not paid; they go hungry, and are often dismissed without any reason. The school teaches religion. The children know nothing about the revolutionary holidays."

Cars came from the city nearly every day. One inspection followed another. The farm was inspected, the office, the museum, the schools. Communists found fault with everything and threatened to have all of us dismissed. Strangers went over the estate, the fields and gardens, the schools. Paying no attention whatever to the administrators of Yasnaya Polyana, they talked with the employees and the students.

"Maria Petrovna, Maria Petrovna!" a rosy-cheeked fellow in the sixth class shouted to the teacher of physics: "I'll tell you something! Did you see that dark man in school today? The one that is around all the time now? Do you know what he asked me?"

"What?"

"He asked me if the teachers spanked us. And do you know what I said? 'Sure . . . they do.' " The boy waited for a moment to see the effect of his words. " 'They spank us every day,' I said, 'especially the teacher of physics, she's wicked. . . .' "

Dark clouds were gathering around Yasnaya Polyana. Every time we heard the sound of a car coming up the drive, our hearts sank.

According to custom, every summer we had a "forest holiday," when we planted trees around our new school building, and then had a picnic for all the children. In the spring of 1924, the Forest Department of the Commissariat of Agriculture arranged a similar holiday for the people in our neighborhood, and invited the peasants of Yasnaya Polyana to take part in it. The head of the Forest Department, a young Communist, delivered a speech. At first he talked of the usefulness of trees; then he began to speak about Yasnaya Polyana:

"Citizens! It is time for us to get rid of all the counterrevolutionary elements that are hiding away in warm corners under pretext of working for our country. Right there," and he pointed toward the high trees of the park at Yasnaya Polyana, rising above the apple orchard, "on this very estate, all the bourgeois exploiters have found a refuge with this rascal Tolstoy at their head! Citizens! You must help us in our struggle . . ." and so on.

I do not think that such speeches impressed the old peasants, but they certainly affected the younger ones, instilling a hostile feeling toward us in their ignorant minds.

Chernyavsky, the "dark man," who was the director of the Communist school in Tula, was trying to influence not only the peasants and students, but our employees, too. The janitors, coachmen, and farm workers would still obey me, but they paid no attention to my assistants and the teachers. They not only ignored their orders but were rude to them. Once when a teacher had to go to Moscow to a conference and told the coachman to harness the horse to take him to the station, the man shouted angrily: "No more tsarist regime now! If you want to go, harness the horse yourself!"

The local Communists with Chernyavsky as their leader built a club house on the outskirts of the village, just opposite the estate, to advance Marxism, militarism, and antireligious propaganda among the peasants. As a sign of derision they set it facing north, so that the back, ornamented with a small wooden toilet, faced toward the estate of Yasnaya Polyana.

At night gangs of young peasants came to the park, and cut inscriptions on the benches, broke the trees, and left the paths littered with paper and sunflower seeds. Sometimes these fellows would come to our windows and curse us on behalf of the Yasnaya Polyana inhabitants. Auntie would start up in bed, eager to drive them out and punish them. I had to beg her to be quiet. She could never really understand the new situation, and I was afraid that with her fiery temper she might make things worse.

The continued restraint of my indignation made me literally ill. But I knew that I could only win by being patient. One reckless word could ruin not only me but the whole organization. There was one hope of salvation, and that was Moscow.

Kalinin listened. He did not say he believed me. It looked to me as if the local Communists had been getting in their word with the Central Executive Committee itself.

"I will investigate," he said.

Time went on and the atmosphere at Yasnaya Polyana grew more charged every day. Many of our teachers had had the experience before of seeing their schools destroyed by ignorant local Communists. Everybody was upset. We discussed the situation repeatedly, trying to find a way out, and at the same time continued to work feverishly. One of my assistants was fighting for Yasnaya Polyana at a teachers' conference in Tula; another was helping me to write a report of our school activity. Sometimes we worked until three o'clock in the morning trying to get our reports ready for the inspection.

The continuous necessity of restraining my anger, the feeling of helplessness and injustice weighed on me so heavily that my heart began to bother me. One night I felt very sick and went to bed. I had hardly closed my eyes when there was a knock at the door.

"Come in!"

A group of teachers entered.

"What is the matter?"

"A meeting is going on in the park. Comrade Chernyavsky has been showing an antireligious movie and now he is talking and persuading the young people to destroy all the bourgeois in Yasnaya Polyana. The young men are excited. They have torn up all the saplings . . ."

Again an unsteady feeling in my heart and a lump in my throat . . .

"We can't bear it any longer!" one of the teachers said. "Something has got to be done. We can't live under the constant threat of being driven out or put in prison. . . ."

"We can't do anything," I said. "We must wait patiently for the committee of inquiry of the Central Executive Committee."

"It will never come . . ." I heard one of the teachers pace up and down the dark room. "But in the meantime they'll ruin our work."

"Alexandra Lvovna! Alexandra Lvovna!" shouted one of the teachers, rushing into my office. "Quick, the committee! An automobile full of people."

"Where?"

"Under the elm tree—five or six! Please take this school bulletin. Show them that the revolutionary holidays have all been observed."

As I hurried toward the front door, other employees nearly rushed me off my feet.

"The investigating committee! Comrade Chernyavsky is with them!"

Six people were getting out of a big car: the president of the Tula Provincial Executive Committee, the head of the Tula Department of Education, the head of the Workers' Inspection of Tula, Comrade Chernyavsky, and two members of the Central Executive Committee.

This was a serious affair. Everybody knew it. The employees were summoned, and I was asked to leave the room. In about an hour I was called into the office.

"Alexandra Lvovna," Comrade Kiselev of the Central Executive Committee said, "what share do you get from your farm?"

Instead of answering, I asked the bookkeeper, who was present, to give me the books of the cooperative. I showed one of the entries to Kiselev. It stated that, having no time to work in the fields now because of school and museum work, Citizen Tolstoy refused to take her share of the proceeds from the farm.

"Hm! Now allow me to ask you: When did you have a banquet with wine that lasted until morning?"

"On the twenty-third of April. It was my name day."

"How many persons were there?"

"About forty."

"How much wine did you have?"

"Two bottles of port."

The members of the committee looked at each other and smiled.

"Is Citizen Tolstoy telling us the truth?" they asked the janitor, Tolkach, who, as I understood, was one of the most important witnesses against me.

"Well, I guess she is."

"Did you have the janitor Tolkach work for you until two o'clock in the morning, making him heat the samovars?"

"No, that was . . ."

"Didn't Tolkach light the samovar for you at two in the morning?"

"Yes, he did, but I will tell you how that happened, and Tolkach will correct me if I am mistaken. That was on the twenty-third of April. Tolkach was on night duty. I invited him to join our party and have tea with us. He seemed pleased, joined us, sang songs with us. At two o'clock in the morning, my assistant, seeing that the samovar was empty, started for the kitchen to have it refilled. He couldn't ask the janitor, who was our invited guest, to do it for us. But Tolkach was very nice about it. He got up, took the samovar and heated it himself, and he was the first to get a cup of hot tea."

"Is that right, Comrade Tolkach?"

"Yes. . . ."

"Comrade Tolkach told me about the incident from a somewhat different point of view," Chernyavsky interrupted.

"When the party was over, about three, I thought of Tolkach's wife and children, wrapped up some apple pie and candy and handed them to Tolkach. I hadn't the slightest intention of offending him, and he did not seem to take it that way."

The questioning lasted for more than an hour and when it was over, I asked permission to speak. I was rewarded at last for several months of patient silence, and suddenly I became the accuser. I told the members of the Central Executive Committee how Chernyavsky tried to undermine the discipline of the students and the employees; how, under his influence, the park was being destroyed; how he took for his confederates the worst and the most dishonest of the peasants and employees and it was they who had been witnesses against us. Anger made me eloquent. Chernyavsky turned red and pale. Several times he tried to interrupt.

"Allow me . . ."

"No, we have listened to you enough," an inspector said. "Now we are going to listen to Alexandra Lvovna."

And when at last the inquiry was over, the Tula officials were asked to leave the room and I stayed alone with the members of the Central Executive Committee.

"What do you want us to do?" they asked.

"I want a retraction of the newspaper article," I said, "and a chance to work."

They promised.

The officials from Tula tried to make me dismiss two of my assistants. I refused, and they let them stay.

Accidentally or not, the administration of Tula changed. A new director of the Department of Education was appointed; Comrade Chernyavsky also disappeared.

The incident of the inquiry made it plain to the local administrators that the persecution of the intelligentsia was not to be practiced at Yasnaya Polyana, and the local Communists became more careful, but their dislike did not diminish.

"Who were those people who came yesterday in a car?" I asked a teacher.

"I don't know. They said they were appointed overseers of the orphan home. They brought presents for the children, and held a meeting with the Komsomols and the Pioneers. I was not allowed to be present."

"You ought to have sent them to me," I said.

"I tried to, but they paid no attention. I couldn't stop them. . . ."

"Telephone me immediately if they come again."

A few days later the same teacher came to Yasnaya Polyana to talk with me.

"I can't do anything with the children," he said. "They are getting disorderly. Their leader goes about complaining that they get bad food and poor clothes. At meals they all make a racket, shouting that their food is stale; they throw spoons about."

"Someone has been telling them to do that. How about those people who came last week?"

"They came again. I telephoned to you, you were in Moscow."

Several days passed. Late one evening the telephone rang.

"Those people from Tula are here. They have brought the children candy and clothes and they've got them all together now in a meeting."

The children were gathered in the assembly hall when I arrived, and a man in a khaki uniform and a woman were on the platform. They stopped talking when I entered.

"We are having a private talk with the children," the man said.

"I am the director of the school."

"But this is a party meeting."

"All right, but before you continue your meeting, I want to know who you are and who gave you permission to come into the school without even speaking to the director."

The man did not answer. He handed me a paper from the government which stated that the Tula branch of the GPU was to supervise the Yasnaya Polyana Orphan Home.

"The Yasnaya Polyana school is one of those bourgeois schools that must be destroyed without the slightest pity. All the teachers in the school are bourgeois and counterrevolutionists; some of them are the sons and daughters of priests.

"Children are beaten in the school. The food is bad. The dormitory food is mixed with worms, glass, and roaches.

"Comrades, watch this hydra of counterrevolution!"

The article was signed "Invisible."

Seryozha Khokhlov came to Telyatinky on an assignment from the local government newspaper, for which he was correspondent, to investigate the conditions in the orphan home. I told the teachers to turn him out. He went as far as the yard, where he began firing a gun in the air and yelling. A few boys belonging to the Komsomol joined him, and then they held a meeting.

"Comrades!" the next article by "Invisible" asked: "When will this damned aristocracy be choked? When shall we clear the way for building up our socialist country?"

More inspections. More officials from Moscow.

CHAPTER SEVENTEEN

Christ is a Myth

All of us—children, teachers, museum workers, peasants—were living two lives, one the official, that is, the Bolshevik life, the other our own, which was being crushed and destroyed and driven far into the depths of our beings.

Even the youngest children were becoming hypocrites.

The old fluffy-haired inspector with the one yellow tooth came again. He examined the third grade in the primary school.

"Well, children, what have you got to show me?"

They brought out their writing and drawings and recited some poetry.

"Can you sing?"

The children looked at each other: "What shall we sing? The 'International'?"

When they finished he asked for some of their village folk songs and they sang several.

"Tatiana Andreevna," they asked their teacher when he had gone, "is the inspector a Communist?"

"No."

"He's not a Bolshevik?"

"Why, no, he isn't a member of the party."

"Oh! Why didn't you tell us? Why did we sing the 'International' for him?"

There were many instances of our hypocritical living. One of the teachers was accustomed to speak against religion at meetings in the club house, but at night his wife would wake up and hear him singing hymns. Museum workers would refer to Tolstoy as a revolutionist who fought against the Orthodox church, and would avoid mentioning his religious ideas. The children burst out laughing when the Acting Commissar of Education, Comrade Epstein, asked if they went to church—and yet many of them were interested in religious questions. Once, as I was passing through the corridor, I heard a number of voices talking loudly in the third grade. I went in.

"Oh, I'm so glad you've come!" the teacher said. "Please tell us what you think about God!"

"God?"

"Yes, yes!" one of the children shouted. "We want to know whether God exists or not."

"Of course He does, children!" I said, avoiding the alarmed glance of the teacher.

"I told you so!" a boy shouted. "I knew He did."

One of the Pioneers with a red necktie jumped up: "No, no, no! It's only the bourgeois who believe in God. And the priests who darken the poor people's minds and then rob them."

"My parents believe in God. They haven't thrown their ikons away."

"Ikons, pieces of wood!" the Young Pioneer shouted.

"Who created the world, if there is no God?"

I stayed for almost an hour. The children wanted to know a great deal: was it true that all priests were greedy? What did my father believe? Did I believe in a future life? I told them frankly what I thought.

"Please come and talk to us again—please!" one of the boys called as I left the room. The teacher followed me. "Well, what will happen now?" she asked.

I did not care. It was such a joy to be oneself. The excited childish voices were still ringing in my ears.

What is the use of trying to keep antireligious propaganda out of the school, I thought, and giving them nothing in its stead? What is the sense of forbidding "godless corners," with the posters of big-bellied, drunken clergymen, the figure of Christ embracing a bourgeois, and the ribald verse of Demian the Poor,* and not daring to tell the children about the teachings of Christ?

The Komsomols proposed to organize a society of "militant godless" at Yasnaya Polyana, and established "godless corners."

On Christmas Eve and the Saturday before Easter, the Komsomols, with the help of the local Communist cells, presented antireligious plays and movies and lectures. The older peasants were indignant; the girls and boys welcomed any kind of a show. Sometimes after the performance the Komsomols would go to the church where services were being held, and shout down the priest and sing ribald songs.

Some of the children had never heard the name of Christ. Others had got their ideas of him from the antireligious posters. Once, in a class in literature, the teacher asked the boys, "Where did Gogol go when he was traveling abroad?"

The children did not know.

"He went to Palestine. You know, of course, why Palestine is so famous?"

Silence.

At last one of the boys raised his hand.

"I know that one of those people who were called saints in the old days lived in Palestine; but what was his name?"

The children were ignorant in religious and moral matters, and the teachers were afraid to instruct them. If a child happened to have an interest in such subjects, the teacher would either not answer his questions or would try to avoid giving a clear answer. Sometimes I thought of my father. I knew that he would have

* A popular Soviet poet.

said: "It is better to let all those children be illiterate than to darken their minds as you are doing!"

And I was troubled.

Every Sunday hundreds of people came from Tula or from Moscow to visit Yasnaya Polyana. We could not show the museum to a group of more than twenty-five at a time, because many of the rooms were too small. Sometimes people were astonished to find that Tolstoy had lived so simply.

As soon as the visitors entered the hall Ilya Vasilievich would say, "Will you please take off your hats in honor of Leo Nikolaevich?" His quiet words always created an atmosphere of solemnity.

The most serious visitors were peasants, workers, and soldiers; the most inane—the so-called "Soviet girl employees." Many of the workers, especially the middle-aged ones, had read Tolstoy's books. Some of the Soviet employees had never heard of him, and I did not know what to tell them. "He was a poet, wasn't he?" they would ask. The young workers knew nothing about Tolstoy's protests against the exploitation of the poor, imprisonment, and capital punishment. His books were only published in small editions in Russia now, and his philosophical works were banned in the public libraries. The teachers at Yasnaya Polyana even debated whether a complete set of Tolstoy's works should be included when we were selecting the books for the school library. I settled the matter by saying we must have them and that there was to be no further discussion.

"Was your father against military service?" a Red Army soldier asked me once.

"Yes."

"Why?"

While I was answering, a group of soldiers gathered. They listened attentively and asked questions, neither laughing nor arguing assertively. I felt a responsibility for what I said, not because I was afraid the men would denounce me for my "radical" ideas, but because they were so eager to know.

Once a group from the Communist school in Tula came to see

the museum. I dreaded their visit. This school was always associated in my mind with disagreeable things: Chernyavsky had
been the director, and all the agitators and secretaries of the
Komsomol who were sent to us came from there.

I showed them the dining room first, and began telling them
about serfdom and my father's attitude toward it. When I stopped
and looked at the boys, I felt that I had their interest.

In the drawing room a copy of the *Thoughts of Wise Men*,
which my father had collected, was lying on the table. I told them
how he read this book every morning before he started his day's
work. "It was like a prayer to him," I said, and stopped short,
waiting for the word "prayer" to produce an explosion. But the
boys were still quiet.

"Let us read it, as he did," I said.

"Yes, please read it!"

I opened to a quotation from the Gospel.

"Who wrote those splendid words?" one of the boys asked.

"Christ said them."

"No! Christ couldn't have said that! Do you really believe that
Christ existed? People prove to us nowadays that the story of
Christ is nothing but a myth."

I gave them some books: *The Teaching of Christ*, *Confession*,
and a few others. We said cordial goodbyes.

Later in the afternoon I had to go to the school. As I passed
through the park, I saw the students. They were all lying on the
grass in a circle and reading aloud—the Bible!

CHAPTER EIGHTEEN

Comrade Stalin

It occurred to me that celebrating the hundredth anniversary of
Tolstoy's birth would emphasize the work we were doing in
his name and might keep the local Communists quiet for a

while. And I thought that by inviting the Soviet authorities and foreign visitors and declaring my "credo" in their presence, I might safeguard the schools and museum of Yasnaya Polyana. I was ingenuous enough to believe that we could continue existing as an oasis in the middle of a desert.

We began to make plans and estimates in 1926 for a jubilee to be held on August 28, 1928. The plans were ambitious, and included the following:

1. The publication of Tolstoy's complete works in about ninety volumes, to be edited by the Tolstoy Society and Chertkov. To include diaries, letters, variants, unpublished works, and articles formerly prohibited by the tsarist censor.

2. The reorganization of the Tolstoy Museum in Moscow and its removal to a stone house.* The construction of a new library for manuscripts; the rebuilding of Tolstoy's house in Khamovnichesky Street; supplementing of collections, and so on.

3. The repair of all the museum buildings at Yasnaya Polyana; the construction of roads through the estate; the cataloguing of the library; the organization of a new museum in the annex to portray "Tolstoy at Yasnaya Polyana"; a new library containing books about Tolstoy; and so on.

4. The building of a hospital with thirty beds, with a surgical department, a child clinic, and nurseries.

5. The construction of the school in memory of Tolstoy. New kindergartens, workshops, a home for teachers, etc.

A jubilee committee was appointed by the government. The chairman was the Commissar of Education, Lunacharsky; the members: Chertkov, Gusev, a delegate from the Yasnaya Polyana peasants, the president of the Tula Provincial Executive Committee, a few professors—the editors of Tolstoy's works—and myself.

All the plans and estimates had to be worked out and passed by the jubilee committee, and approved by the government. We estimated that we would need a million rubles.

In 1926 a small sum of money had been given by the government for constructing the school. Instead of buying bricks for the

---

*This was never done. The museum, with its fine collection of photographs, portraits, books, and other objects, is still where it was.

walls, I bought a forest in Kaluga district, and spent the summers of 1926 and 1927 organizing brick production. About two million bricks were made, a million for the school and a million for the hospital. When I sent my accounts to the Department of Education, they reprimanded me. Why was I buying forests and building brick kilns? I proved that with bricks selling at sixty-five to seventy rubles a thousand instead of ten rubles a thousand, as before the Revolution, it was cheaper to make them. Besides I could not have got enough from the Tula factories; they were all taken by the government.

The walls were built, and the woodwork, doors, and furniture were made in our workshops by the boys and teachers. But there was no money for the roof, floors, or heating system. And there were no funds for the museum. Less than a year was left and very little had been done. I decided to go to Stalin himself and ask whether the government intended to carry through with the celebration or not. After several months spent in vain trips to Moscow, I succeeded in getting an audience.

As I entered the big house in a byway near the old Chinese wall, a soldier standing by the entrance stopped me.

"Excuse me, comrade, I must look at your portfolio."

He peeped between the papers, gave it back, and while he opened the elevator door for me, kept on studying me.

Another soldier met me upstairs.

"Comrade Stalin? This way!"

The reception room was not large. A clerk was sitting at a desk. From here, through a corridor, one might go to any of the three secretaries: Stalin, Kaganovich,* or Smirnov.**

"You will have to wait. Comrade Stalin is busy."

* Lazar Kaganovich (1893–?) had been first secretary of the Ukrainian Communist Party in 1925–28 and at this time (1928–39) was secretary of the Central Committee of the All-Union Communist Party. He continued to hold posts of power under Stalin but was demoted in 1955 by Khrushchev. Kaganovich disapproved of Khrushchev's de-Stalinization program and joined the anti-Party group which tried to depose the leader in 1957. Not much was heard about Kaganovich after that; in 1964 it was announced that he had been expelled from the Party. No source is definite on what actually became of him, but a Western journalist reported having seen his grave in 1963.

** Alexander Petrovich Smirnov (1877–1938) was deputy chairman of the Council of the Russian Soviet Socialist Republic, and secretary of the Central Committee of the All-Union Communist Party in 1928–30. He was later a member of the Praesidium of Supreme Council on the National Economy. He was probably executed in Stalin's purge trials.

I sat down and looked about. People were coming and going. Most of them wanted to see Kaganovich. The doors opened so quietly that I did not hear the secretary come into the room.

"Comrade Stalin is waiting for you."

I was shown into a large room with a desk at the other end. A tall man rose to meet me. Georgian politeness, I thought.

"Sit down, please!" he said with a marked Caucasian accent.

I tried to make my speech as short and clear as possible.

"Your estimates are too high," he said. "We are poor and cannot afford to give you such a sum of money just now. What is the minimum you need for the celebration of the jubilee?"

I did some quick reckoning.

"All right, I will try and do what I can."

"And how about the publication of Tolstoy's works? The Gosizdat has not yet decided to publish and the government has not granted any money for the publication. Perhaps you do not want Tolstoy's books published because of his religious views. . . ."

"We admire Tolstoy as a writer," Stalin said. "We are not afraid of his influence on the masses."

Stalin reminded me outwardly of a noncommissioned officer in the tsar's guard, or a gendarme, with his thick mustache, regular but coarse features, narrow forehead and stubborn, vigorous chin. He was too polite for a Bolshevik. As I was leaving, he rose again and escorted me to the door.

CHAPTER NINETEEN

The Tolstoy Jubilee

It rained for several days before the jubilee. Sinking to their knees in mud, the men tore down the brick kilns and finished the roads. The last exhibits of "Tolstoy at Yasnaya Polyana" were being hung in the new museum. In the assembly hall *The Power of Darkness* and some of my father's stories, made into plays, were being rehearsed. Some of the children were busy making programs. Korolev's bust of Tolstoy stood in a niche at the entrance to the school.

A few days before the jubilee, the president of the Tula Executive Committee sent for me. How were we going to transport our guests from the station? Could we serve luncheon in a brick shed? What would we do for interpreters? It was easy to reassure him on this last question: eight European languages were spoken in our group.

On the day of the jubilee I went to the station to meet the guests at 7 A.M. It was pouring. The station was full of buses and automobiles sent by the Tula Provincial Executive Committee. A crowd of curious people, a few local Communists, and delegates from the Yasnaya Polyana peasants were waiting on the platform.

The special car with the guests stopped in front of the station, and the solid figure of Lunacharsky, the Commissar of Education, appeared, surrounded by a crowd. I noticed at once the pleasant smiling face of Olga Chekhov Knipper*—the wife of Anton Chekhov—and the picturesque head of Professor Sakulin with his curly hair and wide-brimmed hat. The foreigners could be distinguished by their good clothes and shoes, and the cameras slung over their shoulders. They had an expectant look, as if prepared to see this wild country produce strange things. Newspaper men moved quickly through the crowd, pursuing celebrities.

The official meeting took place in the morning. It was long, tedious, and melancholy. Comrade Stepanov, the president of the Tula Provincial Executive Committee, made the first speech. He talked for twenty minutes in a vicious circle, and at the end could not conclude. The longer he spoke, the more entangled he became, until at last, with his face purple, and drops of perspiration glistening on his forehead, he tied himself in an inextricable knot and stopped. The simple, hearty speech of our student Victor Goncharov was very welcome after this. The dean, looking fre-

* Leading actress of the Moscow Art Theatre and wife of Chekhov, who visited the U.S. in the 1920s with that company.

quently at her notes, gave a smooth but rather tedious account of our school work. I was obliged to improvise, and spoke badly. Through all this Lunacharsky smiled and chatted with his neighbors. Suddenly he squeezed my hand and said, "I am very fond of you, Alexandra Lvovna!" This was so funny and so unexpected that I could not help laughing.

Veleminsky, who had known my father, spoke for the foreign guests in a mixture of Russian and Slovenian which no one could understand very well. He concluded by saying that all the foreign guests begged the Soviet government to allow the daughter of Tolstoy to continue her work in the schools and museum in accord with the ideas of Tolstoy. Here his voice failed him, his eyes got red, and he could not continue. I was very much touched. His emotion was obviously genuine.

"Anatoly Vasilievich!" I said to Lunacharsky, feeling that the moment had come to declare my creed. "Allow me to answer."

"What are you going to say?"

"I want to describe the exceptional position of Yasnaya Polyana—how the Soviet government . . ."

"Alexandra Lvovna Tolstoy will speak."

Like a drowning man, I grasped at this last opportunity to make secure the status of Yasnaya Polyana.

". . . the Soviet government so respects the name of Tolstoy, that while militarism and antireligious propaganda are taught in all the schools of Russia, Yasnaya Polyana is privileged, in honor of Tolstoy, to avoid those questions."

As soon as I had finished speaking, Lunacharsky got up, and in a sonorous voice, with the poise of an experienced speaker, delivered a typical Red oration. "We are not afraid," he said, "that the students of the Yasnaya Polyana school will be educated in a Tolstoyan spirit foreign to our aims. We are deeply persuaded that when the youngsters of this school enter our colleges and universities, we shall be able to mold them in our own way. We shall purge them of all Tolstoyanism and make them into strong fighting troops that will support our socialist government."

It was the usual Communist harangue, but it was a catastrophe for the Tolstoyan organizations.

Very pleased with himself, Lunacharsky, followed by the whole crowd, made his way toward the hall, where the guests stood in a half circle on the two wings of the staircase in front of the niche and waited for the official opening of the new school. Here the Commissar of Education delivered another speech. This time he spoke of Tolstoy's influence upon his own boyhood. There was feeling in his words and a tremor in his voice, and when he finished, with a quick theatrical gesture he tore the canvas from Korolev's bust of my father. The ceremony was over, and my hopes with it.

The foreigners were tired and hungry. For several hours they had listened to speeches they could not understand. Stefan Zweig came to tell me that he had always admired my father; the Swedish delegate tried to talk to me in English; Veleminsky told of his former visit to Yasnaya Polyana. One of the foreigners discovered that his camera had disappeared and someone tried to prove that it had been stolen by one of the newspaper men.

A cold and tasteless lunch was served in one of the brick sheds, and afterward we showed the guests the estate and house. We had to give explanations in several languages, which was hard, since many of us had had no opportunity of speaking French or English for years.

The rain had stopped, but the day was still gray when we went to Father's grave. The guests took their hats off and approached the evergreen hedge in silence.

"No monument, no flowers even," someone said.

"He liked the oak trees better than monuments. We tried to plant flowers, but it is too shady, they don't grow."

Veleminsky and a few others knelt. Professor Sakulin delivered a short speech, and we all went back.

The teachers invited the foreign guests to their homes. "You can rest and have a cup of tea."

They refused. One man was on the point of accepting but suddenly he asked:

"And where is Lunacharsky? No, no, thank you. I am afraid he will be displeased."

We got the impression that the foreign visitors were afraid of something. It seemed strange, for we thought of foreigners as free.

In the evening the children's chorus sang music of Beethoven, Tchaikovsky, and Rimsky-Korsakov. Victor read a composition, "The Yasnaya Polyana Peasants' Reminiscences of Tolstoy," which he and another boy had written with the help of their teacher. It was a good job and Victor read well. He stood in the middle of the platform, ruffled his curly black hair, and enjoyed the laughter of the audience.

The last number on the program was the greatest success. The curtain was drawn to reveal some twenty peasant women standing in a circle on the stage, all dressed in old-fashioned, local costumes—white blouses with embroidered sleeves, gold trimmed petticoats, and red, yellow, and green dresses. These costumes had not been worn in the villages for thirty or forty years. We had hunted for them everywhere, dragging them from the bottom of the women's trunks. The best singers and dancers in the village had been invited. An old peasant, Spiridonych, in a glowing red shirt, wide trousers, and high boots greased with tar, and Grandma Avdotya from Kaznacheevka acted out the songs with gestures. The old sad songs were followed by gay dance and wedding tunes. When, during the last song, Vaska Vorobiev darted out of the circle and danced with his sister, the whole audience, including the commissar and the foreign guests, jumped up and applauded wildly.

Meanwhile, downstairs in the teachers' room, correspondents were telephoning to the Moscow papers, although some of them had sent their reports before the meeting began. The next morning we had a surprise: there was not a word of praise for Yasnaya Polyana in any of the Soviet newspapers. *Pravda* criticized the government for neglecting to supervise more carefully a school where half-starved children were forced to sing hymns. Beethoven had sounded like the Christian menace to someone's unaccustomed ears.

CHAPTER TWENTY

The Break from Russia

The jubilee did us no good. Yasnaya Polyana was swept along with the wave of Stalin's reorganization.

The nearest Communist cell was at Shchokino, about six miles away. In order to keep a closer watch over Yasnaya Polyana the Communists decided in 1928 to organize a cell there. At least three party members were required for starting one. Up to that time there had not been a single Communist among the peasants of Yasnaya Polyana, but now a dull illiterate girl was rapidly promoted from the Komsomol into the party. She became the representative of our farm workers in the trade union of the estate, and later was elected one of the administrators of the cooperative.

The second Communist was sent from Tula and given the job of postman. The third, Trofimov, who also came from Tula, was made secretary of the cell. He had no other employment. He was a young worker with a broad, freckled face, a deeply wrinkled forehead, and gray eyes which never looked directly at you. He was the instigator of the antireligious propaganda and military training in the club house, and he acted as if he had the right to meddle with all our institutions. His assumption that he could talk to the children or call meetings without asking permission annoyed me. But what shocked me most was his marching into my father's rooms, cap on head, with the air of master.

Gradually all the high positions in the cooperative and in the club house were occupied by Communists. Veshnev, a writer, was appointed assistant director of the Tolstoy museums.

"I think we can easily use Tolstoy's articles against the Orthodox church," he said to me, as if he had no doubt that I was of his opinion, "and on this basis start antireligious propaganda in the Tolstoy museums."

The schools were drawn more and more into the struggle against the kulaks, and the organization of collectives. The teachers had to explain the difference between kulaks* and bednyaks in theory and illustrate it by comparisons between the children of poor peasants and those of priests in the class. Our committee on admissions, which consisted not only of the administration of the school but also of members of the party, the Komsomol cell, and the local Soviet, made it difficult for us to admit the children of kulaks or of the "servers of cult." One of the duties of the teacher of agriculture was to help the party and the Komsomol cell to forward the propaganda and the organizing of collective farms.

Some of the museum workers, without perceiving it, were drifting away from Tolstoy's ideas, or giving a one-sided picture of them. They described him as a revolutionary who opposed tsarism and the Orthodox church; but they said nothing about his nonresistance, his pacifism, his Christianity, his abhorrence of capital punishment and terrorism.

A circular from the Commissariat of Education suggested that the schools stay open Easter Sunday. I wanted to observe the day as usual, and I called a meeting of the teachers to make sure of their support.

To my surprise all but two voted against me, including my closest friends. In vain I spoke against separating the children from their families on that day, opposing the wishes of the parents and so creating antagonism between the school and the parents. The teachers were terrorized. Yet I knew that many of them, closing their doors and windows, would paint eggs and bake *kulichs* and *paskhas* for their children on that day!

I felt bitter at heart.

"Comrades," I said, "until now you have had faith in me, and believed that I could lead the school in a spirit of independence and freedom. You followed me and helped me. Now I feel that you no longer trust me, and I cannot work with you any more."

* Prosperous peasants who had more than the minimum acreage and livestock.

I could not speak, and left the room. This seemed the last straw. I felt that I was alone, that I was losing the support of my most devoted helpers.

The spring was late in 1929. The ice melted slowly on the rivers, and meadows and fields were full of water. I got up early in the morning and walked through the forest to my father's grave. It was still dark; the sun was just beginning to touch the tree tops. A thin crust of ice cracked, and water gurgled under my feet. I sat on a bench near the grave. There was no sound. Then, as the gold in the trees spread and brightened, a bird twittered and suddenly the woods were vibrant with singing. Here there was peace. All the rest was falsehood, and I had created it in my father's name.

The sun was high when I started home. I did not think, did not decide, but I *knew* that I could not go on living a lie.

I handed in my resignation as director of the Yasnaya Polyana schools to the Department of Socialist Education. It was not accepted. I went to Moscow, saw the Acting Commissar of Education, Epstein, and told him that I could not go on.

"Why not?"

"I do not agree with the government's policy."

"For example?"

"I am against the forced collectivization of the peasants."

"We are not forcing them."

"You are creating such conditions that those who do not want to join the collectives are obliged to. Ignorant members of the party are not only 'curving the line' but ruining people. Not long ago in a village near us, a peasant left a collective, and the Communist cell refused to give him back his property. He had lost everything and was so desperate that he hanged himself!"

"I have just come from the country," Comrade Epstein said. "I visited several collectives. The peasants are all satisfied. They are using tractors, they have bought purebred cattle . . ."

"Where were you? Who told you this?"

"Oh, I went to various places. The peasants told me how happy they were, and, of course, no one knew who I was."

It was another case of not wishing to see the truth—eating caviar and believing that everyone ate it.

I was silent. It was useless to tell Comrade Epstein that a peasant could recognize him a mile away, and that every time he came to Yasnaya Polyana the whole population knew it.

"Please let me resign. I cannot continue working at the Educational Experiment Station of Yasnaya Polyana."

Epstein smiled.

"No, we can't dismiss you—we need you."

In March I petitioned the government to let me go abroad.

"Let me go to Japan for three months to study the schools, and perhaps to America. Then I can come back and work with new energy. I am very tired," I said to Moisei Solomonovich.

"Why do you want to go to Japan?"

"Because you won't let me go to Europe. There are too many émigrés there. It would be difficult for me not to see friends and relatives. And even if you let me go to Europe, and I saw no one, the GPU would accuse me of being in touch with White Russians. There are scarcely any émigrés in Japan."

Everyone at Yasnaya Polyana asked me, "Will you come back, Alexandra Lvovna?" I hinted to a few close friends that I might stay abroad until the end of Bolshevism. At once the rumor spread that I was not coming back. The president of the Tula Executive Committee said, searching me with his eyes:

"You will certainly not come back. If I were in the place of the central authorities, I should never let you go."

"Aren't the institutions to which I have given so much of my energy sufficient guarantee for you, Comrade Stepanov?" I asked.

I no longer cared about the work at Yasnaya Polyana. And the chief work of the Tolstoy Society was done. The manuscripts had been sorted and copied, and most of the editorial work was finished. The publishing of this small edition of one thousand copies in Russian only did not interest me; it was a drop in the bucket. At three hundred rubles a set, who but commissars or foreigners could buy it? Even during the old regime, millions of copies had been printed in penny editions, which could be bought by the poorest people in Russia!

The GPU repeatedly refused to give me a foreign passport, but for eight months I kept on trying. At the same time I was corresponding with several people in Japan, and toward the end of the summer, I received a cablegram inviting me to deliver a series of lectures in Tokyo, Osaka, and other big cities. With this, I went to one of the Soviet officials:

"If you will not let me go," I said, "I shall have to reply that I cannot accept because the Soviet authorities are afraid to let me go abroad."

When at last I held in my hands the red passport book with a crooked photograph of myself on the first page, I still did not believe that I should be able to go. The Commissariat of Education insisted on seeing the outline of my lectures and, after going over them, forbade my speaking about the Soviet schools. Books, letters, an address book, and manuscripts had to be taken to the commissariat for inspection. Then they were sealed so that I could not put anything more in the package.

It was difficult to get a permit to take my guitar with me. It was an old instrument, made by a famous craftsman.

"We do not let works of art go out of Russia," they told me. But I knew that art treasures from the tsar's palace were constantly being sent abroad. "Why do you want a guitar, if you are only going for three months?"

"I take it with me wherever I go."

"All right, you may take it, if you promise to bring it back when you return to Russia."

It was an easy promise to make.

I said goodbye as I would if I were going away for a short time.

"But you will come back?" old Ilya Vasilievich asked.

"Of course I will, Ilya Vasilievich. Take care of yourself while I am away. Don't think of dying!"

"Please come back as quickly as possible."

The old man was crying.

I left late at night. A few friends got up to see me off. As Rus-

sian custom required, we all sat down. There was silence in the
room. Some one sobbed. . . . I could not speak.

My ancient shabby carriage was brought to the front door. One
of the team was old Osman. From the Volkonsky house where I
lived we drove through the orchard to the highway, avoiding the
main house. That was best—not to see, not to think—to break
away quickly. . . .

PART THREE

From Moscow to Tokyo: 1929~1931

CHAPTER ONE

Last Impressions

The train was leaving in ten minutes. We* were waiting on the Moscow platform with our things. There had been a mix-up in the sleeper reservations: no room in the car for us. Our wicker satchel with some French loaves had split, and the loaves had scattered. We collected them and tried to stuff them in somewhere else. They were not just loaves of bread. They were dearer to us than all the candy, flowers, and fruit with which in times long gone we would have been showered when leaving for abroad. These French loaves had been collected by relatives and friends through days and days of skimping on rations.

The little box of *pirozhki*** got squashed. My brother Ilya had brought them. He had also brought a small book in a soft red binding, *Dombey and Son*. "It won't take up much room," he said.

So much to say, but no words came. If only the train would start! "Wait, let me kiss you again!" When women weep, it is painful. When a man weeps, it is unbearable.

Among those seeing us off was a little Japanese woman with sharp features and short clipped hair. She had given us letters to friends in Japan. She herself was staying on in Russia to study the Revolution.

The second bell sounded, then a whistle. The train started. They ran along the platform. We tried to catch one more glimpse to etch them in memory. Perhaps I would never see them again.

---

*Olga Kristyanovich, a friend of mine who had been a teacher at the Yasnaya Polyana school, and her daughter Maria accompanied me to Japan and the U.S. (ALT).
** Little stuffed pies.

The train picked up speed. We no longer could see them. The platform had disappeared. We were on our way to Vladivostok, nearly nine thousand versts distant.

Rain, rain, endless, monotonous, gray. My mind was uneasy. Impossible to cut loose at a stroke from all we had left. My father used to say that, during the first half of the journey, you think of what is behind, and in the second, of what awaits.

Impressions succeeded one another with great speed. The Ural mountains—Siberia. Dirty stations with empty restaurants. Destitution. Ragged people begging for bread.

In our hard-seat coach* there were only a few foreigners. Our neighbor, an English missionary, was surprised that I spoke English. "Would you please help me explain to the porter?" he asked. "I want him to buy me some white bread at a station, but he cannot get my meaning. I tried to eat in the diner, but the food is so atrocious. I have some cheese, but no bread."

"I'm afraid you cannot get any white bread."

"Why?" He reached into an inside pocket.

"I mean, there is no white bread to be had at any station. Black bread is issued on ration cards only."

"I got some, thank you, but I cannot eat it."

At the stops the foreigners would get out to stroll, glancing around with fastidious amazement. There were well-dressed women in silk stockings, Germans, Americans, a Japanese with his wife and two little girls, an ambassador with his family. Most of them were traveling in the Pullmans, they smoked fragrant cigars and wore an air of reserve, looking down on everything. When we reached the harbor city of Vladivostok, one of them, passing a pile of sacks stuffed with beans, gave them a kick. A sack split, the beans spilled out. It was a consignment waiting to be shipped out. "Who needs this stuff?" he sneered.

"Oh, God," I thought in anguish, "why is this food taken away and sold for a trifle when our people have nothing at all to eat?"

All those well-fed, well-washed, self-assured persons seemed

*Third-class coaches without upholstery. Foreigners then traveled in Pullmans, or sleeping cars.

alien, very alien. Those others at the stations and around the harbor, ragged, dirty, bearing everything submissively—those were my own people.

Then where was I going?

In Vladivostok all the hotels were full. "Where are we to spend the night?" The Soviet representatives shrugged their shoulders.

"There's nothing we can do, comrades. You will have to wait at the station."

"But that's impossible. We are terribly tired after nine days on the train, and we have a little girl with us. Give us any sort of room."

But all the rooms had been given to the foreigners. There were no private hotels, they had all been nationalized. We were at a loss.

At last, after I had repeatedly displayed our documents, stating that we were traveling on official business, and had threatened the officials with the Kremlin and all the Moscow commissars, we were assigned a tiny, dirty room with two beds, a broken washstand without water, and a horde of bedbugs.

To find food was even more difficult. The needs of Russians were nobody's concern. We had no foreign currency, and of what use were paper *chervontsy?** Here at the frontier they were being illegally exchanged at the rate of two American cents per ruble.

However, we had had twelve years of good schooling in the Revolution. We were like experienced hunters who can sense where to find game. On the main street we found a confectionery shop where they served coffee and rolls. The rolls were very small. We asked for more, but learned that only one roll was served with each cup of coffee. "Very well, then, give us six more cups."

We got dinner on our food cards, but when we tried to eat it, we felt sick at once. The next two and a half days of waiting for our ship were spent hunting food. In one place we found eggs at

* Formerly gold coins of five or ten rubles.

a ruble each, and not many at that. In another place, pickled herrings, difficult to eat without bread. Here too it rained. The colors of my new waterproof in which I had felt so smart ran in greenish purple and orange streaks.

"The food in that hotel is terrible," said the English missionary from the train when we met him on the street. "It makes me sick."

I wanted to say, but did not: "But you get the best there is." He was an alien. This whole vast country which he had just crossed from west to east seemed to him a dirty land of paupers at the end of the world. How could I ever explain to him? Could he believe there had ever been a time when things were different?

When we boarded the Japanese steamer, the Soviet customs officials scarcely glanced at our baggage. They were busy searching the ship to weed out Russian fugitives trying to escape. Swarthy, nimble little sailors helped us carry our things on board. The cook ran by in a white hat that set off his grayish bronze face. Can we really be leaving, I kept thinking, and could not make myself believe it. It seemed impossible that no one would seize us, detain us.

We were taken to our third-class quarters. There was a raised floor covered with straw mats. No tables or chairs, nothing but the smooth clean floor. In a corner a Japanese man squatted. A sailor conveyed to us in sign language to slip off our shoes before entering. We put down our baggage in a corner, where some good leather suitcases had already been piled, then we also sat down on the floor. It was all so unusual, so interesting, that we did not notice when the ship left its moorings. When we looked out of the porthole, the landing stage was already far behind.

No more regret, no more doubt in my heart as I looked for the last time at what had been my country.

CHAPTER TWO

The Rolling Seas

We were called to lunch. "Is this all for us?" asked Maria. We saw before us soup, fish, vegetables, some sort of dessert, coffee, and best of all, the bread and sugar we wanted. Could this be the food of third-class passengers, we wondered. Perhaps the captain had sent us food from the second-class dining room. It must have been so, for the Japanese next to us was eating rice with chopsticks. I took an old crust of cheese that had come all the way from Moscow with us, opened the port-hole, and flung it into the sea. "To the fishes," said Maria.

It gave us a curious feeling to throw food away.

The captain sent us a message regretting that he had no room left in the second class. He would gladly have offered it. But we liked our smooth, clean platform, the soft mats, and our quiet, dignified Japanese neighbor in the corner with his rice and chop-sticks. In any case, the first- and second-class quarters were equally crowded and stuffy. When darkness came, we spread out our bedding and went to sleep.

The ship was rolling only slightly. Our joy at being released was so overwhelming that it drowned all thoughts of the problem of earning our living, of the hundred and fifty dollars that comprised our whole fortune, of our bad clothes—and chiefly, of all we had left behind.

I soon fell asleep, but awoke with a strange feeling of flying downward. I caught hold of something, only to find myself sliding in the opposite direction. I rolled up to some hard object, sought to grasp it, failed, and was once more precipitated downward. My friend Olga had evidently been awake for some time and was building a barricade of suitcases. Crawling on our knees, we tried to protect ourselves by a wall of heavy bundles, suitcases, and bedding. Just as we settled down again, however, the luggage swayed and plunged, and we went with it. The foghorn screeched, the steamer tossed from one side to the other, everything ringing and rattling. From the second-class quarters came moans and screams. We saw the steward balancing himself between the bunks, carrying soda water, basins, lemons.

All the bags bumped into one another, banged against the walls, tumbling crazily back and forth. A large leather suitcase hit me on the forehead. I grabbed it for support, but it slid and I followed. Finally, I wedged myself behind some projection. My head ached savagely. Then something was sprayed on my face— I smelled eau de cologne. Our Japanese neighbor was bending over me. "Are we going down?" I asked weakly.

"No, no, never," he replied cheerfully. "Very sorry."

For forty-eight hours the heavy seas kept throwing us up and down, to and fro. We could no longer distinguish day from night. My whole body ached from the constant struggling, and my head felt as if everything in it had been knocked upside down and bruised. We no longer rejoiced at bread and sugar, and the steward took away our food untouched. Toward the morning of the second night the sea quieted down a little, and we slept.

CHAPTER THREE

The Beginning of the Fairy Tale

A clear, shining morning. Our eyes blinked from the myriad sparkling facets of the sea. Our small steamer stood calmly at anchor. It seemed unbelievable that only a few hours before the ocean had been beating and tossing her like a matchbox. Fussy little tugs scurried about, snorting and spitting. White sails hung in the haze of the horizon. But I did not care to look at those things. I longed for that high green shore with the curved roofs, where a strange and new life was pulsing.

This was the port of Tsuruga.* Japanese officers in khaki tunics and tight belts boarded the ship with authority. The foreigners with cameras and binoculars got in the way of the hurrying sailors. All these people, passengers, sailors, soldiers, though differing greatly among themselves, belonged to recognized categories, playing their parts in a common life. But when we came on deck and joined the others, I felt we did not belong in any group: we were outside life, like persons just out of prison or an asylum. They stared at my man's hat, my man's shoes. Unacceptable. For my part, they were alien to me, because they did not know what I knew.

All this was years ago; but that feeling, though now subsided, has left its imprint on me.

The look of astonishment on many of those faces intensified when a tug sputtered up to our ship and the captain approached us to point out some Japanese in light suits, who hailed us and waved their hats. "They are newsmen from the papers, the *Tokyo Nichi Nichi* and the *Osaka Mainichi*, and they are coming to interview you. One is Kuroda-San,** and with him are other journalists and photographers."

Their cameras clicked, their questions rained. "Will you stay long in Japan? Where are you going to lecture, about what? Who is this lady with you? Your friend, not your relative? And this pretty little girl? May we photograph them also?"

Presently we were all seated in the first-class saloon, being treated to soda water and fruit. At the request of one polite Japanese, we then and there signed a promise to refrain from spreading Communist propaganda in Japan.

Suddenly a German, who before this had bestowed haughty

* On the west coast of Honshu, a charming little town.
** Mr. Kuroda. He had once visited Leo Tolstoy at Yasnaya Polyana, and spoke very good Russian.

glances on us, approached. "Excuse me," he said, "I do not exactly know who you are or why they are photographing you—but will you permit me to photograph you also?" His camera clicked. "Danke sehr." He walked away to find out whom he had photographed.

Out of a group of newsmen on the landing came an individual in large overshoes, which dragged as he walked. Under his arm he carried a briefcase. Terror seized me. He was one of our own. "I am the representative of the Soviet government," he announced. "I have been informed of your coming."

Is he going to arrest us, I asked myself. But the next moment a thrill of joy passed through me. We were in a foreign country! So we thanked him for his attention, and he departed.

Our automobile moved slowly through the narrow streets of Tsuruga, giving way to pedestrians, women with babies bound to their backs, children playing in the middle of the road, boys on bicycles wearing blue cotton coats with huge white characters on the back, tight trousers, and picturesque white bands tied on the left side of the head. The boys pulled rather heavy loads on the rear of their bicycles or towed huge boxes on wheels. Our ears were filled with strange sounds—peddlers cried, wooden sandals tapped on the asphalt a rhythm reminiscent of a pacer horse's hoofbeats.

My head grew almost dizzy from an unfamiliar spicy fragrance. My eyes tried to look in all directions at once. This street was more like a fantastic stage set than anything real. I had never dreamed that Japan had managed to remain so Japanese. The women with their hair piled high and their silk kimonos printed in strange patterns were like vases tapering to their slender little feet. They wore huge *obi* bows on their backs, snow-white *tabi*, or mitten-like socks, with wooden sandals, and they carried multicolored silk parasols. The men, however, wore only dark kimonos, and their hats were round straws of a European fashion. Everywhere there were lanterns, large, small, round, oval, of every color, inscribed with Japanese characters.

For many, many years I had not seen such an abundance of

merchandise. There were countless little shops showing silks, pottery, fruit, vegetables, all beautifully displayed. The streets were crowded with children in flowered kimonos, their heads black as beetles, shaved in back.

Mr. Kuroda, the newsman from *Osaka Mainichi*, was taking us to Osaka. In his fluent Russian he asked many questions about Russia and myself. But my head was aching, and besides I was staring at the streets. "Excuse me, were you saying something?"

"Yes, what were you doing in Russia?"

"In Russia? I was organizing schools, museums—look, look, why does that man there, the one in the wide-brimmed straw hat, walk in the middle of the street and tootle on his pipe?"

"That one? He is blind, he is a masseur. In Japan, the blind always choose that profession. He is piping to advertise his services."

"Isn't he afraid of being run over?"

"Oh, no, that would never happen. In our country the automobiles run very carefully. But tell me, how many students did you have in your school in Yasnaya Polyana?"

"About six hundred . . ."

"What is that boy carrying on his bicycle?" exclaimed Olga.

"Dinners. Those are trays, one on top of the other, sometimes as many as ten, with rice, soup . . ."

"But how can he carry all that with one hand?"

"Very difficult. The boys pay as much as a hundred yen to be trained to do it. Do you see? He holds his left hand in the back, carrying the stack of trays, and with his right he steers."

On the way to the railroad station, our car stopped at a small wooden house. The paper wall slid open and we entered. A woman in high hairdress, kimono, and tabi stood on a sort of platform bowing and smiling. Her whole being radiated welcome, a feeling of home. We took off our shoes and, leaving them on the polished floor, stepped onto the inner platform. Everything exhaled the same spicy fragrance that had so startled us in the street. Moving noiselessly over the straw mats, the woman left the room, returning at once with a tray bearing tiny cups of green tea and amazingly bright-colored bean cakes.

All this time Kuroda was writing and asking questions. He was to telegraph a dispatch to his paper describing our arrival.

I shall never forget that first day in Japan. It was as if we had been transported into another world, a realm of fantasy, very much as when in childhood our nurse used to tell us bedtime tales that went on and on in my mind after I had dropped off to sleep, so that I went on living among magic visions of "the tsardom beyond three times ninety lands,"* with flying rugs, wizards, fairies, all the things that real, dull life lacks.

Then we were on a train, on our way to Osaka. Wherever I looked, I was enchanted with the vivid coloring, the particular aspect of the people, their clothes, the contrast between their prosperity and the pauperized state of Soviet Russia. It was all wonderful, the speed of the Western-equipped train that carried us, the dust masks of the boys who swept the coaches, the cultivated, fertilized fields where every square foot was exploited, the trees and grapevines burdened with fruit, the picturesque villages of straw roofs and paper walls, the temples with beautifully curved roofs and gates nestling in parks amid thick dark vegetation, the bright red and yellow maples, the rice fields marked in squares by irrigation ditches. I stared unceasingly through the window.

"O bento! O bento!"** boys cried at the stations.

Mr. Kuroda bought us three little boxes. They contained rice, bits of meat, fish, vegetables, chopsticks, and a toothpick. Using our chopsticks awkwardly, we tried to eat but could not. The meat and fish were not salted but sweet, the fruit was tart and bitter, the rice cold and unsalted.

"Don't you like it?" asked Kuroda, adroitly conveying rice to his mouth. "Would you care for tea?"

The tea was green and unsweetened. We were surprised at its being sold at five sen a portion, together with the very pretty earthenware cup.

"May I keep my cup?" asked Maria.

"Yes, of course, they are only thrown away."

* An idiom from Russian fairy tales.
** Rice with seafood and Japanese horseradish served as a box lunch.

In Osaka, Kuroda took us to our hotel. It was clean and comfortable, and we could have rested after our two weeks' journey. But—we longed to dive once more into that realm of fantasy, into those narrow alleys with their strange people, their beautiful handicrafts, their wealth of merchandise, colors, life.

Out we went again, staring without compunction at the passing women with their bright kimonos and high hairdos. "This one must be a geisha," we kept telling each other, "and that man looks like a Roman in a toga!"

At last, exhausted, we lay down on our soft European hotel beds. Sleep refused to come. From the street there came strange guttural speech. Somewhere a string moaned continuously on three notes, long-drawn, unfamiliar. The same spicy, pungent odor pursued us. "Tsoka-tsoaka, tsoka-tsoaka," the wooden sandals clicked in the streets.

CHAPTER FOUR

The Sleuths

As we stepped into the hotel, two Japanese, one short, the other tall, entered the lobby with us. I stole a sidewise look at them. More newsmen? They did not approach us, however, but sat down in silence in the lobby, one on the right, one on the left.

They must have gone on sitting there all the while we were getting settled in our room. When we left the hotel again, they got up silently and followed us. We bought some fruit. They stood by smiling. We went into a pharmacy, and they did too. On returning to the hotel, we went into the dining room. They followed us with their eyes and once more sat down on their chairs in opposite corners of the lobby, one on the right, the other on the left.

The dinner menu was European, also the accessories. The stiffly starched napkins, which I had long lost the use of in Soviet Russia, kept sliding to the floor. Again it occurred to me: the brightly polished silver, the appalling, unnecessary number of plates, the snow-white tablecloth, the finger bowls with warm water—all these were things destined for those other people, the decent cultivated people we had seen on the train crossing Siberia, and on the steamer, but not for us. It seemed as though they must have been given us by mistake.

When we left the dining room, we went out by a different exit leading directly into the street, jubilant over our adroit evasion of our leechlike companions. To make sure, we turned into the first alley, then made two more turns. "Now they'll never find us," we said, walking a little slower, looking at the fine displays of ivory carvings in the shop windows, ships, houses, animals. Then:

"Oh, how awful!" I exclaimed. The two men stood smiling beside us.

Though we were looking for a post office and a place to buy postcards, we did not want to ask directions of them. I stopped a passing Japanese in European clothes. "Could you direct us to the post office, please?"

"Post office!" exclaimed one of our pursuers, instantly at my side. "This way, please." He walked along with us, and presently the other joined us. They gave friendly little laughs, nodding their heads, as if greatly pleased with this opportunity to serve us. "You need postcards? Let us go into this store, it is a good one."

"Please leave us alone," I retorted angrily.

"Here, here, to your right you will find picture cards of Tokyo, reproductions of famous Japanese paintings. . . ."

Now we walked in a group of five. The wide Europeanized streets did not interest us. We kept wandering into typical Japanese alleys, delighting in the colored paper lanterns, the little ship models overflowing with all kinds of goods, and the ever strange people. The two men kept following us, not leaving us until we shut the door of our hotel room.

The next day I asked Kuroda: "Who are these two men who pursue us like shadows?"

"Police agents."

"Detectives! We are being mistrusted and watched. That's unpleasant!"

"It is the custom in Japan. They have been detailed to protect you. The police are especially careful in guarding those who come from Soviet Russia."

"But how can the authorities suspect us? They know perfectly well that we cannot be Soviet agents. Can't we ask to have this surveillance stopped?" I was thoroughly indignant.

"No, it would be useless. They will stop watching you when they become convinced of your reliability. But that will not be soon. You will have to reconcile yourselves to this order of things."

The next day I signed a contract for lectures with the newspapers, the *Osaka Mainichi* and the *Tokyo Nichi Nichi,* and we went to Tokyo, where I was to begin my tour.

One of those police agents traveled with us. He did not try to hide. He watched us openly. He behaved as if he had been glued to us and nothing on earth could shake him off. At Tokyo another one appeared. He called on us daily, even after we moved into an apartment which had no anteroom—its door led right into the dining room. He would come in, take a chair, and sit there from morning to night. I was losing patience. "Don't you understand," I told him on one occasion, "how tactless this is? We want to eat our meals, and here you are, a stranger, sitting by and forcing your company on us."

He jumped up from his chair. "Excuse me, please!" He bowed many times, like one of those porcelain cats with inserted heads that peddlers used to sell in old Russia. "I can sit in the yard."

The next day it rained. Our sleuth sat stoically on the bench in the courtyard, or walked up and down. He was drenched, so we ended by asking him to come in.

One morning he arrived with a very ceremonious countenance, carrying something in his hand. His smile was particularly affable, important. "Excuse me," he said, "I speak Russian poorly, I cannot express my feelings, but you will understand—I love Tolstoy, I am an admirer of his."

He was visibly agitated. His thin, ape-like hand tried confusedly to untie a bundle wrapped in a flowery silk kerchief. Finally, he extracted a large picture of my father. "Here! Sign it, please!"

I signed it.

Several days later he brought copies of my father's books, *Thou Shalt Not Kill, The Kingdom of God Is within Us,* and others.

"I have read all of Tolstoy, everything he wrote, and these religious, philosophical works I like especially. Please sign these."

"But how does your police service accord with what my father wrote in these books? In *Thou Shalt Not Kill,* he says that evil must not be resisted by violence. You know that my father opposed all violence, consequently the police also."

Either he failed to understand, or else would not argue—the Japanese never argue. "I love these books," he repeated. "Tolstoy had a great influence over me. I am glad I can see his daughter. Here is my modest gift to you."

He laid before me another little bundle neatly tied in a silk kerchief.

"Thank you," I said, "but I cannot accept your gift."

"Oh, but this is an insult!" His face went purple, and he looked as if he were about to burst into tears. "According to our Japanese usage, if you refuse a gift, you greatly offend the giver. Please take it."

I had to accept it. The little bundle contained apples and oranges.

Nevertheless, we grew desperately tired of him. "Isn't there some way to relieve us of these detectives?" I asked the elderly Idzumi-San, another correspondent of the *Nichi Nichi,* who had joined Kuroda as our interpreter. "Day in and day out, there is one sitting on a chair in our hotel. He follows us everywhere."

"No, don't try," replied Idzumi, whose Russian was far less

perfect than Kuroda's. "I know this man. A very good man. Let
him come along. You go shopping—let him help you. You need
to carry things, he carries them for you. You need to buy something, he will buy it. Let him come along. He is a good man, a
real Tolstoyan."

Nothing to be done. As a matter of fact, when we were about
to move on, our sleuth did carry our luggage for us, ran for a taxi,
bowing and smiling. He was a good sleuth, a good man, a real
Tolstoyan.

CHAPTER FIVE

The Dancing Slippers

In old Russia there had been little advertising. The established,
self-respecting stores considered it below their dignity to an-
nounce themselves in blatant advertisements or sign boards.
"The firm must earn its reputation," respectable merchants used
to say. "When people learn about the quality of our merchandise,
they will buy." Only a few traders in cheap, trashy goods cried
their merits.

In Soviet Russia, on the other hand, private trade was either
abolished or else existed clandestinely. Only the government and
the Party were advertised by the posters, the press, and the stereotyped slogans of the public speakers.

Therefore I was unfamiliar with what is called business advertising outside of Russia and so was unable to understand the essence of my contract with the *Nichi Nichi* and the *Osaka Mainichi.* That these papers should pay me for my articles was natural
enough, but why they should assume all the expenses of my lecture tour, leaving all the profits to me, I could not understand.

Only later, especially after I had lived in America for a while, did I realize the tremendous role of advertising.

My lectures, arranged by these two newspapers, were a means of increasing their circulation, and the papers were prepared to pay for this. Though Kuroda spoke Russian beautifully, almost without an accent, he was somehow unable to explain this side of the matter. However, I was glad that he was to travel with me as my interpreter. I felt at ease with him. He had lived in Russia a long time, he knew and liked Russians, he wore his European clothes in a natural way, ate European food with relish, and had even acquired something of Russian breadth, frankness, and casualness. Yet there was in him that something which is in every Japanese and remains hidden, inaccessible to Europeans. Every Japanese opens up to Westerners, but he unfolds only one aspect of his being. No matter how we try, we shall never understand his essence, which has been bred through centuries and is his innermost self. Similarly, they grasp our external culture with ease, but do not understand its essence.

It was hard for me to adjust myself to the task of preparing my lectures. What should I say? And how? Evidently, the Japanese ways of expressing thoughts, their forms of speech, were entirely different from ours. From the very first this problem confronted me.

Kuroda and Idzumi called to discuss the plan of my lectures and articles. I named several topics: "The Departure and Death of Tolstoy"; "Tolstoy and Russian Literature"; "How Tolstoy Wrote"; and others. They took a long time discussing each one of these. Then, without saying anything decisive, they took my manuscripts and went away. Two days later they called again.

"Very good," said Idzumi, "but . . ."

"Uninteresting?"

"No, no, very interesting."

I waited. They were silent.

"Perhaps it is not sufficiently profound?"

"No, it is very serious."

"Serious, yes, but it seems to me the language is simple, intelligible to everyone."

Again they were silent. Kuroda smiled. I felt embarrassed. I began to think that what I had written did not answer the purpose, and that they were reluctant to tell me so.

At last Kuroda said, "The editors decided that each of these topics, taken separately, would be too serious. They would like you to talk a little about everything."

"What do you mean, about everything? Each of these topics covers a definite period or a definite issue in Tolstoy's life and work. How could I mix them all together?"

"That does not matter," replied Kuroda. "Put it all into one, that will make a very interesting lecture."

I tried to argue, not yet understanding that it is useless to argue with the Japanese. In the end, I stuck together pieces of all I had prepared and titled it "The Life and Work of Tolstoy." From a Russian point of view, it was a very poor piece of work.

"Very interesting," commented Idzumi, "all people will be pleased."

In Tokyo we moved from our hotel to an apartment. Idzumi took us to it. "Here," he remarked, "European houses, you will be very comfortable."

The "European houses" were built inside the courtyard of an old Buddhist temple. The *bon-san*, or priest, had constructed a sort of two-story wooden barracks, papered it with cheap wallpaper, and rented it out to foreigners. Our apartment contained all the elements of a European tenement: a gas stove, electricity, running water, a total lack of coziness, and even a Soviet government employee living next to us. It was not to our liking; but house hunting with the aid of interpreters was too difficult, and so we put up with it.

Shopping was also difficult. As for finding a ready-made dress to encase my two hundred pounds—altogether impossible. "Such big madame!" commented Idzumi, shaking his head, "Japanese madame all small madame."

American friends helped us a good deal. I had a letter of introduction to an American Quaker couple, Mr. and Mrs. Bowles, who proved to be wonderfully cordial. They had lived all their lives in Japan, they loved the country and knew it well. They took our cares to heart, placed Maria in their Quaker school together with Japanese little girls, and taught us to find our way about Tokyo alone and so gain a measure of independence. Their counsel decided me to buy silk for my dress and have a Chinese tailor make it. So Mrs. Bowles and the three of us went shopping.

We got off the streetcar in the midst of traffic. I felt lost, but it was not Mrs. Bowles's nature to stand and think. "Come on, come on," she cried, hurrying us, it seemed, right under the wheels of the cars. Just when I thought we were about to be crushed, she raised her umbrella majestically. The trucks and passenger cars stopped as if bewitched. We crossed the street.

At last the silk was purchased, the tailor found. I lacked only proper shoes for my appearance. Idzumi called at our "European" house with the car of his editorial office, and we drove to the center of town. The shoe salesmen took one look at my feet, shook their heads pensively, and invariably brought out slippers about three sizes too small. We went from store to store. Everywhere, Idzumi talked at length to the salesmen. I could make out his mention of my father, myself, Russia, Moscow, his newspaper—but the right size of slippers was not forthcoming. The clerks brought out men's shoes, black, tan, with ties, even high boots. "Hard to find," Idzumi said, "Japanese madame have very little feet."

Presently he asked the driver's advice. The latter parked his machine and accompanied us to the shoe stores. Once more endless conversations. Now the two of them talked to the sales people, gesticulated, explained. "What are you talking about for so long?" I asked.

"I must explain everything," replied Idzumi, "about the count, about you, about how the count lived, what he wrote, how he died."

I was beginning to feel exhausted. "Idzumi-San, would you instead kindly ask them whether they have evening slippers?"

"Ah!" exclaimed the old man, overjoyed. "I know, I know! Why didn't you tell me before? You need dancing slippers! Hahaha!"

Once more Idzumi and the driver, interrupting each other, launched into long, detailed explanations. Now there was a group of some five or six, wagging their heads, clicking their tongues, trying in every way to help. I reached a state of despair. In this mood I purchased a pair of men's patent leather evening slippers.

The tailor Mrs. Bowles recommended did not bring the dress in time. So at my first gala lecture in Tokyo, I made my appearance in men's dancing slippers and my shabby woolen dress from Soviet Russia. But Idzumi-San was satisfied. Later he told us:

"Yesterday I wrote an article and sent it to my newspaper. Everybody laughed. I wrote how Tolstoy-San bought the biggest dancing slippers to be had. I also wrote how many pounds Tolstoy-San weighs. Very good article. Everybody was pleased."

CHAPTER SIX

The Lecture Tour

We were a company of three setting out on my tour: Kuroda, a "business manager," and I. Why we needed the business manager I never understood. To be sure, he bought our train seats and reserved the sleepers, ordered dinners and rooms—but why could not Kuroda do it as well? Kuroda told me that the business manager had just been blessed with the arrival of his first child and was very proud of his son. He was a skinny, good-natured little man who tried vainly to give himself an air of importance, to seem European. He ate Western food with visible repugnance, trying to stuff it down his throat with a portion of rice, holding his fork between his third and fourth fingers, as the Japanese hold chopsticks, straining his neck to escape the starched collar that was strangling him.

Idzumi and my friends saw me off at the Tokyo station. I embraced and kissed Olga and her daughter Maria. Suddenly, I no-

ticed such profound astonishment on the faces of Kuroda and Idzumi that I felt embarrassed. They turned their heads away in
great confusion, as if they had seen us doing something utterly
indecent. Idzumi tried to disguise his embarrassment with loud
laughter.

After the train had started, I asked Kuroda, "Why did my taking leave of my friends amaze you so?"

Again the same embarrassment. "People in our country do not
kiss."

"What, never? Never kiss at all?"

"It—it is something that—man and wife, once in a while, when
nobody sees. . . ."

"But—if, for instance, a mother parts with her daughter or son
for a long time—if her son goes to war—don't they kiss when they
say goodbye?"

"Oh, no, never, they only bow to the ground."

Pullman cars, rapid trains, comfortable hotels—I had never realized how far Russia had fallen behind in civilization. In nearly
every city we visited there were large department stores
crammed with goods, with both Japanese and Western restaurants, roof gardens, elevators. What a contrast to Soviet destitution! Not long before in Russia we had been used to saying,
"Thank you humbly," and begging for more when a clerk threw
a few pounds of half-rotten potatoes at us. Here for only a few
cents we could get a large quantity of fruit, bread, rice, fish—and
the clerks thanked us for our patronage.

In all the towns I was startled by the mixture of Oriental and
Western culture. Here were printing plants equipped with the
latest machinery, and thousands of Japanese ideograms to fill the
pages of the newspapers. Automobiles, buses, trams, and rickshaws in the center of Tokyo. Telephones and telegraph offices
(my photograph was transmitted from Osaka to Tokyo by wire-
less), mail service of amazing accuracy and speed, and in the
heart of Tokyo, on the roof of the *Nichi Nichi* building, a flock of
carrier pigeons.

However, neither Osaka nor the commercial city of Nagoya made as deep an impression on me as the ancient city of Fukuoka on the island of Kyushu. The splendid sunshine that streamed through the window of my compartment on the train awoke me. Now we were already at Shimonoseki, where we were to take the ferry to Kyushu.

On deck we mingled with Japanese of all sorts and conditions. As I stared about in fascination, I was startled by the sight of two strange, gigantic women. They walked with the lumbering step of very heavy persons. With their high hairdress, they towered. I could not see their faces until we had got settled on the deck. As soon as we had stowed our luggage, I looked again for them. Then to my amazement I saw that their faces had been shaved—they were huge men, so huge that even in Russia they would have been remarkable. Here among these small people they seemed really to be giants. Strangest of all were their hairdress and their wide kimonos. "Who are those people?" I asked.

"Wrestlers," responded Kuroda. I had a consuming desire to photograph them, but Kuroda advised against it.

"We cannot photograph here, this is a military port. Just now there is construction between these two islands."

"They are working even under water?"

"Yes, they are."

In Fukuoka Western civilization had made scarcely any impression. Not a single European hotel. Kuroda and the business manager were greatly embarrassed, but I was much pleased, thinking that here was my chance to see how the Japanese lived. We stopped at the best Japanese hotel. At the entrance a throng of people met us, bowing and smiling. We bowed too. I was being scrutinized as if I were a freak. In the lobby, where a multitude of *geta* and shoes stood in rows, we took ours off and were conducted up highly polished stairs to the upper floor.

"The host says he has prepared the best room in the hotel for you," Kuroda informed us.

It was indeed a magnificent room, large, clean, with a balcony

on the canal and a view of the town. In the usual *tokonoma**
stood a tall vase with its single flower. On the floor were four
identical large flat silk cushions, a low table—and nothing else.

When one has become accustomed to Japanese life, customs,
tradition, this emptiness conveys so great a sense of harmony and
beauty that any additional object—a chair, table, suitcase—shocks
the eye like an ink spot on a white dress.

After us there entered a woman in a dark kimono, with the
usual high hairdress. Facing me, she bent her knees, her back
arched, and placing her palms on the matting she touched the
floor with her forehead. What was I to do? Kneel also? Or bow to
her while standing? Who was she? I looked at Kuroda implor-
ingly.

He said something to her, then, twitching up his Western trousers, he too knelt, and the two of them, bent double, saluted each
other, their foreheads touching the matting, murmuring a greeting. The business manager followed suit.

We all sat on the floor on the cushions. My feet got terribly in
the way. I did not know where to put them. If I stretched them
out, my back suffered. If I sat on my knees, Japanese fashion, my
knees ached. The easiest way was to sit Turkish fashion, legs
crossed.

Meanwhile the woman went and came, bringing a small stove,
a hibachi full of hot coals. Kneeling, she added live coals, handling them with pincers. In winter there is a hibachi in every
room, and sometimes there is no other heat in the house. One
cannot imagine a heavy European stove in a Japanese house. It
would spoil its harmony and beauty. On the other hand, I have
never in my life met anything as impractical and tormenting as
the hibachi. The glowing coals are put into it before they are
thoroughly carbonized, and this always gives Europeans terrible
headaches.

The first thing the Japanese ever serve is green tea with bean
curd. This tea is taken at every hour of the day, both at meals,
before, and after. The tea and the hibachi had made my room

* Alcove or niche built into important rooms and used for the display of floral arrangements
or paintings.

warm and cosy. The woman took the tea tray, pushed the low
table closer to us, and vanished. When she returned, she brought
other servants carrying three trays and a wooden pail of rice.
Each tray bore tiny porcelain cups, tiny wooden cups, saucers of
fish, greens, salted radishes, fresh grated radishes, and little bottles of soy sauce. As we ate and drank, the woman sat curled up
on the floor next to the pail of rice. As soon as someone's rice cup
was empty, she rose and replenished it. Kuroda was teaching me
to eat with chopsticks. The woman watched, laughing softly, covering her mouth with her kimono sleeve.

After this supper, other women came. They pushed apart the
paper sliding doors of the closet, decorated with pictures of white
storks, and took out thick silken mattresses which they spread in
the middle of the floor. Instead of a pillow, they put down a hard
little silken roll stuffed with wood shavings. Japanese women
place this roll under their necks so as to preserve their hairdress,
which is done only once in several days. On top of the mattresses
they laid several very thick quilts of silk and a voluminous silk
kimono, inside which I found another one of cotton for a nightgown.

In Russia only dead bodies are laid out in the middle of the
room. Besides, I knew that that roll would not stay under my
head without bracing. So I took hold of the whole arrangement
and pulled it up to the wall. The woman watched me, then threw
up her hands, laughing, and ran from the room.

In a few minutes the paper door slid open and in filed women
old and young, men in blue shirts with Japanese characters on
the back, and finally, the innkeeper, his wife and children. They
all stood and stared at the bed, clicking their tongues in amazement, laughing and talking. At last they left.

My fifth and final lecture was scheduled for the next day. Most
of my listeners proved to be young students. The girls had fresh,
velvety, pale faces, and smooth, shining hair; the boys wore black
tunics with brass buttons. Nearly all, male and female, were in
kimonos. For two hours they sat on the floor, legs folded under
them, listening attentively. Probably Kuroda embellished my nar-

rative. What I said in two or three minutes, he sometimes expanded into five minutes or more. He must have spoken well, however, for the women alternately laughed or wiped their eyes surreptitiously with handkerchiefs pulled from their wide sleeves.

Kuroda was pleased with himself. "I spoke well, because this is my home town."

The next day he went to the country to visit his mother, leaving me in the care of the business manager.

I had been craving solitude. I was sick of newsmen, conversation, being photographed. Early in the morning, after writing down the address of our hotel on a slip of paper, I went out alone into the town. I wandered from one narrow alley into another, reveling in the wonderful little shops selling dishes; in this town china was especially colorful and abundant. I bought objects I did not need, I looked, listened, and enjoyed myself thoroughly. By dinner time I was back at the hotel. The business manager met me not far from the door. He looked scared. "What happened to you, where have you been?"

"I went walking."

"Sssss, ah, I was terribly worried." He kept at my side, shaking his head and sighing. At the door, while I was taking off my shoes, he spoke to the innkeeper. When, after dinner, I wanted to go again for another walk, I could not find my shoes. I asked the proprietor for them, but he only shook his head. I grew angry, insisted. By gestures, I made it perfectly plain that I wanted my shoes. He disappeared, then came back with the business manager.

I was no longer allowed to go out by myself for a walk. The business manager always followed me. If I went out onto the veranda, so did he. If I sat in my room, so did he. I was losing all patience. I got up. Hastily, he got up also. "Please leave me alone, I wish to be alone!"

He smiled. So long as I stood still, he waited. As soon as I moved to go, he did also. "Excuse me," I said, "I want to go and wash my hands."

He bowed and smiled. "Please—I shall accompany you."

When I emerged from the bathroom, he was waiting outside. This made me uncomfortable. I did not then know that the Japanese do not see anything indecent about bodily functions. Their toilets are almost always situated in a place of honor near the dining room. I shall never forget the time when we visited a hospital. The senior physician invited us to dine in a Chinese restaurant. Before we left, three Chinese doctors rose and invited us to follow them. All three of us thought they were going to show us something interesting concerning the hospital. However, they led us to the toilet, offered us slippers, and courteously opened the door for us. We were embarrassed, but our embarrassment was even greater when on leaving the toilet we found the three doctors standing by the door, politely waiting.

It was very hard for the business manager and myself to communicate. In theory, he spoke English, but he took a long time pondering each word, and it was not easy to follow him. Those Japanese who learn English without having been to England or America speak a most peculiar idiom almost impossible to understand. He would stop a long time in the middle of a sentence, cocking his head to right or left, trying to express himself. Finally, when he saw I was unable to grasp his meaning, he would break into peals of laughter.

At the end of one such conversation, I understood that he wanted to take me to an art exhibition. It had been planned ahead of time. There were going to be reporters and photographers to learn what I thought of the pictures and to photograph me.

It bored me terribly to look through rooms filled with gilt-framed Western-style paintings—landscapes, still lifes, and nudes: not a trace of anything Japanese in all this. A distressing display. I had seldom seen anything more tasteless: lifeless bodies, soulless studies, crude daubs. The reporters then appeared. They wished to know my opinion. What could I say? "But isn't there any Japanese art at all?" I asked dejectedly.

"Oh, yes, we will show you. But we are very proud of our achievements in the domain of European art." At last they took us to another building.

The first things to meet my eyes were entrancing. Translucent fish, delicate blue shapes in fantastic seaweed growths. One seemed to see the rhythmic movements of their gills as plainly as the stare of their round eyes. One picture was of the flowering cherry, the *sakura*. The leafless twig with its cloud of pink blossoms bowed under the weight of the bright little birds that had lit upon it. I hardly knew which way to look next. What was this? Fog. I felt the chilly dampness. In the fog I made out the outlines of a rowboat with people in strange straw clothing, and on the sharply upturned prow, long-beaked birds. "Fishing birds," explained the business manager. "Those are cormorants, trained to fish. You like this?"

"Very much." I stood enchanted, unwilling to move on.

"This picture has been bought by one of our princes," explained one of the reporters. It was a still life of silvery blue fish in a basket. One had almost jumped out, its scales glittering. "Lucky prince!" said I. "Did he buy any of those European-style paintings?"

"No."

"The prince has good taste."

The next day Kuroda came back. My tour being over, he put me on a train back to Tokyo, where I rejoined my friends. I carried with me a check for one thousand yen,* but still very slight knowledge of the country in which I was to live for the next two years.

CHAPTER SEVEN

One Thousand Yen

The peasants, shopkeepers, carpenters, masons—in short, all the manual workers—amazed us with their dexterity, speed, and technique. However, when something had to

* About $470.

be explained or a decision had to be taken, we found the Japanese distressingly slow. Hour after hour would pass before a Japanese had pondered a matter sufficiently to take action. He had to study every detail, weigh all the circumstances, ask no end of questions about the family situation of the interested parties, even their biographies. Only after long and tortured thinking would he arrive at a decision. On the other hand, after he had once made up his mind, it was difficult if not impossible to make him change it.

Usually, a conversation began at a point remote from the real subject. For a long while one could not guess the trend. So it was when two middle-aged gentlemen called at our house in Tokyo. "Permit us to introduce ourselves," said one in beautiful clear Russian. "This is Iwanami-San, an important Tokyo publisher, and a great admirer of Tolstoy. He has loved and published his works throughout his life. I am Professor Yasugi. I work for Iwanami-San as one of the translators of your father's works."

For a long time we went on bowing to one another, murmuring polite words in Russian, English, Japanese. Then we all sat down around the table in our "European" dining room, which looked more like a dirty bonbon box left over from last year's Christmas tree. The two Japanese sat side by side, and I faced them across the table.

Iwanami-San, the publisher, spoke at length in Japanese. His voice rose and fell. He made no gestures. His hands remained on his knees. Only the rising color in his round face betrayed his emotion. Professor Yasugi, a wiry reserved man with regular features, listened patiently without interrupting, only occasionally nodding his small head. At last the speaker grew so purple in the face that moisture appeared on his fleshy nose. Then he ceased speaking.

Yasugi interpreted clearly, without a shade of sentiment. He said that Iwanami-San had been fascinated by Tolstoy and his teaching ever since adolescence. For a time he had been a vegetarian and had lived very simply, professing nonresistance to violence. As the years went by, however, his youthful fervor had somewhat cooled. Life had forced him to abandon his efforts to live by Tolstoy's ideas, but he would forever preserve his love and gratitude for that influence. Now he was devoting himself to publishing Tolstoy's complete works in Japanese.

The professor finished, and the publisher resumed. He spoke for a long time. Finally, his voice began to tremble and he fell silent. "Iwanami-San has spoken," the professor translated, "of the deep impression made on him by the first book of your father's that he read. Tolstoy's philosophy was a revelation to him." Stage by stage, Iwanami's inner life was unfolded.

What Iwanami had said moved me deeply. Among Russians, I thought, one seldom finds such knowledge of my father and love for him, more seldom than among these seemingly alien people. At the same time, I felt that they had come on business. I wanted to find out what, but a couple of hours had elapsed, and I still did not know the purpose of their visit.

Once more the publisher spoke at length. The interpreter said that he had mentioned my father's repudiation of author's rights. There had been a time when the publication of my father's works had brought a profit. Just now, however, business was poor, publishing had to be carried on almost at a loss. Yet he went on publishing Tolstoy's works.

"Please thank Iwanami-San in my name," I said. "I am greatly touched and pleased to know that the Japanese are so well acquainted with my father's writings and love them so well."

Yasugi interpreted. Iwanami nodded joyously and began to talk very, very fast. Again Yasugi interpreted. "Iwanami-San has read about you, he knows that your father loved you greatly. He is glad to have this occasion to meet you."

Another hour went by. I still could not understand what they were driving at, but I felt a solution drawing near. Now we were speaking of Russia and the Revolution.

"Iwanami-San knows how difficult life has been for all of you lately," said Yasugi. "He knows, too, that at present living in a foreign country is not easy for you, without funds, without friends, and he considers himself obliged to come to your assistance."

Iwanami glanced at Yasugi and began searching for something in his briefcase. Presently he pulled out a long piece of paper, covered it with his hand, and steadied his eyes expectantly on the professor.

"And so he has brought you a present, a check for a thousand yen," Yasugi concluded.

An awkward pause ensued.

"Please tell him that I thank him very much," I responded, "but I could not accept such a gift."

The chair squeaked under the publisher's portly figure. He fell into great agitation. "Why not?"

"Because I cannot accept money I did not earn."

"But your father earned it."

"No doubt you know that my father willed to me all his manuscripts and his author's rights with the understanding that I would protect them as he would have wished, that is, grant to all those who so desire the right of printing his works without compensation. How could I possibly break his will and accept money for his writings?"

The two Japanese sat thinking.

"But couldn't you accept this amount from us as a gift?" asked Iwanami.

"No, I thank you, but I cannot."

The publisher was even more agitated. He alternately opened and closed his briefcase. When finally he lost hope of persuading me, he clicked it shut and smiled broadly. Then he asked a new question.

"He wishes to know whether you would accept an invitation to all three of you to come to dinner. He would be greatly offended if you refuse."

We gladly accepted.

They bowed a long time before they left. A few days later an automobile called for us, and we were taken to a Chinese restaurant. In a little private room about twelve Japanese were awaiting us. They all spoke Russian. A few were professors of the Russian language in various universities and colleges. I was astonished to learn how well versed they were in Russian literature. Most of them had translated Russian classics for Iwanami's publishing house.

At about six we sat down to dinner, and rose about nine. What a dinner it was! One course followed another in seemingly endless succession: soup, game, meat, fish, lobster, salads, swallows' nests, pigeons' eggs, sea cabbage, shrimp, and the famous carp, an obligatory part of every festive Chinese dinner, fried in such a way that even the fins, the head, and the tail are eaten. I counted more than twenty courses. "Eat as little as you can," our neighbor whispered, but we could not easily shake off our Russian habits.

The portions were served on plates almost as tiny as those little girls give their dolls, but we were far from expecting twenty courses, and by the time the carp appeared, we were sated. At the very end, when all of us could hardly breathe, rice was again served with green tea. Every one of the Japanese ate a tiny cup of rice, drank the tea, and rinsed the cup now empty of rice so that not a single grain should be wasted. Such is the custom: it is a sin to waste a grain of rice.

Finally the dinner came to an end. The Chinese waiters brought hot damp towels. Our companions unfolded the towels, wiped the sweat from their faces and necks, and then their hands. Iwanami was especially amusing. He puffed, closed his eyes, rubbing his neck and bald head with pleasure until he shone like a samovar.

Among the translators present were Professor Fukami and Professor Yasugi, who later translated my book, *Torusutoi no omoide* (Recollections of Tolstoy) published by Iwanami.*

---

*This was published in English as *The Tragedy of Tolstoy* (New Haven: Yale University Press, 1933; reissued 1973). It also appeared in numerous other translations around the world.

CHAPTER EIGHT

The Student

Little by little we learned how to find our way in the streets of Tokyo, to use the street cars, to say a few of the most necessary Japanese words, and we also managed to make ourselves understood somehow and sometimes, in English or Russian or French or German.

Despite the difficulties and privations, life seemed an uninterrupted marvelous holiday. Our walks in the town were always interesting. We loved to gaze about us, trying to penetrate the secrets of this alien but beautiful life. One evening, for instance, a street suddenly came to life with lots of lanterns and candles. Peddlers of all kinds lined the sidewalks, selling toys, dishes, goldfish, drygoods, flags. They were cooking sweet potatoes on the spot and roasting chestnuts. We moved along with the crowd, which thickened all the time, until we came to a small Shinto temple lighted by multicolored paper lanterns. A celebration honoring this particular temple was in progress. The whole street was taking part.

Sometimes when walking in the street of an evening, we found ourselves looking into the interior of some modest Japanese home with paper doors. Squatting on cushions on the floor, the family would be having supper around a low table. The clean matting shone, and the electric lights emphasized the spotlessness of the place. The family would sit quietly, ceremoniously, eating their rice with chopsticks out of tiny porcelain cups. Such calm breathed from their figures in their wide kimonos, from their earthenware hibachi with glowing coals. What taste and beauty in these surroundings, in the customs, of even a plain, poor Japanese home.

At the end of December people began preparing for the new year, the chief Japanese holiday. The shops were decorated with long ropes of rice straw in tight plaits, neat as a girl's braids. These plaits either dangled, ending in tassels, or were made into wreaths, in the center of which hung oranges with their green leaves. Here and there amid the greenery hung a huge red lobster. The horses and cars were also decorated. Along the streets rows of bamboos and pines were improvised. In the florists' windows dwarf plum trees in blossom appeared.

Every one of these objects had its own significance. Thus the pine tree symbolized long life; the bamboo, steadfastness; the plum tree, endurance. Certain shops exhibited pictures of the horse. That year, 1930, was dedicated to the horse. The years are reckoned in sets of twelve, of which the first year is dedicated to the mouse, the second to the cow or bull, followed by the tiger, the hare, the dragon, the serpent, the horse, the sheep, the ape, the cock, the dog, and finally the boar.

The Japanese have a system for characterizing a person according to the time of his birth. The symbol of the year in which a person is born is important in choosing one's future husband or wife. It is bad to marry a man born in the year of the tiger to a girl born in the year of the cock or hen. That marriage will not be happy. A marriage is ideal when both have been born in a year dedicated to the same animal. This guarantees that their temperaments will suit each other. If, however, the husband was born in the year of the horse, but the wife in the year of the cow, that is not so bad, since these animals get along with each other.

The anniversary of a birth is celebrated nine months earlier than with us. Maria was overjoyed when she found that out. "Mama," she exclaimed, "that means I'm not fourteen, I'm already fifteen!"

About this time, just before New Year's Day, a college student well and neatly dressed called on us for the first time. On entering our dining room, he removed his shabby student's cap (shabby caps were considered chic among Japanese college boys), bowed, and laid a bundle of fruit in a pretty kerchief on the floor. Then he took a stand by the door and made a long speech in

Russian. He spoke as if reciting a lesson, pausing at certain syllables and rolling the r's in a queer manner, as if strained.

"I wish to study RRRussian literraturre and language," he declared. "I love Tolstoy, I have rrread many of his worrks; most of
all I love *RRResurrrrection*. I should be verry grrrateful if you
could give me lessons in RRRussian language and literrrature."
Concluding, he inhaled with a whistling sound, as the Japanese
often do from a feeling of modesty and shyness, and fell silent. Of
course I replied in Russian.

"I do not understand," he said. I repeated, speaking every
word very distinctly. Obviously he did not even try to understand.

"I do not understand," he repeated the Russian sentence se-
renely. Then his whole face creased in mirth, no longer solemn
and plain, but childishly lovable. He burst out giggling. Now we
all laughed, Maria, Olga, and I. We understood that he really
could not speak a word of Russian. The speech he had just made
had been memorized with the aid of a dictionary. Somehow, by
gestures and again the dictionary, which he thumbed with his
thin fingers, we came to terms. He was to come twice a week.
Maria would teach him Russian in return for lessons in Japanese.

The youth became a constant visitor to our little apartment in
Minamiteramachi Street. A few times he happened to drop in
during dinner. Once we offered him some dishes, but he found it
almost impossible to eat Russian food. "Spasi," he apologized—
for some reason abbreviating the Russian word *spasibo*, thank
you—"I have had enough." Since Japanese courtesy does not permit leaving anything on one's plate, he choked, but managed to
swallow all the food.

The next time, we offered him a bowl of borshch. Keeping at
a safe distance from the table, he said, "Spasi, I have had
enough."

Maria-San, as the student called her, loved the cinema, and he
used to take her to movies. Sometimes when they failed to return
by nine o'clock, her mother was worried, but invariably it ended
well. He took good care of Maria, treated her to Japanese dain-
ties, and if it rained he brought her home in a taxi.

Maria and he came to understand each other completely. Sometimes she lacked the patience to listen through to the end of his long, prepared Russian speeches. With extraordinary facility, she had picked up a few score of Japanese words, with which she managed to be so talkative that as often as not she reduced him to silence.

He never embarrassed us, was never intrusive. Sometimes he dropped in on his way home from classes, his books still with him, and if he found us busy and Maria had not yet returned from school, he sat down at the dining room table and studied. Learning Russian cost him great pains, though writing seemed to come somewhat more easily than pronouncing. It was time-consuming to converse with him. He obviously struggled hard to compose a sentence in his mind; then he would trace with his finger on the table the words he intended, whisper to himself, and finally speak.

"I love—very much—Katyusa. You know song 'Katyusa kawai'?" At length we grasped that he meant the Russian song, "Milaya Katyusha," sung by Katyusha Maslova, the heroine of my father's novel *Resurrection*. The "sh" sound was quite beyond him, and the Japanese word *kawai* replaced *milaya*, both meaning "dear." He closed his eyes and sang, "Katyusa, Katyusa, Katyusa kawai. . . ." Like some other Japanese we knew, he was convinced that in emitting these strange sounds he was singing a Russian song.

One day our student shared his troubles with us. His father, a merchant, had wanted him, the eldest son, not to study but to prepare to be a merchant like himself, for the eldest son had to carry on his father's trade or profession. Because his son wanted to devote himself to literature, the old man constantly objected with growing anger.

In a Japanese family the eldest son is the hope and support of the whole family. Next to his father, he is the senior member of the household. If the father dies, he assumes responsibility for all. He is given much, but much is also asked of him. A favorite topic in literature and drama is the eldest son who strays from the right path and causes his parents grief. Yet not a few tragedies occur because the eldest son is deprived of the freedom of choosing a profession to his liking and is forced to do what his father did all his life.

While I was writing the book that Iwanami was to publish, we had moved to the village of Ahsia, on the ocean, halfway between Osaka and Kobe. Our student came to see us there and brought his younger brother. This boy looked very different from his elder. His high school tunic hung on him like a sack, he did not know how to wear his foreign footgear. On entering our house he would kick his dirty, heavy, laced shoes off his bare feet as though they were geta. His sunburned face was unwashed, but its expression was charming, childish yet pensive and earnest. He too did not want to be a merchant but a painter. Shyly and worshipfully gazing into Maria's eyes, he spread on the floor before her his drawings of the actors of the famous Kabuki theatre: shaven faces under female wigs, long trains, brightly colored kimonos. His drawings were neat and precise, on fine Japanese paper. Possibly they were copied from theatre magazines.

"We have come for advice," explained the elder son as we all sat down on the cushions. We had just finished a Japanese dinner brought in from a restaurant. "We ask your counsel, as from our mothers." Again he was tracing his words with his fingers on the matting before he spoke. "We have left home. Our father is angry, he does not want my brother to be an artist, or me to study literature. He says we must be traders. We don't want to be traders." He gazed at us in question.

We did not know what to tell them. Yet the two boys had traveled about a hundred miles to ask our advice. They were visibly upset. They waited.

"You must try your best to secure your parents' permission. It will be hard on you to go your own way without your father's consent."

The boy nodded. Again he traced some words on the floor. "Very hard," he said finally.

They stayed with us for two days. The younger brother drew many pictures of Kabuki actors for Maria. The elder asked me to write out a saying of Tolstoy's as a memento. Finally we took them to the train. They bowed low many times before leaving. Resting their hands on their knees in the old manner, they thanked us. We felt, though, that we had been unable to help them.

As it turned out, it seemed they had managed to get their father's consent, for when we returned to Tokyo from Ahsia, both brothers met us there. We had opened a school for teaching the Russian language, and of all our pupils the elder brother was the most punctual, the most assiduous. Our friendship grew. When he could speak Russian a little, we read Turgenev, Dostoevsky, and Tolstoy with him. He often called on us, and took Maria to the cinema. Her mother no longer worried about letting them go out together, and the boy became almost a member of our household.

One day, however, he failed to appear in class. We were told that he had fallen gravely ill and had left for home. Several months passed, still he did not appear. "He is not coming back any more," a friend of his told us. "He has been very ill, in the hospital. Now he is better."

"What was his illness?"

"Seriously ill, nervously ill."

We could get no more information out of him. Later, only a short time before our departure for America, I received a letter from him, a lovable, tender letter, full of modesty and humility. He begged us to forgive him, for Christ's sake, he was such an "unjust" one, he called himself, using a Russian word partly self-manufactured, because he had dared to love Maria-San, and would love her always, the pure Maria-San, pure as the sky. Recently he had seen us all in a dream—Tolstoy, Olga-San, Maria-San, and myself. In that dream we had all forgiven him and loved him. When he awoke, he was sobbing for joy.

CHAPTER NINE

Fencing

We came to love old Idzumi. He was so like a Russian that we forgot that he was of another race, another culture. Perhaps that was because he had lived in Russia a long while, but in spite of that, his Russian was so comically defective that we rocked with laughter whenever he talked. He often chided me for being impractical, unbusinesslike. "Tolstoy-San, big fool," he would say.

I made believe that my feelings were hurt. "Why, Idzumi-San?" I asked.

"There, not know how to make money, big fool. Count, he too, big fool." Noticing my astonishment, he added, "There, big wise fool. Need nothing, need nothing. Give away everything. Big fool!" Idzumi would go away laughing, showing a mouthful of gold teeth.

"And you, Idzumi-San, are you clever?"

"I very clever, very sly!"

"And you know how to make money, do you?"

"Money—I have little. I have wife, son—all time, 'Give money, give money.' And money is little, there isn't any money!"

One day the old man came in looking very sad indeed. We asked him what was the matter.

"There—I, 'Living Corpse.'* Eldest son—no good son—doesn't want to study. Drinks sake, and says 'Give money, give money,' all the time. I want—like the count, like 'Living

* Tolstoy's drama.

Corpse'—to leave my house—want no family, wife, children. There, I leave and go away, like Tolstoy."

Such depresssion visited him but seldom, however. Usually he joked and laughed—mutilating the Russian language unmercifully, laughing at us and at himself. Some of my articles for Japanese newspapers and magazines Idzumi himself translated. "Tell me, Idzumi-San," I asked sometimes, "have you heard any favorable mention of my article in the papers?"

"Yes, they praised it much. Photographs good, I translated good, everything good, they praised very much."

"And how about—how about what I wrote?" I inquired hesitantly.

"*Nichevo* *—not bad. I translated, made over everything my own way, they praised it very much."

Idzumi looked older than his age, his head bald, his face wrinkled like a dark, very ripe pear. He dragged his feet without lifting them from the floor. He always looked exhausted. We were surprised then to hear that the old man was a great expert at samurai fencing.

"When fencing, I am like young," he would say. "Forget all, bad son, work, little money. When fencing, I am honest, clean, and brave—like God!"

We had believed that fencing lessons brought Idzumi additional earnings, but when we asked him about it, he was shocked. "Money—no, no money! When Idzumi fences, he thinks not of money. Brave, clean, honest!" he repeated.

It is a Japanese custom for a man to get up from bed about three in the morning for a period of several nights in midwinter to practice some noble sport or art. Adherents of the ancient theatre sing and play antique instruments. In Idzumi's case he gave fencing lessons.

"But why in the middle of the night?"

"Must be strong—strong character. It is cold, not want to get up. But—Idzumi-San gets up, fences—like samurai."

Once he invited us to come and see some fencing. A huge Jap-

---

*Nichevo, a Russian word meaning nothing, never mind.

anese in a dark kimono and a wide gored skirt called for us. He
had a beard. Japanese men in general wear no beards, so this
young man looked more like an Ainu* than a Japanese.

The fencing hall was crowded. Idzumi's wife and daughter were
making bustling preparations for tea and supper. All the men
present except Idzumi were young, mostly students, in Japanese
dress, some in gored skirts. We were given seats on a platform
and were served tea. The performance began.

Several pairs of fencers came out simultaneously. They all wore
helmets, mailed shirts, gored skirts, and white tabi. The various
adversaries bowed low to their opposites, crossed their rapiers,
and stood motionless. We watched them intently, seeking Idzumi, but without success, though we recognized our "Ainu" escort at once: he was the tallest in the room.

Suddenly the fencers leaped forward with savage yells. Blows
rained on heads and shoulders. The figures darted with incredible
speed and agility over the floor covered with matting, hurling
themselves upon one another with wild cries. Their impact was
terrific—then they sprang apart.

"Ah-h-h-h-a! U-u-u-y!"

Sometimes they paused for a moment, rigid, like fighting
cocks, then resumed their blows with even greater force. They
looked as though they bitterly hated one another and were determined to cut one another to shreds. One! Two! The rapiers fell
on the opponents.

"Is it possible that such blows are falling on old Idzumi?" Suddenly, we spotted him. He was making strange jumps sideways,
he took tiny mincing steps, he leaped, darted hither and thither,
shouted—and like all the rest, got blows on the head. "Doesn't
that hurt him?" Maria worried.

Then the battle ended. Idzumi had lost. All the adversaries
bowed very low to one another. After changing their clothes, they
joined us. We were surprised to find no trace of excitement in
them, let alone hatred. Spreading out their wide skirts, they sat

---

*The Ainu people inhabit the island of Sakhalin, north of Japan. They are believed to
have lived there since prehistoric times. A Paleo-Asiatic people, they differ racially from
the Japanese.

down with us. Only old Idzumi was breathing hard. His bald head had not suffered in the least. It only shone more brightly.

"There—tired," he commented.

One fencing match followed another after that. We even tired of watching them. Idzumi's wife and daughter came and went, bearing trays of refreshments. The men drank a great deal of sake, their faces glowing. Their blows seemed ever fiercer, the cries more savage. In the intermissions between matches, the fencers sang and played various instruments.

Two boys sat down next to Maria, treated her to refreshments, importuned us to sing Russian songs. It was getting late. We thought it time to go home, but our "Ainu" escort was having such a good time drinking sake that we could not detach him.

Gradually the fencers' movements became less certain, the songs less harmonious, the conversation freer. Suddenly, the electricity went out. In the darkness everyone jumped from their seats, hot bodies collided against us, Maria cried out, clutching her mother.

"Nichevo, nichevo," Idzumi tried to reassure us. But we decided to go home immediately and began to make our way to the door. Not until we were well outside the crowd of silk kimonos, the wine fumes, the tobacco smoke, did we feel relieved. Now our tall "Ainu" appeared as if out of air. He conducted us toward the station. "Thanks, thanks, Idzumi-San," we called, hastening to keep up with the big bearded fellow.

Thereafter Idzumi did not appear for something like three weeks. Then one day a postcard came. I could hardly decipher the rambling script. He informed us that he was in a hospital, very ill. He begged us to cook some Russian *kisel* * and bring it to him. I immediately went to see him. Weakly, he pressed my hand.

"There—Idzumi dying. Fenced much. Tired. Inflammation."

The doctors said he was too old for the vigorous activity of fencing. He had caught pneumonia, complicated with pleurisy.

Our *kisel* was the last food he took.

---

* *Kisel*, a custard-like dessert made of fruit juice, preferably cranberry or raspberry, eaten cold or hot.

CHAPTER TEN

In the Country

It was early January. We drove up to a massive gate, its tiles curving downward like the eaves of a thatched roof. We walked in the dusk through a large courtyard to a long country house with gleaming white paper walls and wooden doorsteps. We expected a warm indoors after our trip in freezing weather, but an icy chill at once closed in on us. Ishida, our young host, said, "Please come in, take off your coats."

No one closes the sliding paper doors—but why close them? There are no stoves whose heat should be saved. However, we obediently took off our coats, and shivered. The Japanese do not even try to heat their houses: they heat themselves. We were given warm quilted kimonos and invited to sit on the cushions on the floor around the hibachi, itself covered with a large quilt. "A *kotatsu,*" said Ishida. "You will feel warm right away."

We all crept under the quilt almost to our waists. A woman brought in the inevitable green tea. In a few minutes the warmth crept around our feet, then our bodies, and soon we were entirely warm.

Professor Nabori, who had come with us from Tokyo, and Ishida both spoke Russian. Two years earlier, Ishida had visited Russia, including Yasnaya Polyana. I had shown him through the school, the museum, the village, and arranged an evening of popular songs and dances. Now he was repaying my hospitality. Nabori had also come to Yasnaya Polyana for the celebration of my father's hundredth birthday in 1928.

Both Nabori and Ishida had changed into kimonos, and at once they were transfigured. They became themselves: that is, two

Japanese gentlemen. They too crept under the kotatsu. It is hard to describe how a Japanese changes when he dons his national dress. Even the puniest, most unprepossessing man appears taller, broader in his kimono, and his gait assumes dignity and assurance. European dress becomes neither man nor woman in Japan.

Ishida's sister brought in the ceremonial New Year's supper on individual trays with legs. The central place on the tray belongs to the January dish of soup in which are sweet mushrooms and lumps of a special white dough of rice flour. We had seen this dough in tremendous quantities in every provision store in Tokyo without knowing what it was. Nabori and Ishida sucked in the gluey substance with great relish and swishing sounds, but we could not manage either to chew or swallow it.

Ishida's father, a stern old man with a long drooping mustache rather like a Chinaman's, did not eat. He sat near the hibachi in a kimono of coarse gray silk, smoking a long pipe with a gilt edge. He remained silent, but once in a while his wise, confident eyes flashed with humor. What was he thinking? Was he proud of his intellectual son, who understood nothing about farming but loved literature? Or was he disappointed that this son would not help him grow mulberry trees and raise silkworms? One glance at the large new house, the courtyard and outbuildings, showed that this was an excellent homestead, and the old man a thorough farmer.

After supper we all went into the next room. It was likewise without tables or chairs, only silk cushions on the floor, but there were bookcases and shelves along the walls. The books were mostly Russian. We were all eager to look at them, Professor Nabori because he taught Russian literature at the university, and we because for several months we had not seen a single printed Russian word. "In Moscow books are very cheap now," observed the young Ishida, modestly lowering his eyes, "so I brought some back."

His choice was excellent: classics, histories of art and literature, art albums. Ishida told us we might borrow some, so, creeping over the floor, we selected what interested us.

The old man with his pipe had also come into the library. He sat motionless on his cushion near the hibachi, smoking and smiling ironically. What is he thinking?

In the courtyard there was a commotion, the sound of many geta clicking on the cobblestones. Outside someone ran from window to window, peeking in. We heard whispers and subdued giggling. "The peasants have come," Ishida told us; "the men want to show you their folk dances."

The walls slid apart. In the cloudless sky the cold moon made the courtyard bright. Beyond, the black silhouettes of cypresses. On the left rose the tall tiled roof of a two-story building, the loft where the silkworms were kept. The courtyard was teeming with women and girls carrying their babies on their backs as if they grew there. Evidently these young nursemaids were freezing, for they shuffled and stamped their feet, their geta clicking, the black heads of the drowsy infants wobbling. Some small boys in dotted kimonos, their noses dripping, chased one another, pushing and fighting.

Then the crowd grew quiet, gathered. A man came into the courtyard. With quick movements he constructed a platform before the open door of the house wall. He rolled up an empty barrel and stood it bottom up on the platform. The people pressed closer, in a semicircle. They were awaiting entertainment—as for us, we had been enjoying a spectacle all the time. Then eight men in vivid kimonos with pink ribbons and bows around their heads leaped onto the platform. Only then did we realize that all we had seen so far had merely been the ordinary activity of daily life.

There were five musicians, holding musical instruments such as we had never seen before. One looked like a double-headed whirligig topped with a drum skin. There were a bamboo flute, a rattle, and of course the barrel drum. The musician with the rattle intoned a melancholy, drawling song. It changed from a soft pianissimo to a mad fortissimo, then fell ever softer, as if about to die off—then all eight performers interrupted with savage cries. The musicians beat furiously on their instruments, the flute wailed, the drum barrel sounded the measure. Three of the performers, carrying colorful parasols, jumped down from the platform and began to dance, folding and unfolding the parasols with extraordinary grace. The musicians were in a frenzy. Everything danced, hands and feet, instruments, parasols with a soft rustling. Yet no matter how abrupt the contrasts of the sounds, the movements of the dancers were calm and flowing. When the music changed to something passionate and tempestuous, however, they gave savage guttural cries.

Following the parasol dance there was another, in which the dancers were adorned with plumed hats. The moon rose higher and cast a bluish veil on the bright colors. Again, reality was transformed into magic, a fantasy.

"Now they will show you the dance of the samurai," said Ishida. "Whenever our emperor is in danger, we shall all go and defend him with our lives under fire." Yes, they certainly will, I thought. This farmer's son, who does not want to work on a farm, would forget his books, ready to die for his emperor.

A man carrying a doll came out. He was a samurai called to war. He must leave behind many children, the youngest in his arms. His expression, his gestures, depicted the struggle between love and duty. To keep from sobbing, he put a handkerchief between his teeth. He shook his head, clasped the child, danced over to the door, then returned in despair. He put down the child and very haltingly danced out. Love of country had won.

Sweat was rolling down his face, the muscles twitching. "Is he very tired?" I asked.

"No, he is not tired, it's only that he has put his whole soul into this dance, for he has lived it all."

I was told that the peasants wanted to ask about Russia, they were very interested. Eight men sat in a row on the kitchen floor. Before each one stood a little bowl of rice and a little plate of salted radish. They no longer wore their pink hair ribbons. Their black hair was as smooth as if oiled. They sat perfectly still, their thick hands, used to heavy toil, resting on their knees.

"They want to tell you that they have read Tolstoy's works, that they are glad to see you, and would like very much to know more about the Revolution. They read the newspapers and hear rumors, but they are unable to judge true from false." As Ishida finished, he cocked his head, glancing first at the peasants and then at us.

At the end of the row a tall sinewy peasant with silver-streaked hair (evidently the oldest of the group) put down his rice bowl. As he bent, the heavy silk sleeves of his kimono drooped like great wings. He spoke.

"They wish to learn what the Five Year Plan is," Ishida interpreted. "Do the Russian people need industrialization? What does the government do for the peasants?"

I answered.

"They are also interested in knowing how the election takes place, and is it true that most Communists are Jews?"

They were surpised to hear that there was no secret ballot in Russia. When they asked about compulsory education, I replied that it was only in the planning stage so far. Ishida observed with pride, "In Japan universal compulsory schooling was introduced sixty years ago."

They were most eager to know: "Must the oldest son in a Russian family carry on his father's profession?" When they heard that all sons in Russia have equal rights, they were amazed, laughed loud, mouths wide open, like children.

"It isn't so with us," commented Ishida. "Even if the father drinks all his money away, the son is obliged to stay with him and do his farming. Not far from here is a cliff overlooking a chasm. Once an unfortunate son threw himself down because he could not go on living with a bad father."

Next morning Ishida took us for a walk. We were followed by a crowd of boys and girls, the latter carrying swaddled babies on their backs, the geta clicking. We came to a wooden Shinto temple. At first I thought its walls were mottled, but as we came closer I saw they were covered with Japanese ideograms, with ornaments, figures, scenes. One scene represented a young Japanese holding a pitcher, standing by a mighty stream gushing out of a cliff. "What is that?" I asked.

"It tells the story of an eldest son who was very good and loved his father greatly. The father liked beer, but the son was too poor to buy any. Sadly, he wandered off into the woods. Suddenly he saw a spring issuing from a rock and smelled—beer. God had rewarded him for his great love and made the spring flow with beer."

There was an extraordinary quantity of inscriptions on the walls. "Poems," explained Ishida, "some expressing submission to God's will. For instance: 'We do not wait for the rains to cease, we work on with zeal in the rice field.' "

We walked around the temple. In a neglected corner stood a hideous figure with a red-painted, one-eyed head, larger than life. "What is that? Why one eye?"

"It is a saint, named Dharma-San," replied Ishida. "Originally he had no eyes at all. This head was given one eye because the people had a very good tobacco crop this year. If there is a good mulberry season, they will give him a second one."

"But where are the saint's feet?"

"He hasn't any. For seven years he prayed without rising, and so he lost his feet. The peasants adore this saint, his image is often found near the temples."

For ten sen Ishida bought us two small Dharma heads with blank areas instead of eyes. I made a vow to give one eye to my saint when I had written the book I planned about my father, and a second eye when I returned to my own country. I still have the head. He got his one eye, but the other is still blank. Shall we, the saint and I, see the day when he receives his second eye? I am not sure. The cardboard of his head has begun to crack, and the paint is peeling.

We had to go back to Tokyo. On the day of our departure there was great activity in Ishida's house. Even the old man, always sitting on his cushion smoking, smiled cheerfully. Ishida's sisters decked Maria out in a wedding kimono, laughing happily. The Japanese, especially the plain people, laugh like children when they are happy.

Just before we left, a caller came. "My friend, a poet," Ishida explained.

The poet, it transpired, loved my father's books and had read many. I gave him a picture of my father. He laughed happily. We asked him to write a poem for us. "I have already written you a poem, I wrote it long ago in the autumn, as soon as I knew you were coming." He produced a sheet of thick Japanese paper and read:

> The mountains of Haruna are all in autumn colors,
> The morning fog is creeping into the gorges.

When we took leave of our hosts, the evening was beautiful. The mountains of Haruna were now clear, the morning fog had lifted. They stretched in a deep purple chain across the horizon.

CHAPTER ELEVEN

Rice

Why do I love the fields so much, the gardens, peasant huts, and yards smelling of dung, the barns, the serene, sunburned people eternally working from dawn till night? And why do the cities with their glamor, their shady parks, comfortable houses, stores flowing with goods, their important, active people—why do they seem to me the vanity of vanities? I want to escape as soon as possible.

Perhaps it is my father's love for the village that has influenced me. It is precisely love that I mean, not any rationalization about peasant labor as the most honorable of all, or about the peasants being our providers. These things I understood only much later. My father's love for the peasant could not possibly leave me untouched.

The rural life of Japan, the peasants, the houses were, like everything else, different from anything I had ever seen, and I tried to learn as much as I could about them. The sight of the broad tanned faces of the women planting rice, the men in wide straw hats tilling the soil, these gave me the same intense feeling of pleasure as did the sight of peasants working in Switzerland, France, America, or Russia. I felt their genuine essence, devoid of artificiality. It was expressed in their calm, their dignity, their weathered bodies, the beauty of health. The life of the peasant, it seemed, merged with the life of the earth, miraculously nourished by the sun.

Yet it was strange that here, as everywhere else, these peasants were the most disinherited of the population. I never saw people work so intensively and for such long hours. At that time, there were hardly any machines. The farmers worked the fields by hand with huge spades, hoes, and crowbars, turning over the earth sometimes to a depth of three feet or more. What did the Japanese peasant receive for such toil? Copper pennies. Without outside jobs, he would starve. The total net income of all Japanese agricultural workers in 1931 (numbering 5,500,000 farm families) came to about $16.20 per family.* The peasants sent their daughters to work in factories. They themselves were craftsmen, making toys, earthenware, *tatami* ** and geta. Even so they remained very poor.

I believe there were many reasons for this condition. Comparable circumstances existed—and probably still do in many places—in Europe and America, for the root of the whole evil was that the profits from peasant labor went to the wholesaler, the middleman. The progressive Japanese understood this well and started a cooperative movement which has spread far and wide.

The average Japanese farmer had very little. Therefore there was no advantage in owning big expensive machinery. Furthermore, the peasants were crushed by high taxes, whereas the government supported artificially low prices for produce. A propa-

Fortune magazine, September 1936.
** Straw mats.

ganda leaflet once published this statement by the Ministry of War:

> From the point of view of the masses, who represent the majority of consumers everywhere in the world, it is desirable that products should be available under the most favorable conditions possible. Japan enjoys the great advantage of a lower cost of living.
>
> The English and the Dutch favor the small controlling minority in industry and sell their goods at a high price to the colored populations of the colonies. This is contrary to the interests of the masses and to a spirit of fairness.

When I was staying in Japan, the Japanese liberals and socialists lived largely in the cities, knowing nothing of peasant life, interested rather in the industrial workers. This situation was much like that in Russia before the Revolution. One evening in Moscow, a group of prominent liberals came to bid farewell to several prominent socialists whom the Bolshevik government was exiling as counterrevolutionaries.

"They are driving us out," said one, his grief evident. "We have given our lives to the service of the people. The sad thing is not that we are banished, but that there is not a man among the workers and peasants who will remember us, care about us."

He was right. Nobody pitied, nobody remembered these men who had given their lives to serve "the people" and the hoped-for revolution. It is my belief that if someone had explained to the Russian peasant who these *narodniki** were, the *muzhik* would have spat through his teeth: "Serves them right, the sons of bitches. They've overthrown the tsar, murdered him—and our life is a hundred times harder than before."

It would hardly have been possible to explain to this peasant exactly *who* overthrew the tsar, explain the relationship between those who killed the tsar and the revolutionists now being banished. The people never knew these theorists, just as the latter had no true knowledge of the millions of Russian peasants. Just

* Populists; a social movement that agitated Russia from about 1860 on, advocating the peasant commune as a means of bypassing capitalism.

so the Japanese socialists did not know the peasant population, numbering half the nation.

My friend Take-San, a Communist woman writer, and others like her were perfectly informed about the life of the workers—but they knew nothing of peasant life. They would tell you everything about industry, wages, housing conditions, working hours, and all the rest—but ask them about peasant earnings, the price of rice, tobacco, silkworm cocoons: they did not know, or if they knew something, it was all theory. The life of the peasant remained infinitely alien and remote.

Working the fields in Japan was terribly hard. Deep cultivation was necessary. If rice is the crop, then abundant water is essential, as are great quantities of fertilizer; otherwise, the soil in Japan yields nothing. We watched the peasants spreading the white powder of herring meal. The fishing industry produced an enormous amount of herring, more than could be consumed, and so it was converted to fertilizer. But the best of all fertilizer was human excrement, especially for vegetables. When we learned this, we were dismayed. "This fertilizer is not used in Russia," I told a friend, Konishi-San.

"They just don't know about it," he reponded with an air of superiority.

"But, you know . . ." I began to argue timidly. In his presence I always felt as I had when I was a little girl and he used to come to my father to work on the translation of the Tao-te-ching by Lao-Tze. "Mechnikov said . . ."*

"Silly things he said, your Mechnikov," Konishi interrupted, "you should know better. By the time the stuff has fermented for six months in hermetically closed cement tanks, it is entirely harmless. The Japanese have used human fertilizer since time immemorial, and they are much healthier than you Russians."

I could not argue. It would have been pleasanter to know that the fertilizer was another; also I felt slightly insulted about Mechnikov, whom I had thought the Japanese esteemed. I knew that

---

* Ilya Mechnikov (1845–1916) was an eminent biologist who won the Nobel Prize for physiology and medicine in 1908.

Europeanized Japanese liked fermented milk prepared from his formula and gave it to their children. Every morning a boy on a bicycle delivered this yoghurt to Japanese homes, shouting, "Iria, Iria!"—the Japanese pronunciation of Ilya, Mechnikov's first name.

Japanese fields consisted of square plots, divided by irrigation ditches. Before spring planting time, the peasants pumped water into the fields with a water wheel. If the region was mountainous and the fields were terraced, a complicated system had to be used to keep the water from running off. There was a whole science of irrigation, making the water spread from one field to another, the manner and degree of its evaporation regulated. Dykes had to be erected on the slopes. "Today they would never build such fields," Konishi told me; "it's immense work, and people are spoiled nowadays."

When one surveyed these terraces from above, they were like a descending series of flat dishes brimming with water. It was a wonder how the water remained on the terraces. The surface was still; the dark tufts of the rice stalks stood in rows. Every atom of soil was in use. Once in a while one noticed an irregular patch of some twenty square yards surrounded by rocks, planted with wheat or rice.

When I was there, the Japanese used oxen or horses to plow. Their plows were strange, large and awkward, not at all like European plows. It was awesome to watch the men and animals ankle-deep in liquid mud, moving slowly, painfully. At each step the water splashed up, plastering man and beast with mud. When they came to the end of a row, there was an added straining effort to turn the plow.

Soon the stalks would sprout, bright green, so thick the water could no longer be seen. Then the seedlings were pulled up and replanted. This was largely the work of women, usually without any tools to even the spacing, yet the rows were regular. I photographed them. How they laughed! Peasants always think it odd and humorous that one wants to photograph them. What is there in it? Dirt, hard labor, day after day—nothing more. "Is it hard?" I asked.

"No," replied one woman, stepping out onto dry land. She pointed to her feet, explaining something. We could not understand. Her ankles were covered with dark objects. When she took them off, we saw spots of blood. They were leeches. She laughed at our horror.

The harvesting was not easy either. The rice was cut with sickles, then tied in small sheaves. The main problem was drying the sheaves. First they had to be carried off the field. Then, if there were trees handy, the sheaves were hung on them; if not, poles were driven into the ground, other poles placed crosswise, and thus the sheaves dried.

On small farms the peasants did the threshing, winnowing, and husking by hand. They used the simplest hand threshers or even flails. They also winnowed the grain, with primitive winnowers like fans. They told us that once, long ago, the rice was not polished but eaten "black." Then beri-beri, the vitamin deficiency disease, was far less prevalent.

Before I went to Japan I did not care much for rice. In our childhood we were fed rice when our stomachs were out of order. Rice, therefore, was to be avoided, and so were noodles and macaroni. In Japan, however, rice suddenly assumed great importance, like bread in Russia. Perhaps because of the recent famine in my country, I developed a great respect for rice. I learned that it must be boiled in the Japanese manner, without salt. Though rice may be eaten with anything—fish, meat, eggs, horseradish, even fruit—it never should be mixed with anything. That would defile its snowy purity. It was a sin to drop even a grain on the floor, just as at home we thought it a sin to drop a crumb of bread. Nor should any rice be left in the bowl. It must be eaten to the last grain. Then I began to understand and appreciate the place rice has in the East.

Rice has many names in Japan; in the field it is *ine;* black rice is *gemmai;* white, *hakumai;* boiled rice is *kome*, more often *gohan*. It is eaten morning, noon, and night. Only the poorest who cannot buy it do not eat it. It is relished equally in a hut or a palace. It is used to cure illness, and to feed nursing infants. It is the staff of life. Nothing else grown in Japan is a staple food.

We were amazed by Japanese vegetables, such as were unknown to us as food. We saw in a garden regular rows of burdock, that weed so rank around neglected houses in Russia. We cooked it with sugar and ate it. Then we were startled by the long radish, like ours in taste, juicy and sweet, but so huge it sometimes grows to a man's height. At the foot of volcanic mountains, where there is lava in the soil, it grows so immense that sometimes a packhorse could carry only two. It is eaten raw or grated, cured, or salted, with rice, fish, and when spiced, with soy sauce. In the stores one saw salt radishes, two feet or more in length, thick as a man's fist, baked in dough. One could buy it in slices, one, two, or three sen's worth.

Outwardly, peasant life was beautiful, with its houses, gardens, fields. Sometimes one saw wonderful flowers in the fields, or an arbor covered with wisteria, a tiny pond with fat carp and white or pink water lilies.

Peasant social life had much that was charming. As in Russia before the Revolution, communities of peasants lived one for all and all for one. Weddings, funerals, family celebrations of all sorts concerned the whole community. There were no beggars in the villages: the peasants would not allow anyone to beg.

They kept their holidays, their traditions, their customs as sacred. These beautified peasant life and contributed to the charm felt constantly throughout the country.

CHAPTER TWELVE

Beauty Undisplayed

I could not imagine Yokoy-San as part of the paper factory where he was employed. Work benches, offices, printed stationery—these things did not seem to belong to him. I had never met anyone who seemed so Japanese, and who, though contaminated by Western civilization, yet preserved all of Japanese culture, together with a love for the antiquity of his country. No one had helped me so much to understand the special beauty of Japan that remains hidden from most Westerners. I know that what we discerned more or less superficially is far from being true understanding. Yokoy raised a corner of the curtain, however, so that we could perceive the immense, rich world behind it, a world we shall never know in its full reality, but at least we knew it existed. Thanks to him, our enthusiasm was not limited to the pretty lacquer articles or the flowery kimonos. This was our good luck, for not even all Japanese have access to the painting, the music, the tea ceremony, the Noh dances—all the treasures of antiquity.

At first glance Yokoy's place looked modest, even rather drab. I did not understand why he was so solemn as he led us into a little house when alongside it he possessed a much newer, larger, more magnificent one. I said nothing, however, and afterwards was glad of it. Had I shown such lack of understanding, it would have been like praising furniture copies without noticing genuine Louis XVI pieces in the same room.

Okakuro Kakuzo has written of the aristocracy of Ashigawa:

> They like to live in small cottages, modest as peasant dwellings, but built on lines, with proportions, worked out by such geniuses as Shojo or Soami [fifteenth-century architects]. The posts of such houses were carved of precious fragrant woods from distant Indian islands; the bronze hearths, with drawings by Sheshu [a fifteenth-century artist], were perfection. They used to say, the beauty and worth of a thing is more often what is concealed than what appears.

This was a novel idea to us, but gradually we perceived that the hidden beauty is greater than what is seen.

The Japanese language has a difficult word, *shibui*. Try as I might, I could not penetrate the full meaning of this word. It had a degree of fineness that resisted comprehension. If a dress is ordinary looking, it cannot be shibui, nor can a tasteless flower arrangement. Simple enough. I thought I had begun to understand until one day, a Japanese said, "How can I explain? Well, imagine evening, sunset, a lake, motionless. All at once the stillness is broken by a splash; a frog has jumped into the lake. Circles spread ever wider on the glass surface. That is shibui."

In his book on Japan, G. B. Sansom has characterized shibui: "The Ashigawa shoguns, we have seen, developed a form of luxury so far the opposite of the rich and cloying that it is termed by the Japanese *shibui*, or 'astringent,' an idea which can perhaps best be understood by comparing a sweet fruit with one of slightly acid flavor."*

Sometimes it occurred to me that shibui is nothing other than concealed beauty, the beauty that is not displayed.

A Japanese lady gave me as a present a little black lacquer box. Inside I saw amazingly fine gold tracery on the inner cover. The inner lining of a Japanese costume, the *haori*, is usually handsomer than the outer surface. The samurai would never carry their precious swords in full view but kept them sheathed. Yokoy's little house, therefore, was unquestionably shibui.

It was of unplaned wood darkened with age. "I brought it over from one of the northern islands. It is a simple peasant house, but it is seven hundred years old."

In each room the furnishings were different. In one there was capriciously bent bamboo. In another, mahogany and camphor wood. In a third, the *kakemono** was set off by a frame of some exceedingly picturesque wood with the bark still on it. There was no symmetry anywhere, but complete harmony everywhere. In the first and largest room, Yokoy showed us some court records placed on the wall. They represented litigation with a neighbor over an ox. It had taken place seven hundred years ago. The rooms were almost empty, but whatever they did contain was an antique. Some things were over a thousand years old.

The general harmony was broken only by a portrait of my father. It was drawn in black ink on a kakemono and was hung on the wall that day in honor of my visit. "See," said Yokoy, "he is looking at us as if he were alive."

*Japan: A Short Cultural History.
**Scroll of paper or silk with a picture or inscription.

In the smallest of the rooms Yokoy treated us to tea. Not the tea ceremony of Japan, for we all sat on the floor any way, stretching our legs out or bending them under Turkish fashion, as Europeans usually sit when visiting a Japanese home. But we were having the same kind of thick, strong, green tea always served at tea ceremonies. It made one's head swim.

Yokoy pushed the windows apart. "Do you see those bamboos, those mountain plants and grasses? I brought them from distant mountains where men rarely penetrate. Every Saturday I come here to Odewara from Tokyo. If it rains, I sit here quite alone. I look at these mountain plants, the rain rustles the leaves of the bamboo, the wind sings. In my thoughts I am far, far away. I think for hours, and sometimes I write a *tanka*.* This is 'the room of the night rain.' Sometimes, though, I sit in another room."

That room was slightly larger and faced the ocean.

"Do you hear how the sea is heaving? Do you hear the whispering among the rocks? This music, the rhythm of the surf, goes on for hours. What I love is when the monotony of these sounds is suddenly broken by the booming of the gong from the Buddhist temple."

Yokoy's face was always still, but wise. He seldom smiled and never laughed. "Not long ago," he continued, "I wrote a poem." Closing his eyes and swaying slightly, he chanted in a voice that seemed to come deep from within.

"What is it?"

"A poem about your father, 'The Old Man.' Hard to translate, it has a play on words. It speaks of the grass called *okina gusa—okina* also means old."

He did translate it, and it ran something like this:

> What a cold cold evening tonight!
> It must be the same at Yasnaya Polyana—is it, I wonder?
>
> On this late autumn evening
> Does the tomb of the Great Old Man
> Stand serenely in the drizzling rain?

* Poems of thirty-one syllables.

The leaves of *okina gusa* we picked
Recall the days of other times,
And we talk on about Okina, the Great Old Man,
Until late into the night.

Alas, the *okina gusa* leaves have long since withered,
But the seeds sown by the Great Old Man
Fell on the soil of the Land of the Rising Sun.
May they grow, may their leaves thrive, for ever and ever.

Look! The *okina gusa* lives again!
It has taken deep root in the Land of the Rising Sun.
Come forth, you leaves, come forth, you buds!
I pray that you soon shall come into blossom.

Yokoy also had a small garden, with ancient lantern posts of gray stone. Covered with velvety green moss, they looked like huge mushrooms. There was a little pond, shaped irregularly, where waterlily pads floated. There were rock piles, as if accidentally fallen. Orange trees and tangerine trees planted by Yokoy's forefathers were heavy with fruit. At the far end was a gate of plain bamboo and tree bark. It was all so delectable I did not want to leave.

"Just a little garden," murmured Yokoy modestly, "some day I shall show you a genuine Japanese garden."

Once he took us to the curative hot spring of Atami, to spend the night. It was only a few miles from his home. Atami was a marvelous place on the seashore, though it had many times suffered from earthquakes. We stayed in a large, uninhabited European house with five stories, at the edge of a steep cliff. In its luxury, it reminded me of villas on the Riviera. We were shown into a spacious room with a roofed verandah, excellent beds, handsome furniture. A Japanese woman, the housekeeper, showed us to a lower story to which hot water from the springs was piped, where bathing tanks had been installed.

It had been a very long time indeed since I had enjoyed this sort of pleasure. I was overcome by the sensation of bliss. Hot baths. A delicious supper. A splendid kimono to rest in. My friends and I sat on the verandah, gazing at the plumes of steam rising from the springs scattered throughout the village, at the ocean glittering beyond the pines. "Who is the owner of this house?" we asked Yokoy.

From his laconic replies we understood that it belonged to a rich and powerful man named Fujiwara, and had been built for his guests. He did not live in it, because such European luxury was not to his liking. Nearby he had an ancient Japanese house, which he sometimes visited, sleeping on the floor and eating his rice with chopsticks.

Our endless queries must have been annoying. All three of us constantly wanted to know something, and it was a trouble for Yokoy to reply in English. Appreciating this, I refrained from asking whether our unseen host was descended from those Fujiwaras who in the eleventh and twelfth centuries kept Japan in turmoil.

After breakfast the next morning we went to see the Japanese garden. It had endless winding paths, bordered with the rarest tropical plants and exquisite flowers. Every possible thing had been considered. It was entrancing. We paused on a little humped bridge over a rapid brook. Yokoy was taking pictures. "There's a turtle," exclaimed Olga, pointing.

"Oh, so you have noticed it!" Yokoy was visibly pleased. "It is a very ancient turtle—a thousand-year-old stone."

"But why is it placed under the bridge, where one can hardly see it?" I asked tactlessly, peering down. It was barely visible in the watery shadow. Between its flippers goldfish played.

"Oh, that is exactly why it is precious. Beauty must not leap to the eyes. You see, you noticed it, didn't you? So will others."

Yokoy then took us to the little house in which the tea ceremonies were held. It stood on a tiny islet, surrounded by a quiet ring of water. Fat gold carp lazily waved their gills, staring at us fearlessly with their round eyes, expecting tidbits. Yokoy indicated a huge hollowed stone nearby filled with water. "That is for washing your hands before the tea ceremony," he explained. "This stone was brought from a thousand miles away. For centuries water had dripped on it and formed the hollow."

We emerged on a broader path. Through a thatched gate we walked toward Fujiwara's ancient house. Yokoy again stopped to photograph. "This gate is extremely old and very Japanese. The one you saw at my place is nothing in comparison." It was indeed beautiful, dark with age, magnificently proportioned.

Then we arrived at Fujiwara's house, the one where he enjoyed living. Again very clean, quite empty rooms, simple and chaste. No doubt only a connoisseur's eye could fully appreciate the treasures we saw; but everyone could delight in them, just as the music of Beethoven or Mozart may delight persons who have never studied harmony. Everything we saw—the precious fragrant wood, the ancient dishes, the stones, the plants from distant places—each thing had its history. When a Japanese gazes at the hollow stone near the tea house, what he really contemplates is a waterfall at a far mountain and the stream that over countless years formed the hollow. He sees the temples and villages long since gone.

We returned to Tokyo by way of Odewara. On our way to the station we stopped near a large Buddhist temple. One approached by a high, wide staircase, strewn with the red and yellow leaves of the maples. At the foot a camellia bush bore rosy pink flowers. Higher, next to the temple, a leafless plum tree blossomed.

The temple itself was closed. Before the stairs a thick rope stretched. Yokoy pulled on it to invoke the deity. A low bell rang. I thought of Yokoy at night, sitting alone, listening to its velvety tones.

On the upper landing of the stairs was the statue of a youth with a bundle of firewood on his back. The knees of his trousers were patched. His long hair was pinned on top in the old fashion. "This is Ninomia," explained Yokoy, "he is a saint. He lived comparatively recently, and taught our people simplicity and thrift. A Japanese Tolstoy."

Shortly before we left for America, we again visited Yokoy at Odewara. We did not stay long, only for dinner with him, a farewell dinner, as he said. In the main room in a place of honor the kakemono contained a tanka taken from the famous Buddhist temple in Kamakura. It spoke of respect and devotion for parents.

Mine tsuzuki Hana yori Hana ni asobikeri
Matsuran Oya no Kokoro shirazuni.

An approximate English version would be:

My dear ones! I have been a bad child
Playing with flowers on the hillside,
Spending all this time with others,
Forgetful of my anxious parents awaiting me at home.

For Yokoy this poem was meaningful. "Let Tolstoy-San go away, far away," he said, "never mind, she will not forget her parents and her native land. The time will come when she will return to her country, just as the little girl in this tanka hastened back to her parents, for she understood that one's own home is one's greatest joy."

CHAPTER THIRTEEN

The Tea Ceremony

One day, Yokoy came to us with an interpreter. His bearing was as solemn as if he had come on business of very great importance. As a matter of fact, it was an important occasion for him, as he was an expert on the tea ceremony. He worshipped this ceremony. Probably it was he who had arranged for us to be invited by his friend Yui to attend one. The latter had just built a new country house in the suburbs of Tokyo, and the ceremony was the equivalent of a housewarming.

Yokoy delivered a regular lecture about it. He had brought some books so that we might acquaint ourselves beforehand with its meaning and importance.

On the appointed day there were six guests, Yokoy, Professor Yonekawa, a Russian married couple, Maria, and myself. We had put on our best clothes. The Japanese wore kimonos of black silk with their family coats of arms on the backs and sleeves. The Russian ladies wore dark silk dresses.

After a five-minute walk from the station, we came upon a small house half-hidden among trees. Taking off our footwear, we entered a bare room. We were already filled with a sense of the significance of the moment, and silently, fearing to offend by unwittingly taking some liberty, we crouched round the hibachi, which was filled with crackling coals. "Take the most comfortable position," Yokoy recommended, "we shall have to sit like this for quite a while."

A long time passed. The longer we waited, the greater the solemnity. Voices were hushed. Faces grew more and more concentrated and meditative. As I was the guest of honor, I was especially afraid of forgetting to do any of the many small things Yokoy had instructed me to do, and which I had read about in the books he had given me. Yokoy was to be my model of behavior, and I was to repeat every gesture of his.

From outside there came a rustling sound. We stopped whispering. The sound approached. Oddly, it roused an acute expectation. "The host is sweeping the path on which he is to meet his guests," whispered Yokoy. With deliberation he rose, went to the door, and slid it open. All his movements were measured, graceful. By the entrance there hung a large gong in the shape of a fish. Yokoy struck it thrice, and it sounded a low, soft call. "I am informing our host that his guests are ready."

Another gong rang in response, one, two, three. The first one repeated its call, and the host entered. Yui was a short, sturdy, attractive man with a high, intelligent forehead and a prominent chin. He was wearing a dark silk kimono with a coat of arms in white, on his feet, special white tabi. Silently we greeted one another, bowing to the ground, and then, in silence, we left the house. The Japanese slid their feet easily into their geta, and the big toe with its separate loop held them firm. But the geta were never meant for European stockings: we kept dropping them off, hopping on one foot trying to catch up. All our movements, it seemed, were awkward and ridiculous, breaking the solemnity.

We proceeded down a path, our host ahead, then Yokoy, the rest of us following. At the entrance to the new house stood a large vessel of water, clear as dew, and a dipper. Each in turn washed face and hands before entering the tea room. The men changed their black tabi to white ones. We slipped off our geta and followed our host through a very small door. To get through it, we had to bend. This was to express humility. I almost stuck, hitting my head against the frame. I saw stars and, suppressing a cry, rubbed a swelling bump. When we had entered a tiny room, about seven by nine feet, the door was closed behind us. Now I was to watch every movement of Yokoy. He knelt reverently before the niche—the tokonoma—bowing to the floor. Then, crouching, he gazed long and intently at a certain small object, took it up and turned it over, with an expression of surprise, almost rapture. Then he returned it to the tokonoma and, still on his knees, moved closer and began reading aloud the Japanese characters on the kakemono.

Then my turn came. Clumsily, I fell on my knees and, like Yokoy, gazed at the little object—it was a tiny turtle. Conscientiously, I tried to appreciate the value and beauty of this minute thing, probably worth thousands of yen. I copied every gesture of Yokoy's—feeling grotesque at aping him without being able to feel what he felt. I did not do it well. Too quickly, I returned the turtle to its place, and of course I could not read the ideograms. It was a puzzle how to manage my big European body. It disrupted the harmony, I felt.

The others repeated the same gestures. I kept watching Yokoy. He slowly rose and moved to an opening in the floor filled with coals; over it stood a tea kettle. Yokoy gestured his pleasure with the wood of the frame. It was a piece from the ruins of a thousand-year-old temple, brought from far away. Again each took his turn to examine and admire.

The tea ceremony had not yet begun, but already my legs and feet were aching. I could not imagine how I could endure more hours of sitting. The host came and went. He blew on the coals,

warmed the water, always with exaggeratedly slow, smooth gestures. Everything had been ritualized. If I had trained for de-
cades, I could not have achieved his grace. I had not even participated properly so far.

The tea was terribly strong, and the heat from the hibachi was
already giving me one of those blinding headaches. Through the
second half of the ceremony I sat in a daze. I dimly remember
Yui sitting before the tea pot, hands folded, as if pondering. I
remember his putting the tea into the pot, then lapsing into meditation after stirring the green powder with a brush.

Indistinctly, I was aware that there was something classically
beautiful in his posture on the tatami before the ancient pot. I
remember the puckering taste of the thick liquid. With elaborate
slowness, punctuated by pauses of stillness, Yui poured it into a
dark earthenware bowl of irregular shape and thus, holding it in
both hands with the tips of his fingers, bowing to the floor, he
served each guest.

In the same manner, they received the bowl with the tips of
their fingers and thanked him, bowing low. Yokoy drank each
draught with relish. Etiquette prescribed three and a half swallows. Holding the bowl, he admired all its sides, then wiped the
place his lips had touched, and turning another side, handed it to
me. I repeated each of his gestures. It was only a mechanical
performance, however. I was almost beyond all understanding,
and could hardly force myself to keep up. My legs were like
wooden blocks, unfeeling, my head swam.

The day before I had read in a book Yokoy had brought, "The
first cup moistens the lips and throat. The second breaks solitude.
The third aids the search for one's inner self, so that one might
find the meaning of five thousand of the most complicated characters; the fourth elicits a light perspiration; the fifth cleanses one;
the sixth summons me to meditation of the eternal; the seventh—
but alas, I cannot take in any more, I only feel the breath of cool
wind in my sleeves. . . ."

All this is undoubtedly true to those Japanese who, like Yokoy
and Yui, adore antiquity. Their sixth cup of tea plunges them into
a meditation worthy of the eternal. Visions of ineffable beauty

appear as they crouch, slowly sipping draught after draught of the narcotic tea. To me, however, the tea ceremony was an ordeal exacting all one's will to endure to the end, not to faint, not to groan—or simply not to unbend stiffened limbs and run out and away, as straight as the eyes can see, as a Russian proverb has it.

At last the end did arrive. We rose and went to another room. Fresh air drifted from the garden. Yui's wife came in. The mystical was left behind, we returned to actuality. But I could not regain my senses at once. I went home, to bed. There I remained for twenty-four hours with a cold poultice on my head.

Yet why, when I recall the tea ceremony, does a strange emotion arise in me? It is like the emotion awakened by a painting, a description of a place I once visited, where I experienced much that was beautiful.

CHAPTER FOURTEEN

Tokutomi-San

My father wrote as follows in 1906 to a well-known writer, Konjiro Tokutomi.

I should be very grateful to you if you would explain your religious views to me. . . . By religious views, I understand the answer to the basic and very important question for man: what is the significance of the life he must live? . . .

I thank you cordially for your letter, for the books, and for your sympathy. Give my greetings to your wife, and ask her to write to me, if this is not asking too much, a few words about her own religious beliefs. What does she live for, and what to her is the highest law in life?—the law to which all human laws and desires are to be sacrificed?

Your friend,
Leo Tolstoy

Some time later Tokutomi himself came to Yasnaya Polyana. His visit gave my father considerable emotion, as he was at that time interested in Oriental religions and had come to the conclusion that the essence of all religions is one and the same for all peoples, and that only external forms and the interpreters of these forms, such as Christ, Buddha, Mohammed, and Confucius, are different.

Tokutomi had long since died. When I visited Japan, however, his wife, whom my father had asked to tell him "what she lived for," still lived in her house near Tokyo and devoted herself to the publication of her husband's works. When she learned I was in Tokyo, she wrote that she would like to see me.

Hori-San, her secretary, called for us in a car. Though Japanese, he looked rather Spanish because of his large dark eyes and long nose. We drove for about an hour, the last ten miles or so between beautiful fruit orchards, bamboo groves, rice, and radish fields. Hori, speaking English, pointed to the mountains. "There is Fujiyama."

Though the day was clear and frosty, the mountains were shrouded in haze, and Fujiyama could not be seen. The car wound right and left on the narrow roads. Finally it stopped, and reversed up to a house. Several women ran out to meet us. The smallest, the oldest, and the most modestly dressed in a dark kimono, took my hands and pressed them to her bosom. Her eyes were warm with kindliness. "Thank you," she said in English, "thank you for coming."

Taking off our shoes, we entered, to find ourselves in a European room with tables, chairs, doilies, and photographs. All those things one usually never sees in a Japanese house. The kakemono hung in the most prominent place—a legend executed in beautiful chirography. "That is my husband's favorite saying: 'Always strive ahead,' " said Tokutomi-San as she noticed my interest.

It was both difficult and easy to converse with her. Difficult, because she had only a slight command of English; easy because I felt her close to me in spirit, as if I had known her for years, and also because she had traveled a great deal with her husband

and therefore was acquainted with Europeans and European customs.

We walked out into the garden. Throughout there was an endless variety of maples, some with fire-red leaves, others yellow, or brown, purplish, all shapes of leaves, pointed and rounded, large and small. At the far end of the garden the green-gray branches of pines spread under flattened tops over the verandah, where wisteria wound its old thick trunks, like boa constrictors.

We wanted to tell Tokutomi-San that we liked the garden, so as to open the conversation, but she could not understand us. Yet I wanted to tell her a great many things about my father, that I remembered and esteemed her husband, and I wanted to tell her about Russia. She, too, however, wanted to talk. She tried to understand me, she listened earnestly, her hollow cheeks grew flushed, but the more agitated she became, the less she grasped. After long moments of struggle to think, she managed, "To translate what I wish to tell you is not possible, but I shall try." She began to speak in Japanese.

"She wants to tell you many—many things," Hori-San interpreted, "she wants her heart to speak to yours." Tokutomi-San nodded, but it obviously went against the grain to have to speak through an interpreter. Again she pondered, whispering to herself. At last she spoke.

"My husband and I loved your father as though he had been our own." She laughed soundlessly, an inner laugh, which to the Japanese expresses joy yet hides emotion. With rapid little steps she reentered the house, then returned with a letter her husband had written to my mother. He had never sent it, because it was during the Revolution, and he feared it might go astray. He wrote of his desire to come to Yasnaya Polyana and "bow before the grave of Tolstoy, uniting his heart to all those hearts close to him." He wrote, too, of his grief for the Great War, and then the civil war, and hoped that our country was moving toward better times.

The hours until dinner flew by. Tokutomi's second secretary, a modest young Japanese girl with slightly affected manners and a little bow-shaped mouth, invited us into the dining room. We bowed our heads while Tokutomi read a Christian prayer in Japanese. Then she treated us to a dinner partly Japanese, partly Western. There was soup, accompanied by bowls of rice, also a big turkey, roasted, as in the West. Maria and I were startled, however, to see a huge fruit, the size of a human head. We took it for a melon, but when it was cut open, it turned out to resemble a giant orange. "It is a *zabon*," she explained, "it comes from Formosa."

After dinner she took us for a walk. On the way we met a group of girl students on an excursion with their teacher. The faces of young Japanese girls wear an amazingly clear, bright, and pure expression, and these were smiling, cheerful. When Tokutomi-San pointed to us and said I was Leo Tolstoy's daughter, they first registered surprise, and then laughter—so much so that I was embarrassed, though they laughed from pleasure. From somewhere a camera appeared, we were all photographed, and then we walked back.

Trying to choose the simplest English words, I told Tokutomi-San about my life in Russia, about Yasnaya Polyana, and the difficulties I had encountered in carrying on my work under the Soviets without betraying my conscience, until, in the end, I had to leave. She understood me, not so much by words as by feeling. She took my hand into her small cool hands, and when I spoke of sad things, she pressed it. She did not let go of it until we arrived back at the house. We entered the garden from a different gate. There she showed us a simple grave. It reminded me of my father's. There were many flowers. She must have brought them daily.

In the evening we left. As we said goodbye, Tokutomi-San seemed to want to kiss me, without knowing how. She merely pressed her cheek to mine.

As the car left the village behind, Hori said, "Look! Look! Fujiyama!" The entire cone of the majestic mountain was visible.

CHAPTER FIFTEEN

The Buddhist Temple

The Chinese sage Fu was once asked whether he was a Buddhist priest. He pointed to his Tao hat. He was then asked whether he professed Taoism. He then pointed to his Confucian footwear. And when he was asked whether he was a Confucian, he indicated his Buddhist scarf. "Christians, Buddhists, Shintoists—we are all children of one family," a Japanese Christian told me.

Japan has an endless number of sects or religions. Even a specialist might find it difficult to trace all the religions in Japan. I found that whichever belief a Japanese professes, he will do so in the Japanese manner, that is, the Shintoist. Shintoism is the flesh and blood of the Japanese people. One sentiment seemed to prevail in every Japanese: his love for his country and for his emperor.

We knew an old Christian priest, a man of profound faith. It might have seemed natural that he should have discarded all ancient Shintoist beliefs—but he had not. As a Japanese, his prejudices were so deeply rooted in him that he would never have thought of discarding them.

Once we brought him a little present of Russian fruit preserves. It was quite an event for him. He called in all his friends and relatives, since, according to Shintoist beliefs, to taste a new food means to prolong one's life span. This idea has survived since ancient times, when the tradition of sacramental tasting was still active. That included the first tasting of the sake made from the new crop of grain or rice. The emperor himself was invited to that ceremony.

"Are not Christianity and Shintoism the same thing?"Another Japanese once asked us this. He was a well-educated man of considerable culture and a converted Christian. "Doesn't Shintoism teach love of one's neighbor, as does Christianity?"

After a stay of some length in Japan, my original impression of the strength of religion in its culture persisted. I was constantly amazed at the number of temples throughout the country, large and small, rich and humble, in the mountains, the woods, the fields, in ancient parks, on teeming city squares, in remote corners, on the banks of lakes and rivers, on the ocean shore. No matter where you rode or walked, all roads led to a temple. They attracted us by their mystery, which we could not fathom, and by their dissimilarity to Christian churches. We searched them out in the most unexpected places, sometimes far from the beaten path. When found, we rejoiced as though it were something most unusual.

I remember one bicycle ride on a hot summer's day. We turned off the paved road and followed a village lane, past hamlets where black-haired children played in the sunshine and women were busily hanging out their winter kimonos to dry. We rode past carpenter shops exhaling resinous fragrance, past warehouses filled with rice, past vegetable gardens, fields and groves, and flooded plantations of lotus, their huge leaves and pale pink blossoms hiding their hearts from the fierce heat of the sun.

We came to a footpath and started uphill. The trail narrowed as it skirted a noisy brook. On the right was a steep mountain slope overgrown with pine trees. The front wheels of our bicycles struck rocks, we swayed and jumped off, but it was impossible to turn back. Irresistibly, we were drawn on, pushing our bicycles ahead of us. We had to find the source of that clear mountain stream. Under the baking sun, over fallen trees, we dragged on up the slope. Unexpectedly, the trail widened, and we came upon a level space. On two sides maple trees overhung the path so that the sun penetrated only here and there. The air smelled damp. The path turned. Cliffs on either side. On the right were statues of gods wearing red and blue children's caps. A red, curved gate came into sight. Behind it a little Shinto temple grew, it seemed, right out of the cliff. There the trail ended.

Complete silence reigned. Only the stream could be heard playing with pebbles out of sight. When, and from where, did anyone come here? We had not met a single person on our way. Yet someone came daily, for there were little bowls of fresh rice at the threshold of the temple.

Few persons visit these little rural temples, and tourists never see them. At Kyoto, at Nara, at Nikko, we saw the celebrated ancient Zen temples of Ameda, Nicheron, and other Buddhist sects. Each one has its own history. Every day processions came to visit them, to see, not to pray. We encountered an endless number of these revered temples, beautiful, mysterious. Some of them housed huge grotesque statues of Buddha, others, figures of the sun goddess Amaterasu, who looks no less formidable. Whenever you saw long lines of colored lanterns half a mile ahead, you knew you were nearing a temple. Some of these were surrounded by veritable forests of long paper strips with Japanese characters on them, hung about on the tree branches. These are *ofudo*, epitaphs or prayers brought by the faithful.

On the yearly holidays particular to a specific temple, a lively trade went on. There were booths with all sorts of curious displays or amusements, and there might also be a traveling circus. Such festivities occur once a year.

Sometimes as we rested in the shade of the park surrounding a Buddhist temple we would watch the worshippers. First, a man would remove his hat, then as he drew closer, he would clap his hands once to invoke the deity. At the entrance he would pull a cord that rang a bell. The man would bow, drop a coin in the box placed there for offerings, and go back to his normal business.

Prayer took on a simplified form, especially in certain sects. Some five hundred years ago a priest named Sin-ran founded a sect that gained many followers in Japan. He affirmed: "The entire depth of your faith may be expressed by merely uttering the name of Buddha. Repeat 'Nami Amida Butsu' with deep faith, and your sins will be pardoned." The priests of this sect have been especially influential in Kyoto. They are considered as nobility. The rank of a senior priest is inherited, son from father, and there have even been cases of priests marrying princesses.

One of the most interesting temples we saw was one at which the worshippers vowed to run a certain number of times round the temple, in the belief that otherwise their prayers would not be heard. Panting and wiping the sweat from their faces, they would run without stopping, women, men, old, young, pot-bellied, skinny. Those in European dress ran more easily, but others in their long kimonos were impeded by their skirts, while the geta caught on the pebbles. Each runner held a bunch of small sticks, and every time he passed a large urn he would drop one into it, thus keeping count of the laps he had done. Some vowed a hundred laps, others five hundred or a thousand. The runners stayed at a nearby hotel, and if they could not run the full number in one day, they stayed for as long as necessary, even weeks.

Besides such naïve rites as these, I also witnessed instances of profound faith among the Japanese and an earnest desire to perform feats of sacrifice for its sake. Just as a Japanese is capable of hara-kiri for the sake of his honor, so will he not hesitate to sacrifice his whole life once he is convinced of the creed he has adopted.

"My second son is a follower of your father," old Konishi told me in a voice of deep sorrow. "He lives alone high up in the mountains inaccessible by railway, a terribly remote place. His mother grieves heavily for him, she pities him."

"What is his occupation?"

"Basket weaving. His earnings are small, but even so he gives away nearly all. 'Whatever a man does for another will come back to him,' he declares. 'If you give away your last bit of rice, someone will offer you work. If you give away your last beans, someone will give you rice.' "

The old man sighed. "He lives in great poverty, eating only beans, rice, and vegetables—and that not every day." Konishi bowed his head. The mother was not alone in her grief. "I greatly esteem your father," he added, as if in apology. "But I cannot understand why the boy had to sacrifice his whole life for love of him."

CHAPTER SIXTEEN

The Sect of the Ittoen

I had not known about the sect of the Ittoen, and so I was surprised one day when three guests knocked at my door. One was dressed in good European clothes; he wore dark glasses and stepped cautiously, testing the ground with his feet. A youth in student uniform supported him by the arm. I recognized him as a blind professor I had met at the Bowles's house in Tokyo. The third was dressed like a workingman in a russet blouse, sleeves out at elbows, a faded round hat, and trousers torn at the knees. Obviously, he was indifferent to his torn clothes. His manner was serene, very dignified and assured. He proved to be a member of a religious society called the Ittoen, and had come to invite me in the name of his society to lecture in Kyoto.

I heated tea and spread on the table all the food we had in the house. The three men seemed hungry, for they ate with relish, but they refused cold meat. This did not surprise me, for many Japanese are vegetarians, possibly because of a Buddhist influence. "We feel that all living creatures are our kin," they would say. I was amazed, however, when the man with torn trousers informed me that their sect had been founded in memory of my father. "We live by his ideas, we profess his teachings, and try to live as he taught. We should like to learn as much as we can about him, especially what is not in the books."

I fully expected that the lecture for this humble society would draw a small group in a small hall. The Ittoen engaged Kuroda as interpreter. When we neared a large building and our car cautiously made its way through a mass of persons, I was astonished. The hall accommodated three thousand people and was overcrowded. Student girls and boys sat on the floor in rows, stood in the aisles, on the platform. The members of the society who were in charge were in shabby torn clothes, but their faces were joyful as they scurried about helping to seat the audience. My acquaintance with the torn trousers rushed up to me. "Do you need anything?"

"Could I go somewhere to change my dress?"

To my alarm, he dragged me through the crowd to the other end of the hall, crying, "Obenjo doko desuka?" (Where is the toilet?) People craned their heads, laughing.

In half an hour the lecture was to begin, and so the Ittoen chairman, a tall, handsome old man, invited Kuroda and me to tea. He told of my father's influence on him. "When I read *A Confession* and *My Religion*, I understood I could not go on living as before. I resolved to try to live as he taught, a simple life of work. Since you are coming to us, do not say, 'I have come,' but rather 'I have returned'."

More than ever Kuroda and I wanted to speak effectively that evening. We were both carried away. The lecture lasted two and a half hours. It was already very late when, afterwards, Olga, Maria, the blind professor, Kuroda, and I were taken to the house of the Ittoen society.

It was a small house. Behind it, scarcely visible in the darkness, loomed a cone-shaped mountain. Somewhere close by a stream gurgled. We entered a room that reminded me somewhat of a Russian peasant *izba*.* In the middle was a table with benches. The room was bare, almost impoverished. We were offered real tea, bread, and crackers. Clearly, these things were not the daily fare of our hosts; rather they were luxuries to honor European guests.

Now we learned that the Ittoen society had been founded twenty-five years before, and that the title, Ittoen, means "one

*A cottage.

lantern." This signifies, Kuroda explained, "sacrifice at least one old paper lantern for the sake of your faith. Thus you will enlighten your life."

At that time the society had about a thousand members, and about seven acres of land, where some hundred and fifty persons lived. Theirs was a very austere life. They neither drank nor smoked. Not only were they vegetarians, but they ate only "black" rice, unhulled. "What are the rights of your society?" asked Kuroda.

"We have no rights or privileges," the chairman replied with reserve, "we have only duties."

I wanted to know whether they called themselves Christians.

"We call ourselves neither Christians nor Buddhists nor Taoists. We take from all religions whatever is closest to us in spirit, whatever has meaning, whatever helps us live."

"That is like my father," I commented. I told them that in his collected works, in his reader, *Stories for Children*, and in *The Way to Live*, he had tried to assimilate and express the essence of all the great teachings of the world.

"This is why we feel your father to be so close to us."

Kuroda asked, "How, though, do you earn your living? How can a hundred and fifty persons live off seven acres of land?"

The chairman smiled. "We often read the story, "Ivan the Fool." We too rub leaves, and gold appears. But we need no gold, we are always fed, we are always content, we have everything. This land was given to us, this house and these shops were built for us."

"Do you have to work for others?"

"Yes, we do, but we take no pay from those who do not understand us, only from those who do and sympathize with us."

"Very well, tomorrow I need a workman."

"We shall send you one."

"Would you send such a workman to anyone?"

"Yes, if we are asked. Usually, we clean toilets, because nobody else likes that work."

I stared at that solemn dignified man. Impossible to imagine his doing anything of the kind. Japanese toilets were not like those in the West, where sewerage systems exist. As a rule a man would come around once a month on an ox cart or a horse-drawn wagon, with about twenty clean barrels with hermetically sealed lids. This man had a long-handled scoop with which he transferred the contents of the toilet receptacle into a barrel. He was paid thirty sen, against a receipt. His hands, his clothing, were always clean, he was very neat, and no one would ever guess his occupation. Certainly it was a most disagreeable job. We used to run out of the house whenever he came. I marveled how anyone would do such work for only thirty sen—fifteen American cents.

Nonetheless, our old friend Konishi seemed to think the sum was outrageous. "People are spoiled today," he would say, "now they want thirty sen to clean out the toilets. In the old days one never paid anything. People only wanted to cart the stuff away for fertilizer."

We spent the night at the Ittoen house, sleeping on clean *futons** on the floor. Next morning when I awoke, the sun was already high. We were shown into a yard, where we could wash up with icy mountain water. The chairman wanted to hurry breakfast so as to be on time for morning prayer.

The temple looked like a large but simple Japanese house. Some hundred persons were kneeling in prayer. One standing in front beat on a gong. The voices of the congregation hummed like bees, chanting a Buddhist prayer. Then the chairman delivered a sermon. I heard the name "Tolstoy" repeatedly. After this, I spoke—greatly hampered by having to express myself through an interpreter, for these people were hanging on every word about my father, whose teachings had so influenced them. To communicate through a third person makes it almost impossible to create a genuine bond between audience and speaker.

We went out of the temple with the men, who returned to their work. The whole place was alive. There was activity everywhere. The chairman pointed to a group working the ground with picks. "They have come to us to learn how to live in poverty and

* Comforters, used as blankets or mattresses.

toil. I am the only one who knows their names. That man," indicating a slender handsome man in a coarse workman's kimono and a white head band, "was one of the richest men in Japan. He gave away everything he owned and came to us. That other man, with the shovel, is a graduate of two university departments."

On our way back we dropped in at a beautiful Japanese house. The Ittoen chairman led us to an upper story, clean and empty, flooded with sunlight, as if translucent. The sole decoration was a single red poppy in an earthen jar. The chairman slid apart a little door. We faced something like an altar. It held a portrait of my father. Above it, a circle.

"This is our emblem," explained the chairman. "It signifies all—that is, infinity—or zero. This room is for anyone who desires to concentrate on his inner being, the light that comes from God, and to love kindness."

We descended to the lower story. From the anteroom a low door led to a room like a coffin, empty, with only straw mats on the plank floor. One had to crawl in, one could neither stand nor sit, only squat Japanese style. Kuroda explained. "This is the chairman's room, where he receives visitors."

Outside, sunburned children and their mothers were passing. Beyond soared the mountains, covered with a dark pine forest. Below, the stream gurgled. For a moment, I wished to stay here. We sat down on a little bench on a bridge over a canal. Barges loaded with rice floated noiselessly by. Hundreds of miles long, this canal connected Kyoto with the large Lake Biwa.

Photographers broke the spell. Where had they come from?

Now it was time for us to return home to Ahsia. We asked our host to send us back by barge. Two members of the society, a young man and young woman, came with us. We sat down on a huge bale of rice that creaked softly. On the prow a man steered with a single oar, and we floated slowly downstream past green banks, blossoming gardens, villages and, beyond, the lofty peaks. We had already traveled for scores of miles when suddenly a steep cliff curved over us, and we were in darkness. The bargeman lighted a lantern. Its yellow flickers reflected on the moist, slippery vault overhead that dripped water on us. Other barges were being drawn upstream in the opposite direction by men hauling on a rope along the wall. Greetings were exchanged, voices echoed above the dark water.

For a few moments we emerged into blinding sunlight, then, almost at once, another overarching cliff. For a little while we floated through the darkness, then out again—and a harbor lay before us. This was Kyoto.

"We would like to show you a little house we built for travelers," offered the young man of the Ittoen. "Not far from here."

"For travelers? What travelers?"

"All those in need of shelter. Many poor persons travel these roadways without any place to lay their heads. Our cottage is not luxurious, but the wanderer will find all he needs."

We slid past steep banks overgrown with azaleas, white, orange, pink, and on landing, we climbed up a steep road. Crossing a wooden bridge over a brook, we faced a mountain gorge, where a hut stood among old shade trees. Taking off our shoes, we stepped inside. The ends of burned-out logs lay in the fireplace. On the floor stood a little kettle, a pan, and a bowl of salt. On the shelf were a few dishes. "Someone has spent the night here," observed the young man. He went out into the courtyard, chopped a few faggots and put them in the stove. The cottage grew warm. He brought in a pail of water, filled the kettle, put in some rice.

"How often does anyone stay here?"

"Nearly every night."

"And could we stay here overnight if we come to Kyoto?"

"Of course, we'd be delighted. Water, wood, and rice will always be here ready for you."

CHAPTER SEVENTEEN

Dorobo-San

We had found a seamstress, who called for our work and took it home. She asked an impossibly low price, but, except for kimonos, her work was poor. When she had to deal with plain percale dresses, she blundered along for better or worse; anything that required thought, anything unfamiliar, threw her into such confusion, such embarrassment, that she did not know what to do. She was very young and rather pretty. Her plump figure was nicely narrowed by the dark full kimono and the obi.

We needed to have a great deal of sewing done. The rags we had brought from Soviet Russia were beyond repair. We had neither dresses nor underwear nor bed sheets. We needed nightgowns above all, for the weather was growing cold, but also blanket cases, the envelopes buttoned on the outside. But our seamstress had never in her life seen either blanket cases or nightgowns. Our request perplexed her extremely. Again and again, she shook her head. With her plump little hands, she daintily lifted up our material, unfolded it, refolded it, measured it, pondered, fingered the material, stretching out the sleeves of our model nightgown. Then she folded everything together, carefully, tied the whole into a scarf, laid the bundle down on a corner tatami, and bowed herself out, saying, "Very sorry."

That evening she returned with her husband, a clerk in a dry-goods store. He unlaced his Western shoes, she slipped off her geta, placing them both side by side in the anteroom. Blowing and inhaling noisily in token of modesty and respect, they entered our apartment. The husband's face showed resolve. Hitching up his European trousers, he knelt, unfolded our blanket case, and began to take its measurements with his own yardstick.

He measured every side separately, every corner, every space between the buttonholes. On a slip of paper he took notes that looked to me like stenographic symbols. Several times he sat up, stroked his forehead, then heroically resumed. "S-s-s-sh-ah," he breathed, sounding like a plugged water pipe. He measured the blanket once, twice, a third time, crossed out some of his scrawls, rewrote something. At last, as if exhausted, he rose. I brought out the nightgown. His face showed despair. He took it from my hands, clearly intending to hand it back at once, felt it, pulled the sleeves, gazed through it against the light, and said resolutely, "Very sorry," returning it to me.

When a Japanese says, "Very sorry," that means the case is hopeless.

Desperate as we were, we insisted that she do the work. The house we occupied was too cold to sleep Japanese fashion in kimonos. Nothing ready-made could be found to fit us. All such clothes were far too small. Once more we began negotiating. No one understood anyone else. The couple again took measurements. After two hours of to-and-fro-ing, they left, bowing and mumbling something incomprehensible.

It seemed they had agreed to try, but they ruined the work. The blanket cases were too short, and not a single button fitted the buttonholes. The nightgowns were too tight, the sleeves too short, the necks too décolleté. A width of material had to be inserted. The seamstress treated this problem kimono-fashion, adding several folded thicknesses of material, so that the yokes of our nightgowns resembled the collars of draft horses. "Sorry," she kept saying, "very sorry."

Nevertheless, we went on giving her work. One day she came in, hardly recognizable. What had happened to her plump charm? Her stubby figure was encased in a blue, abbreviated Western suit. Her creased little neck was wrapped in scarlet gauze, on her head sat a purple hat shaped like an inverted flower pot and adorned with a bright pink flower.

What happens to the natural good taste of the Japanese as soon as they begin to imitate the West is beyond understanding. Most puzzling is the fact that when Japanese women in Japanese clothes mix their colors—discordant to us—the effect is beautiful. Yet somehow I have scarcely ever met a Japanese woman who looked well dressed in European clothes.

"I hardly recognize you today," I murmured, "you are all dressed up." She smiled, but sadly. Her eyes were red and swollen. She blinked as though trying not to cry. "*Dorobo*," she managed, "bad man, robbed. . . ."

With great difficulty she succeeded in telling us her story in bad English. Her husband had gone away on business for a few days, and her mother had stayed with her. At night, a thief (dorobo) had sneaked into the house and taken all her own and her husband's clothes, watches, and jewels. Fortunately, there was only a little money in the house, but the women had been badly frightened, especially when the baby awoke and cried. The thief had said he would harm no one if they made no noise.

"But what would have happened if you had called for help?"

"Abunai, abunai, impossible," the girl protested, "very dangerous, he would have killed us, he had a big knife with a long thin blade! Oh, very abunai!"

Though the dorobo had not killed them, he did tie all their clothes into a large bundle, so heavy that he could hardly lift it. Seeing that the thief did not intend to leave a single garment, the girl had bowed to the ground pleading, "Please, please, Dorobo-San, be kind, leave me one dress, so I can go out of the house tomorrow morning!"

So the Dorobo-San had left her a single dress—the Western costume we saw. All her best kimonos, and those of her husband—all gone. Her story moved us very much.

The next time a Japanese friend called on us, we asked him about thieves. "Yes," he answered, "I am sorry to say, this does occur. But usually they don't kill anyone. Only one must keep quiet."

"Mmm." I had a vision of that long narrow blade.

"I know of cases when a thief came into a house at midnight or a little after; he took what he wanted, and then declared that he was going to wait until the first morning street car."

"And what did his victims do?"

"Nothing. They sat up with the thief. When it was time for him to go, he bowed, thanked them, and vanished—not without warning his hosts not to make any noise—very politely. Once, when a thief entered, he was hungry, and the housewife brought him rice, fish, salt radish—she fed him as she would have served a guest. Dorobo-San bowed to the floor in thanks. . . ."

"Didn't he steal anything?"

"Oh, yes, of course he did, he took all he wanted, then went. Fortunately, they are scarcer nowadays, the police have weeded nearly all of them out."

"How do they get in, do they break through the doors, or climb in through the windows?"

"Sometimes they climb the walls and the balcony, or they break the locks. Whatever is most convenient."

Our imagination was working. "What shall we do if a Dorobo-San comes here?" we wanted to know.

"He won't come, there's nothing he'd want to take from you. But if he comes, be polite to him, that's all. He won't hurt you."

From my recently acquired stock of Japanese words I began to compose a speech if we had a visit from a Dorobo-San.

"Gomen kudasai, Dorobo-San." (I beg your pardon, Mr. Thief.)

"Kane arimasen." (No money here.)

"Gokhan arimasu dozo." (There is dinner, if you please.)

Thank heaven, Dorobo-San never came.

CHAPTER EIGHTEEN

The Japanese Idea of Decency

Mother, mother, look!" exclaimed Maria. We were on a train journey. "That man is undressing!"

And so he was. The other passengers paid not the

slightest attention, as if his behavior was quite natural. He had been wearing a kimono, no doubt because that costume is comfortable for traveling. Now he was changing before arriving at the city. City employees in offices and stores are obliged to wear Western dress. With no haste, the man slipped out of his kimono, pulled on his trousers, buttoned his collar, and replaced his geta with European shoes.

Once when we were visiting our friend the professor, he suddenly remembered that there was a flower exhibition in Tokyo, and invited us to go. He called to his servant for his European clothes and went on talking with us while he changed.

In the European sense, the Japanese had absolutely no idea of decency. In hamlets remote from large cities, one could often see naked people in the summer. Nobody attached any significance to it. They had no nudist societies, they simply did not wear clothes. The Japanese summer is intolerably hot, and farm workers toiled hard in the fields. The women everywhere were naked to the waist. When we were bicycling, we often wandered into villages, and at first we were astounded, but after a while we no longer noticed.

When we stayed in Ahsia, the little fishing village on the ocean, we were awakened early every morning by the fishermen singing a little tune, always the same one, its notes emphatic. Sometimes we went to the shore to watch them. At first we would see two boats far apart, then gradually the triangle between them and us shrank until by the time they reached the shore they were rowing side by side, pulling a heavy net. Some wore a loin cloth, others not even that. All around us people were bathing or promenading, but no one paid any attention to those shining brown bodies tempered by sea water and the sun. The fish poured in a silver torrent into wooden vats. The housewives crowded round to buy five sen's worth of herring.

There were always lots of people on that beach. Sometimes old men, their kimonos kilted up, or women with babies bundled on their backs, came to fish for oysters and to gather mussels, or sea kale, which is dried for food. In the summer there were crowds of bathers. Boys dove from landings, played ball, swam far out from shore. On the beach were tents displaying sweets, toys, ices, and other edibles. The ladies' parasols flitted about like butterflies. As our house was near, separated only by a pine grove, we would go several times a day to swim and sun ourselves.

Perhaps out of deference to Westerners, a law had been passed several years earlier requiring all bathers to wear suits. Thereafter men and women came to the beach dressed, leisurely removed their clothes and, with the obedience to law characteristic of the nation, put on bathing suits. They had no conception that there was any indecency in a naked body.

When bathing indoors, the Japanese like the water so hot that a European cannot stand it. The first time I tried it, I thought I would be boiled alive. In fact, I looked like a cooked lobster. Repeatedly I asked for cold water, but the attendants looked so pained that I finally gave up. They had a distinct aversion to tepid water.

Every peasant cottage had its *ofuro*, its bath tub, or rather, a large tank, into which water was piped. The fire box was underneath, stoked with wood or coal. If the water got too hot, it could not be cooled except by adding cold water. There was a stopper at the bottom, and a round wooden platform to prevent your skin from touching the hot floor of the tank.

The Japanese bathed daily. The whole family used the same water. First came the head of the house, then the eldest son, followed by the other sons in order of seniority. Last came the wife, the daughters, and servants. In winter the bath was a means of keeping warm. If the rooms were chilly, the people crept into almost boiling water and stayed there, until their bodies steamed like a hard-driven horse. They scrubbed with towels, then wrung them out and wiped themselves off. The air in the room was so chilly and the towels so hot that evaporation was quick. I was astonished to discover that even small rural theatres were equipped with baths. In winter the audience were in very thick kimonos, whereas the actors were sometimes dressed very lightly. During the intermissions, therefore, they warmed themselves in the steaming baths.

The many hot springs provided one of the greatest pleasures of the Japanese. Our friend Ishida took us for the first time to a winter resort in the mountains. I must confess that, though we enjoyed the beauty of the scenery, the mountains, the lakes, the houses on the slopes, the picturesque narrow streets lined with curio shops, we could hardly endure the bitter cold of the un-heated hotel, with frost on the walls and window sills. The only way to get warm was to creep into the steaming water of the ofuro. We had to bathe several times a day. When we emerged, we put on heavy quilted kimonos. The warmth would last for two or three hours, then we would have to bathe again. At first we thought the contrast between hot and cold was too sharp, but we finally found it delightful to sit in a hot bath with the window wide open on a frosty, snow-clad countryside.

At curative watering places the customs were even more prim-itive than elsewhere. A Russian woman told us of her visit to some sulphur springs. She was quietly dozing in her bath when she was startled by a naked man about to enter the same tank. She made a great commotion, which caused only wonder among the Japanese.

We had no bath in our house in the Tokyo suburbs. When we returned from Ahsia, we therefore went to a public bathhouse nearby. We put on kimonos and geta, and thus clad walked down the street to the bath establishment, hurrying so as to be among the first to get in. At two every morning, the bathhouse was scrubbed and the water changed. The first time we were a little embarrassed. We did not know the customs, and our knowledge of Japanese was sketchy. In front of the door sat a heavy woman and there were various signs. We removed our geta and went in.

We knew enough Japanese to ask how much it cost. It was five sen. Our budget could stand that. We undressed and entered the bath chamber. Low marble benches stood along the walls. Every-thing was immaculate, and there were both hot and cold faucets. At the far end was the tank. We were just about to step in when an almost naked man came in. We waved to motion him away, but to our consternation he came toward us. We waved franti-cally, but still he approached, and then began speaking. Not until long afterward did we learn that to wave your hands away from you signals a person to come nearer, whereas waving your hands toward you warns him away.

At that time, however, we shouted, "Sayonara! Sayonara!"— meaning goodbye. It was the only word in our limited vocabulary that seemed appropriate. We went on shouting until finally he disappeared behind a partition. We began to wash, but were not finished soaping ourselves when the Japanese looked in, asking, we supposed, if he could help us. We shouted and waved again. At that moment, a Japanese woman with a high hairdress entered. The man descended the steps and spoke to her. She stretched out on the floor, and he began to massage her and wash her body and her hair. We had already slid down into the tank, waiting for him to leave.

After this first customer, another woman came, then a third. The man served them all. Each woman after her bath got out a hand mirror and began to make up, starting at the nape of the neck* and putting on layer after layer of powder on her steaming skin. The result made them all look like bisque dolls.

All this time we had been crouching in the tank. It was getting crowded with women and children. The little shaved heads and unwiped noses of the youngsters spluttered, they thrashed and knocked against us. The water was now too cold for the women, and they demanded more hot water. We could hardly stand it, yet we did not dream of getting out because the man was still working. In desperation, I finally fled to the dressing room, my friends following. It was all very disturbing to us, but in the interest of cleanliness we continued to visit the bath house.

* An erotic zone to the Japanese.

CHAPTER NINETEEN

The Samurai

The rainy season is the worst season in Japan. It begins in June and continues for a few weeks. It is called *nyubai*. The country is seized by stifling heat, such heat as people living outside the tropics can hardly imagine. A heavy, thick rain falls almost ceaselessly, but it does not refresh. It merely charges the already laden air with more moisture. To make the slightest motion causes one's body to break out all over in a sticky perspiration. Day and night, one's throat feels constricted. Impossible to take a full breath. There is no hope of respite. The nights are worse than the days. Around one's bed—or more exactly, the futon—hangs a net curtain. Screens for the sliding paper doors that serve as windows are out of the question. If you are not careful enough in tucking in the edge of the net at bedtime, gnats and mosquitoes eat you alive. To sleep at all is hard, but if you do doze off in the first part of the night, you only awake later, suddenly, wildly, sitting up in bed, trying to get more air into your lungs. Your nightgown, hair, and pillow are wringing wet. Useless to change, for in five minutes you will be drenched again. The sweat streams down face and neck, between your shoulder blades.

When the nyubai caught us, Olga, Maria, and I were staying in a small place near Kobe. They both suffered, but not so desperately as I did. At times I was in despair. I felt suffocated, like a fish out of water. My head ached constantly. I longed to run away, to break through that solid mass of humidity—but there was no place to go.

The nyubai was still prevailing when a young man came to see me with a letter of introduction from a Japanese friend of mine. The letter said that the young man was active in the cooperative movement. With others like himself, and with the support of the municipality, he wished to arrange a lecture about my father in the little town of Gifu. "I recommend him to you," wrote my friend, "he is a fine young man, a noble descendant of the samurai."

Timidly, the descendant of the samurai fumbled for his English words. He stated that the mayor of the town and the members of the cooperative invited us all to Gifu. They offered to reimburse us for our traveling expenses, our hotel, and in addition would pay a hundred yen for the lecture. Moreover, they hoped we would accept their invitation to observe the night fishing on the Nagara River—a spectacle for which their town is famous.

We thanked the young man and promised to come. However, a few days before the proposed date, I felt so ill that I telegraphed to Gifu that I was unable to manage the journey. Then the sun came out. What a blessing! The air was no longer steaming but clear, though hot. We saw people hanging out their kimonos and quilts in the sun, spreading out their damp rice, flour, sugar. Every single article of any sort was saturated. Shoe leather had begun to mold. I felt much better, and so sent a second telegram that we were coming.

The descendant of the samurai met us at the Gifu station. He wore a strange, distracted expression. He seemed hurried, upset. Incessantly, he smoothed his rumpled hair. The wide sleeve of his kimono revealed as it fell a very thin forearm with a sharp elbow and blue veins. I could not tell why, but I pitied him.

We were taken to a hotel and shown a room with a verandah overlooking the Nagara River. Foaming and whirling, the water was rushing headlong down its course. Through the crooked pine boughs we could see the long rowboats with their uptilted prows speeding downstream, while others, struggling madly with the fierce current, contrived to cross to the other shore, where steep wooded mountains beckoned. A little downstream from the hotel was a landing where large, roofed boats with colored paper lanterns swayed gently: floating tea houses.

Our young man returned with a fat bespectacled man in a greasy Western suit with a shiny waistcoat. He looked like an inferior sort of commercial traveler. "This is the interpreter," the young man told me, "he will translate your lecture."

"Yes, I know Tolstoy," said the interpreter, "he was a famous Russian count." Having thus impressed us with his erudition, the fat man glanced complacently at the young man and me, and laid his dimpled fist on his flank. Having asked me for the manuscript of my lecture, he then and there began translating it. His questions, his comments, made the blood rise to my head. His thick moist lips transmuted simple statements into naked ABC's. Things that had been left to be understood were turned into vulgarities as blatant as the man's white-dotted purple tie. How, I asked myself, could that tie, those flabby cheeks, this vulgarity, exist beside the mountains, the pines, the rushing river, and the descendant of the samurai?

I was to begin my lecture at three o'clock, but by three no one had come for me. Half-past three. Four. I began to worry. Something must be wrong. At half past four they arrived, put me into a taxi, and we drove off to the lecture hall. It was half empty. The audience looked strange, a motley crowd of shop boys advertising their firms on the backs of their kimonos, peddlers with their baskets, both men and women, and a group of very old people. Persons dropped in, walked out, with no regard for what I was saying, as if they had come for a short rest, then hurried away on their own business.

The interpreter waved and shouted, pounded on the table. Two or three times there was a burst of coarse laughter, though there had been nothing funny in what I had said. This laughter cut me to the quick. Never had I felt in so foolish a position. There was absolutely nothing in common, it seemed, between my words and the shouts of the purple necktie. At the end I made a final effort to rouse my audience. In vain. They sat with the same bored expression. I concluded. Neither the interpreter nor the audience seemed aware of it. I could not bear to remain on the platform another minute and left. The interpreter, failing to hear me speak, turned and noticed I had gone, so he also descended the steps. Once someone clapped irresolutely, but no one supported him. Stretching and yawning, people began to leave. The young samurai came up, twisting his locks, smiling a wry, pained smile.

What can it mean, we asked ourselves. Where are the leaders of the cooperative? The municipal authorities? What was this weird audience? We decided to go home at once, but all evening long we waited for our samurai. He had vanished. When we told our hotel manager that we wanted to leave, he shook his head firmly, giving us to understand that it was impossible. Next morning, the young man finally appeared. I demanded that he should send us home at once. "I can't," he returned, and two bright spots flared on his cheeks.

"But why not? If you have failed in the lecture enterprise, we will pay the hotel bill, but we cannot stay here. We must go!"

"I beg you, please, don't! Don't disgrace me! I must fulfill my promise— I cannot tell you everything, but please believe me! I am grieved, terribly grieved—compared with the loss of friends, anything is easy. I had trusted them, but if you leave now, that will be the last blow for me, a terrible blow—please, I implore you!"

We could understand nothing. But the samurai had the look of a man on the brink of despair. His cheeks glowed, they were sunken, there were dark circles under his eyes. "Forgive me—I must be ill. I haven't slept for several nights, I can't eat. . . ."

Again he vanished. We waited a whole day. Then another day. We felt abandoned. The hotel bill was mounting, and we had very little money with us. We had no idea how it all might end and began to worry in earnest. We were being served three meals a day, but each meal became more frugal. When we asked the hotel manager when he expected the young man to come, he only waved his hand.

Rain alternated with bright weather. When the sun was out, the heat was so intense we could hardly breathe. From morning to night we ambled along the banks of the Nagara. Already we were indifferent to its beauties. We had one desire only: to be released from our captivity.

We watched people, looking like porcupines in their straw rain-coats and straw hats broad as umbrellas, crossing the river in their long narrow boats with the uptilted prows. Peasants dressed like-wise mowed the thick grass along the banks, their scythes hardly larger than sickles. Tipsy groups passed the time with geishas in the tea houses along the shore. We had made the rounds of the town, we had visited all the temples, looked in all the stores. We no longer knew what to do with ourselves.

On the fourth day our young samurai reappeared. He seemed a little more cheerful, he smiled, ordered a good dinner, and dined with us. Maybe everything is all right, we thought, and it only seemed that there was some trouble. "Where have you been?" I asked.

"I'm sorry to have kept you waiting. A friend had fallen ill and summoned me in a hurry. I have ordered a boat for tonight. We are going to see the night fishing."

How strange these people are, I thought, we want to go home, we don't feel like being amused. "Can't we go home today?"

"Tomorrow I'll put you on the train."

He spent the whole day with us. After dinner we went boating. I say "boating," but in fact men dragged our boat upstream past steep banks with high thickets. The way back, however, took only a few minutes. At about ten at night, a procession led us from the hotel to the landing, paper lanterns lighting the way. Two servants carried a basket with apples, melons, fruit drinks, and pastries. We stepped onto a houseboat with glowing paper lanterns. Then several boatmen leaped into the water and started dragging the boat against the stream, panting noisily, the water foaming and beating against the boat. If for a second they had let go of us, we would have been borne off in the opposite direction. After an hour and a half of this progress, we reached a broad part of the river overgrown with weeds, where the current was not so swift. Our boat moored alongside other floating teahouses. One heard laughter, the tinkling of dishes, and merry, excited voices. A good deal of sake was being drunk. The high hairdress and the powdered faces of the women made us conclude they were geishas.

Our boatmen also warmed themselves with sake, exchanging cheerful shouts with other boatmen.

All these people, we noticed, were peering expectantly into the darkness upstream. Clearly, they were waiting for something. Suddenly, a small light leaped out of the black, then another, and yet a third, approaching at high speed. Great excitement. The boatmen jumped to their places. From a bend of the river a pillar of light swept down toward us, shooting sparks, then another, and another. Before we had collected our wits, our houseboat and its fellows leaped from their moorings like unchained beasts and were precipitated downstream.

There were three fishing boats, and we followed the first. On its prow there burned a bonfire of birch logs in an iron grill. Its light fell on a tall, slender man in a short straw skirt and a round cap, holding a clutch of reins controlling twelve cormorants swimming ahead of the boats, so swiftly that they seemed to be towing, controlled only by the man on the prow, looking like a mythical god in flight. At times a bird would dive after a fish, and one feared the boat would overturn, but the bird always surfaced, dove again, and reappeared.

Another man, less handsome and adroit than the one on the prow, stood on one side of the boat, governing several birds, four or six. Now and then a fisherman pulled a bird out of the water and squeezed its throat; the bird disgorged its prey, then was freed.

It was all so exciting that the watchers on the houseboats could hardly contain themselves, shrieking in rapture. Everything streamed in the same direction, the water resounded, the birds dived, the flames of the bonfires flickered—the only static figure was the man in straw garments on the prow, whose motions controlling his birds were barely perceptible.

It seemed as if we had been gone only a few minutes when suddenly the boat cut into a sandy bank and stopped. The cormorants ceremoniously took their perches on the boats. "Each bird knows its place," the samurai told us. "The best fisher takes first place, then the second best, and so on. If the third tried to take the second's place, there would be a fight. They mean to keep their right order."

When all the birds were settled, the men began harvesting the fish by pressing the birds' throats so they disgorged their catch. "They all wear neck bands just tight enough so that they cannot swallow the fish, except for the very small ones. The larger remain in their crops. Fish are expensive. The men's earnings come from this exhibition and from their sales of fish."

After a little our boat started back to the hotel. Each hour of this diversion had cost a lot of money. The next day the samurai saw us to the station, and we left Gifu.

"Whatever happened?" I queried my Japanese friend who had sent us the letter of recommendation about the samurai. "Why did you write me that the municipal authorities, the president of the cooperative association, and other notables had invited us, yet we saw only that young man? He seemed terribly embarrassed."

"Yes, I know all about it. A misunderstanding. The people at Gifu had received your first telegram, but not the second. One of the members of the cooperative had forgotten and left it in his pocket, so that the lecture had been canceled. When they finally discovered your second telegram, it was too late. It was impossible to get an audience together. Seeing that the lecture project had failed, the president of the cooperative and the others lost their courage and went into hiding. The young man resolved to try to overcome all obstacles by himself. He had to pay for the lecture hall even if there was no audience, so he dragged people in from the street—free of charge, of course. With immense trouble, he secured an interpreter, since the interpreter previously engaged lived in another town and could not come."

"But why didn't he simply cancel the lecture? Why didn't he telegraph me?"

"In his opinion, you were not to blame, and so he could not tell you. In order to pay your hotel bill, he had to go to his native city to see his father. The father had been wealthy, but had lost his fortune. The only things of value he had left were some ancient paintings. He sold one of these to pay the hotel. To make matters worse, the hotel keeper would not let both you and him go without payment, so he had to leave the three of you as security while he went to raise the money. He still owes you for the lecture."

"Oh, no, please tell him he is not to dream of it."

However, the samurai returned. Confused and flushed, he handed me an envelope tied with red and white cord, the sign of a gift. Inside, money, a hundred yen. I could not take it.

A week later he came again. Bowing to the ground, he laid down on the tatami a longish package again tied as a gift. It contained an ancient Chinese kakemono. It was impossible to refuse this gift. I accepted it. It is a drawing of a small house in the mountains. Whenever I look at it, I recall the rushing Nagara River, the pillar of fire, the rain of sparks, the harnessed cormorants, the man in the straw skirt, a figure from legend. And behind the gorgeous spectacle, the shy, perturbed face of a noble youth descended from the samurai.

CHAPTER TWENTY

The Professor's Family

Every morning the *shoji** slid open in the house across our street and a small creature emerged on the veranda. The boy looked like a spring flower in his vivid kimono with a little white apron, the back of his head shaved smooth. In a high voice he would shout, "Torutaya-Than, Torutaya-Than!" That was as near as he could come to "Tolstaya-San."

"Ohayoo, Kaju-Chan [Good-morning Kaju]," I'd reply.

* Sliding panels forming walls.

This was the home of a professor, a large semi-European house with a terrace and balconies, a front lawn, and masses of flowers.

A little later the nurse, the good-natured, laughing Sumi-Chan, came to see us, carrying our little friend on her back. Hard to say who had the greater—or more exactly the smaller—vocabulary, Kaju-Chan or we, but in either case the stock was sparse. We could scarcely converse at all, only smile at one another.

Kaju-Chan would determinedly get off his nurse's back and totter on his tiny bare feet across the tatami. He had learned to walk only a short while before. Since he and I wanted very much to talk to each other, this conversation was repeated daily: "Kore nani [what is this]?" he would ask, poking his little fingers at some object unfamiliar to him.

"Kor pan [It's bread]," I replied, happy to be able to do so.

"Kore neko [It's a cat]," declared Kaju with great seriousness, pointing to our Debu-Chan, the tomcat asleep on the floor. He liked to sleep on the tatami in the sun, sometimes turning up his black and white belly to feel the warmth coming in through the window, shading his muzzle with his paw. He had been given us by the professor's sister, and we were immensely fond of him. His Japanese name meant "fat mister." We used to talk to him in Russian, and he understood us very well. He often went out for a walk with us, but he was afraid of automobiles and street dogs, so he would follow us along fences and roofs, though never far behind.

One day an accident befell us, after which we were even fonder of him. He liked to lounge on the wooden lid of a well in the neighboring courtyard. We tried to break him of this habit, but nothing succeeded. On this day the neighbors forgot to replace the lid after drawing water. We heard muffled wails, a cat's wails, and at first could not find the source. Debu had fallen into the well. We tied a board to a rope and dropped it down, but he must have been there so long that he had weakened, for he could not get a good grip. I ran to the next street, where there were some workmen. I did not know the words to explain, and, out of breath, repeated, "Irasshai dozo, hayaku, irasshai! [Please come, quickly!]"

Two men came running. Maria tried to explain to them, almost in tears. One tore off his jacket, tied a log to a rope, and had his comrade lower him down the well. It was a deep one; the water must have been no less than thirty feet from the surface, and I now feared for the man. Meanwhile, Debu was undoubtedly much weaker, his cries were fainter, and sometimes ceased. At last we could hear the man shout something, and his friend began to pull him up. Ah! The cat was in his arms! Stiff and motionless, we were sure he was dead. His eyes were closed, his ears were flattened, his fur drenched, his long full tail now very thin.

We hardly knew how to thank the two Japanese. I gave them some money, and begged them to go at once and have some sake, for the one who had gone down the well was soaked, but they only looked shocked. "No, no," they protested. They said something else, too, but I understood it only in a general way, that they could not take money for saving the cat, because that was their duty. They had done it out of respect for Neko-San, Mister Cat.

We took turns warming Neko-San in our arms, we poured sake and medicine into his mouth, gave him warm milk. By some miracle, he survived.

When Kaju visited us, Debu-Chan could never lounge in the sun for very long. Smiling and wobbling on his shaky legs, Kaju would approach and pull his tail. Debu-Chan would leap into the air screeching and flee, with the boy running, tumbling, after him.

Kaju was incredibly thick round his middle. If his heavy kimono had been removed and European baby clothes substituted, he might have looked like a slender little boy, but the Japanese keep several yards of flannel wound around their children's stomachs winter and summer to ward off colds. As a result, he looked very clumsy, but this only enhanced his irresistible charm.

Suddenly, though, we lost the joy of his company, owing to my own foolishness. I often carried him in my arms. Once, unable to resist his loveliness, unexpectedly even to myself, I forgot all prudence and put a smacking kiss on the nape of his neck. Why had I done it? I caught myself at once, but too late. In a flash, I understood from Sumi-Chan's face what I had done. I would never have believed that an amiable Japanese girl could have worn such a stinging, hateful look. She reddened. All friendliness vanished. In its place, contempt and hatred. I felt like a criminal, as she seized Kaju in her arms and ran home across the street, mumbling something of which I grasped only one word, "Kitanai, kitanai [dirty, dirty]."

From that day on Kaju-Chan no longer called, "Torutaya-Than." He never came to our house. We had become kitanai. With my guilty conscience, I felt that even the attitude of the professor's wife, the gentle Oka-San, had changed. Her smile was not as friendly as before, and whenever she spoke to us her manner was reserved, cool.

The eldest son is the hope and pride of every Japanese family. The professor's eldest son had died, and his father told us how it happened. The boy had gone with some comrades to bathe in the sea, and had been seized with cramps. When his father received the first telegram, he thought nothing grave had occurred, but after the second telegram both parents hurried to their son, but found him in bad shape. They took him instantly to a Tokyo hospital, but it was too late. The boy died of peritonitis.

"I was in agony, for I blamed myself for my son's death." The professor smiled in a way. "If I had only gone after the first telegram, we might have saved him. But—" smiling again, "I did not think it serious, I was busy, too, so we did not go." Suddenly his voice broke. The fixed smile remained.

It was painful to see and to hear. I could not refrain from asking, "It hurts you to speak of this—why are you smiling?"

"Because we consider that we have no right to trouble others with our own grief, therefore, when we feel like weeping—we smile."

While his son was still alive, the professor had gone on a trip to Russia to improve his knowledge of the language. He spoke it very well, almost without an accent, with only a slightly exaggerated care in pronouncing. He knew not only the classics but also

Soviet writers, and we found a well-chosen library of Russian books at his house.

In Moscow he had made the acquaintance of the well-known writer, Boris Pilnyak.* At that time there was widespread hunger in the country. It was hard to find food, especially if one had children, since milk and fats were scarce. Pilnyak had a nephew living with him, an orphan of about seven, undernourished like everyone else. "Let me have your nephew," the professor said to Pilnyak. "He can talk Russian to my eldest son. I want my boy to study the language and become a teacher of Russian, like myself."

"Well, why not? Take him with you," responded Pilnyak. Though it was all hardly more than a joke, still there are times when even a joke takes on gravity and may even decide a man's fate. Thus the boy's fate was decided. The professor brought Anatoly—or Tolya—to Japan. There he at once became Toru-Chan. At first he pined and wept and could eat nothing but rice. Later he grew acclimatized. In school the Japanese children named him "Green Eyes." The Japanese chirography was very hard for him, but he quickly learned to speak and soon began to forget his Russian. The professor's eldest son and he spoke only Japanese to each other. When the son died, there seemed little sense in the Russian boy's staying on in the professor's family.

I was sorry for Tolya. His was not an easy position, though I never noticed that the family were in the least unkind or unjust to him. On the contrary, it always surprised me how evenly and impartially Oka-San behaved to a child who was not only a stranger but an alien as well. Nevertheless, Tolya was lonely. Big and broad-shouldered, with large gray-green eyes set off by long curved lashes, his cheeks rosy as apples, he bore no conceivable likeness to a Japanese.

Olga gave him Russian lessons. He would fumble for words, pronounced with a Japanese accent, and wrote with many mistakes. He seemed uninterested, probably because he felt the les-

* Boris Andreyevich Pilnyak (Vogau) (1894–1937?) was a novelist and short story writer. His novel, *The Naked Year* (1922, tr. 1928), which concerns the social chaos following the Revolution of 1917, attracted wide attention. *The Volga Falls to the Caspian Sea* (1930, tr. 1931) was severely criticized by the Soviet government as bourgeois. Pilnyak disappeared in 1937, and is believed to have died in a concentration camp.

sons useless. Several times a month he received long tender letters from his Moscow grandmother. Unable to read them, he
would come running to us. She wrote how she and his sister often
thought of him, hoping he still remembered Russia. She begged
him not to forget the Russian language, to read it, and to write
her oftener. Tolya's sister, she said, was going to school, where
she did well, and she hoped he did likewise.

Tolya could only decipher his grandmother's letters with great
difficulty, almost syllable by syllable. I do not know what his feelings may have been. Was he lonely for his native land, his grandmother, his sister? To judge from her letters, his grandmother
was thoroughly Russian. Did she, could she, realize that by now
her grandson was virtually Japanese? That he wrote in Japanese
characters, ate stewed burdock and raw fish with chopsticks? That
he had almost forgotten the Russian language, finding it far easier
to slip on geta than struggle with those Western shoes that had
to be laced and unlaced? That he called the professor "Uncle"
and his wife "Auntie?"

Many an evening, when the professor and his wife left the
house, Toru-Chan stayed home as the senior member of the family, together with Sumi-Chan. She liked the phonograph. He liked
music also, but he did not want her to put on the record of the
Japanese patriotic song celebrating the victory at Port Arthur over
the Russians. "Don't you dare put on that song!" he would
shout—but it amused her to tease him.

"Stop it at once!" he would yell, beside himself, stamping his
foot. "If you don't, I'm going out, and you can stay alone all evening." As she was afraid to be alone, she gave in. What if a
Dorobo-San came. . . .

One day Tolya came to us straight from school, very much excited. Like a child, he began at once to tell us what had happened
in school. "They were telling us today about the Japanese people,
how very courageous they are, how every Japanese is ready to
die for his country, how they fear neither suffering nor death, and
that it is splendid that Japan won over the Russians, that the Russians are all cowards! The boys began to plague me because I was

a Russian and a coward. Horrible! I was nearly out of my mind, I was so angry, I flew at them, punching them. . . ."

"What did the teacher do, punish you?"

"No, he didn't, he didn't even reprimand me. I had to show them, didn't I, that we Russians are not cowards?"

I do not know today where Toru-Chan is, whether his uncle ever took him back to Russia, or whether he stayed on in Japan, or whether he has now grown up as a Japanese or a Russian.

The mother or housewife must always remain unnoticed in a Japanese family. Oka-San moved about gracefully, silently, never shouting, never angry, never protesting. When a man and a wife go shopping the wife always takes the packages out of the clerk's hands and meekly carries them home. One often saw such a couple in the town, the woman carrying the heavy bundles, holding a small child by the hand, with a baby on her back, while her lord and master walked beside her, unburdened, smoking a cigarette. In a street car, a woman will make sure of a seat for her ten- or twelve-year-old son. If there is no other place, she remains standing, balancing on her geta, clinging to a strap, even if there is a baby on her back.

In general, Oka-San, like other Japanese women, had no idea of what it is to live for oneself. She was entirely preoccupied by the needs and desires of her husband, her *dana-san*, and her children. In Japan few women dared claim their own rights, their own wishes. Though the professor was a cultivated man who tried in every way to develop her mind, allowing her much freedom, she was not eager to use it. The freedom of Western women did not appeal to her, nor did European or American furniture or food. If in some ways she adapted to foreign customs, she did so only because it was her husband's wish, because all his work was related to European life.

She looked with abhorrence at the noisy, graceless women from that other world. They laughed aloud, unrestrainedly, they walked with their toes turned out—something considered monstrously ugly by Japanese women. From babyhood on little Japanese girls are taught to walk with the toes turned in. She was horrified at those women who dared ride bicycles on the street alongside delivery boys from the shops. Despite her great restraint, more than once I caught her exchanging a glance with Sumi-Chan, followed by suppressed laughter. To them we appeared utterly absurd, uncouth.

We were not at all offended, though, to realize how distant we must have been in Oka-San's eyes from the Japanese ideal of submissiveness in a woman. Some time later, during a stopover in Honolulu, we saw some giant native women who struck us much as we struck our Japanese friends—except that the difference between Japanese and European women is even greater.

We used to feast our eyes on Oka-San. Smiling gently, she would move soundlessly throughout her house, always occupied, taking her bath last of all, after husband and children, eating her dinner after all the rest, when the fish and rice were already cold and the best portions had been consumed. The last to go to bed, she was the first to rise, so as to prepare breakfast for her husband and her boy. Probably it never occurred to anyone in the family that she was the principal person in the house.

CHAPTER TWENTY-ONE

Jinn-Rickshaw

The man would fling his legs out like a good trotter. His feet flew between the slender curved shafts, faster almost than the eye could follow. His muscles were like steel springs, they rolled in his calves as he ran. His feet were shod in black cloth slippers with rubber soles. A thong held the big toe separate from the rest, so that his foot looked like a hoof. In winter the rickshaw men wore black jackets and trousers, in summer, white. Their wide hats, flat as a tray, shielded their gaunt sunburned faces. There were no fat rickshaw men.

The old Konishi could not understand why the idea of a rickshaw tormented me. "Cheap," he would argue, "cheap and comfortable." To be sure, it was both fast and easy. Seemingly, the man-horse conveyed his fares through the streets, in and out of the path of the cars, without strain. Only when he stopped did you notice his panting. He wiped the dripping sweat from his face and neck with clean paper handkerchiefs.

"Of course, they have a hard time now," Konishi continued, "big competition. The cars have taken most of their employment away. Everyone prefers taxis. Many men have had to go back to their villages, nothing to do here any more."

Nevertheless, the rickshaw men worried me. I often studied their passengers. The heavy well-nourished Europeans especially annoyed me. I kept thinking (though without malice) how nice it would be to make them change places, harness the rider between the shafts, order him to run a few miles. Was it possible, I wondered, that the Revolution had corrupted me, that the sight of a fat European with a thick cigar in his mouth riding a rickshaw provoked the same detestation in me as it would in a Bolshevik proletarian? I wanted to know more about these men, but it was hard to get anything out of Konishi. "Do they fall ill?" I asked.

"Like anyone else. They die young. Few live to be over sixty. Most of them have enlarged hearts and lungs."

"You have used them a great deal, Konishi-San, tell me about them."

"What is there to tell? There's nothing to tell. Well, when the first railroad was built, it ran only between Tokyo and Yokohama, or Osaka and Kobe. People usually traveled by water, on the lakes or the sea. In general, traveling was uncomfortable, so they invented rickshaws. That improved matters a lot."

"And after that?"

"Nothing. People liked the *jinn*-rickshaws; the name means 'man power.' We have another name, *kuruma*, meaning wheel or carriage. It was a wise man who invented the jinn-rickshaw, very wise. The people esteemed him greatly, and the government valued him so much that it paid him royalties for the rickshaws."

"But why didn't people use horses, as we do in Russia? Are they more expensive?"

"No, not more, perhaps less."

"Then, why . . ."

"Well, how can I explain? The rickshaw is more comfortable than a carriage. The horse walks slowly—the rickshaw goes at a trot. Then there is more fuss and trouble with horses, they have to be housed, groomed, fed, watered, and so on."

"But why should a horse walk all the time, doesn't it know how to trot?"

"Oh, the horse has to be urged, whereas the man runs of himself." He said no more. He evidently was not interested, and our questions bored him.

Wishing to be tactful, I changed the subject. "You were going to tell me of your travels, Konishi-San."

"There's nothing particular.to tell. From Osaka to Nagoya it's about eighty or a hundred miles. A nice, comfortable ride. The rickshaw makes about five miles an hour. Every ten or fifteen miles there are posting stations where you change rickshaws and a new man takes you on."

"And how about the baggage?"

"What about the baggage? We took it along. Each person is allowed about fifty-four pounds. And after all it didn't cost very much. The rickshaw man charges fifteen or twenty sen for about one *li*." *

"And how did you get uphill?"

"How? If it was very steep, we got out and walked, otherwise he went on pulling. In the mountains, also on Formosa, people use a *kago* **—a palanquin, you call it, don't you? Two men have to carry that, so it costs more."

The old man ceased. Our silly questions obviously had begun to irritate him. He closed his eyes, indicating he was tired of such

* One li equals about 4 kilometers or 2.45 miles.
** A litter suspended on poles and borne by men.

a conversation. There was no hope of eliciting anything more from him.

When we stayed at the hot springs, I had a chance to see the kago. I was climbing a steep hill on foot by a narrow twisting trail, and was nearly at the top. On my right, a precipice, on the left, a torrent of boiling water. I saw some people boiling eggs in it. The summit was out of sight, veiled in a thick yellowish vapor. Throughout the gorge there was the rotten-egg stench of sulphur. Puny shrubs grew along the yellow-gray cliffs. There were no birds, no grass—everything looked blighted. If hell exists, the thought flashed through my mind, it must look like this. Anxiously I edged my way along the rim of the precipice, sickened by the evil odor, and stopped at a level place to rest.

Below me on the trail a procession appeared about to overtake me. Four brightly upholstered palanquins were being borne along on poles. The passengers were shouting and laughing as if tipsy. There were two men and two women holding colored parasols. The bearers labored solemnly with a firm sure step along the edge of the cliff. I could see that every twist of the trail, every rock, was known to them. They earned their living carrying merry tourists uphill like this.

Later I learned that such men were the *eta*.

CHAPTER TWENTY-TWO

The Eta-Outcasts

We had learned of the eta from a foreigner who had lived in Japan for many years. The Japanese themselves do not like to talk about them, but we were intensely interested and tried to discover their origin. To us the eta looked exactly like everyone else, but the Japanese assert that they can always be recognized and that they have an altogether special appearance.

There are various versions of their origin. Many Japanese believe that once they were captives from another country and that this is why they look different. There is another version, however, that seems more probable.

During the eighth and ninth centuries, when Buddhism dominated Japan, the Buddhist law against eating flesh of any kind was strictly observed. In time, however, that religion became somewhat weakened, but the habit of vegetarianism had become so ingrained that people persisted in it. To kill a living creature filled them with extreme repugnance.

In the tenth century, when internecine wars spread, there developed an overwhelming demand for leather for all sorts of military equipment, for saddles, harness, boots, straps, etc. Yet hardly anyone would undertake the slaughter of animals. Those who would became anathema to the Japanese. This distinction continued from generation to generation, from father to son. No one would associate with any of the butchers, and these men were so universally despised that gradually they became a separate caste, with their own settlements. They were entirely segregated socially, and it was unthinkable for a young Japanese man or girl to marry an eta.

For many years the eta were deprived of all civil rights. They had had to form their own administration and their own criminal code. They were ineligible for government service. They established separate schools for their children. In 1868, when the Meiji dynasty came into power, their civil rights were restored, but certain trades or professions remained forever reserved to them: butchering, tanning, blacksmithing, the dirtiest sanitary work in the hospitals, the care and upkeep of cemeteries.

Somewhat later, another occupation was granted them, when plague and famine swept the city of Kobe so that it became deserted. One ancient little Shinto temple stood unattended. The only persons who cared for it, cleaned it, and kept it in order were the eta from a neighboring settlement. They brought flowers to it, and so they were allowed the right to be florists.

Though officially the eta had been restored to full citizenship, nevertheless other people remained aloof. The liberals in the government in vain made speeches to prove that the eta were exactly the same as other persons and must be respected. No one wanted to have anything to do with them.

"Is it possible that such prejudice can still exist?" we asked a progressive friend of ours.

"Yes—and no," he replied hesitantly, increasing our wish to inquire further.

"How would your son feel, for instance, if he were to sit next to an eta in school?"

"S-s-s-s-a-a-a-!" The question was obviously displeasing, for all his liberalism. "Yes—I dare say he would not like it. Frankly, no one would. When an eta delivers meat to the door, that's all right, but he is not allowed to enter the house."

By now our curiosity was great. "Could you show us an eta in the street?"

"Every time you go to the butcher shop to buy meat, you see an eta."

"But what about an educated eta, a cultivated eta? Would you invite him into your home?"

"Some people do." He evaded a more direct reply. "But in most cases they do not know he is an eta. Yes, unfortunately, the prejudice is still active. To tell the truth, the eta are seldom appointed to government positions, for this would exasperate the other employees. No one wants to work in the same office with them."

"But why? After all, everybody in Japan eats meat nowadays. Are the eta dirty? Are they all poor?"

"No, many of them are wealthy, with fine houses, servants, and cars. It's hard to say just why people feel such a revulsion, but they do. To us, they seem to be an entirely alien race."

"And you, you don't like them either?" I asked.

"Well, how shall I put it?" His eyes narrowed, his face puckered, and he went off into peals of laughter. We stared at him, amazed, but his laughter was so contagious that involuntarily we smiled.

"Oh," he said finally, still hardly able to speak, "I have just remembered an incident with my neighbor. He is a very nice man, he comes from a very good family, only he is poor. One evening he came home befuddled. We heard lots of noise, he was shouting, so was his wife, the sons were swearing. I ran over to them to see if I could help—ha-ha-ha! They were all beating him, the whole family! Hard, too!"

"Because he had come home drunk?"

"No, no, because he was keeping company with an eta, and it was the eta who had got him drunk. Oh, how my neighbor's wife hates them! She says she can always recognize them by their smell, that they stink."

"And so you don't like them either?"

But you can never get anything out of a Japanese if he does not want you to. The liberal shrugged and was silent.

CHAPTER TWENTY-THREE

The Miraculous Doctor

That Hori-San should have such a large family did not fit in with his general characteristics. He would talk with animation about half-serious subjects. In a merry company he would drink warmed sake. He interested himself in fantastic projects to an even adventurous extent. He had an ardent though transient interest in political and public affairs. He had a certain artistic flair and something of a literary taste. He wore a velvet jacket. Yet despite all this, and often unexpectedly, it seemed to me he had a fund of common sense. His wife, however, was an

exhausted, careworn woman with eight children ranging from an
infant in arms to an eldest of fifteen. Except for one, they were
all girls. The family lived in a degree of poverty bordering on
destitution.

"Where did you learn to speak English, Hori-San?"

"In America."

"Is that possible! You have been to America? And what did you
do there?"

"I tramped!" he replied, his big un-Japanese eyes sparkling. I
could see that he liked to reminisce about his life as a tramp.

Hori was very fond of his family. He tried hard to provide for
them, but he did not know how, and so he drowned his cares in
sake. Far too much sake. Perhaps that is why he lost the secre-
tarial position he once had and decided to go into chicken farming
and garden produce.

However, he did not know how to manage these things either.
His vegetable garden was choked with weeds. He had only a few
chickens, and they looked very scrawny. He had bought them at
a bargain from a street peddler in Shinjuku. The peddler had
culled out all the pullets and sold him only roosters.

In the beginning of our acquaintance Hori's wife was reluctant
to invite us to their house, she was so ashamed of their poverty.
Gradually, though, she grew used to us and saw that we were
almost penniless ourselves. We all went bicycling together, Olga,
Maria, Hori, Toru-Chan, and I. Hori showed us the most beautiful
spots in the vicinity and took us on visits to his friends. Usually
he would speed ahead with the younger ones, Maria and Toru-
Chan, his hair waving in the wind. He would ride on the right
instead of the left side of the road, laughing and talking incessantly. These trips were always a perfect delight.

At Hori's house we made the acquaintance of Naruse-San. Hori
had invited us all to tea. The torn tatami were disguised for the
occasion by cushions. There was a motley set of dishes, tiny Japanese cups, European glassware. Hori's wife was continually apol-
ogizing, growing more embarrassed at every step, but we liked
everything in the house, the lovable, modest little girls in their
kimonos, the only son, the tired, worn-out wife. The boy was a

year and a half old, still crawling. We liked the guests, too, the animated, handsome, young Naruse-San, who displayed a keen interest in everything, and her friend Akaba-San with her round, simple, kind face. Naruse-San had brought another friend, a painter with a portly figure and a cheerful expression.

It seemed extraordinary to have chanced into this company. Who were these people, I wondered, without reaching a conclusion. For one thing, Naruse was an enigma to me. She appeared to be more broad-minded, more developed, than most Japanese women I had met, yet she could not be categorized as "emancipated." Her dress, her elegance, and her love of family life contradicted that characterization. Twice I had an opportunity of seeing her husband and her son. The latter, as I remember, was a lawyer. Both husband and son were employed, and seemed not to enter into her personal life to any great extent. She was concerned with public affairs, with literature and art. Her spirit appeared to be striving after something beyond home life.

All this we felt rather than knew, for we could not converse with her. Besides Japanese, she knew only a little French and was timid about using it. We had only a few words in common and could conduct only the most elementary conversation. Nor was it possible to approach understanding her through an interpreter. She was too complex a personality. Even if she had been willing to express herself openly and earnestly, Hori would inevitably simplify and blunt any subtlety in her thoughts, such complexity being to him quite superfluous. All we could do was to observe her, especially when we visited her home.

She always had a stream of visitors, doctors, artists, poets, writers, who came and went without anyone bothering to entertain them. Those who came oftenest were Akaba-San, Hori-San, and the fat artist. They felt perfectly at home, carried the tea in and out, set the table. Before we were aware of it, we too found ourselves feeling equally at home. Once we even helped cook a Japanese dinner of *o tempura gohan.** We made a sauce to go with raw fish and boiled rice Japanese fashion.

* Fried shrimp and vegetables.

That was a very gay meal. Even her sober husband and son smiled and drank sake with Hori and the artist. It must be said that Hori's manner of drinking was unusual. He would hold the tiny cup for a while before his long nose, gulp it down, then nod happily to everyone present, beaming with pleasure.

There was also a more solemn occasion at Naruse's house. She invited some thirty friends to hear me speak about my father and about Russia. When I had finished, the guests kept asking questions, and as usual I was carried away. Hori could hardly translate fast enough. Suddenly a strange sensation in my spine made me turn around. A burly man in a coarse gray kimono was sitting behind me. He was holding out his hands toward me, and the odd warmth was coming from them.

"Docteur, très fameux," explained Naruse introducing us. The doctor and I bowed to each other. He still held out his hands toward me. Suddenly he placed them on the small of my back and involuntarily I bent over: he was pressing a place that had been hurting me. Two years earlier, while I was still in Moscow, I had fallen on an icy sidewalk, striking my back against the curb. Ever since then, despite massage and hydrotherapy, it had remained sore.

In a low voice, laconically, it seemed to me, the doctor explained something to Naruse.

"What does he say?" I asked.

"He says that this spot has been hurting you considerably and that it hurts a little now. If you wish, he offers to treat you by the touch of his hands. Don't fail to let him do this, for he is a most remarkable man. He can cure anything. He only has to touch you, and you will feel relieved."

The doctor's hands went on moving about me as if seeking something. He raised them higher, encircling my neck, my chin and cheeks. Unexpectedly, he pressed a spot on my left cheekbone. Again he murmured a few words.

"He says," Hori interpreted, "that you had a bad toothache, and though the tooth was pulled out, it still hurts."

The room was hushed. Everyone's attention was on the doctor and me. They were waiting for my answer. Akaba's kind face was flushed, and Naruse herself was visibly excited. They were all admirers of this strange man.

"Yes," I replied, "I had an inflammation of the gum, and the day before yesterday the tooth was taken out."

"Docteur fameux!" Naruse again exclaimed.

"And you too can learn to diagnose and cure diseases," proclaimed Hori, "I tell you, he is a remarkable man! We are all learning from him now. In three or four lessons you will have the same power—well, perhaps not quite the same, but in any case you can learn to treat all diseases. You should not have had that tooth extracted. He would have cured it."

"But if there was pus at the root . . ."

"That makes no difference, he has such power."

Meanwhile the doctor kept silent, his hands on his lap and his eyes shut. He seemed not the least interested in what was going on round him.

I discovered that the whole company, Akaba, the painter, Hori, and Naruse herself had been taking lessons in healing from the doctor. It was decided that Olga and I would also join their circle and learn about the laying on of hands. Hori told us that the doctor was a very learned Buddhist, that most of his life had been spent in meditation, prayer, and fasting. He ate only once a day, in the evening, and then only vegetables, rice, beans, and so forth. Before the laying on of hands, one must not eat at all, but concentrate and pray. Every morning he washed in cold water, as this not only cleanses but also hardens. He possessed nothing—but he needed nothing. He saw his patients at Naruse's house. Sometimes he accepted gifts in grateful return for his treatment.

When Olga and I came for our first lesson, the disciples had already gathered, Naruse, her friend Akaba, and Hori. We sat on the floor in a half-circle, facing the doctor. We were all terribly serious. He ordered, "Close your eyes." He began to read Buddhist prayers.

I had a burning desire to see his face, so I opened a slit in one eye. The doctor then walked around the half-circle, taking the hands of each disciple and folding them together. When he came to me, I shut my eyes fast. He took my hands, spread them out, raised them to the level of my nose, folded the fingers into the palms, and pressed them, to show me how to hold them. At last we were allowed to open our eyes.

It was fearfully hard to keep sitting motionless on our heels. Legs and arms grew numb. Elbows tended to droop. Palms opened. Now and then the doctor took a disciple's hands in his, to catch the current flowing between them. Every time his hands touched mine, I felt a slight prickling, as if from an electric current. Even before he touched me, I felt the wave of warmth nearing me. The closer his palm was to mine, the sharper the prickling sensation.

When the séance was over, we all tested one another. No matter how Akaba tried—and her attitude throughout was one of awed rapture—I must say frankly that I never felt any current from her hands to mine. Nor did I feel anything emanating from Hori, though he too was zealously trying to master the science, pressing his hands together hard and gazing down his long nose. His wife had urged him to acquire the skill so that there would be no need of any expensive doctor ever for their large family.

I failed to sense any current from Naruse's delicate little hands. Yet whenever the doctor so much as raised his hands, I did feel a force proceeding from him. As I understood it, that force helped him locate the disease and then cure it. A normal human warmth does not flow from a diseased area. It is lifeless, as it were. To revive it and bring it back to health, the healer must develop the power in his hands that emits a miraculous wave of heat.

At home I practiced for several days. At times, I did seem to feel the desired prickling in the tips of my fingers. Repeatedly I importuned Olga by moving my palms close to her face, but every time she skeptically declared that she felt nothing. However, the lessons went on. I do not remember how many I took, but each time it was a little easier to keep holding my arms outstretched. My elbows no longer drooped, there was no need to prop them against my chest.

I confess that doctor interested me greatly. I do not know how true it was that he had cured numerous sufferers who came to him for treatment. Naruse asserted that he had cured cancer and stomach ulcers. Nevertheless, whenever I fell ill, I was reluctant to consult the famous Buddhist magician. I wanted to be treated by an ordinary European doctor.

CHAPTER TWENTY-FOUR

"Very Sorry"

A person who has lost his wealth must do without his accustomed comforts and niceties. On the whole, he experiences the same sort of change as one who has lost his heavy fur coat in winter: he feels lighter and more agile, but he must work to keep warm.

We were feeling thus unencumbered. Nothing tied us to any place. We lived where we chose, how we chose. We "kept warm," so to speak, by some work or other. We wrote articles, gave lessons. I lectured. We organized courses in Russian in Shinjuku, a lively little place near Tokyo. But there were periods when we had no work. Then keeping warm became a difficult problem. We cut our needs down to a minimum. We were living in a tiny house of two rooms. We ate fish, chicken—and veal kidneys and liver, since, as the Japanese eat no internal organs, they sell these very cheap.

We also ate rice and fruit "on little plates." The latter was something I had never known before. If apples, pears, or bananas got even slightly bruised in the shops, they were put aside on little plates and sold for very few pennies. Often such fruit tastes even better than that of perfect appearance, priced higher, because it is riper. Thus, for the equivalent of forty dollars a month in those times, the three of us managed to live and also pay tuition for Maria in an American school.

Even so, forty dollars was a sum hard to earn. An enterprising Japanese opened courses in Russian just opposite ours and in the same street. He advertised them far and wide, and charged three yen per month instead of our five for each student. Gradually our pupils deserted us for him, until only seven remained. We had to close the school, and our remaining students came to our house for lessons. Our financial equilibrium therefore became very unstable.

To make matters worse, I fell seriously ill. It began with angina; then my gums became infected. My temperature rose astronomically, and I grew delirious. I could neither eat nor drink, tossing on my futon on the floor. Olga insisted on calling a doctor. I protested, because the five yen we would have to pay him was our total reserve capital.

It may be said I was fairly miserable. The tatami were too hard, the futon too thin for comfort. A noxious draft came in through the low window. It irritated me to have my drinking glass, thermometer, and watch on the same level as my bedroom slippers. Thoughts of tomorrow assailed me. What would become of all of us when the five yen went in the market?

For about a week I lay ill, when suddenly there was a knock at the door. The postman! He brought a letter with French postage and a postal order for one hundred dollars! It was like a miracle. It came from a friend in Paris as a share from an old publishing enterprise.

Then Olga and I decided to call a doctor—but whom? There was not a single Russian physician in Tokyo. An American? But the only American doctor we had heard of in that city was a specialist in nervous ailments.

Our neighbor, the professor, declared resolutely, "I shall ask our doctor to come see you. He has been our family physician for many years. He is a kind and conscientious man, and he charges only a little."

To be sure, he was a good-natured fellow, rather fat and round, in a gray European suit; he hitched up his trousers, squatted on his heels, and began examining me. From his waistcoat pocket there hung a watch chain, and every time it touched me a chill ran down me. Several times he stood up and inhaled breathily with a loud "S-s-s-s-aa!" He tormented me for a long time. I opened my mouth, I closed my mouth, and then was asked to open it again.

"S-s-s-s-a-a-a-! Very sorry!"

The doctor called in the professor. The both squatted before me and discussed me at length, wagging their heads. As far as I could gather, the doctor was consulting the professor of literature as to the best way of treating a European patient. After all, the professor had a lot more to do with Europeans than the doctor, therefore he had to understand them better. Finally, the doctor prescribed some powders. I suspected they were aspirin. But I failed to get better. The next morning the doctor called again. He seemed more perplexed than ever. I watched him as he twitched up his trousers and sat down.

"S-s-s-s-s-a-a-!" The doctor inhaled noisily, pondering.

"Wakarimasen!" [I don't understand.] He left and never returned.

Our friend the professor explained, "The doctor told me that it would be useless for him to visit you. He can't help. He can't understand what the ailment is, so he doesn't want the responsibility."

As the professor had already told us, the doctor was not expensive. He had charged only one yen. Meanwhile, I felt worse and worse. We did not know what to do. At last the professor said that he had a friend, a very talented young physician, a man with a brilliant future. He would be glad to come to see me: he needed no fee. A medical case that was more or less complicated would interest him from a scientific standpoint. He would be grateful if I would permit him to come and examine me and try to diagnose my illness.

So the doctor came. Very youthful. Like a boy, he itched to display his erudition. At his very first questions, I almost drove him out of the house despite my weakened condition. With some hesitancy, the professor interpreted questions concerning my heredity. He wanted to know about the health of my parents and grandparents. He wanted to know how many children my mother had had, and how many my grandmother. He asked why I had not married. He examined my throat, pressing my tongue down with a wooden chip. He then examined it without the chip. He took a sample of my sputum. At times during his examination he remained silent, squatting on the tatami in the classical Japanese pose, completely immobile, hands on his knees. He was thinking.

At last: "Infection!" he pronounced and ordered me to gargle with hydrogen peroxide. For days Olga had been trying desperately to obtain this very medicine, but could not, because she did not know how to ask for it in Japanese.

Whether it was from the doctor's questions or from the peroxide, I soon felt better and gradually recovered.

CHAPTER TWENTY-FIVE

Sakura-Cherry Blossom

The air was saturated with fragrance. Rosy-white clouds of blossoms floated against the blue of the sky. Heavy branches, leafless, overhung the rapid mountain stream. The loveliest time of all was the early morning, when the birds had just awakened. They could not be seen in the thick blossoms, only their jubilant, imperative little voices dominated the air. Silently, delicate airy petals parted from their boughs, slowly, they settled on the water, then slowly disappeared.

All during April, Japan is one fragrant garden. Last of all the *sakura* blooms with its weight of tender pink compound flowers. Everywhere sakura. Along the roads, on the fences, in the parks, the forest outskirts, its petals fall, strewing the fields, the highways, the shores of the lakes, the rivers. It adorns the houses of rich and poor, the temples, the peasant huts. From all sides people flock to the larger parks and gardens, where sakura is abundant. Just as on New Year's Day, people are dressed in their best, rejoicing. A great holiday, for the sakura is in bloom.

In that time, nice people in Japan did not ride bicycles. To launch such an endeavor, a respectable professor would have needed courage. It would have meant a descent, as it were, to the level of errand boys delivering packages. However, our friend was a progressive, cultivated man and paid little attention to conventions. The professor therefore disregarded—or even disapproved of—the surprised glances of his wife and walked his new shiny bicycle from the shed. We were off.

The weather was magnificent, hot in the sun. The narrow village lanes had just dried and there was at first no dust. Our bicycles rolled fast and easily. After about two hours we reached a wide brimming river. A ferry took us across. Beyond the river, as far as the eye could see, was an immense expanse of foamy pink bloom, endless, merging with the horizon. Cherry blossoms! We flew toward them, to feast our eyes and breathe their fragrance.

The road became so crowded that we could ride no further but had to get down and push our wheels. A horde of cars crept along in single file. The hard-trodden footpath was crowded too, littered with papers, tangerine peels, cigarette and cigar stubs. Families with children, couples, groups of friends—all were merrymaking, for this was the annual festival of the sakura. Now, though, one could neither see nor smell it for the crowds and the dust.

Some ambitious peddlers had exploited the holiday and put up portable shops along the rows of old trees. There were shops doing a brisk trade in sake. Others sold peanuts, bean curd, roast chestnuts, and toys. The women peddlers, tipsy themselves, seized people by their sleeves and pulled them to their shops with cries. Some women (a type I had never seen in Japan) were dressed in exceedingly bright kimonos, with a high hairdo, and they too uttered cries with licentious gestures. One accosted some children and got them to repeat their lewd gestures, to the tolerant amusement of the equally tipsy crowd. I noticed one young student leading a girl, also a student, by the arm, smiling a shamed, stupid smile and swaying—both tipsy.

The Japanese people were celebrating. Even if a man stayed perfectly sober all the year, on that day he relaxed—or if he could not drink at all, he pretended he had, for how can one celebrate without drinking?

We had stopped to photograph this mad crowd, but were immediately surrounded. They shouted and clutched at us, so we turned around to hurry home. We went by a different route, but for several miles we had to maneuver among the merrymakers and countless taxis passing us. At last we could turn off onto a village road that skirted a canal bordered with sakura. There we stopped and sat down to rest in the divine serenity, breathing the scented air. The petals were fluttering down onto the clear water.

CHAPTER TWENTY-SIX

Advanced Women

What? You mean to say that there is more freedom in Japan than in the USSR? That all depends. Freedom for whom?" Take-San protested vigorously.

Her narrow eyebrows rose over her huge dark glasses, her thin fingers nervously playing with a pencil. "You simply do not know what you are talking about. Let us take women. In Japan women are slaves. Fathers sell their daughters into factories and—well, bad houses."

"Houses of prostitution?"

"Yes. Do you know how many such girls there are in Japan? *Shoji*, as we call them?"

"Prostitutes?"

"Yes, yes. Fifty-two thousand, not counting the eighty thousand geishas."

"But geishas are not prostitutes, are they? I thought they were, well, something different."

"Of course they are all the same thing. A geisha always has—how shall I say—well, a rich man . . ."

"A man who keeps her?"

"Well, yes. Sometimes this man buys her out of the geisha establishment, but then it's the same as prostitution, only the geishas are more refined, better educated, more intelligent than a common *jore*.* But it's all a horror. Tiny children are brought up to be geishas. Their fate is already decided. Haven't you seen them?"

Indeed I had seen them at concerts and theatres. Little girls of ten or twelve, their faces whitened and painted, wearing loud-colored kimonos. They were always with a modestly dressed Japanese woman with a high hairdress, for geishas always dress modestly. A foreigner would never discern any difference between them and other women, but a Japanese could not err. It was painful to see these doll-like little girls, trained from childhood to become a source of entertainment for Japanese men. On this question, I thoroughly agreed with my friend Take-San.

"Can't they change and lead honest independent lives if they want?" I had understood that prostitutes were free citizens in Japan.

"Oh, that's only on paper. Very well: imagine the parents who have already received money for their girl. They have contracted an obligation. How can she ever go away? To be sure, among progressive people today, especially among women, there is a strong movement on foot against prostitution, and to an extent it is solving the problem. But that is only a drop in the bucket. The point is: prostitution in Japan is legal. And you say there is no freedom in Soviet Russia! Prostitution there has been liquidated! Women have obtained all their rights—but here . . ."

* A prostitute.

"In your country," I answered, "everyone knows that prostitution exists and is being combated. In Soviet Russia, though, it exists still in hidden forms. The women employees in Soviet offices who receive beggarly salaries—even teachers in the schools—are forced to go out into the streets at night. And the wild children*—if you only knew how they live! There are thousands of them. Little girls of only eight years sell themselves."

"Well, if something is wrong in Russia, you know what a heritage the Soviet government received from tsarist times. How could it possibly liquidate the problem of homeless children all at once?"

"There never were hordes of homeless children under the tsars."

"But—the Soviet government is poor. It cannot immediately raise the salaries of its employees. But is that the important thing? The Soviet government is trying to improve the lot of the proletariat. It has given women all rights. It has organized aid to mothers and infants. It has introduced the eight-hour day in the factories—whereas our girls are being sold to factory owners! And under what working conditions! And the niggardly wages!"

"But what about the mass shootings, the requisitioning of their last supplies of grain from the very people who produced the grain? What about the deprivation of personal freedom, the abolition of the secret ballot? What about destitution? Famine?"

"Famine? Look at our peasants. They have no rice, they have to eat beans. They have no clothes. But in your country, all such matters are temporary. Wait until a few years from now and look again. So far, they have been able to destroy capitalism and the bourgeoisie."

It was hopeless to argue with her any longer. Like many others, this girl was deceived by the beautiful slogans of the Soviet government. She believed in Soviet theories, but she was absolutely blind to Soviet reality. She clearly perceived all the defects

---

*The *bezprizhorny*, homeless orphans, were a terrible social problem for many years after World War I. Numbering in the thousands, they overran the country. The government instituted measures, and in time the problem was overcome to a large extent, but after World War II it reappeared.

of her own country. Like many other admirers of Bolshevism, however, she neither wanted to see nor could see that long ago socialism in Russia had degenerated into totalitarianism—that the rights of every human being had been abolished.

"You are a Bolshevik, Take-San," I commented.

"Who, me?" She laughed. "No, please don't call me that."

"But isn't it so? Everything you have been saying I heard very, very many times from Bolshevik speakers."

"Yes, but I am not a party member. And please, I beg you, don't say I am—and never tell anyone that I sympathize with the Bolsheviks." A scarcely perceptible shudder. She frowned. "If you only knew how they torture prisoners here, especially Communists. They beat them, they beat them so it makes them cry out."

"In Russia people are tortured *by* the Communists."

But she let this remark pass unnoticed. She was far too full of the injustices of her own government. "In prison they can neither stand nor lie, only squat all day long. And how they are beaten!" Again she said, "Oh, I'm so afraid. Many times I've wanted to enlist in the party, but could not bring myself to it. I know it is bad, very bad, to be so afraid, I know I am not loyal, but I can't— I can't."

She was pathetic, but also funny. Her full rosy mouth, her broad intelligent forehead that did not match her lips, the flattened nose, the brilliant narrow eyes—and the affectionate womanly nature that shone through, no matter how she tried to hide it under her boyish shirt and tie, her generally mannish appearance.

"Well, then, why didn't you stay in Soviet Russia? Why did you come back, if it's so bad here?" She had just returned from the USSR.

"Yes, you are right." She spoke sincerely and earnestly. "There they are seeking new forms of life. They are moving ahead—but here? I couldn't stay in Russia any longer, though."

"Why not?"

"Nothing to eat."

"How so, nothing to eat? Everything is being done for the

poor, for the proletariat—yet you say there is nothing to eat?"

"Yes, they are doing everything for the poor," she repeated with conviction, "but temporarily there are difficulties. There is no rice—that is, it could be had, but it is very expensive."

"Well, you ought to be able to work for the Revolution without rice. Russian workmen lack not only rice but also bread. Our old revolutionaries—Breshko-Breshkovsky, Morozov, and many others—they were willing to sacrifice their lives for the Revolution. For twenty years on end they would sit in prison, for their idea—and you are afraid not to have rice?"

"Yes, you are right."

"You are a poor sort of revolutionary, Take-San," I remarked. She was too sincere, too straightforward, too naive. I lost all desire to tease her. "You should get married, Take-San, have children, and bring them up."

"What, me get married?" She burst out laughing in a high little voice, like that of a boy whose voice is changing. "Ha-ha-ha, I could not possibly get married."

"Why not?"

"Nobody will want me." Flustered. "I am too homely."

Whenever she came to see us, the neighbors gaped at her. From the professor's house Oka-San with Kaju-Chan on her back peeped out. Sumi-Chan, the nurse, wiped her red hands, loosened the sleeves of her kimono, tied up when she was working in the kitchen, and ran out into the street, crying, "Look what a pretty boy!" The Japanese women were laughing, covering their mouths with their wide sleeves. They would whisper among themselves, staring half-enviously at the boy-girl as she passed. She, however, in her black suit, her man's hat, and flat-heeled shoes, a briefcase under her arm, walked by purposefully without looking. She was used to being jeered at.

Take-San often spoke to us about a friend of hers, a woman writer, very advanced and very popular among the young who sympathized with the Bolsheviks. "She is very intelligent," she would say, "much more than I am."

According to what I had heard, that woman writer was a popular leader of socialism among the younger generation. She despised the old ways, the old customs. She was struggling for the total emancipation of women, for equal rights. She professed free love and atheism. She despised bourgeois family life and—as she said—their petty interests. The usual modesty of a Japanese woman was quite absent in her. She was very sure of herself, very confident.

My impression of her intelligence, however, differed from Take's. In talking with her, I several times recalled one of my father's favorite comparisons: a man is like a fraction, the numerator representing his real attributes, the denominator, his opinion of himself. This woman's denominator was immense.

"Good day," she greeted us when we first met, not waiting for Take to introduce us. Evidently that was a superfluous formality. She held out her hand, turned out a little. "How long from home?" She spoke Russian fluently.

"It will soon be a year."

"When do you think of going back?"

"Well, I am not thinking of it, so long as the Bolsheviks prevail."

"Is that so?"

Her eyes searched mine, and I met them full on. As is sometimes the way, one does not know why, just as love suddenly springs up, so does hostility. I sensed this not only from the shadow that ran over her face, pasty, even puffy. I did not like her either. Her manners lacked any reserve. Her mannish clothes, her incessant smoking, holding her cigarette between two fingers and blowing a jet of smoke to the ceiling—every single thing about her showed how long ago she had dispensed with the modesty of a Japanese woman—a stupid and superfluous trait in her eyes.

"I thought you sympathized with the Bolsheviks, you worked with them for so many years. And your father, wouldn't he have sympathized with the liberation of the people from the tsar's yoke?"

"But what is there in common between the Bolsheviks and the liberation of the working classes?" I asked.

"What? What did you say?" She was up in arms at once, ready

for battle, her cigarette in her short fingers suddenly poised. "You know that the Bolsheviks have broken the shackles of the working class!"

I could not hold back, and we fell into a foolish, unnecessary argument. We both shouted, not listening to each other. Bad feeling flared. Her style of contention was as deficient as my own, and was also rather Russian, that is, unrestrained and harsh. Sometimes I quite forgot that it was a Japanese woman before me, not a Bolshevik agitator.

"You tell me they have exiled the peasants!" she cried. "Not the poor peasants—only the kulaks! And right they were! They ought to crush into dust all those who oppose the Soviet government!" Her plump little fist pounded the table. "Perhaps you'll say next that the bourgeoisie should be revived and the tsar set up again! Oh, but . . ." smiling ironically, "I don't know why I am arguing with you. What does it matter what you say? You whom the Revolution deprived of everything you had?"

"The Revolution gave me a lot, it taught me to work for society, it gave me a public post and a good salary. The trouble is not mine, but the millions of workers and peasants . . ."

"Peasants? Petty bourgeois, owners of property, smug ingrates who cannot understand their own interests!"

"So you would teach them to understand by ruining them, exiling them, shooting them?"

"Yes, yes, and yes," she screamed, frenzied, "and they should be shot if they stand in our way . . ."

Finally, Olga and Take, who had not taken part, separated us.

The woman writer left and never returned. I was only too pleased. Thank God, there were few such women in Japan. The Japanese women did indeed struggle for their rights, but not in that way. There was then a very strong and sound movement for the liberation of women, and the leading role was played by American women. Japanese girls educated in the United States were bringing back to Japan the knowledge of American education, customs, and manners. Japanese women too were freeing themselves from domestic serfdom, from their *dana-sans*, their lords and masters.

While I was in Japan, there were already American YWCA workers, Quakers, and others from similar organizations who were making an enormous effort among Japanese women. In every large school and college there were American teachers. The English language, European and American ways of living, even manual skills were being taught. The young girls were leaving off their lovely kimonos and obis and instead were wearing uniforms—white blouses, navy blue skirts, clumsy shoes in which they shuffled as if they were shod in geta.

Another profound change had also been taking place. The Shinto and Buddhist creeds had begun to give way to Christianity, taught by American teachers. It was apparent everywhere that the Japanese were rapidly assimilating Western civilization. The Japanese women, however, retained a gentleness and refinement I have never observed in any other country, whatever their position, and regardless of what religion they followed or what clothes they wore.

CHAPTER TWENTY-SEVEN

End of the Fairy Tale

On the third of February 1931, after almost a year and a half in Japan, I received the following official communication:

February 3, 1931

Citizen Alexandra Lvovna Tolstoy:

I am requesting you herewith to come to my office at 12:00 o'clock noon on Friday, the 6th of this month, to discuss a question connected with your residence abroad.

Consul General of the USSR in Tokyo,
Podolsky

Just prior to this I had written a letter to Deputy People's Commissar for Education Epstein, asking him to extend my mission, since I was writing a book about my father and wished to finish it while in Japan. In addition I requested him to promise me that the school and museum in Yasnaya Polyana would continue to be managed in accordance with the same principles that had been in effect under Lenin, i.e., that no antireligious propaganda would be conducted on their premises. In answer to my letter Epstein stated that, although there was much work to be done, he would nevertheless permit me to extend my mission until September; as to arrangements covering matters of principle in the Tolstoy organizations, we could agree on that when I returned. Having received this paper from the Deputy People's Commissar, I immediately reached a decision: to sever relations with the Soviet government permanently, and never to return to Russia unless there was a change of regime. I wrote the following:

To the People's Commissariat for Education

Alexandra Lvovna Tolstoy

Statement

On February 3 of this year I received an official notice from the Soviet Consul General in Tokyo requesting my presence in order to clear up the question of my delay abroad.

The principal reason for my delay is the impossibility of continuing to be active in an occupation devoted to the memory of my father while residing in my native land.

Even before my departure for Japan I more than once made written and oral declarations asking to be separated from my position as director of the Yasnaya Polyana Experimental Station.

I wished to retire because the school was gradually ceasing to differ in any way from ordinary schools, and I as my father's daughter could not remain at the head of an institution which was opposed to all his teachings. By this time the school in question has completely ceased to take into account the fact that it is a "memorial" to Tolstoy—they have introduced militarization, antireligious propaganda, etc.

If the above is unavoidable, I cannot continue to be in charge of a "memorial" to my father which propagates views in direct opposition to his own teachings and which instructs children in the handling of firearms.

Before I went abroad, the subject of antireligious propaganda had already been raised in connection with the Tolstoy Museum. Now they write in the newspapers about a thorough reorganization of all museums.

Finally, the question has come up of liquidating the Society for the Study and Dissemination of the Works of Leo Nikolaevich Tolstoy, which has spent thirteen years toiling over my father's manuscripts, accomplished the tremendous task of putting in order his archives in the Lenin Library, and volume by volume prepared my father's works for their first complete edition.

The Government knows very well that, as long as it maintained the policy of excluding ideology from the Tolstoy institutions, and of protecting them conscientiously, I worked my fingers to the bone. Now when Comrade Epstein answers my letter with a "Come, we'll reach an agreement," at a time when in fact all the Tolstoy institutions have not only been turned into run-of-the-mill Soviet organizations but also have as their prime purpose the spreading of anti-Tolstoyan doctrines, I as Tolstoy's daughter cannot work in them and consequently shall refrain at this time from returning to my native land.

Alexandra Tolstoy

February 4, 1931

On April 7 a paragraph appeared in the newspaper *Posledniye Novosti* in New York: "We are informed from Tokyo that Alexandra Lvovna Tolstoy, having applied for a Canadian visa, has received instructions from Moscow to return to the USSR. A. L. Tolstoy has stated that she will not comply with the order and will not go to Russia."

Olga, Maria, and I had lived in Japan for twenty months, and had become friends with many Japanese; but we felt that it was time to make a choice and settle on a permanent basis, in some other country, where we could put down roots and where Olga could give her daughter a decent education.

However, it was not so easy to disengage ourselves from Japan. To whom did I not turn! To the ex-Russian ambassador in Tokyo, Abrikosov, to the influential Americans, to our Quaker friends, asking them to take the matter up with the American consul. I wrote to the Dukhobors in Canada. It seemed to me that they might help me, in remembrance of my father who had donated to them his entire proceeds from the first printing of *Resurrection*, while my brother Sergei helped them resettle in Canada, accompanied them on their ship, and guided them as far as Saskatchewan, where they settled down permanently. But from them too I received an unsatisfactory answer. They wrote that the immigration authorities had recently become extremely strict and were not allowing anyone to enter Canada.

Although I judged by the newspapers that the situation in the United States was rather disturbing—Communists stirring up trouble there too, the hunger march to the New York state capital at Albany, the depression, dissatisfaction, the rise in the number of unemployed, which had reached five million—I still naively believed that I as Tolstoy's daughter would easily be able to earn something by giving lectures about Russia and about my father. We had no doubt that Olga, with her knowledge of several languages and her college education, would find work in universities or libraries.

The situation was also somewhat alarming in Japan: the war with China, the occupation of Manchuria, the widespread poverty and lack of earning power. But it was even harder for us because, as soon as the Japanese, especially the liberal intelligentsia, learned that we had broken with the Soviet government and refused to return to our country, our position changed radically; interest in us faded and was replaced by condescending pity. From "fully privileged" citizens of Soviet Russia, we changed into "refugees." We found ourselves people without passports, without rights.

I was astonished when our friend Professor Yonekawa, almost choking from excitement, told me about the writers' conference to be held in Japan, to which all Soviet authors would be invited—Sholokhov, Fadeev, Romanov,* etc. To my question as to whether writers such as Bunin, Zaitsev or Kuprin** would be invited, he answered with a crooked smile:

---

*Mikhail Sholokhov (1905–) is officially regarded as the greatest Soviet prose writer. A loyal Communist Party member, he is best known for his epic novels, *And Quiet Flows the Don*, *The Don Flows Home to the Sea*, and *Harvest on the Don;* Alexander Fadeev (1901–1956), novelist (*The Nineteen*) and short story writer (*Leningrad in the Days of the Blockade*), served as a leader of the Russian Association of Proletarian Writers from 1928 to 1932 and as head of the Soviet Writers Union from 1946 to 1954; Panteleymon Romanov (1884–1936) was one of the most popular Soviet writers of the 1920s, attracting a wide public following with sketches of his countrymen in *Without Cherry Blossom* and *The New Commandment*.

**These last three Russian writers all fell out of favor at one time or another with the authorities. Ivan Bunin (1870–1933), author of "The Gentleman from San Francisco," *The*

"Oh no, they don't interest us, they are emigrants."

"Why don't you go back home?" the Japanese asked us. They did not believe it was dangerous, that we might be exiled somewhere in Siberia, or rot in prison, perhaps even be shot.

Part of the Japanese intelligentsia were opposed to their Mikado and the war party that supported the monarchic regime, and, as a possible counterweight to the conservatives, saw salvation in Communism. They considered Communism a most interesting experiment by the Russian people, and greatly admired it. It had freed the Russian masses from the tyranny of a tsarist government; it had opened the road to freedom and prosperity.

We were in despair, fearing that we would never be able to leave Japan. But unexpectedly the three of us received an invitation to dinner with the American ambassador.

The ambassador and his wife received us most graciously, trying to do everything possible to make us feel comfortable. But—we were people from different worlds. They lived in a world of decency, respect for the individual, prosperity, self-confidence; we came from a world of violence, lack of human rights, poverty. After twelve years in that Soviet world, we had lost touch with civilization. In the USSR, people dressed God knows how, only to be covered, froze beside the diminutive, wood-burning stoves, lived without hot water, with no baths.

Now in Japan, while things were much better, we lived very simply: a tiny house of three rooms, in the larger of which Olga and her daughter stayed, another smaller one, mine, and a third, a kitchen, where we cooked and ate. We went to the bathhouse to wash, returned home in tabi, and slept on the floor like the Japanese, since there were no beds. There was only one table in the whole apartment—on which we ate, wrote, and Maria prepared her lessons—and three chairs which we would move from one room to another.

Village, and *Dry Valley*, opposed the Soviet regime and was forced to emigrate in 1920. Boris Zaitsev (1881–1972), a writer of lyrical and impressionistic short stories and novels, left Russia in 1922. Alexander Kuprin (1870–1938), associated for a time with Maxim Gorky, gained public attention with his indictments of the evils of industrialization and military life, *Moloch* and *The Duel*. Kuprin left Russia after the Revolution but returned in 1937, the year before his death.

As a result, no matter how hard we tried to dress and do our hair properly for the ambassadorial dinner—I in my overly long black silk dress with its long sleeves and high collar (my "lecture" dress) and my patent leather men's shoes (still the only ones I could find in Japan to fit my foot)—we must have looked extremely odd. At table, our clumsiness showed how we had got out of the habit of napkins; we dropped them on the floor and dived under the table to pick them up (in Soviet Russia they made sheets out of napkins). I did not know why they served little cups of warm water after the dessert. In our home in old Russia we would serve cups with small glasses of warm water and mint to rinse the mouth after dinner. I watched the others and saw that they wet their fingers after the sweets and wiped their lips with the moist first finger, and I, although I saw no sense in this activity, did the same. In addition I noticed that Americans, when cutting meat, shift their fork into the right hand, put the meat in their mouth, then pass the fork again to the left hand and the knife to the right. Our governess did not teach us this when we were children. A frightful waste of time, especially when you're hungry, but I soon mastered this wisdom too. One had to be civilized!

During dinner the ambassador asked me a great many questions about Soviet Russia and listened attentively to my story. After coffee he rose and, saying that he must have a very confidential talk with me about an extremely important matter, asked me to come into his study.

I was terrified. What could this be? Perhaps something connected with the Soviets? Maybe they are insisting that we not be given United States visas? Various silly thoughts came into my mind, thoughts which could occur only to a Soviet citizen who had lost all trust, whose psychology was so different from that of someone living in a free country.

The ambassador let me precede him, pulled up an armchair for me, and we sat down at a huge desk. He opened a drawer and pulled out a letter.

"This letter was addressed to me," he said. "Read it, and give me an answer. I already know the contents."

Dear Mrs. Tolstoy,

The newspapers say that you are in Japan, do not want to return to your native Russia, and would like to come to Canada if the immigration authorities will permit. You would be able to accomplish this if you were to marry a Canadian or an American who had property in Canada. I am an American who has property in Canada, and also in the United States, which would give you the opportunity of settling in either of these countries. I should like very much to meet you, and if we did not suit each other, I, like a friendly husband, could choose a partner for you who would be suitable, since I am a student of physiognomy, phrenology, palmistry and other sciences. There are very few women here. I will marry only for love, and for no other reason. There are people here who have seen you and know you, who think you are a miracle. They say you are about thirty years old. I am forty-nine. If we found, after having married, that we had made a mistake, I would do all in my power to arrange an amicable divorce. Send me your photograph and biography. I will do the same if you choose to try the novel kind of romance which I am proposing. Go to the American consul for further information if you are interested, and in this way you will do a great favor to the friend who sends you his invitation.

(signature)
Saskatchewan, Canada.

"What do you think of this?" asked the ambassador.

"How do you mean? Write him a letter, refusing and thanking him."

"But you don't want to consider the proposal seriously?"

I burst out laughing.

"What do you see funny in this?" asked the ambassador, sounding a bit offended.

"Pardon me, but one thing seems funny, that I might get married at my age; I am already forty-eight. And then too, what a funny idea to write to a complete stranger!"

"But I still don't understand you; this would be a way out of your situation, and he suggests that in case you don't suit each other he will immediately give you a divorce."

But the ambassador could not convince me. I took the letter home and answered the Canadian, thanking him for his proposal but saying it was impossible for me to take advantage of it.

At about this time a good friend of my sister Tanya arrived from

Europe: Madame M.,* a very nice, lively, well-educated native of Luxembourg, a pleasant person. She had promised my sister to look me up and find out how she could help me, and she immediately offered me some money. I said that at present we had no visas, but that if we did receive them I should very much like her to lend me enough for the three of us to travel third class to America.

Finally, at the end of April 1931, we were summoned to the American consulate. They handed us an "Affidavit re: Unavailable Documents." This consisted of documents on plain white paper, which we should sign, in which it was stated that the papers were issued to us in place of passports, which we did not have because we did not recognize the present regime in our native country, Russia.

It seemed as if our difficulties were over, but this was not the case. When we ordered third-class tickets to San Francisco on the Nippon Yusen Kaisha line, the company refused to make reservations:

> Our Hong Kong office received an order from the United States Consul General in Hong Kong on June 2, 1931, stating that immigrants who receive U.S. visas must have sufficient resources to support themselves for the rest of their lives; and that only persons who present concrete evidence that they are financially independent and will not look for gainful occupation may receive permission to go to the United States.

Again dismay, bothering American friends and the American consul.

"They are afraid," a Japanese friend said to us, "they are *very* much afraid. You go to America. In America they ask: does Madame Tolstoy have money? No, she does not. Madame Tolstoy returns. Madame Olga, Mademoiselle Maria, all go back to Japan. And who brings them back? Steamship company. No money, so it takes them free, it loses money. They are afraid. But we go on petitioning, make more requests." And we resumed the endless petitioning. Then finally all the obstacles disappeared. Madame

---

*Exact names for some of the people Alexandra met are impossible to trace. The editors have therefore decided to use initials in these cases.

M. gave us seven hundred and fifty dollars, out of which we paid six hundred for the tickets.

We boarded the steamship. Confetti flew through the air, they threw us garlands of flowers made of different colored paper, we hung on to them—our last real contact with this splendid country, which had given us the chance to live happily in it for twenty months. The third blast on the ship's horn, the paper chain breaks. A group of Japanese men and women waved to us, many had tears in their eyes, yes, and we too came very near crying.

Goodbye, kind and beautiful Japan, goodbye dear Japanese friends. We will never forget you.

Calm weather, a cloudless sky, a quiet sea. The ship slowly pulled away.

What was awaiting us now?

CHAPTER TWENTY-EIGHT

How Pineapples Grow

It was not bad aboard the ship, the something Maru. A cabin for four, a bathroom adjoining, salt water. Clean on deck, a heterogeneous crowd, the majority Japanese or Filipinos. There were few Europeans in our third class, and two Russian businessmen from China.

Very quickly half the journey was over.

Land. Honolulu. Dark-skinned, slender men wearing only shorts, superbly built and as agile as monkeys, clambered aboard the ship. First-class passengers threw coins into the sea. The Hawaiians dove into the ocean like ducks and within seconds swam up with the coins between their teeth. On the shore a number of large, rather plain women had lined up, adorned with garlands of flowers and looking like a flock of birds. We hardly had time to look before the women draped flower leis over us, the cloying scent of which made our heads swim.

Warm but not sultry; one breathed easily, free and happy in spirit, with nothing oppressive, the future ahead, and meanwhile twelve hours on land at one's disposal to see everything one could in this paradise, and a chance to swim. We found bathing suits for rent on the beach. The water was warm, the caressing waves rolled by, one after the other. Young people slid over the waves on water skis, sail boats, yachts moved in the distance, and along the shore the fronds of palm trees gave out a harsh rustle. "Bananas, real bananas," shouted Maria in ecstasy, "red bananas . . . and what is that?" It was a mango, very sweet, almost too luscious.

Leaving the sea behind, we had a keen desire to see how pineapples grow. Seeing a policeman we asked how far it was to a pineapple plantation. The policeman was surprised, but nevertheless explained to us very politely that one had to take a street car to the edge of town, and then walk six miles. A long way, but we wanted so much to see how pineapples grow. There would not be another such chance in our lifetime.

We walked for a long time. Rain fell. It would sprinkle, then stop within a minute, then start again. We would get wet and quickly dry out in the hot sun. We must have gone three miles when we saw a farm on the right side of the highway, a house, and cows grazing in a field next to it. We decided to go in and ask whether it was very much farther to a pineapple plantation. We had only begun to approach the house when a pack of dogs rushed out, each one different, black, white, small, large, shaggy, smooth-coated, some with drooping and some with pointed ears. We stopped.

A woman came out of the house and asked, "What can I do for you?"

"We would like to see how pineapples grow," we said timidly. "You don't raise pineapples?"

She laughed.

"No, my farm produces milk. The pineapple plantations are

much, much farther, you may not make it. Three miles anyway from here."

"But we want very much to see one."

"Then go straight on along the highway."

We thanked her and wandered on. Maria was already tired, but we stubbornly kept on walking. Several automobiles passed us. One of them stopped.

"Hello!" In the car sat a lady who looked very much like the one on the milk farm, only somewhat younger. "My sister told me that two ladies with a girl want to see how pineapples grow, and I decided to give you a lift."

We overwhelmed her with thanks, climbed into the automobile, and sped off. It was the first time in my life I had seen a woman driving a car.

"Who are you? Where from?" asked the lady. We replied that we were just now coming from Japan, but were Russian refugees bound for America.

"That's a coincidence," she said. "For I have just finished a book by the Russian author Tolstoy—*Anna Karenina*. You probably know it?"

"Yes," I said, "I have read it many times, the book was written by my father."

"What? What do you say?"

The brakes screeched and the machine stopped abruptly. The lady turned and looked directly at me with her gentle gray eyes. "What? Here in Honolulu I meet a woman on the road who wants to see how pineapples grow, and she turns out to be the daughter of the man whose book I have just finished reading and which I admire so! This is amazing, most amazing!" I even felt she did not believe me at first.

We talked. By evening we already knew one another, who was who and from where, and passed such an interesting day that it long remained in our memory.

The pineapple plants were like big artichokes with sharp, prickly leaves. And I had thought that pineapples came from large, beautiful bushes! We were disappointed. But how many there were! Acres and acres. They grew in as much profusion here as do cabbages or potatoes with us.

The kind American lady then took us to a sugarcane plantation, from there to a sugar factory, and we ended the day with the factory director, who served us tea.

The next morning we sailed away. Our cabin was adorned with whole branches of bananas, with fragrant mangos and pineapples, as sweet as sugar, which we had bought for a song.

Goodbye, Honolulu, marvelous city! Goodbye, dear American lady! She was my first experience of the kindness and hospitality that I later came to know so well in the United States.

CHAPTER TWENTY-NINE

Landing in America

In San Francisco we were met by a representative of my lecture manager, Mr. Feakins, with whom Jane Addams* had corresponded about my lectures.

Many years ago, when I was only eleven, Jane Addams had visited my father. I could remember her only hazily; but when I was in Japan I asked her by letter if she could arrange some way for me to earn money in America; it seemed to me that the best and perhaps the only way I could do this, except by simple physical labor, would be by giving lectures about my father and Soviet Russia.

Mrs. Stevenson, who met me, was a very pleasant, active American of about fifty, whose intelligent, lively, dark eyes spar-

---

*Jane Addams (1860–1935) was a distinguished social worker who in 1889 founded Hull House in Chicago, one of the first social settlements in the United States. In 1931 she was awarded the Nobel Peace Prize.

kled with humor or perhaps amusement on perceiving such wild Russians in their odd get-ups, which in no way suited conventional Americans. Probably she had never met a lecturer so poorly dressed, traveling in third class. But her embarrassment was plain when it developed that they would not let us disembark immediately, as they did all the others, but took us to Angel Island.

We were indignant. Why such unfairness? Why are they sending us to that island when they let the first- and second-class passengers go directly ashore?

They explained to us that everyone coming from Japan by third class is inspected for worms. In Japan, because the fields are fertilized with human manure, very often people are infected with worms, so before letting immigrants go ashore the American authorities must be convinced that they are not worm carriers.

But why would worms not dare to make the acquaintance of rich people, but instead prefer to live with third-class passengers, I asked. No one was able to answer that question for me, not even Mrs. Stevenson.

A small steamship took us to Angel Island. In the distance was what looked like a little round island—the Alcatraz prison.

A one-story house. Clean rooms, beds neatly made, no speck of dust. But bars over the windows. "Like being in jail," I thought. A nurse brought in three chamber pots.

"Mama, but I don't need it," squealed Maria.

None of us needed it. But that did not make it any easier. It was very tiresome. I went outside. A steep bank, like a breakwater. Fishermen. I had hardly time to approach them when I saw one of the anglers pulling out a huge salmon. My fisherman's soul jumped for joy. I went closer to have a look.

"Back!" cried one of the guards. "Don't go near the water."

"But why? I'm not arrested."

"Go back! You're not allowed to go near the sea."

I felt bitter. I remembered Soviet Russia. But well, we are still not in America, I consoled myself.

"Mama, what are they going to do, hold us here the whole day?" asked Maria. "My stomach is never going to work."

We were very dejected. Though Olga and I kept silent, we felt the same as Maria.

Finally we passed the first examination—we were clean and could not infect the United States with worms! But our troubles were far from over.

They tested our eyes. They made us read letters and words. Olga and Maria passed the examination easily, but it was a bit more complicated with me. "But you can hardly see anything," the doctor said. "How are you going to make a living?" "I will write, and give lectures." "Yes . . . well, perhaps your vision is good enough for that." He let me through.

But even this was not all. The immigration authorities had to be convinced that I would not infect the country with Bolshevism.

Well now, everything will go simply and easily, I thought. I came to America to fight Communism, to give lectures against the Bolsheviks, and of course they understand this and will let me through right away.

But it was not like that. At first the official who questioned me was very severe. "I don't understand," he said, "why, if you are so opposed to Bolshevism, you lived freely in Soviet Russia for twelve years and the Bolsheviks never touched you!"

I had to tell him how I was arrested five times, how Lenin helped me,* and how a decree was issued to the effect that the Tolstoy institutions should remain free of antireligious propaganda in memory of Leo Tolstoy.

"Then how did it happen that they finally let you go?"

I told him how I was able to outwit the authorities, promising to return within a few months, saying that, as director of the Yasnaya Polyana Experimental Station, I had to study schools in Japan and America. I described the life of the Russian peasants and workers, and the massive repressions. I talked for about two hours. This was the first and perhaps the most difficult lecture that I ever gave in America.

---

* Lenin helped through the decree of the Praesidium of the Central Executive Committee concerning Yasnaya Polyana, signed by Kalinin (see p. 138). This decree gave Alexandra official sanction for her development of Yasnaya Polyana.

The longer I talked, the more intensely the official questioned me. By now he was not alone but had called in his assistant, who also listened to my tale with the greatest interest. When I finished, both smiled. "Now I will admit," said the senior official, "that I never heard anything more interesting. You have acquainted me, as no one else has, with the real situation in the Soviet Union. I am glad that you reached the USA, and hope things go well for you in this country, and that you will be able to clarify the question of Communism for our people. But one last question," he added, pausing. "Do you wish to declare your intention of becoming an American citizen and take out first papers?"

"No," I said, and felt at that moment that I had done something terrible. Now I'm lost, they won't let me in, I thought.

"What? Why don't you want to become a citizen?" he asked severely. "Do you have a poor opinion of our country?"

"No, no," I hastened to say. "But how can I declare my intention of becoming a citizen now, when in my soul I am still Russian, I live for the best interests of my country, I still hope that maybe two, three, or ten years will go by, but that the Bolsheviks will be finished then and I can return to Russia? How can I deceive your government? Take out papers, become a citizen, and then return to my country? No, I can't do that. When I have lived in and grown used to this country, gotten to know it, love it as my own, then and only then will I declare my intention of becoming an American citizen."

I stopped. The official too was silent. Then he turned to his assistant. "What do you think of this?"

"The question was answered in a most original manner, but from her standpoint she is right," the assistant said. "I wish everyone who came into our country would take the matter as seriously as she does."

"I think the same," said the chief officer.

And so we stepped onto American soil—legally. America had accepted us. Mrs. Stevenson took us to a first-class hotel, paid for by my manager. This was at the beginning of September 1931.

PART FOUR

First Steps in America:
1931-1939

CHAPTER ONE

San Francisco

In San Francisco my manager, Mr. Feakins, sent his representative, Mrs. Stevenson, to meet us. After talking with her, I realized that the depression had curtailed the chance of any substantial earnings from lectures. Unemployment had touched not only the working class but also the well-to-do and the intelligentsia. Everywhere Americans were having to be close-fisted. Women's clubs and similar organizations were cutting down or canceling their plans for such events. Mrs. Stevenson could arrange for only one about my father in the San Francisco Town Hall.

This was a daunting discovery. In Japan, through my sister Tatiana,* I had been lent the sum of seven hundred and fifty dollars toward traveling expenses by Madame M. Little remained of this. Yet I was in urgent need of clothes in order to appear anywhere. I had to buy a coat, hat, gloves, and shoes at once. Anxiously I went shopping. Finally I acquired a black silk dress with a stylish neck, shoes, a coat with a dyed fur collar, and a brown hat to match.

Outside the store disaster struck. A gust of wind blew off the precious hat and cast it into the street. I rushed to save it, almost falling under a car, its brakes screeching. All traffic stopped. The drivers swore at me. I saw only the hat. For a second its mad dash was checked. Just as I was about to grab it, the wind gusted again, and the wretched thing rolled on directly in front of a car. Instantly there was not a hat but a pancake. I smoothed it out as

*Tatiana was my eldest sister. A widow at the time of the Revolution, she had escaped to Italy with her daughter. Tatiana died in Rome in 1950 (ALT).

well as I could, dusted it off, and set it back on my head. Impossible to buy a new one. But could I lecture in it? In those days, all women wore hats.

Somehow, some way, I had to earn some money. For sixty dollars we rented a three-room apartment. Maria registered in a public school. Olga was invited by some Molokans,* who lived on one of the hills in San Francisco, to teach Russian to their children.

The extraordinary contrast between the older and younger generations of Molokans surprised me very much. The elders were huge, bearded, handsome, and serene, holding fast to their faith, neither smoking nor drinking; the women wore kerchiefs, were plump from fatty cabbage soup and tarts. The young girls, however, had rouged lips and painted nails; the young men smoked cigarettes.

"Come with me, sister," said a Molokan with shoulders as wide as a door. "I will show you how we live. I have a new car. I've bought my house on installments. I've already paid for up-to-date furniture."

One evening there was a gathering in the apartment of a Molokan. I was invited to tell them about Russia. Since I knew that they had been peasants in the past, I tried to throw light on how difficult it was then for peasants in Soviet Russia. I described the collective farms, how the farmers were not allowed to consume their own produce or sell their surplus; I told of the prohibition against moving from one place to another, or going to the city to earn something. When I closed, some young people jumped up to argue.

After two years away from Soviet Russia, I had grown unaccustomed to these commonplace agitators. Excited, smoking one cigarette after another, they set forth how everything I had said was untrue. The peasants had never lived so well as today. The peo-

*The Molokans (from *moloko*, meaning milk) were one of the many anti-Orthodox sects that proliferated in recent centuries in Russia. They drank milk during Lent, unlike the Orthodox, and had been extremely puritanical in Russia. They revered only the Old and New Testaments—all subsequent theology was meaningless to them. They derived from the Dukhobors, a sect Leo Tolstoy helped emigrate to Canada through the proceeds from his book *Resurrection*.

ple had liberated themselves from the tsarists and the landowners who had exploited the working class. The people are free, they said, the Soviet government furnishes the collective farms with all necessary machinery.

It at once came back to me how barrels of molasses used to be carried over a bridge in Moscow across the Moscow River. Once one barrel split open as it fell onto the pavement. Immediately dozens of persons threw themselves onto the oozing molasses. They scraped it off the pavement into little cups, or even into their hands, swallowing it on the spot.

Olga began her lessons on the hill where the Molokans lived, and every day she came back tired and upset. "You can't imagine," she said, "what these children are like. Undisciplined, spoiled, they swear, they spit during lessons. At the same time the girls paint their nails and the boys smoke."

All this was very strange to me. Nothing of the kind existed in the Russia we knew. I did not think I would ever be obliged to do anything with these youngsters, but once Olga turned her ankle. In order not to lose her salary, I set off for the Molokans' hill to teach the children.

We began with dictation, but I had not pronounced the first sentence before a boy on the back bench with great dexterity suddenly flung a piece of chewing gum against the wall. I reprimanded him—he did it a second time, a third time. A nutshell came flying at me.

Then I took one of the boys and two of the girls who were guilty of all this, and after shaking them by the collar, I threw them out of the door. The noise stopped. I went on with the dictation. When Olga recovered and could resume her duties, I was very glad.

Olga would say to the parents, "You're too restrained with them; give them a good thrashing, that's what they do in American schools—how else can you manage them? The other teacher knew better how to handle them." She did not know that corporal punishment of students had been done away with in America.

The children complained of me to Olga: "Don't you let that fat one come here any more, she fights."

I must admit that in San Francisco I was struck with the behavior of the young. Never had I seen anything like it, for in Soviet Russia, though many women smoked, to smoke on the streets or to embrace in the parks or in automobiles was unheard of. Not even in Japan had I seen a single woman smoking. And there kissing in public was considered the height of indecency. In America there was certainly another code. "A port city," I thought, "perhaps it's different elsewhere." All this was bewildering a generation ago.

CHAPTER TWO

San Quentin

Mrs. Stevenson introduced us to John Barry, a man of about fifty, a correspondent of a San Francisco newspaper and a radio commentator. We became very good friends. He often dropped in, to ask us questions about Soviet Russia and our former life. He may have used some of our information either in the press or on radio. At this time I was preparing a lecture for the San Francisco Town Hall. Striking a pose, I would repeat and repeat. Poor Olga did not know how to escape. She closed the doors, but the apartment was small, everything could be heard. Moreover, Mr. Barry took on the task of teaching me speechmaking. For hours on end I crammed, like a student, again and again repeating one sentence after another.

The day of the lecture at last arrived. The place was crowded. In the first row sat my teacher, John Barry. This was not in the least conducive to composure. I was so frightened that I do not remember what I said. In my agitation I forgot all his instructions. The audience kept applauding, I kept bowing. John Barry said it wasn't so bad, but I had not addressed the last rows, as he had taught me, only the first rows. Several times I had said "it" at the end of a sentence.

Often he took us around the city to acquaint us with life in America. "Would you like to visit an American prison?" he asked me.

"Yes, it would be very interesting to compare American jails with the Soviet variety, where I spent some time."

The next day we went to San Quentin. As one of America's largest prisons, it was very interesting to me. The gray buildings were tremendous. There were not many guards around them, considerably fewer than in the Soviet Union. They seemed clean. Most of the inmates went to work daily.

We were led into a sort of office-reception room, and several prisoners were brought in. They were told that I came from Soviet Russia, that I was the daughter of a great Russian writer, Tolstoy, and that they might ask me some questions. As always happened, they did not know where to begin. They stood first on one foot, then another, and everybody felt uncomfortable.

"I know," I said, "how difficult, how painful, it is to look at the same wall, study the same cracks and scratches on that wall, and to know that every day the same routine will be repeated, every day you will see the same people who will tell you the same things, every day you will see the same bit of sky from your cell."

"But how do you know this?" one of the older prisoners interrupted.

"Because I experienced it all," I replied, "I was in prison under the Bolsheviks."

"Well, that means you're a fellow jailbird," said an elderly chap, clapping me on the shoulder. The ice was broken. The prisoners interrupting one another, asked me questions. Why had they put me in jail? How long did I stay there? What was the prison regimen like? How did they feed us?

"In the morning," I told them, "a half pound of soggy bread and chaff, which had to last the whole day. Watery tea. Dinner was soup made out of frozen potato peelings, unwashed, so that we had to wait for the dirt to sink to the bottom of the dish before eating it. And dried Caspian roach!"*

I had to explain what this fish was and how one had to beat it before one could eat it. "For supper sometimes the same dirty soup, sometimes millet gruel with no butter. And that was all."

The prisoners looked at one another. "We sometimes even get ice cream on Sundays."

"And how were the beds?"

"No regular beds. Three planks, badly put together. Skimpy mattresses stuffed with wood chips, which would sink down between the cracks and cut into you. That hurt. I used to put a pillow under my side, to avoid getting bed sores."

"And we have comfortable beds," said the prisoners.

"Still, life is over for us," said a very young blond lad with naive, sad, blue eyes, blushing deeply. "I studied, I went to college, now I have to serve time for three years. My youth goes by, I'm out of the habit of working, my life is ruined."

"Your life is not ruined," I protested. "Of course I don't know what you have on your conscience."

"I forged a check," the boy said simply.

"Well, then, you see, we all stumble in life, even fall down. But that doesn't necessarily mean that we stay down. You fell— but why can't you change your life for the better, begin to walk with a firm step, try not to stumble in future? Make good use of this period. I knew a wonderful boy in Moscow who was sentenced to jail for five years, only because he was a prince. During his five years he completed a full university course. Why don't you do the same? Go on with your studies so you can take examinations later?"

We parted friends. The lad kept shaking my hand. "I promise you, I will study, I give you my word." Evidently, he needed to give his word for his own self-assurance.

It was already twelve o'clock. We went into the women's dining room. It was clean and bright. They were serving soup and some

---

*A very cheap coarse fish called *vobla*.

kind of meat with vegetables as a second course. Like a restaurant, I thought, remembering Soviet jails.

We were allowed to visit some cells of prisoners with life sentences. One struck me especially. A clean, light little room. A canary was warbling at a barred window. Everywhere books, a multitude of books. The bed, clean and comfortable. The occupant was a very young girl, sentenced to life for murder. I tried to talk with her. No answer. By her compressed lips, her bitter, hostile expression we understood that our visit was unwelcome.

Afterward, John Barry told me that a number of the men I had talked to that morning had asked permission for me to give a lecture that evening to a larger group of prisoners, but that the supervisor had not allowed it.

CHAPTER THREE

Salt Lake City

A little money had accumulated from my lecture and Olga's lessons, so we moved east of California. I was to give a talk in Salt Lake City to the Mormons. On the money to be received from this appearance, we planned to go on to Chicago, where two more engagements awaited me and where I was invited to stay with Jane Addams. Olga and Maria were to continue to Philadelphia, where an American lady and her niece had promised room and board in exchange for household work.

Salt Lake City is a very special town. Located near a large lake with deadly dull, salt shores, it contains one of the largest temples in the world, the Tabernacle, with a huge organ. My imagination had pictured these strong if terrifying people led by their founders, Joseph Smith and Brigham Young, overcoming all sorts of hardships in their struggle with nature and the rest of humanity. Theirs was called the Church of Jesus Christ. While professing Christianity, they accepted polygamy, until it was finally prohibited in accordance with the law of the United States.

We were met by a short, energetic, elderly lady with smooth hair. She was Susa Young Gates, then one of the still living younger children of the fifty-six born to Brigham Young. She won our hearts at once, she was so kind, affectionate, and interesting. She took us to various beautiful historic spots, showed us the house where she was born, where once there lived the seventeen wives and fifty-six children of her father.

"Did the wives quarrel?" I asked.

"No, they lived in peace. Though actually, I was still very small then and I don't remember much."

It interested me to know to what extent the young people lived up to the Mormon prohibition of smoking and drinking. The answer was not long in coming. When we were returning by train from a trip with Mrs. Gates a young man of about twenty entered our compartment and sat down. He knew Mrs. Gates, and they exchanged a few words. He came from a Mormon family, and Mrs. Gates had known his father. Suddenly she leaned toward him. "Let me smell your breath!" she cried. "You smell of tobacco! And you a Mormon! Get out of here, I don't want to see you!" He left, his head hanging.

The Mormon temple had a capacity of two or three thousand people. The pulpit was elevated. I had never seen one like it. Looking down, I saw a tremendous crowd. It was frightening. Then the organ struck up "God Save the Tsar," and my fear left. They are playing our national hymn for me, a Russian, I thought, how good of them! Then the organ played "Ochie chorniye." * "Dark eyes, passionate eyes, fiery eyes and beautiful," I sang to myself. Does the Mormon pastor know the words, does he know it is a gypsy song heard in all Russian cabarets? I was no longer

* *Dark Eyes*, a song known to every gypsy violinist in Europe and the United States.

afraid. I concentrated on my subject, "Tolstoy and the Russian Revolution."

In the *Minneapolis Tribune* this paragraph appeared:

The tremendous economic and political experiment in Soviet Russia must eventually collapse, since it is founded on purely materialistic conceptions and moves by force alone, declared Countess Tolstoy, daughter of the great Russian writer, Count Leo Tolstoy.

CHAPTER FOUR

Chicago and Hull House

I reached Chicago in the evening. The taxi driver helped me to drag my numerous pieces of luggage into the large entrance hall of Hull House. Immediately I was surrounded by a group of elderly women. I could not figure out at first who was who. Miss Rose Smith, the director, told me that her friend Jane Addams was not there just then but that she was delighted to have me as her guest and looked forward to meeting me.

From the moment I saw her I fell in love with Rose Smith. Her face was beautiful, serene, with almost classical features. She had lovely, tender gray eyes and naturally wavy silver hair. Tall, she moved with grace. Evidently everyone adored her—Annie the maid, and another Miss Smith named Eleanor, the cook, and the rest. Eleanor was quite different from Rose, also tall but heavy; she had large blunt features and a deep rumbling voice.

"We must leave your things here until tomorrow," said Rose Smith. "Tomorrow the furnace man will come to make the fire and he will carry them all up for you. Meanwhile Annie will take whatever you need upstairs for the night. Come, I will show you your room."

As Annie climbed the stairs, I saw that she was breathing heavily, asthmatically.

After tidying, I descended. My things lay in a jumbled heap in the hall, Russian carry-alls, Japanese baskets, old suitcases. I decided to rid the hall at once of this clutter. Shouldering a heavy suitcase, I carried it upstairs. When I came down again, all the old ladies had gathered in the hall. Annie had seen what I was doing, ran for the cook, then both Rose and Eleanor Smith appeared.

"Leave them here, why are you doing this?" cried Rose Smith in dismay. "I never saw such a thing, she is doing a man's work, this is terrible," protested Eleanor Smith.

They watched me until I had carried everything away, hoisting them one by one on my shoulder, much amused at their astonishment.

The next day I met Jane Addams. "Why, I remember you as a child with braids in Yasnaya Polyana, where I saw your father. You were eleven then," she said. "You ran into the room while we were talking. Your father said, 'This is my youngest, Sasha.'" We both laughed.

Miss Addams asked me what arrangements I planned for living in America, offering any possible assistance. She lived in Hull House in a not very large apartment of her own. To me it seemed rather dark, the furniture antique and somewhat worn. A fire was burning. I soon understood what an influence she had on those around her. Her word was law. Without giving orders, she managed people. Hull House *was* Jane Addams, and Jane Addams, Hull House. Nor was this her sole domain. Rose and Eleanor Smith lived only for Jane Addams.

Very soon I realized that Miss Addams and I disagreed on politics. I felt she was disappointed in me as the daughter of a great humanitarian and liberal. I did not hide my convictions. My father's pacifism, his love for people, his desire to improve their lot represented a religious philosophy formed over the years. If some violence should be done away with, then so should all violence.

Pacifism can mean only the pacifism founded on Christ's words, "Do not kill." It was my belief at that time that the Soviet government talked of pacifism only because it was not prepared for war, and it hoped thus to trap naive American liberals. In America at this time there was a movement of sympathy for the Revolution, especially among the intelligentsia. Miss Addams' clever, lively eyes clouded when I made several observations of this kind.

She thought that, despite the imperfections of the Communist regime, the road to a new freedom had been opened up, that the Revolution deserved credit for having overthrown the monarchy and having deprived the landowners and capitalists of the means of exploiting the workers and peasants, and that the greatest merit of the Bolsheviks was their striving for peace. It was necessary to achieve peace at all costs. As for United States recognition of the Soviet government, there could be no question; from her point of view, this was essential, for it would guarantee peace.

I comprehended very quickly that it would be impossible to convince Jane Addams of the contrary, to make her understand the horrors of Bolshevism. She was surrounded by a tight circle of professors, scholars, archetypes of the liberal and the pacifist. Eleanor Smith told me how Catherine Breshko-Breshkovsky, "the little grandmother (*babushka*) of the Russian Revolution,"* had come to Hull House. While she was living there, she censured Communism right and left. It was arranged for her to lecture on behalf of Hull House and its wards.

"Then something awful happened," Eleanor told me, laughing. "On hearing that Grandmother was going to speak against Bolshevism, a terrible racket arose in the hall. The crowd became frenzied, they screamed, people jumped from their seats and rushed onto the stage. If it had not been for Jane Addams, it would have

---

*Catherine Breshko-Breshkovsky (1844–1934), who came from a noble family, was famed as an organizer of the Populist movement and the Socialist Revolutionary Party. She was an early supporter of methods of terror against tsarism. She began the education of the peasants and other social reforms on her father's estates. After more than thirty years of imprisonment and exile in Siberia as a result of her reform work, she was released by Kerensky after the Revolution of 1917, and she fought the new regime. Going into exile, she was active in anti-Soviet campaigns.

gone badly with Grandmother. She was led off the stage and never delivered her lecture."

I was glad I was not living in this ideological environment at Hull House. I sat in Rose Smith's apartment and wrote about my life in prison.

Eleanor Smith was a good pianist. Her task at Hull House was giving free music lessons to poor children. I happened to say to her that music always inspired my father, especially that of Chopin, and that I had the same taste. When influenced by music, one's thoughts are higher, clearer, one's images are brighter. After that she played for me each morning, mostly Chopin and Mozart, while I was writing.

It was a long, long time since I had lived in such quiet, such comfort and cosiness. My room was tidied, excellent food was served on time. Beautifully trained servants moved about the house. They had been there for years, growing old along with their mistress. All this time I was writing. Sometimes my hostesses helped me search for English expressions, for I was writing in English.*

Once, however, we found ourselves at a loss. In a certain chapter of my book I was describing the filthy swearing and fighting between two prostitutes in the prison camp where I was confined. Though I had learned the entire lexicon of obscenity in Russian jails, I was ignorant of English profanity. The old ladies exchanged glances, as helpless as I. When we asked the furnace man, he laughed, covering his mouth with his hand, and muttered, "Perhaps bitch is good enough." So "bitch" went into the book.

In the evening I would read to the old ladies what I had written. Eleanor would quietly wipe away her tears. She often helped correct my English. Jane Addams also read my accounts of prison and discussed with several journalists the question of publishing them.

There is an end to everything in this world, however. My bliss-

---

*I Worked for the Soviet (New Haven: Yale University Press, 1934). Parts of this memoir, dealing mainly with the prison experiences and school at Yasnaya Polyana, make up part 2 of the present volume.

ful life in Chicago came to an end too. I bought a railroad ticket with the proceeds from my lectures. Saying goodbye to my dear friends, I moved on to Philadelphia.

CHAPTER FIVE

New York and the Settlement House

No, no, not four or six but exactly five," a housekeeper in Philadelphia told Olga. "If there are four holes, too little powder comes out, and if six or seven, too much, you waste it. Trust me, five are exactly right." Obediently, Olga took the can of scouring powder and punched five holes. All day either Mrs. X. or her emaciated niece, an old maid with pursed lips, reprimanded Maria. "Don't stoop, hold yourself straight. Maria, you eat too fast, we don't eat that way here. . . . Don't rock back and forth in your chair. . . . Put your books away."

Not only Maria but also we grown-ups had something to learn. Mrs. X.'s system of housekeeping was worked out with extraordinary precision. Not a superfluous movement. We had to learn how to make an American bed. In Russia the pillow is covered with a pillow sham. Here it was done differently. Here the table had to be set in another way; we had to know how many and what kind of plates to put out, on which side to lay knives, forks, and spoons. We disorderly Russians found all this impossible to master and were unable to develop much interest in these new areas.

Olga and her daughter Maria were provided with food and a room with bath. It was taken for granted that there was no salary. The work did not go easily. Most of the time I was away on lecture tours, but occasionally on my return I saw how hard it was for Olga, not so much physically as psychologically. We began to dream of having our own place.

My next lecture was in Town Hall in New York, where I stayed for a while. On Jane Addams' recommendation to her friend Lillian Wald,* I took quarters in the Henry Street Settlement House in the poorest Jewish district. Everywhere there were bazaars and peddlers' barrows with all kinds of vegetables, fruit, the cheap necessities of life. There was a general smell of onions and garlic. Not only Yiddish but also Russian words were sometimes heard. Dirt and poverty prevailed.

When someone spoke to me in Russian, I was pleased, but I soon understood that here many Jews did not know that it was the Provisional Government** that had done away with the Pale of Settlement, confining Jews to specific provinces in the west of Russia, as well as with the quota restriction on Jewish students. They believed the Bolsheviks had done all this. I ran into the same pro-Soviet ideas in the Henry Street Settlement House as in Hull House. Lillian Wald made me tell her many things about Soviet Russia. She would listen attentively, her dark intelligent eyes sometimes gazing in astonishment. "I never thought things were so bad."

New York depressed me. It was a long while since I had experienced such gnawing pangs of loneliness, worst of all amid a crowd of strangers. People, people, hurrying, cold, indifferent, with tired faces. I walked endless streets, rode the buses, got lost in the subways—always observing. The stamp of vice was already evident on some young faces. The hard experience of life had marked them before their youth had had time to bloom. Women smoked on the street, gum-chewers shoved one another at the subway stops. One stream of people gave way to another. Everyone in a rush. No one concerned for others. The faces worried, anxious. Could they have souls? It was frightening to me.

In the Henry Street Settlement it was less disturbing. Here

---

* Lillian D. Wald (1867–1940) was founder of the Nurses' Settlement on Henry Street in 1902. This was the first city nursing school in the world. She also originated the Federal Children's Bureau and expanded Red Cross Nursing.

** Established March 2, 1917, under Prince Georgi Lvov, a wealthy landowner and social reformer (see p. 19). He resigned on July 24, and Alexander Kerensky headed the government until the October Revolution of the Bolsheviks.

people were occupied with helping others, giving advice, taking a woman in childbirth to the hospital, visiting the critically ill, assisting children in their school work; but still loneliness would sometimes gnaw at me and, sitting alone in my room, I would cry. I cried at being torn from my native home, at the fact that Bolshevism had penetrated so deeply into free countries . . . and because everyone was foreign.

One day there was a knock at the door.

"May I come in?"

The tall broad-shouldered figure of a bearded man appeared. "Ilya!" *

"Well, well! Let me see you! Have you changed? Grown older? Oh, still nothing to mention, good girl. How did you manage to find this slum?"

My brother overwhelmed me with questions, probably to hide his emotion. He so took my breath away that I could say nothing. It was twenty years since we had seen each other. He had gone to America before the Bolshevik Revolution. In all that time he had become even more like his father. The same gray eyes, only larger, the same wide brows, broad nose, heavy beard. Only the expressions of his face, his mouth, were different.

How to begin a conversation after a separation of twenty years? While he was still in Russia, I knew, he had formed a relationship with a woman whom he had married after a divorce from his previous wife. He was already sixty-five and lived here in New York with his wife Nadya. We spoke of Russia, the family, our relatives. The longer we talked, the closer we became. He had changed a good deal, grown wiser, more like his father in his convictions. We had no disagreements on the subject of Communism either. He hated it as much as I did. When we parted, he said simply:

"Sasha, I am very happy."

In the same tone, scarcely holding back tears of joy, I repeated:

* Ilya was my elder brother (1866–1933), my senior by eighteen years. When Hollywood filmed my father's book, *Resurrection*, he played the role of a cobbler who exactly resembled his father (ALT).

"I am very happy too."

We pressed each other's hands and he left. I no longer felt alone—I had a brother in New York.

CHAPTER SIX

The Lecture Circuit

M y manager, Mr. Feakins, was a most agreeable man, witty and jolly. Throwing his head back, he laughed heartily when I told him about John Barry and my lecture in Salt Lake City.

"I should like," he said, "to introduce you to a gentleman for whom you are to give a lecture in a very aristocratic New York suburb. He is extremely demanding, this man. He questioned me at length about your personality, as to whether you could give an accurate picture of life in Soviet Russia, and whether you had a good command of English. He has not quite made up his mind to invite you, because the fee is fairly high, and he wants to be sure that you will suit him."

A meeting was arranged. Mr. N. proved to be a portly, elderly individual with a smooth rosy face and a reddish-gray crew cut. We met in Mr. Feakins' office and went out to lunch.

"Don't cross the street until the green light comes on," he instructed me. "Here, quickly now, we have to hurry, the green light shows for only half a minute on side streets. Quick, cross over, or they'll run over us."

"What a peculiar man," I thought, "why is he so excited?"

In the restaurant the food stuck in my throat. Mr. N. stared at me with piercing eyes. All during the meal he turned me inside out with his questions about my life, my opinions, my habits, plans for the future. Later my manager, Mr. Feakins, described with amusement how he had gone to hear me at Town Hall. Only then did he decide to invite me to give a talk at his club.

"Now then, just try, do your best, speak loud, because there will be deaf people in the audience, and don't hurry. Give a picture of Soviet life." A well-built man said this as I was about to go on the stage. I am always nervous before an appearance, especially at the beginning. Now I was so scared I trembled all over. Mr. N. introduced me as a "brilliant" speaker who handled the English language beautifully. This sort of description always has a very bad effect on me.

From my opening words, I felt I was a failure. To get back on my track, I looked at my notes, my hands shook, and there were dark spots before my eyes. The lines on the paper jumped about. I could not make head or tail of anything. To gain time, I kept repeating, "Well . . ." Mr. N. was sitting in the front row and never took his eyes off me. During the question and answer period, I did recover somewhat.

A real fiasco. I decided that my career as a lecturer was buried for all time. What a surprise, when a few days later I received the following letter from Mr. N.:

Dear Countess:

I had not expected to let a whole week go by without writing you to say what very great pleasure your listeners derived from your lecture last Thursday in Summit. The Directors of the Athenaeum even criticized me for not leaving enough time for questions after your speech.

The accuracy of your statements and your understanding of the situation in Russia were most instructive. Many people told me how much they enjoyed and benefited by your report.

And this morning I met a friend on the train who had lived for two years in Russia, and ever since has continued to follow carefully what happens there. He is an engineer, and in this capacity he has had occasion to come into contact with many officals. He agrees completely with your statements.

If you are interested in some press reactions to your presentation, I should be glad to send them to you.

Thanking you again for giving the members of the Athenaeum an opportunity to hear you, I remain,

Respectfully and devotedly yours,

[signature]

The next lecture was scheduled for a very elegant women's club in Summit. I pulled myself together, made preparations, put on my best clothes, and set off.

Only women were present. They were dressed simply but very well. The lecture hall was not large, seating three or four hundred, and it was full. A young lady sitting in the front row was knitting. This irritated me. If I am any good at all, you are going to stop knitting in front of me, I thought. This time the lecture was a success. When I remembered the lady in the front row, I saw that her work lay in her lap, she was bending forward, listening attentively.

The next lecture took place in Boston. Henry Wadsworth Longfellow Dana, grandson of the poet, had attended the celebration at Yasnaya Polyana in 1928* in honor of the hundredth anniversary of my father's birth. He had invited me to stay with him on the present occasion. He met me at the station and took me to his home in Cambridge, once the famous poet's, a magnificent house with large high rooms, antique furniture, and a huge library.

We chatted over a cup of tea while Mr. Dana reminisced about his trip in 1928 to Yasnaya Polyana with Stefan Zweig and other eminent visitors. When he said he planned to go again to Russia, I understood that he sympathized with the Soviet government. Once more the same pseudo-liberal judgments that drove me to despair. What have I got into, I thought. I felt ill at ease in that historic house. On his side, Mr. Dana was also disappointed, seeing in me such an implacable enemy of the Soviet regime. We immediately began a vigorous argument. The next day I decided that I would leave his place.

"I am going to your lecture at the Ford Auditorium,"** he said. "Be careful, or I will heckle you."

My theme was "Tolstoy and the Russian Revolution." The hall was filled to overflowing. It was a very heterogeneous crowd, intellectuals mingled with ordinary workmen. Presiding was a sixty-year-old minister, a rotund, ruddy, bald, benevolent man.

*See p. 163 above.
**The oldest forum for debating ideas in the United States.

The first part of the lecture, in which I told of my father's convictions, went smoothly. When I turned to the Communist "experiment," however, and described life in Russia after the Revolution and how the Bolsheviks distorted even Marx's theories, I felt that the audience was growing restless. I knew there were many socialists in the hall.

When I finished, a violent uproar broke out. Part of the audience applauded wildly, another part hissed, whistled, and shouted insulting epithets. The unfortunate minister bounced around the stage, not knowing how to calm the public. Then the question period began.

How many acres of land, how great a fortune did I have before the Revolution? Did I have the title of countess? Was it taken away? Were religious sects persecuted in old Russia? I gave answers.

One fellow jumped up, shouting rudely, spitefully, "Madam speaker, how do you explain the fact that you come from that famished land of Soviet Russia, as you call it, but are so well fed that you probably weigh two hundred pounds?"

The minister waved his arms. "I do not permit any questions here that touch on the personality of the speaker," he said.

"Allow me, I will answer," I rejoined. "This is why, comrade," I said laughingly. "From hungry Russia I went to capitalist Japan, where I spent twenty months. I have also been here, in another capitalist country, America, for several months now and have stuffed myself with capitalist food."

A roar broke out again. Part of the audience laughed boisterously, another part muttered. Another comrade rose and called out, "Madam speaker, kindly explain why we do not hear of gangsters, kidnappers, and all the other kinds of crooks in Soviet Russia, when there are so many here? How do you explain that?"

"Why, it's very simple, comrade," I answered. "In America they put criminals in jail, but in Soviet Russia they run the country."

Again an uproar, applause, laughter, catcalls. It was time to close. People climbed on the stage, some smiling sympathetically, others furious, their faces contorted in anger. From all sides they came, forming a closed circle about me. The little minister ran to me, pulled his hat down over my eyes, threw a coat over me, and shoved us through the crowd out onto the street. Mr. Dana followed us. "Why didn't you ask any questions? I was waiting for them," I said.

"There were enough questions without mine," he replied.

Although the lecture had gone well enough on the whole, I thought, still I felt depressed. I could not digest the idea, not only that the Western world was unable to rid itself of the Bolsheviks, but also that conditions in almost all the free countries were not encouraging. In America, depression. In all European countries, dissatisfaction. In England, hunger demonstrations organized by Communists. In Japan, terrorist killings, war with China, Manchuria occupied. In Spain, growing discontent. Naive to think that the Russian people could expect help from anywhere. Public opinion? Leaders? Famous writers like Stefan Zweig were flirting with Moscow, as were Bernard Shaw and Lady Astor. Romain Rolland found excuses for Bolshevism and violence by maintaining that people must be led against their will to happiness and prosperity.

Hope for deliverance in Russia had been my incentive. It had given an overriding meaning to my life. Gradually, it evaporated. The Western church, Protestant or Catholic? Only the Catholic Church carried on its struggle against Bolshevism. I was glad on hearing that Pope Pius XI had decreed a week of prayer and fasting in opposition to Communism and atheism.

CHAPTER SEVEN

The Farm Near Philadelphia

Mrs. X. introduced us to the Makarovs. He was Russian, she American, a kind-hearted social worker who took part in the Neighborhood League activities. One day, when Olga and I were their guests, we mentioned how we dreamed of living somewhere on a farm, independently.

Some time passed. Suddenly and quite unexpectedly, Mrs. Makarov informed us, to our great delight, that through the Neighborhood League it would be possible to take over an old, run-down farm without paying a cent. No one was living there, and the owner would allow new occupants to do whatever they chose. It was situated near Newtown Square, not far from Philadelphia.

However, when we reached this farm, what we saw was beyond any conception of "run-down." All the windows in the house were broken. The floors had caved in. Dirt everywhere. The cobwebs had probably not been swept away in years. The tarpaper roof of the little hen roost was in shreds. The only thing left of the shed was three stone walls. Next to the house was a running spring, cold as ice, where, we learned later, milk was once kept cool. Concrete walls had once surrounded it, forming several sections, and evidently there had been a roof. Now only one wall remained, covered with moss.

The landscape seemed to us very poetical, the overgrown fields, the babbling brook below the hill, the few old trees around the house, woods in the distance. It was spring. Our hearts longed for the outdoors, for physical exercise, and even more for our own nook. So we moved with all our belongings to this "farm."

Putting in the windows, repairing the roof, cleaning the interior—all these were matters of the greatest urgency. Eagerly, we settled down to business. Since we ourselves could not cope with the carpentry, we asked Mrs. Makarov to send us a man to work by the day. At that time wages were low, and there was a prospect of getting such a man for five dollars a day. To us, however, even that seemed a fortune.

One morning at about eight o'clock—of course we had risen much earlier—a man drove up in a shining automobile. We were much surprised, as no one lived within a mile and a half of us. "What can we do for you?" I asked.

"How do you mean, what can you do for me?" He was surprised in turn. "I thought you wanted me to do a job for you. If I am not mistaken, this is the place, and you are the Russian ladies of whom Mrs. Makarov spoke."

We were overjoyed. He worked unusually quickly and conscientiously. Soon our home began to look lived in. The windows were in place. Some sort of furniture made its appearance, donated by Mrs. X. and the Neighborhood League. Rose Smith, Jane Addams' friend, sent us beds, rugs, and armchairs from a country house she was liquidating.

We began to cultivate the vegetable garden. As we had no sort of plow, we did our digging by hand. The whole garden was full of large rocks. It was hard to bury them in the ground, for the stony soil did not let us dig down very far. To lift those great rocks, we had to use a lever, gradually shoving small stones under a large one until it rolled over. It was the work of Sisyphus, but we surmounted it and planted our garden.

Sometimes, though rarely, someone wandered into our domain. "Do you know where Countess Tolstoy lives near here? Where is she now? Is it possible to see her?"

At this point I was struggling with stones, heaving and digging, soaked with perspiration, and very scantily clad. "I don't know," I muttered, "there is no countess here."

Sometimes elegant men and women rode by on horseback, and hunters in red coats galloped over the fields as autumn approached.

In the fall Olga sent Maria to school in Philadelphia, and the two of us stayed on the farm. Often I was away giving lectures and Olga remained alone. All our friends in Philadelphia thought that for two women to live by themselves on a farm was not without risk, and that it was especially dangerous for Olga to be there entirely by herself. Someone told us there was a lonely old Cossack in Philadelphia, now unemployed, who would gladly come to us and help with the work in exchange for room and board, no salary necessary, only a little pocket money and tobacco.

This Cossack, whose name was Fyodor Danilovich Gamalei, took his obligations seriously. He asked for a revolver, and an American acquaintance provided one. Whenever strangers came by, he appeared as if out of the earth, standing silently, stroking his mustache, until he was convinced that these people were neither Bolsheviks nor dangerous in any way. He was a huge man, broad-shouldered, with graying hair. He was constantly twisting his grizzly mustache. In fact, he was perfect Gogolian type, so we called him Taras Bulba. He was bowlegged, probably from incessant sitting on a saddle. His conversation was brief and terse.

"Oh, how sore my back is!" we sometimes complained.

"Well, what of it?" he retorted. "It's not fatal."

We could not contradict him.

The Neighborhood League gave us a heavy, cast-iron cook stove, which would take wood or coal. "We must ask Mrs. Makarov to send us two or three men to set it up," I remarked. The Cossack just waved his hand. When Olga and I came in from the vegetable garden a little later, the stove was already in place. To this day I do not understand how he managed it.

Another time they sent us a huge, old-fashioned bathtub, of a kind no longer in use. I tried to move it. Impossible. "Don't even think of setting it up," I told the Cossack, "you will strain yourself."

"Well, what of it?" he returned.

After we had gone out, he had somehow put the bathtub where it belonged.

A friend related how several years ago this Cossack could not find work. A fellow laborer brought him to a contractor, who was demolishing a house. "I don't need any workers," he said.

"But just try him. There you have four men struggling to tear down that wall. Give this fellow the job of knocking it over."

"Oh, well," said the Cossack when this conversation was translated (of course he could say neither yes nor no in English), "let's try." He hit the wall so hard with a sledge hammer that it collapsed.

We bought a few chickens, so we now had our own eggs. Gradually the vegetables sprouted. All we lacked were cows. There was ample grass. We began to make inquiries. On a large neighboring farm small purebred Jerseys were being raised. They were beauties. We were dazzled. The prices, though, were frightening. Hundreds and hundreds of dollars for one cow. We were dejected. Such prices were out of reach. Then the manager showed us several, saying, "I can sell you these, they are slated for the slaughter house."

"But why? Don't they give milk? Are they old?"

"No, no, they are young, and they give plenty of milk, but they have undulant fever in their blood."

We had no idea what undulant fever was. "Is that harmful to people?" Olga asked. "I have a twelve-year-old daughter."

"No, no, it's not at all dangerous for people, but these cows often can't give birth, their calves are stillborn."

One wonderful cow had great, gentle eyes and a snub nose. We fell in love with her at once and bought her for about fifty dollars. Now we had milk, butter, sour cream, and curds to our hearts' delight. We never suspected that we might get ill ourselves. Later we learned undulant fever was what we called Malta fever in Russia, a dangerous illness, hard to cure.*

Soon our family increased still more. An American lady gave us a beautiful black Belgian sheep dog, a six-month-old puppy. We called her Vesta. Along with her came her menu: half a pound of meat per day, two egg yolks, carrots, and something else. In a word, her fare was more sumptuous than our own. We could not have afforded it. So we tore up the note, accepted the dog with thanks, and fed her on porridge. Her natural passionate liveliness was in no way affected by this diet. When she grew to be nine months old, our garden was besieged by dozens of canine suitors of every breed, size, and age.

We did our shopping in the village of Newtown Square, a mile and a half away. There we got our mail and bought provisions, often in a full contingent; first went Maria when home, then Vesta, dragging the little cart for our purchases, then Olga and me, with the cow bringing up the rear. She would stand in a

---

*Medical sources suggest that the cow may not actually have had brucellosis (undulant fever), or else that all of us may have at some unknown time acquired a degree of immunity to the disease (ALT).

corner of the wood while we shopped, waiting patiently, never going out into the highway. We marched back in the same order.

Our bucolic life was satisfying. The hardships and physical difficulties did not frighten us. Olga and I had both been well trained in Soviet Russia. But when we thought of our native land, we were depressed.

CHAPTER EIGHT

How to Speak Out and Be Heard?

Not to think. Just not to think. Not to think of Russia, of those who stayed behind, of the peasants with whom I had been such good friends, whose property had been nationalized, who were sent to Siberia only because they were thrifty, not drunkards, knew how to manage their own farms, working with their sons to expand their holdings. Not to remember a brother, relatives, friends. Such thoughts hurt like an exposed nerve.

In order to suffer less from such recollections, one had to be active, to struggle—but how? My anti-Communist lectures gave me some satisfaction. Naively, I still thought I might influence somebody. But it was not much.

When my tales of prison life, written in Rose Smith's home, appeared in the *Pictorial Review*, the Yale University Press took my book *The Tragedy of Tolstoy,** for publication. It had first been published in Japan. Now it was to come out in several lan-

---

Torusutoi no omoide [Recollections of Tolstoy].

guages, including a Russian version in *Sovremennyya Zapiski* and the Paris newspaper *Posledniye Novosti*.*

Gradually our circle of acquaintances was increasing. We formed a particularly close friendship with a pianist and professor of music, L. L. Swan, and his wife. They lived not far from us, and he taught at colleges in the vicinity. Through him we came to know other families.

Toward the end of 1932 all we Russians were shocked by the news of the execution of twelve hundred rebelling Cossacks in the Kuban. Women and children were killed as well as men. Forty-five thousand were exiled to the far north. My friends said to me, "There is no point in your keeping quiet, with your name you can speak out, and what you write will be published." Our Russian friends the Voronovs were particularly stirred up. "Write, write, we will find Americans to help you publish in the papers."

In 1908 my father wrote "I Cannot Be Silent," in opposition to the death penalty. I took the same title. Here is a portion of my article.

When the Tsarist government condemned a number of revolutionaries to death in 1908, a cry burst from my father's lips: "I cannot be silent." And the Russian people took up this cry in sympathetic protest against the death penalty.

Now when a barbarous revenge is being taken in the northern Caucasus, and when thousands are being executed and other thousands banished daily, and my father is no longer among the living, I feel I should raise my feeble voice against these evils, the more so since I worked with the Soviet government for twelve years and saw with my own eyes how the terror spread each day.

But the world kept silent. Millions were exiled, many died in prisons or concentration camps in northern Russia, thousands were shot on the spot. The Bolsheviks began with their old enemies, old priests, simple believers, professors and scientists, but now they have reached out to the workers and peasants. And again the world is silent.

Annals of the Fatherland and Latest News.

For fifteen years a nation has been living in slavery, suffering from cold and hunger. The Soviet government robs the people, takes from it its bread and all it produces, and sends it abroad, because it needs foreign exchange, not only for machinery but also for Bolshevik propaganda. If the peasants protest and hide bread for their hungry families, retribution is swift—they are shot.

The Russian people can no longer stand these conditions. Now here, now there, uprisings occur. Thousands of famished peasants, abandoning homes and farms, are fleeing from the Ukraine, where death from starvation threatens.

What does the Soviet government do? It issues a decree banishing hundreds and hundreds of thousands of persons from Moscow (a third of the entire population) and punishes rebellious workers and peasants with bullets and deportation. Even the days of Ivan the Terrible never saw such cruelties. And now when the Cossacks living in south Russia have rebelled, the Soviet regime has organized a fearful campaign of extermination against an entire population, unheard of in its cruelty. Whole families of Cossacks have been shot down. Forty-five thousand people, including women and children, have been sent on Stalin's orders to certain death in Siberia.

Is it possible that the world will again remain silent? Will the governments really continue calmly to sign trade agreements with the Bolshevik murderers, so strengthening the latter's position and undermining their own countries? Can the League of Nations quietly discuss the question of world peace with the representatives of a power whose principal goal is world revolution based on terror and rivers of blood? Is it really possible that such idealistic writers as Romain Rolland, who so perceptively understood the souls of Gandhi and Tolstoy, two of the greatest peace lovers of our time, and others like Henri Barbusse or Bernard Shaw will go on praising the socialist paradise? Can they not comprehend that they bear some responsibility for spreading that Bolshevist contagion which threatens the whole world with catastrophe and ruin? Is it conceivable that people still think a bloody dictatorship led by a group of persons bent on destroying world culture, religion, and morals can be called socialism?

Who will cry out to the world, "I cannot be silent?" Where are you who preach love, truth, and brotherhood? Where are you Christians, you genuine socialists and pacifists, writers, social workers, why do you remain silent? Do you actually need more proofs, more witnesses, more statistics? Can you not hear the cries, the prayers, for your help? Or do you perhaps also think that happiness may be achieved through violence, murder, depriving an entire nation of its freedom?

I am not addressing my appeal to those whose sympathy for Bolshevism has been bought with money stolen by the Soviet government from the Russian people. I am directing it to those who believe in brotherhood and human equality, to the religious, the socialists, the writers, to social workers and public figures, to wives and mothers. Open your eyes! Unite in a single protest against the torturers of a hundred and sixty million helpless persons!

Alexandra Tolstoy

My article provoked a wide variety of answers. Some requested my autograph. One letter from a woman, president of a literary club, informed me that her club was studying Russia and planned a luncheon at which they would like to read my article—but they did not know what to prepare for food and asked me to draw up the menu.

A retired "member of the Black Hundred," * as he signed himself, wrote:

"One must say that the guilt for fifteen years of suffering by an innocent generation of 'revolutionary' Russian people should be laid at the door of that weak-willed tsarist regime, which in its day did not have the intestinal fortitude to send your papa and your whole family and all Russian prophets like him to the insane asylum."

An American from New York State wrote: "I am very much alone. I should like to correspond with you."

An American women from Portland, Maine, wrote:

"In the December 24, 1932, issue of the *Saturday Evening Post*, W. Durant claims that Russia [has] achieved extraordinary successes under Lenin and continues to live happily under Trotsky's guidance. Is this true? It seems to us that Russia became helpless soon after the Bolsheviks took over. There are groups of us scattered throughout America who are opposed to Communism, but such groups are accused of militarism."

A most interesting letter was received from a young Jew. "I am sending you only a few lines . . . to compliment you on your article. . . . The whole world is against the Jews, and uses all possible means to attack them. The ignorant, uneducated Jews who support Communism [here] make matters worse for all Jewry. An end should be put to Communist activities, even if it

---

*This was a reactionary and anti-Semitic organization founded in the Revolution of 1905. It was particularly active during Stolypin's premiership (1906–11).

means using measures of the greatest severity. Such activities will eventually lead to a world crisis if energetic steps are not taken immediately."

A high school student wrote: "We are discussing the question: 'It is resolved that Russia is now in a much better situation than it was under the tsar.' "

Hundreds of such letters were received.

The Democrats had won by a large majority in 1932. Franklin D. Roosevelt became president and recognition of the Soviet Union followed.

CHAPTER NINE

The Connecticut Farm

I had only read about how the banks were failing: how people, rich people, or laborers and farmers who had perhaps accumulated small sums of money in their lifetime, counting on a tranquil old age, had become poverty-stricken in a single day. It had never been my lot, however, to witness such a catastrophe. When such rumors began spreading in our area, I rushed to my bank in Philadelphia. I had had on deposit a total of only about fourteen hundred dollars, received for my book* and some short stories. Fortunately, friends had advised me to put a thousand dollars into postal savings, so only something over three hundred was in a checking account.

I saw a crowd gathered before the bank. Women were crying. The men were nervously smoking. The bank officials had simply vanished. All the tellers' windows were closed. Behind the grat-

*The Tragedy of Tolstoy.

ings people were moving, but nobody would talk to us. Impossible to get any explanation.

One old farmer in working clothes struck me particularly. He was tall, bony, sunburned. Probably he had jumped into his car just as he was when he heard the awful rumors. He leaned against the wall of the bank, helplessly, his arms stretched out as if appealing for understanding.

"This can't be so, there's some misunderstanding, something we don't see," he said to the man next to him.

"No misunderstanding at all," snapped the latter. "We've lost everything. The bank's declared bankruptcy."

"Yes, but I worked hard, I worked hard, my whole life's savings are in here, how can I tell my wife? She won't be able to bear it, I can't face her."

The general consternation was appalling. I thought, Americans do not know what it means to lose one's property. What is property? What is far more terrible is to lose a family, a country, everything.

Nevertheless, I must admit I was upset. I had long known what it meant to lose property. The sum of three hundred dollars, however, was a goodly sum, very necessary precisely now, when we had again turned into homeless vagabonds. Indeed, after we had put the farm in order, after investing so much money and toil in it, the owner had demanded such a high rent that we were in no position to pay it. Three years later I passed by this farm. Nobody was living there. It was in a worse state of disrepair than when we had taken it over.

Again we had to look for some kind of corner of our own. Fate now took pity on us. It must be said that people seldom came to see us. We were living about a mile from the main road. Only an unpaved country lane led to our place. After even a little rain, a car would get stuck. Every arrival therefore was an event.

Elena Varneck, the friend who had translated my book, *The Tragedy of Tolstoy*, had been staying with us for the summer. She hunted for a secluded spot where she could take sun baths and found one, near our house, by cutting a high swath in the weeds—"in the nettles," as she said. There in the heat, as she was blissfully sunning herself, a voice suddenly sounded. "Are you the countess?"

"No, no, please go away."

The voice turned out to be that of a newsman, not at all taken aback by her appearance. He kept pressing Elena to tell him where the countess was. Finally, he went away.

One fine day a splendid new car drove up to our house. In it sat a beautifully dressed woman and two young men. "Sasha! It's you! How happy I am to see you!"

The face was familiar. I had certainly known it—but where? When? My thoughts ran back, ten, twenty years ago, to World War I—then I remembered: a small group of us on the way to the Turkish front. I saw the scene: it was hot, sultry, the sky was cloudless, a deep dark blue, the grass was thick and tall, juicy; six horses, unsaddled and hobbled in Caucasian style, were eating ravenously. With me were two male nurses, an orderly, and a sanitary aide. We were resting under the shade of some bushes, very tired; it was already the fifth day of our journey. All of us were in gray, we still wore our dusty Caucasian coats and caps of lamb's wool, our revolvers in our belts; our faces were dark from riding in the sun, the skin was flaking off our noses and foreheads. Then, as now, an elegant lady had arrived in a marvelous automobile, like an apparition in that wilderness, asking, "Are you Countess Tolstoy?" The countess had got up off the grass, embarrassed, in her dusty coat and wide trousers. Now I knew who this was.

"Jane! Jane Yarrow!" I cried.

"Yes! How happy I am to find you! This is my second son, Mike, you remember, he had just been born then, and here is Ernest, my youngest, he hadn't yet arrived in this world."

We sat outdoors, drinking tea, recalling the past, interrupting each other, bursting with recollections. What a lot we had to remember! Those days in Turkish Armenia in the city of Van during the terrible conditions of World War I, starvation everywhere, typhus and malaria were epidemic. Jane had come down with typhus, while her husband was already cyanotic when our Russian troops arrived with an army doctor. "You saved our lives!" Jane declared. We were friends from then on.

And now here was Jane, telling me how they once found me lying stricken on the steppes of Turkish Armenia, and how her husband had searched me out when I was in a Moscow prison and brought me a bountiful American food package. She had come now with a particular proposition. A friend of the Yarrows, their closest neighbor, had found a small farm in their area of Connecticut. It was for sale for a thousand dollars. There was a little house, two hen roosts, and seven acres of land. Our own nook! Our own land! What could be more heavenly!

We wasted no time, we went and inspected. A wooded state park surrounded the place. The house was small, with three rooms, a tiny vegetable garden, an old dilapidated cow shed, even several slender, bending birch trees—not like those in Russia; still, they were birches.

We hired a large truck, loaded it with furniture, suitcases, and baskets of chickens. We ourselves went by train to Meriden, where Jane picked us up. Our dog Vesta traveled in the baggage car with her puppies, their eyes not yet open. We had had to sell our cow, for Connecticut excluded cows having had undulant fever. That was a heavy blow for us, for she had been a member of our family.

There were two so-called houses on the farm. The main house had three rooms: two bedrooms and a sitting room. From the latter a trap door let down into the kitchen by a steep folding ladder. "The owner of this house was a sailor, so he built it like a ship with a hold," our new neighbor, Uncle Joe, told us. He had come to make our acquaintance, but not alone, for two little goats followed him, like two dogs, and Vesta promptly chased them off.

Olga settled into this "large" house. I moved into the little one, which had been the brooder. In time, our Cossack put down new floors for me, painted it, and made a partition, which produced two tiny rooms: one, the bedroom, with room for one bed and a wardrobe, in the other, space for a desk, armchair, and bookshelf. It was cramped—but it was my own.

Around our farm there were wooded hills, a mile and a half below us, the wide Connecticut River. In the forest were quantities of berries and mushrooms. We arranged a loan at the local bank, bought some pullets, and began our new country life.

CHAPTER TEN

Lectures in America

When I recall those first months of my life in America, I think how naive I was to hope that I might convince anyone. When I said in my lectures that life in Russia under the tsars was much easier than life now, I heard only incredulous silence. Probably people thought, "She is a monarchist, of course she wouldn't recognize any social reforms." Or: "How could a countess, a former landowner, think any differently? No doubt she imagines that her estate will sometime be given back to her."

In truth, there were very few who understood what I was talking about. Since we are so constituted that every person must have purpose in life, I took it into my head that my life's aim was to tell the Western world everything I knew about the Soviets and to warn against the deadly danger of Bolshevism. I knew much that the free world did not know. The problem was how to get that information across. I spent sleepless nights thinking about lectures, articles, letters to the President. I talked in all sorts of halls, in women's clubs, auditoriums, forums. I could make people laugh and cry. When I told of the frightful life in

Soviet Russia, I saw women wiping away their tears on hearing of the poverty, the prisons, the tortures, and the hunger. This made me think I was achieving my goal.

"But still, hasn't life become better for the working people?" they would ask. "Don't you find that there are many more schools and universities under the Soviets? Under the tsars, there was ninety percent illiteracy."

"Forty-five percent illiteracy," I corrected. "It is true that there are now more schools and universities, but the quality of education is lower."

"And how should one pronounce the name, 'Anna Kare*ni*na,' or 'Anna Ka*ren*ina?'" A beautifully coiffured woman startled me with this query.

I answered questions, shook thousands of friendly hands but sometimes thought in despair, it is hopeless, they can't understand.

Once I was invited on one of my tours to a meeting devoted to the League of Nations. They asked me to say a few words.

> In 1909 my father was invited to a peace conference in Stockholm. He did not go, but he had no regrets, for he learned later that, though one part of the conference was devoted to disarmament, another part was focused on the problem of defensive armaments. The League of Nations cannot contribute to world peace. All the nations, beginning with Soviet Russia, are energetically building up their armaments. A genuinely Christian attitude toward war is impossible, especially with the participation of the Soviet Union, which refrains from attacking the free countries only because it is not yet strong enough. I do not believe that the League of Nations can exert any serious influence on the course of world events.

The response I usually received was polite silence. The possibility of my influencing American liberal circles was clearly nil. I could not understand how these goodhearted, well-intentioned Americans, often carried away by a passionate if ignorant defense of liberty—a free people who had never known starvation or tyranny—could fail to realize that at that moment hundreds of thousands of peasants were dying of famine artifically created by those very same leaders who were seemingly promoting peace in the League of Nations. Did they not know that millions were dying of forced labor? How could the Western nations still believe in peace, believe in the possibility of good relations with the Soviets? How to explain the truth?

I wrote to President Roosevelt, asking for an appointment. It was of no use. I believed then that people are governed by logic. It offended me that the Russian immigrants did not join in unanimous protest against the brutality of the Soviet regime. Honest indignation was swelling in America at the Nazis. Why not at the Soviets? On the contrary, public opinion increasingly supported American recognition of the Soviet regime. Naively, I believed that this attitude came from ignorance of the conditions in Russia. Therefore I wrote to anyone I thought had influence, and to Clarence Pickett, secretary of the Society of Friends in particular, asking him to protest against the atrocities in the Kuban and to oppose recognition by the United States.

He replied, inviting me to speak to a meeting of the Quakers in Philadelphia in March 1933. Thirty persons attended. I spoke for about twenty minutes. At the end I was troubled in spirit that I could not speak further. The Quakers were silent.

Later I received a letter from Mr. Pickett. He said in part:

> Of course I am completely opposed to the persecutions which the present government inflicts, not only on your own but on other religious groups in Russia. However, just now a protest based on this fact will be extremely helpful to the most conservative and reactionary elements in our country. . . . The majority in our group supports recognition of the Russian government, not because it is in sympathy with what it does, but because it is an *established* government, and in addition because there is no way of influencing a government which we do not recognize. . . .

In my reply I argued that it was not an "established" government but one that had seized power contrary to the will of the Russian people, and that the uprisings throughout the country testified to this fact.

Having had no luck with the Quakers, I then wrote to Jane Addams, asking her to intercede with President Roosevelt in opposition to recognition of the Soviet regime. Her reply was very kind but disappointing:

The group of pacifists to which I belong has felt from the very beginning that a de facto recognition of the government of Russia would be more likely to lead to peace between nations than to hostility. Perhaps we are mistaken; but in any event the governments which have tried other methods have not avoided the unseemly situation in which we now find ourselves. . . . Since I have argued in favor of recognition for so long . . . I simply cannot refuse to put my signature on the petition being addressed to the new President. . . .

Once on returning from a journey, I was met by Olga. She told me that a man had called with two others. He had given his name as Captain MacKenzie, saying he had been in Moscow, and had brought a message from my brother Sergei.

"Well, did you find out when he will come back, or his address?"

"No."

I was angry. "But why not? This is so important to me!"

"Just listen, Sasha," she calmly interrupted, "I didn't ask him any questions because he and the other two seemed to me very suspicious."

Two weeks went by. At nine o'clock one morning I was sitting at my little desk writing. Vesta was lying at my feet. Suddenly she began to growl, her hackles rising, and jumped at the door. I was frightened for some reason. I turned the key in the lock. A knock on the door.

"Who's there?"

"I'm selling Persian carpets, I'd like to show them to you."

"I don't need any carpets, and besides I haven't the money."

"But just take a look. If you don't want to buy, you don't have to; they are beautiful carpets."

The carpet salesman spoke English with a Russian accent. The door handle grated. He was trying to open it.

"Go away, I tell you."

"Open the door."

The door rattled, some dried paint fell off. Opening a drawer, I took out a revolver and cocked it. Vesta was yelping at the door.

"Open up!"

I waited, trembling, not taking my eyes from the door, holding the revolver on my lap with my finger on the trigger. Vesta was growling less, her teeth chattering. All at once the tension ceased. Vesta came away from the door. I heard the sound of a car starting up. Within seconds Olga was calling, "Sasha, Sasha, open the door, Captain MacKenzie has gone!"

"What captain?"

"MacKenzie, MacKenzie, the man who came days ago saying he had a message from your brother Sergei! That was he!"

"MacKenzie? He's gone? What happened?"

Before she had time to reply, I saw a truck in the yard—our butcher and his helper had brought us our meat. Below our hill, rolling down the road, was a big black car with a large luggage compartment. Three men were in the car, and I could see that one of them had a beard and wore a cap. They were traveling very fast.

"Quick, call the police!"

But the police were seventeen miles away. By the time we had telephoned and the police had grasped what we were saying— perhaps they did not actually believe us—Captain MacKenzie, alias the Persian rug dealer, alias Comrade Communist, and his accomplices were already miles away.

CHAPTER ELEVEN

The Blessed Sense of Freedom

Our life on the farm was hard but serene and happy, with no fears or feelings of depression. We would rise early. Sometimes, as the sun was lifting behind the wooded hills, the bushes were hung with dew, gleaming with a thousand lights, the flowering grape vines or the fresh-mown grass scented the air. I would run to the hens' roost with pails of fresh water from the well, scatter their food, and return to the house to sit down at my desk. Silence. All I could hear were the chickens cackling and Vesta's teeth chattering as she tried to catch the flies that were pestering her. In the "big" house porridge and borshch would be cooking on the iron range. Our Cossack would be hammering on something new or in need of repair.

We had plenty to eat, all the eggs and vegetables we could want, for we raised our own. Even the melons were ours. The woods were full of mushrooms and berries, raspberries, dewberries, blueberries. We did buy meat, butter, and milk until we acquired another cow, as well as fish, tea, coffee, and sugar. The prices were low then: eleven or twelve cents a pound for fish, sixteen or seventeen for the best ground beef, twelve or thirteen for a quart of milk. On the other hand, we hardly got rich on selling our eggs for fifteen to seventeen cents a dozen. The most important thing, though—incomparable—was the blessed sense of freedom. We could do what we wanted, fearing no one and nothing. If we wanted, we worked; if we wanted to wander out for mushrooms, we could, or write a book.

After the midday meal and until late at night we were working, cleaning the hens' roost of their droppings, putting grain in their trough, gardening. In the evenings we cleaned and inspected the eggs and packed them for sale. Gradually we expanded our operations. By spring we had a thousand hens and between twenty-five hundred and three thousand chicks. Our two cows and a vegetable garden brought us in a little income, and in summer we made a bit more selling our wild blueberries to our rich neighbors at a good price. The aristocrats lived below us on the banks of the Connecticut river, but poor people like ourselves lived up on the hills.

Next, there appeared a handsome husband for Vesta, a gift from my brother. Mitka was a large gray police dog. Vesta fell in love with him at first sight and remained faithful to the grave. The dogs roamed free. Once in a while they brought home a rabbit, and once Vesta fetched us a partridge, which we cleaned, cooked, and ate with relish. They also hunted for skunks. I remember being awakened by a terrible smell. When I went out to investigate, I saw Vesta sitting by the door with a triumphant expression. Right in front in the yard lay a dead, chewed-up mother skunk and her three offspring, in a row. We buried the skunks and washed the dog.

Our cows were first-rate. One, a purebred Jersey, was given me by Albertini, the husband of my sister Tatiana's daughter, who had come over from Italy. The second cow was born on our place. As was natural to a pedigreed lady, the Jersey was quiet and modest, like the cow we had had in Pennsylvania. She too had great, sad eyes and a snub nose. Her young heifer was mischievous and clever, and several times spoiled our garden. To get round the wire fence that protected it, she would throw her full weight against it and flatten it. Then she would step over the fence and complacently graze on the corn. Her Jersey mother, unmoved, would watch the destruction, not daring herself to cross over the fence. This was not the sum of her child's mischief, however. She found out how to get into the hen roost. With her horn, she would lift up the latch on the gate, get inside and eat up all the hen food, overturning the trough. Then she would turn on the faucet, again with her horn, drink the water, and take a shower. We had to change all the bolts and reinforce the fence.

Sometimes our huge dogs and the cows would alarm our intellectual visitors. "The dogs don't bite," we told them, "don't be afraid." "But will the cows butt us?"

"No, no." The cows were very sociable. As soon as they saw people, they would come up to them, to the horror of our city friends. "Don't they bite?" one learned professor asked us.

Now our Cossack often absented himself. The dream of his life was to marry, buy a small farm with his savings, and settle there with his wife. "I'm going to Philadelphia," he informed us one day.

"Some business?"

"Oh, well, maybe it will work out, the Cossacks are trying to find a bride for me."

He departed. A week went by. Our Cossack came home highly incensed, but he would say nothing. On being queried, he merely waved his hand. "Fyodor Danilovich, what about the bride? Tell us, did you like her?"

"Oh, well, so what? Nothing to tell. What bride . . . ?" waving his hand. He looked very unhappy, even his bold mustache had a pathetic droop. He looked older, shrunken. We let the matter rest, but in a few days again questioned him. "Now tell us, Fyodor Danilovich, how was the bride. Didn't anything work out?"

"Oh, what's there to say, it didn't work out, that's all."

"But why?"

"A good-for-nothing girl . . ." he stopped. "Lopsided," he muttered with an effort.

"But maybe she's a good woman?"

"Good, good!" he sneered. "She's lopsided, besides, she has asthma, she breathes like a broken-winded horse." A deep sigh.

"You ought to take an American for your wife," I suggested.

"An American! Do you think I'm out of my mind? An American—they're no good, what sense do you get out of them, sitting all day long in a drug store, swilling down soda water. They come home, take a can of something off a shelf, slop water over it—and give their husbands that! 'Eat it,' they say. American women . . ." he snorted, "trash."

One of the most memorable events of our new life was the purchase of an automobile. It cost eighty-five dollars, plus registration and insurance. To us that was a fortune. Never—not even in later years when I bought new Fords—did any machine seem so beautiful, so luxurious. It was a small, old black roadster. I tried to learn to drive it by myself, without a teacher, going back and forth in our yard. I knocked down a post, I almost ran over Vesta—who promptly became jealous of the car. Whenever it started, she would seize a front wheel in her teeth and yelp.

Nevertheless, I had to learn to drive. My brother Ilya had been taken seriously ill. I had to visit him, and it was very complicated to reach him by bus or train. Next door to us there lived an Estonian family, whose elder son, aged eighteen, sometimes gave us a ride in his car. "Albert," I asked him, "can you go with me tomorrow to see my brother in Southbury?" The town was some seventy miles away.

"Why not, if you pay me."

"I'll pay you, on one condition: I must drive."

"But you don't know how!"

"Maybe not yet, but you will teach me."

He thought a minute. "Well, all right, only on condition that you do just what I tell you."

"Of course, but now I put another condition: we leave at 3:30 A.M., when no one else is on the road."

"O.K."

It was a beautiful morning, cool, fragrant. The sun had not yet risen. The stars were dimming in a transparent pale sky. The grass glistened with dew. My little black Ford grumbled, having got too generous a dose of gas, but I held on to the wheel with both hands. Nothing now existed for me but the road.

I thought I would certainly run into every post on the way, every tree. We traveled like a snail at twenty-five miles an hour. Meriden was the first city on our way. From time to time trucks overtook us. The next large town was Waterbury, fifty miles from our starting point. By then it was seven. The perspiration was rolling off me, drenching my underwear.

"Albert," I said at last, "I'm exhausted." We changed seats.

On the return journey, however, I drove the seventy miles by myself. In a few days I took the driving test in Middletown. Jane Yarrow went with me.

CHAPTER TWELVE

Joy in Death

One question recurs constantly to all normal persons: does our life end with our bodily existence? For long years I pondered this question, recalling the deaths of those closest to me.

The answer is no. The I, the soul, does not die. All the religions of the world confirm this belief—Christianity, Judaism, Buddhism, Taoism, and the rest. I believe that the soul does not die. It is immortal, it crosses to a new unknown life.

My father wrote, "Life is a dream—death, the awakening."

Even in extreme old age it is hard to part with life, with those nearest to us, with our animal friends, with nature itself. In my lifetime I have suffered a succession of such bereavements, an endless succession.

So it was with me when I lost my father. For twenty-six years I had lived his life. He alone was the center, the purpose, of my own life. To work for him was my sole aim. I had loved him more than anyone else in the world.

In youth one cannot understand the beauty, the majesty, of death. One also cannot understand the significance of illness, its purpose, when God in his wisdom sends suffering. Suffering marks the glorious transition of the soul into the unknown.

When my old nurse was describing the death of my little brother Alyosha, I did not understand her. Only now in my old age do I realize the wisdom and significance in the death of that four-year-old child. He was dying of croup—though I do not recall knowing this, for I was only two. At the last moment he suddenly opened his big brown eyes. Gazing into the distance, holding out his little hands, he whispered, "I see! I see!" His eyes closed, for the last time he sighed.

For a long time I did not realize the meaning of that moment. When I see the photograph of that beautiful child, it seems I knew him only from the stories of our old nurse, my father's contemporary. Then, involuntarily, I ask, what did he see? What does anyone see at the moment of death? What did that little child see?

What did my father see at that moment? His favorite daughter, Masha. Before her marriage she had been his disciple. She helped him in everything, she copied out his works, she wrote his letters. She died while my father was yet alive, and it was a very heavy grief to him. When he himself was dying, suddenly, he saw her. "Masha! Masha!"

His last words were: "Truth—I love—" adding with difficulty, "much."

I did not know what to live for after the loss of my father. I could feel only an abysmal void. I had lost everything. The fulcrum of our household had gone. Everything had collapsed, there was nothing to live for. Stunned, I could not conceive of any further step.

Not until later did I comprehend the meaning of death—its beauty, its majesty—the necessity for suffering, which makes a creature grow in spiritual stature.

When my mother lay dying, it was my lot to nurse her and at the end to close her eyes. Never had I loved or understood her so well as in the hours before her death. We both wept and asked each other's forgiveness. She had become wonderful, all-understanding, close—how I loved her then!

I remember another joyous death, that of my brother Ilya.

I used to visit him in his woodland cottage on the banks of the Zoar River near Southbury, Connecticut. Three months earlier I had visited him on my way home from Boston. He was then in good shape. He drove about in his little car, chopped wood for his stove. He was almost entirely alone; his second wife, Nadya, was constantly going to New York. This time I found him in serious condition. Ilya had greatly changed since my last visit. He had lost weight, he complained of pain in his side, and he moved with difficulty. Again he was alone. The cottage was dirty, flies everywhere. There was no food on hand. I tucked my city dress up, tied my head in a kerchief, washed, scrubbed, and carried out trash. The bath was full of soaking clothes. In the ice box, moldy boiled beets. I did the laundry, shopped for provisions, prepared a meal.

Now he was smiling, happy to be no longer alone. I called a doctor in New Haven. After examining his patient, he took me into the little garden to tell me he believed my brother had cancer and should be taken to the hospital. When the doctor had gone, I went to Ilya.

"Well, have I cancer, Sasha?"

I was silent.

"No need to hide it, I want to know, I ought to know."

Our eyes met. However hard it was to tell the truth, I could not lie. "He doesn't know yet, you must go to the hospital for an examination."

"But very probably it is cancer."

He spoke hesitantly and with difficulty, then closed his eyes. I knew what he must be living through. He had so loved life and knew so well how to enjoy it. He could not speak more.

My eyes filled with tears, and so I slipped out of the house to walk in the woods along a path by flower beds, fruit trees, birches. He had so loved all this. The quiet woods smelled of decaying leaves. Here and there I saw the little brown hat of a mushroom eaten by snails, a paler mushroom growing out of moss, a birch mushroom with a spotted stalk, an aspen mushroom with its reddish-brown cap. I took my kerchief off to hold the mushrooms, and went back to the cottage.

"I'm so happy you came," Ilya smiled warmly. "Don't worry, he's already in my hands."

"Who?"

"Ilya Tolstoy."

After a moment's silence: "Thy will be done. . . . What lovely mushrooms!"

In the New Haven hospital Ilya lay dying. He suffered greatly. The pain in his liver caused him to gasp for breath. His once strong body was being consumed by cancer. I tried to come as often as possible. It was moving to see how happy it made him. "Sasha, it is too late to help me to live, so help me to die."

At first, he said, it was hard to accept the fact. "I was hoping to make something from an invention. I had planted these fruit trees, and was waiting for them to bear. Now there is nothing to wait for, I must die. I keep thinking, to whom have I been guilty in my life? In my thoughts I ask pardon from them all. I was very guilty toward. . . ." He told me a long story. "If you ever meet that person, ask him to forgive me."

He dictated letters to all his relatives, letters of farewell, asking their forgiveness too.

Once he seemed strangely happy. "Sasha, I've figured out a new occupation for myself. I'm not going to live, so there's nothing I can want. This is what I've been thinking: I've been counting over all my close friends, considering what each one needs, what I could wish for each—and so I lie and think."

Evidently he did not want to use the word pray. His thoughts and his words grew from deep within him and were transformed into his Holy of Holies.

Another time he said, "Sasha, you know Semyon's death made a terrible impression on me." My mother's godson had been a childhood friend of my older brothers, and until the Revolution had been our chef. He died in Yasnaya Polyana from cancer of the liver. His last days were passed in frightful torment, in complaint, without submission. "I should be submissive, accept what is sent me."

He was very upset on one occasion. "Listen! My neighbor—do you hear him? This is how he goes on for hours, days. Sometimes he cries out at night. It's awful."

However, when that man quieted down after an injection of morphine, Ilya too grew calmer, and we could talk, as only those in the presence of death do talk—that is, before God. We spoke of death. We both believed that there is no death. I knew how intense were his thoughts, how profoundly he was preparing for transition. His every word was weighted with meaning. This knowledge evoked the same formation of mind in me. To the utmost I strained to match his mind, to travel his way with him.

His suffering was terrible. Nadya tried to persuade him to accept the morphine injections, but he refused. Realizing the spiritual process through which he was passing, I knew I also would have refused it. We understood each other perfectly. He said quietly, "I have sinned much in my life. I have been sent this suffering in atonement, so as to prepare myself. I must bear it, for the sake of God."

Throughout the last three days he insisted on refusing the morphine. I was with him the whole time. Nadya came and went. Ilya no longer wanted to get well. He seemed to see a kind of injustice in the idea of getting well. He said to the nurse, "Sister, sister, why are you bringing me the enema? It's not necessary, I am dying anyway."

"Oh, come now, you'll get well yet."

"No need to say that, sister, no need, I already know."

Two days before his death I asked to spend the night with him in his ward, but no matter how I begged they would not permit it, for he had not yet been placed on the critical list. What I dreaded was that at the end he would again be alone, without me.

The next day Nadya came. "Sasha, I am going to New York."

"Don't," I urged, "stay here, Ilya will die tonight."

She would not listen, however, and left. That night I did stay with him. He was only half-conscious, but he took my hand and held it for a long while. By now he could take nothing but liquids, and I fed him with a spoon. At about one in the morning he began to toss, groaning, with a gurgle in his chest. "Ilya," I whispered, "be calm, this is the transition you have been waiting for with so much agony." I began a prayer, I don't remember which.

Suddenly, he raised his hand to his forehead, then let it fall. I finished the sign of the cross for him. A few seconds, minutes, passed. Then he opened his deep blue eyes wide. Such rapture and astonishment were on his face that I knew he saw something hidden from me. I felt infinitely insignificant. A last sigh.

At two in the morning I left him. I was crying, but not from grief. I was happy. I had been present at the greatest of all mysteries.

"How is Ilya?" my friends asked when I returned in the morning. "How is Ilya?"

"He is dead."

They stared at me, speechless. I did not know why. My face apparently had no trace of grief, I was smiling. Inconceivable. How could anyone be glad at the death of a beloved brother? They well knew what friends we had been.

I could not explain why I was smiling, why in my soul I rejoiced. How could they have understood? For the first time in my life I had comprehended why suffering was necessary for death, and how wonderful was the transition. "Life is sleep— death is the awakening," as my father had said. I had seen how my brother grew in spiritual stature during these weeks of terrible suffering. Finally, the joy of release, the joy of transition.

Sometimes an old man, feeling his age, stops working both mentally and physically. Then the muscles lose their elasticity, so also do the heart and brain weaken, his spirit begins to disintegrate, he resists the idea of leaving behind the daily nonsense of living. Yet that nonsense conceals what should be the foundation of life, everything genuine and spiritual.

How foolish, how blind we are at times! Often we tread into the mire what we should preserve. We seek happiness or glory or pleasure in senseless pursuits. So one's life passes. It is too late to rectify, though—one cannot turn the clock back. "Si jeunesse savait, si vieillesse pouvait"—if youth but knew, if old age only could. Before we take leave of this world, let us bow in the old Russian way to all those yet living, all those one has sinned against, saying, "Forgive me!"

CHAPTER THIRTEEN

The New World and the Old

In those days I was living a double life—at the farm, and on my lecture journeys. At the farm, heavy physical labor, old tattered clothes, roughened hands, bulging muscles. On my trips, the attempt at an urbane appearance.

Someone told me I should wear gloves on my glycerine-softened hands. Not very pleasant, but what else could I do? One's skin splits, hangnails appear, nails break, fingers get stiff. And at the same time one must appear in an elegant dress with sheer stockings, open shoes, a tilted hat. Or in full evening dress of velvet or lace—and white gloves over those rough, reddened, calloused hands.

For three days before a lecture I would begin nursing my hands, soaking them in hot water, oiling them with all sorts of fragrant salves, wearing gloves at night. Sometimes I would be gone for several weeks. There might be speaking engagements every other day, or better, twice a week. In time, I came to know the American people, their families, their children. In the western part of America they seemed simpler and more cordial than in the East. I felt freer, less constrained in the West. Wherever I spoke, the people greeted me warmly. They were interested in what I had to say about Russia. The halls were always filled to overflowing.

Once, in the winter of 1934, I had to travel from a small town in Michigan to Terre Haute, Indiana, and had to change trains several times. At one station I noticed a man of about thirty-five sitting opposite me, smoking. For some reason I was uneasy.

"That man is a Russian," I thought. Then I chided myself for such silly ideas and forgot him. I remembered him only when I had to change trains again. He was sitting at a little distance, snapping his cigarette lighter. Where have I seen that kind of lighter, I thought. In Russia!

Again, in the confusion of changing trains, I forgot him. Once settled in my proper car, I saw him sitting in the adjoining section. My next destination was Des Moines, Iowa, and I asked the porter to call me a cab. It was already about eleven at night. The station was dark, badly lit, and a good distance from the town. A taxi drew up, the porter began stowing my baggage, when I saw my fellow traveler already sitting in the far corner of the cab. Like a shot, I drew back, the porter pulled out my bags, the car drove off. "Didn't you see that man sitting in the car?" I shouted to the porter.

"Excuse me, madam, I didn't know, the gentleman pointed to you and said you were together."

On reaching my hotel, I called the president of the club that I was to address. Within a few minutes she came with her husband. I told her the story, and she notified the police. Neither that man nor his taxi could be found. Was he really a Communist pursuing me? Or was I suffering from a persecution phobia? Could I be seeing Bolsheviks where there were none? The political events attending the American recognition of the Soviet Union were not designed to reassure me. Such thoughts gave me no rest.

I traveled from city to city, giving lectures. Between talks, I read the newspapers. In Des Moines, there were four thousand people in the auditorium. I was to confront three Communists, vociferous, middle-aged men, speaking with an accent. During the debate they hurled questions at me, but though they were outwardly confident, they were easy to defeat. They were local American Communists, completely ignorant of Russian life, whereas I knew the facts to refute their arguments. The audience gave me an ovation. On leaving, I saw a group of my opponents at one side of the hall, gesticulating wildly, glaring at me.

Often I felt alone and dispirited in my travels, especially in hotels. Strangers everywhere. But I did enjoy the trains. You could ask the porter to bring you a table, you could write letters, prepare a lecture, read, or simply gaze out of the window. Once on a trip to Chicago I noticed a man sitting in my compartment, but soon he stepped out, and I was alone, which was very pleasant. At six I went to the dining car. Walking through the car, I heard Russian. Three men at the end of the car were in lively conversation, one of them my neighbor. They were so preoccupied that they did not notice me. When my neighbor returned to my section, I asked him if he was Russian. "I don't understand," he replied with a heavy accent, and went out.

When the train reached Chicago, it was already midnight. Almost all the passengers got out, but the Russians stayed. Hoping they would go too, fearing that they might follow me, I delayed getting off, but the car was almost empty, and I had to go. I felt that those three Russians were following me. At the exit, however, I was met and warmly embraced by the kindest of Americans, with whom I had once stayed. "I knew you would be alone," she said, "and that it would be dull for you, so my son and I came to meet you. Our car is here."

My relief was immense. I began to ask myself, was I growing paranoid?

By a turn of fate, America in the 1930s became a leader in the politically free Western world. Some of the democratic countries followed the lead of the United States. France concluded a treaty of mutual assistance with Soviet Russia. Since America had recognized the Soviet Union, Belgium, Czechoslovakia, England, and other nations did also. Ambassadors were exchanged. New representatives of the USSR were playing a role in American life. From France Pierre Laval went to visit Stalin. So did President Beneš of Czechoslovakia. The activities of the Communists increased.

Soviet agents were boring in everywhere, into the labor unions, the schools and universities, Protestant church circles. They infiltrated the black masses, organized demonstrations in

Harlem. Probably Browder,* Foster,** and their comrades had their instructions from Moscow. I do not doubt, however, when Browder asserted that there were thirty thousand Party members in the United States, that the figure was grossly overstated. Perhaps it was enlarged in his mind by the unknown number of so-called liberals who advocated the cultivation of ties with the USSR through commerce, education, and travel.

The newspapers, the radio, the official government publications referred to Soviet activities as *Russian*, implying the assent of the Russian people. Stalin's power kept expanding through torture and expropriation. The Kirov assassination in 1934 strengthened his tyranny over the old Bolsheviks, Lenin's comrades, as well as over the masses.

At the same time the star of Hitler rose higher and higher. Nazism was as ugly, as frightening, as Bolshevism. Both were the enemies of Christianity. Fifteen thousand celebrated a pagan holiday in the Berlin Sports Palace. I outdid myself in trying to explain to Americans how I viewed the Soviet regime, but with little effect.

Once I was to give a lecture in Richmond, Virginia. My friends Nadya Danilovsky and Alice Davis lived in the vicinity, and I stopped in to see them. That morning they happened to say that they expected on the following day a visit by Eleanor Roosevelt. This gave me, I thought, a chance to speak with someone near the seat of power. I helped my friends prepare for the luncheon, I made some *pirozhki* to accompany the soup course, and fried a chicken.

During the meal I raised the question of Russia several times, but each time Mrs. Roosevelt was either talking with someone

---

*Earl Russell Browder (1891–1973), an American Communist, was secretary general of the Party in 1930–44 and president of the Communist Political Association in 1944–45, which briefly replaced the Party. He was the Communist Party's candidate for President of the United States twice, 1936 and 1940, and editor-in-chief of the *Daily Worker* in 1944–45.

**William Zebulon Foster (1881–1961) was also an American Communist leader. He directed the famous steel strike of 1919 and was the Party's presidential candidate in 1924, 1928, and 1932. He was succeeded by Browder in 1930 as head of the Party.

else, or she changed the subject. After lunch, coffee was served in the living room. Again I tried to turn the subject to Russia, but in vain. I tried once again and for the last time when we took a little walk in the garden. "Look," she said, "what a charming view. I love Virginia, don't you?"

Life on the farm followed its diurnal course. The measures instituted in Washington had their indirect effect on us. The wild, neglected woods were turned into a splendid park, with fine new roads past forest lakes created by new dams and bridges. Now, every day, at about eight in the morning, trucks full of young people roared by to some job sponsored by the Works Progress Administration. At about five they would return, singing and shouting.

"They're not so terribly tired," commented a neighboring farmer. All day he worked on his vegetable garden; he plowed, while I guided the horse along the soft, friable furrows. "Five o'clock—and they're already going home, the loafers. Let them ask me when I finish my work! I thank God if I get through by ten! And who pays the taxes to support them? You pay, I pay!"

Once a truckload of young men stopped at our farm on the way home. "Hello," cried one, "you seem to keep animals. We have some meat stew left over. Would you like it?"

They passed us several pails of their stew. None of our animals, cows or chickens, got any of it. We ourselves and the dogs appreciated the WPA donation. We ate and ate for three days, sharing our dinners with Uncle Joe. Still we could not finish it all. From then on we were often fed at government expense—or, as our neighbor observed, at the taxpayers' expense.

CHAPTER FOURTEEN

The Egg Business

I had just learned to drive when my little black Ford we called Zhuk (beetle) was smashed to pieces. It happened like this. Olga and I had decided to sell some eggs to the Hamden cooperative near New Haven. We packed the eggs in the baggage compartment and took off. On approaching Hamden we had to cross a river, and just beyond the bridge there was a sharp turn. I was going very slowly and on the bridge I slowed down more. Suddenly a car shot out from around the curve, traveling fast on the left side of the road, heading straight for us. A collision was unavoidable. I slammed on the brakes, and we took the whole force of the blow. The glass shattered, there was a loud crack, everything was tossed about. Olga's face was bloody, I had blood on my arms and legs. We were taken to a doctor.

"He's a good man," a witness reassured us. "He'll tell you what you should do. Most of his practice comes from accidents on this corner. Collisions are constantly occurring. Of course the road commission ought to do something—but then the doctor would lose his practice."

The doctor examined us, gave his evidence, and poor Zhuk was towed to the nearest garage. I looked at him for the last time. It was a sad sight. The radiator was flattened, the front fenders crushed, the wheels knocked out of line. A thick yellow stream was leaking out of the luggage compartment—our eggs.

It turned out that an entire family had been riding in the other car, including three young children but, thank God, none of them was hurt. The car's owner carried insurance, so we received full compensation for our car, the doctor's services, and our lost time.

Olga could not work for a while, but after her wounds healed, she claimed that the terrific blow had cured her rheumatism.

We bought another car, a second-hand station wagon, much more convenient for transporting our eggs.

At about this time Alexander Kashchenko came to see us. He and his wife were our close friends, and they had just bought some land on which to raise chickens also. To learn the business, he often visited us, staying for several weeks and helping with the chores. Sometimes he marketed our eggs for us. At first we sold them to the fraternity houses at Wesleyan University in Middletown.

We took the extra seats out of the station wagon and replaced them with boxes. Either our Cossack or Kashchenko usually loaded these, but when I delivered them at the houses I had to carry them into the kitchen myself—not hard but inconvenient. The students would stand on the porch smoking, never offering to help. To them I was merely "the egg woman," their source of fresh eggs. Since I was being paid, it was my job to carry the boxes. Though the houses gave two or three cents more per dozen than the commercial markets or the cooperative at Hamden, and though it was a forty-mile trip to Hamden, I decided not to deliver to the houses any more. The following exchange confirmed this decision.

"The boys are kicking about your eggs," the housekeeper at one house told me one day. "I don't know why, they don't like them, they say they are rotten."

"Rotten! But they are only three days old!"

"Maybe so, but you know how boys are."

Sometimes Kashchenko delivered the eggs to the fraternity houses. He was a bit deaf. Somehow he managed understanding Russian by watching people's lips, but in English he was at a loss. Once he returned rather puzzled. "I didn't understand what that housekeeper wanted, she was trying to explain something at great length. Well, not to irritate her, I smiled and said, 'Yes, yes.' "

The next time I went myself. The housekeeper almost slammed the door in my face. She was almost too angry to speak. "Take back your eggs," she shouted. "They're rotten, the students won't eat them."

"That's not true, I'm bringing you the freshest ones there are."

"What? You dare say that? Your deaf man came, he's more honest than you are, he admitted that these eggs are very old. 'Yes, yes, you are right, they are old,' he said—and you still dare argue! Get out of here, I have no time to talk to you."

Kashchenko's deafness explained what the trouble was. But in addition, I had not yet mastered the arts of the professional egg woman. It seemed that with each delivery we were supposed to bring an extra dozen or so for the person who received them. So I refused to deliver any more to the fraternity houses, and instead brought them to the Hamden cooperative. After delivering them, I would stop in at the Yale University library and bring back books on loan.

Farmers like myself came to the cooperative. They would arrive in big handsome trucks full of cartons, or the poorer ones would be driving an old car or a station wagon like mine. We all exchanged ideas, we shared our experiences, our opinions of the best breed of hens, of how they could be induced to lay more, the prevailing prices. Now I seldom had to carry in our boxes; usually the farmers helped me; one in particular made it his business to help me deliver. By now I was well used to driving, and I enjoyed these trips. In the winter, of course, it was much harder, if the roads were covered with ice or a heavy snowfall.

Once, on the return from New Haven, half a foot of new-fallen snow lay on the ground. The sky had been overcast and flakes had already started falling when I left home. Now I had to put on chains. Six miles from home, the chains got loose and twisted around the wheels. I got out my jack to lift the wheels and unwind the chains, but the deep snow caused the jack to sink deep, and I had no boards to steady it. For about an hour I struggled, but in vain. I could not pull off the chains. It was growing frostier. My feet were so chilled I could no longer feel my toes.

Obviously, I now had to abandon the car and seek help. I knew that a blacksmith lived about half a mile back on the road. Walking in the deep snow was arduous with my numb feet. The smith lived in a little house of two rooms, one of them his smithy. He was a tremendous man with a head of dark curly hair. When I entered, his blackened hands were working his bellows. His wife sat nearby, a baby on her lap, while children of various ages were romping about. I described my trouble.

"We'll take care of that right away," said the smith. Putting on his jacket, he left the house. I sat near the fire and took off my shoes.

"Good God," exclaimed the woman, seeing my whitened toes. "You've frozen your feet!" She put her baby in his cradle and began rubbing my feet, which began to hurt excruciatingly.

Soon the man returned with the broken chains and quickly began to solder them into shape again. When he had finished, I was warm again. I held out three dollars to him "for his lost time," as I put it.

"I'd be offended," he returned, "we're all Christians, it's our duty to help each other."

What a wonderful thing to hear! I could not insist. All the way home I felt light in spirit, happy. Those simple, kindly people had warmed me, not only physically but also spiritually. However, I still could not get home all the way by car. The chains again broke. I walked the last mile, abandoning the car.

The next Sunday I went back to those kind people, taking them some produce, chickens, eggs, butter, jam. Forty years and more have gone by since then, but I shall remember that family all my life.

One day the elderly farmer who regularly helped me carry in my eggs asked me, "Haven't you a husband?"

"No, I live with a friend, and a man who stays with us helps us."

"I live alone, too," said the farmer. "My wife died two years ago. As she was very ill in her last days, I got used to doing everything myself, even the cooking and cleaning. But I have a nice house, five thousand hens, and a hundred acres. The farm does well, I have no debts—only it's not good living alone."

The next time I came with the eggs, he said suddenly, after

getting all the crates in: "I see that you are a good worker, and strong, I've seen how you carry the crates. But you need a man, it's not a woman's work to haul those crates. Let me make you an offer, without any obligation: we're both chicken farmers, we both know our business. I promise I will never let you do the heavy work, but you could help me with the farming. Would you like to be my wife?"

I thanked him, but said I did not plan to marry, I was too old. There the matter ended.

CHAPTER FIFTEEN

The Flood

Another spring, March of 1936. Heavy rains had washed away what was left of the snow. Though the ground was still saturated with water, the rain poured down. The roads were flooded. One day Isaac, our cheerful baker, who delivered bread three times a week, came running in. He always brought us the latest news.

"The water has risen five feet in the Connecticut River, in some places it's even nine to fourteen feet higher. I had to detour, the main road is swamped. The railroad tracks are under water."

In order to get through to the Hamden cooperative, I now had to travel more than a hundred miles instead of the usual forty. The main highway was a disaster. Both bridges and buildings had been carried away, road beds were utterly destroyed, whole enterprises were submerged. The damage was in the hundreds of thousands of dollars.

For all chicken farmers March is the critical month. If you get the chicks out in March, they are old enough to begin laying in September and eggs get a good price in the fall and winter. We had prepared in advance. In February we had bought Leghorn roosters with high combs and a proud gait. We had culled the very best hens and put their eggs in the incubator.

In March, just at flood time, the chicks began to hatch. We could hear them peeping while still within the shell, while others were boring holes for their escape. Our electricity was still functioning. We went peacefully to bed.

Later that night I heard Vesta howling mournfully in the kitchen cellar, where she lay with her newborn pups. Half asleep, I opened the trap door, climbed down in the dark, only to find myself ankle deep in cold water. I turned on the light. The water had nearly reached the corner where the puppies were. We hoisted them upstairs, then Olga and I began bailing out the cellar water in buckets. Soon we realized that the level was already so high that our well water was overflowing through the pipes into our kitchen. The situation was desperate. Then the cook stove went out. But that was nothing compared to the next calamity: the electricity went off. The incubator! Its temperature had dropped from 102 to 80 degrees.

Olga rushed to light kerosene lamps under the incubators and to cover them with blankets. Now we remembered that our new little chicks were over other stoves, half of which were heated by electricity. So we had to transfer them all to places heated by coal. We were frantic, what with the crowded space, the crush— we threw out little yellow corpses by the dozens, the hundreds.

The financial loss we suffered from that flood was far from trivial. We had lost almost all the incubator hatch and at least half those in the brooders. Two weeks later, the road had gradually dried out, the river had receded, the electricity had been restored. We were exhausted, yet there was still a tremendous amount of work to do. The storms had torn down trees, swept away roofs, in addition to our losing the chicks. Moreover, we had no money.

We considered selling the farm and hiring ourselves out on wages. We wrote Jane Addams of our problem. She was then visiting a professor at Harvard University. We said we wanted to find work, perhaps as administrators of someone's estate.

Soon we received an answer that a place was open. On a certain day our prospective employers would come with their proposal. Before long a beautiful car rolled up to our little house, two persons emerged, a professor and another lady.

"I'm delighted that I could find you this new place," said the professor, "I'm sure you are tired of living here in such circumstances."

When we heard the conditions, however, we showed no such joy as was expected.

"I have a large dairy farm, with seven laborers on it," the lady told us. "They have to be cared for, their food prepared, the cleaning done, the beds made, laundry—I have a washing machine—ironing."

"Excuse me, but how much do you feel you could pay us?"

"You would have two nice rooms, a bath, good food three times a day—oh, yes, I forgot to say, on Sundays you will sell ice cream at the highway stand."

"Yes, and . . . ?"

"Along with everything else I'm offering you, you will receive fifteen dollars a month."

"Thank you," I said.

"You will be provided with everything you need, you will have no worries, everything will be at your disposal, and the main thing, you'll have excellent rooms with bath."

"And no dirty work," added the professor.

"Thank you again, but I would rather clean up the manure of my cows and chickens. Here we are our own masters—don't you understand?—we can do as we like, and as for salary, the two of us have been making at least two hundred dollars a month."

Though Olga was silent, I knew she absolutely agreed with me.

Evidently offended by the ingratitude of Russian women, the two ladies got into their car and drove away.

We went on looking for work. We asked Sam Yarrow and his influential friend Mr. P. to help us find employment.

"Are you perhaps familiar with cooperatives?"

Hope soared.

"Yes, I worked a good deal with cooperatives in Russia, I organized a variety of cooperative societies in Yasnaya Polyana, I was a member of several of the larger cooperatives, and studied the theory of Scandinavian as well as Russian cooperatives."

Mr. P. told me that he was just then developing a project for cooperative societies to be funded by the Works Progress Administration. In New York they were looking for personnel to man this endeavor. I went to New York. The lady who received me asked endless questions. Finally:

"I have no doubt you will be accepted. I must confess, I know much less about cooperatives than you do. I've enjoyed our talk. You have cleared up a number of things for me. For example, I never suspected that thirty percent of the Russian people were enrolled in cooperatives during the war, or that in general such organizations are so highly developed in Russia."

We parted as friends. I did not doubt that I would be accepted. The salary was not large, only eighty dollars a month, but the work was very appealing to me. To my surprise and disappointment, I was informed I had not been accepted.

"Just drop this business," advised our neighbor, Mr. P., a resident of the aristocratic area on the high banks of the Connecticut. "They won't let you into the cooperative movement under any circumstances. I heard from a friend in New York that this movement is infiltrated by Communists. Tell me, were you ever in trade?"

"Yes, not in Russia, where I only exchanged old clothes for flour in the second-hand market, but here, as you know, I've been selling vegetables and eggs from the farm."

"Not that kind of trade, I'm thinking of real business."

"Well, what kind?"

"Could you sell houses, ready-made houses, to be assembled and shipped?"

"Why not?" In my imagination I was already picturing how I would describe the advantages of such houses, their comfort, their readiness.

"Well, I'll think it over," said Mr. P.

A young American girl was engaged to trade in houses. The business did not work out and was soon closed. What to do next?

CHAPTER SIXTEEN

Freddie

In our kitchen cellar we were sitting at supper, our Cossack "Taras Bulba," Olga, and I. It was already dark. Our bodies ached from head to foot. It had been a tremendous effort to get ourselves up to make a cup of tea. After supper we still had to clean the roosts and inspect the eggs. Suddenly the door opened. In walked a tall, blond, very good-looking boy of about seventeen.

"Good evening," he said, "I came to ask whether you might need someone to work for you."

"Where are you from, and why do you come so late?"

"I've left a workshop in New Haven. Would you take me on? I'll work for only board and keep."

He had been glancing at our own food. "Would you like to have supper with us?"

"Thank you." He began to eat with the avidity of a hungry man.

We arranged for him to spend the night. Next day he began to work. Two days went by. Freddie—as we called the lad—tried, but he did not know how to work. There was something about him hard to explain, something ill—but what? He was very nervous, he avoided the company of people, preferring that of the animals, especially the puppies.

On the third day after he came I had to go to town to buy chicks as replacements for those that had been killed. I took the boy with me. After the flood the roads were so bad I could have gotten stuck at any moment, and so it was risky to drive alone. It was raining again, and the car careened from one rut to another. It was hard to keep it on the road, and I kept it in second gear.

"You aren't afraid of me?" the boy asked unexpectedly.

"No, why should I be?" The car sank into a deep rut, my only thought being how to get out of it. Once out, I stepped on the gas.

"You're not afraid?"

"Why afraid? Oh, the car is leaning to the left now, can we have broken a spring?"

"You've been so good to me, I don't want to lie to you."

"Ah, apparently there's nothing wrong, the car has straightened out, it was only the road that slanted. . . . But why shouldn't I be good to you? What are you trying to say?"

"I wanted to tell you . . . I've run away from an insane asylum."

God! I thought, he is insane, and I am driving alone with him. Involuntarily my foot pressed the brake, but I gave no sign of fright. "What do you mean, from an insane asylum? Why? Tell me the whole truth, Freddie. . . ."

"Yes, I ran away from there, I know you won't give me away, I beg you. . . ."

He told me his story. His father was a fisherman. He did not remember his mother, she had died when he was an infant. His stepmother detested him. Once when his father went to sea, a storm came up, and his father did not return. Within a few days his stepmother dragged the boy to the morgue. The boy could hardly recognize his father—his nose, his whole face, had been so eaten by crabs. The boy was carried unconscious out of the morgue.

"I can't forget it, it was terrible, terrible."

He had grown up quite alone, his only companions the boys of the street. His stepmother thought only of getting work out of him, making him wash the dishes, and so on. She began to think of ways to get rid of him, for the father had left a considerable amount of insurance for the benefit of his wife and son. Finally, an opportunity came. Since childhood Freddie had been interested in automobiles. For hours he would stand about in shops watching the mechanics at work. Once when he was fourteen, he started up his stepmother's car and took off. The road ran downhill, he did not know how to brake the car, and ran into a tree. The car was smashed, but he was unhurt. He was put in a home for teenage delinquents.

It was a harsh place. The other boys beat him up. The guards were brutal, perverted. He twice escaped, was caught, and ultimately was put into an insane asylum, where the lunatics had persecuted him. "I would even crawl under the bed to get away from them," he said, trembling all over. "Save me, don't give me away, I can't lie to you any more."

I glanced sideways at the boy. He had large, naive blue eyes, long lashes, the delicate complexion of a girl, an attractive smile. He seemed to me so helpless, so unhappy, so youthful, his mustache not yet grown.

"I stayed there for fourteen months. I'm normal, don't you see I'm a completely normal person? They kept me there because I had nowhere else to go. I was alone, completely alone in the world."

I was silent, thinking what I should do.

"Please don't give me away, I can't go back there, I'm the youngest in the whole hospital. It's an awful place, at night people pound their heads on the wall, laughing out loud, crying, fighting. Thirty men in the ward with me, dirty, horrible, they chase me—I hide from them under the bed—I can't go back, I'll go crazy. . . ."

"No, I'm not going to give you away." I pressed the accelerator.

But what if he really is crazy, I thought—he could grab me by the throat or jump out of the car—what shall I do? My right foot shifted from the accelerator to the brake. Oh, God, tell me what to do. The poor, poor boy.

"Oh, if you only knew what a terrible place it is! There were two murderers in with me, violent, they beat me, they—I can't tell you—don't give me up!"

We arrived at our destination. I took the key out of the car and went into the store, saying, "Wait for me, I'll buy the chicks and come back."

Ignoring the clerk, I went straight into the office, picked up the telephone and called my friend Sam Yarrow. "What?" he exclaimed, "escaped from the insane asylum?"

"Yes."

"Well, then the only thing you can do is to advise the asylum immediately that the boy is with you. In this country anyone who hides an insane person is criminally liable."

"But he doesn't seem at all crazy, he's still a child."

"That makes no difference. If he has escaped from an asylum, you are obliged to report it. If you don't, I will myself."

I hung up the receiver. The sweat was pouring off my forehead. I went to the door. The boy was leaning against the back of the seat. He looked very, very pitiful. Pale, thin, like a little chicken.

A crime against the government—how do I know he is not crazy?—he was in the hospital—no, no, I mustn't give him up—but Yarrow will report him anyway. . . . Suddenly I reached a decision. "The hospital? The doctor on duty, please. Immediately, on a very important matter."

As soon as I had hung up, I felt the whole baseness of my action. I had followed the law. But another feeling rose within me, stronger than all arguments about legality, or justice—the sense of my own falseness. It was almost a physical sensation.

Two men burst into the room. "Where is he?"

"In the car, you see, that Ford standing by the door."

I could see how the boy's eyes widened as if in deathly fear. He struggled, they seized him. I went home alone. It was raining. The car stuck in the mud.

At home there was a lot of work, everywhere water, the roof leaking. We had to clean up hundreds of little corpses, dirt, mud—but the worst, the stickiest mud, the most odious, was inside me. I did not sleep the whole night. Next morning, in spite of my fatigue, I took the car out of the garage and went to the asylum. A huge, handsome building with a fine view, broad lawns, trimmed hedges and trees. A wide corridor, with a polished floor. "Freddie?" said the attractive woman in the entrance hall, "yes, yes, I know, a very nice boy. So you've come to see him? Sit down, wait a minute, I'll call him."

Strange people were walking along the hall. One was stepping carefully, as if afraid of falling through the floor. He was smiling gently. Others shouted and swore.

"Who wants to see Freddie?" A man called out. "Come here, please."

Freddie was sitting on a chair. He wore the look of a hunted animal. His hands were folded on his knees, his head hung.

"You!" he cried. "That means you didn't give me away, they found me themselves!" He flung himself on me and began to kiss me. "And I thought I was alone in the world again, that you had abandoned me!"

"Freddie, I couldn't keep you any longer without the authorities knowing about it, but I give you my word that I will do everything possible to get you out."

"But I trusted you, I trusted you," he repeated, "but you gave me away. Now I will never get out."

In three months, after much trouble, I got Freddie out. He settled down with us on the farm. It was hard for us, two women, to be with him. His life in correction houses and asylums had psychologically crippled him in many ways. Later on, when Olga and I decided to leave the farm anyway, I was able to arrange for Freddie to work for the WPA, but he ran away, was again caught and shut up in the asylum.

Several years later I met him again. He came to see me, and told me that he hadn't been able to stand the asylum and had escaped once more. He was now married, had a child. He had been working in an automobile shop and was happy. But he did not tell me where he was living, afraid I would again report him. His fear was unfounded. Freddie was more normal, healthier, than many who live in perfect freedom, and I was no longer responsible for him.

CHAPTER SEVENTEEN

A Hard Decision

At about this time, Marta Knudsen came from Sweden to join us. Like Olga, Marta had worked in the school at Yasnaya Polyana, where she had been my first assistant. Teaching was her greatest joy, and she put all of herself into it. When I saw her now I remembered how, when among children, her blue-gray eyes shone beneath her blonde lashes with infinite goodness and gentleness. She was an altogether happy person.

She told us how everything had changed as soon as I left for Japan. The Bolsheviks promptly introduced antireligious propaganda in the school and the museum—not the case so long as I was there. The intensive collectivization of the peasants was under way. The best of them were sent to Siberia simply because they were good farmers and hard workers. Drunkards and loafers were in command.

It was particularly sad to hear of Ilya, Sasha, and their son Misha. Sasha had been my friend since early youth. She was often in our house, and I had spent many hours with her. She had a gay, affectionate nature, and I was very fond of her. When she laughed, her little upturned nose would wrinkle and her eyes squinted. Her hair was light as flax. She had married early, and then we saw less of her.

Ilya was an entirely different type. Handsome as a picture, the kind of man often seen in portraits. Healthy, well-built, with dark, curly hair, he had a ruddy complexion and dark blue eyes. Misha, their only son, studied in the Yasnaya Polyana school during the day. Evenings and holidays he helped his father. Together they built a brick house with their own hands, shaping and baking the bricks themselves. Modern-minded, they discussed with the school doctor how to place the windows to let in the maximum light, they arranged for adequate ventilation, and roofed the house with sheet iron. Such foresight, however, was exactly what was frowned upon in Soviet Russia. It had become bourgeois. All three were exiled to Siberia.

Marta told us how everyone in the village of Yasnaya Polyana saw them off. A crowd assembled at the station. Though hunger was everywhere, each one had nevertheless brought what he could, a few lumps of sugar (the greatest luxury), a slice of lard, some hard-boiled eggs. Many were weeping. Such exiling was called in Soviet terms "dekulakization," from the word kulak, meaning prosperous peasants.

One by one the Communists brought their own people into the administration of Yasnaya Polyana. The atmosphere became so painful that Marta emigrated to her relatives in Sweden. Though she had been born in Russia, she was a Swedish citizen under law because her parents were Swedish.

Olga and I had long hoped that Marta would come and help us on the farm, so her arrival not only delighted us but also lightened our own labor. She very soon adapted to our tasks and to our privations. Despite her aid, things were hard. Not enough money. I was giving fewer lectures. Olga missed her daughter, who was at school, and worried about how to earn enough to enable Maria to finish her education.

The immense loss of our chicks had affected us both materially and psychologically. We no longer had the same energy as in the past five years of struggle. I recall how I used to stand up to my knees in the icy water of a stream to collect bushels of pebbles for cement, and how we mixed the cement with shovels—no one dreamed of a cement mixer—to lay the floors in the hen roosts. Whatever we had accomplished was only by the greatest effort. Through Jane Addams' generosity, we had laid on water for the house and the hen roosts (though we ourselves had no bath), built a fine new hen house and a little house where the Cossack had lived earlier and where Marta now settled.

All this we managed thanks in large part to a tempest and a

flood. When the Connecticut River rose during heavy rains, part of Middletown was submerged. The lumber yard where we traded was destroyed, and its stock floated down the river. Some of it was rescued, but it was already stained by the water and was sold at half price. This was the material we used.

In spite of all this, we were really very tired, and, sorry as we were to liquidate the stock of our farm, we finally decided to sell the chickens and cows and move to Florida. Understanding this radical step, Marta moved to the home of our neighbor, Mr. P., to help his wife, who was not well, with the housework. She took our police dog Miki with her, while Vesta accompanied us. The young pullets had turned out very well, plump New Hampshires, already laying by September. Our neighbors set a high value on them and they sold fast.

An old man in Middletown who had previously bought pullets from us and was highly satisfied came to see us. We had several hundred chickens left, and he bought them all, transporting part of them himself while I delivered the others in our little truck. We hauled the crates out of the car and resettled the birds. When we had done, the old man asked me to step in. "Maybe I can offer you something?"

I did not feel like going in, but we had to settle the accounts, so I did. At the threshold I halted. Good God, what a room! Gogol's Plyushkin, I thought—no, Dickens' Scrooge. The old man even looked like Scrooge, tall, thin, his nose like a buttonhook. He kept giggling, raising his left eyebrow as if winking. His thinning hair was yellow with dirt and tobacco smoke.

Once this room had no doubt been the living room, but now it was cluttered with rubbish, sacks, pictures in gilt frames, old pails, down-at-the-heel shoes, pieces of iron. Evidently he was too used to this condition to notice it.

"Can I offer you a cup of tea?"

"No, no," I said a little too quickly.

"A glass of wine, or cider?"

"No, thank you." I was nauseated at the thought of drinking anything there. All I wanted was to get out as fast as possible.

"You know what?" the old man suddenly remarked, winking.

"Your life is no good at all, no good." I was silent. "But my life too is no good."

"And why?"

"Ha, ha, ha!" He burst into hearty laughter. "You are alone," poking a finger at me, the nail long and yellow. "Women shouldn't live alone. I live alone. A man shouldn't live without a woman. It's no good. Let's join up, I have money. But I'm alone, and that's no good."

I was so disgusted that I stood up abruptly. "Give me the money for the chickens." The money in my hand, I fled as if scalded.

Gradually the farm emptied. I had not thought it would be so sad to dismantle what we had created with such toil—especially parting from the animals. People came for the cows. A big truck was backed up to a low mound so they could climb aboard. They balked and were whipped. The cows mooed. I cried. "Don't cry," said the buyer, who had arranged for installment purchase. "Calm down, I'll pay you the whole amount next week."

"Yes, it's not that, I know you will pay me."

Our little old station wagon of 1929 vintage was already in bad condition, tires worn, the top broken in places. To reach Florida in that would be impossible. I looked at a station wagon with eight cylinders, paid a few hundred dollars for it, and drove it home.

When I passed the prison at the foot of the hill where the sheriff lived, I gave the car more gas and shot up the grade. Parallel with me, not looking to either side, tail between his legs, ran a mongrel pup. Suddenly he threw himself directly under my wheels. A jolt, I knew I had run over him. I stepped on the accelerator and within a few minutes was home. I telephoned the sheriff. "Just opposite the prison I've run over a dog. I'm not trying to avoid responsibility, but I can't bear that dog suffering. I beg you, send one of your people to see. If he's hurt, I'll pay for his care, and if he is dead, I'll pay whatever his owner asks."

In a few minutes the sheriff called me back. "Don't be concerned. Thank God the dog is dead—by the way, I think he committed suicide. Three days ago his ninety-year-old master died, and since then he hasn't eaten or drunk, just kept looking for his master, he acted as if he had lost his mind. It's a good thing you ran over him. He died instantly, without suffering."

A long time passed before I lost the feeling of having run over a living creature.

The day before we left, I gave a lecture at a nearby college. That night at home I felt a sharp pain in my stomach. All night I tossed, with no sleep at all. By morning the pain had quieted. What to do? The electricity was turned off. Our things were all packed. We got into the car. Vesta lay down on the back seat, and we took off.

CHAPTER EIGHTEEN

Edens in Florida

My health kept getting worse and worse. While we were staying with friends in Washington, another attack of sharp pains hit me. When we reached Richmond to visit other friends, I was so ill that there was no thought of going further. I could eat nothing solid, only milk and bouillon. The tiniest piece of bread, fish, or vegetables produced the same inhuman pain. I felt as if everything inside me was afire. The Richmond doctor said I should go to the hospital and have x-rays. But that would mean spending our entire capital of a few hundred dollars. Impossible.* Our friends did all they could to help, but we felt we were imposing on them and must move on, ill as I was.

Those who have gone to Florida by car know the blessed feeling of leaving a damp cold climate behind and moving gradually into southern warmth. Heavy winter clothes packed away, you

* Later Alexandra was operated on for a large stomach ulcer.

take out bathing suits. Hurry into the water! The hot sun bakes you, you breathe the salt air with rapture. The shallow caressing waves, the sands of Daytona Beach, hard and white. All right, car, how fast can you go? Fifty, sixty, eighty miles an hour—I never expected our Ford was capable of such speed. They let you drive at any speed, even a hundred and twenty miles an hour, for the sand was as hard as asphalt and the beach was wide. The ducks and the seagulls flew up before our wheels.

After Daytona we went inland, past orange groves and lakes, to the west coast, where the calm waters of the Gulf lap the shore, to Tarpon Springs, where Greeks cultivate sponges. Finally we reached Ozone, a little town between Tarpon Springs and Clearwater.

An American friend had acquired two tents for us and obtained permission for us to set them up in a citrus grove belonging to an acquaintance. We camped among orange and lemon trees, while by one tent hung branches of guava heavy with almost ripe fruit and to the right rose a tall graceful clump of bamboo. The warm air was filled with the pungent scent of oranges; under the trees the ground was scattered with lemons, oranges, mandarins, grapefruit.

We lay down to sleep. Olga and Vesta were so tired that they quickly dropped off, but I was excited, my heart flooded with happiness, I felt the joy of existence, of being surrounded by nature. A pity to sleep!

Such feelings come in youth—when one is in love one cannot sleep. Now I was in love with the sea I adored, with the hot sun, with the fruit trees, and also perhaps with the sensation of freedom. The moonlight lay in patterns on the floor of the tent. All at once I saw the door flap moving. A small pointed face poked its snout inside, entered, and began eagerly eating Vesta's food. It squeaked and champed, but Vesta heard nothing, she was so worn out by the journey. What animal could this be?

In the morning I saw it sitting high up in the bamboo, its rat tail hanging down, while Vesta dashed madly around, barking, digging at the roots of the bamboo, trying to bring it down. The opossum calmly watched.

For about a month we were blissfully happy in our tents. We swam, fished, ate all sorts of fruits. The guava reminded us of wild strawberries. We cooked on a little kerosene stove, went about half clothed, and enjoyed ourselves to the utmost. Only Vesta suffered. There were thousands of thorns growing on the ground under the trees, and she constantly got them caught between her toes. She would whine piteously, come to me on three legs, and lift her hurt paw for help.

In time, however, our paradisal life came to an end. Through the Roger Babsons I was invited by a Protestant church at Babson Park, near Lake Wales, to give four "sermons" on consecutive Sundays on evangelical topics and to lecture at the college. I knew Mrs. Babson already, as I had given several talks at Babson College before. Mr. Babson offered us a small cottage and a tiny stipend of a hundred dollars.

Olga did not accompany me to the church. She teased me about my new vocation of preacher. But I took my obligation very seriously, I prepared conscientiously, put on my only white dress, and preached. To tell the truth, I contributed very little of my own. I took the Gospel for my theme and tried to interpret it according to Tolstoy's teachings. The elegant ladies in white silk dresses, white hats and gloves, the men in light suits with sunburned faces listened attentively.

My diary for March 2, 1937 records: "In the South they practice discrimination against the blacks. You hear conversations like this in women's clubs:

" 'Tell me,' I asked, 'don't you think that not letting Negroes use the same cars, having separate washrooms at stations, and so on provides a fertile soil for Bolshevik propaganda among colored peoples?'

" 'Oh, no,' one lady quickly objected, 'we are very fond of the Negroes, they can be the most wonderful servants, so devoted, gentle, naive as children. I love the Negroes—only they must know their place.' "

This attitude was incomprehensible to me.

From my diary for March 9, 1937:

"A Rolls-Royce automobile with a chauffeur at stiff attention, his hand on the door. A lady in a white embroidered dress; a man, smooth-shaven, in an impeccable light gray suit, his hair shining white. Where they live—Palm Beach, Mountain Lake— these are the chosen people. They speak of their houses as modest, comfortable, and their life as simple."

At Mountain Lake, where the Babsons had invited me to attend a Quaker service, there was a watchman at the gate. "Where are you going? Why?"

Probably only black servants traveled in cars like my old Ford.

"Whom are you coming to see?"

"Mr. Roger Babson."

He saluted, wondering, no doubt, who is this woman in the old Ford, but he warned me politely, "Drive carefully, it's slippery after the rain."

Never had I seen such luxury. A sea of flowers, magnificent tropical trees, lemons the size of my fist, wide lawns, Japanese cherries. In the famous Bok Tower, the carillon was ringing— Chopin's "Funeral March." Now and then one heard false notes.

All Florida communities must have churches, I had thought, some rich, some poor, where people go on Sundays and come home to eat a chicken dinner. Here there was no church, only a club. Several Quakers had arranged a Quaker meeting in this small community. No need for a church, a preacher, or a service. You just sit quietly for half an hour, then, if one of the silent congregation is inspired, he speaks out.

How the roses scented the air! On the tables China roses, creamy pink. What lovely dresses the women were wearing, rose, green, white, turquoise, all of silk, their shoes white or cream. I badly needed shoes, but couldn't afford to buy any. We had to live on one hundred dollars for three months, pay for the license for the car and the taxes. What radiant complexions the women had, what stunning hats!

Once settled in their seats, they grew quiet. Time passed.

Someone's stomach rumbled. In the first row one old man slept, his mouth open. I looked at my watch. Twenty minutes had gone by. A lady in a gauzy pink hat hid a yawn. Twenty-three minutes.

An elderly man in a gray suit with a rosy, good-natured countenance rose. "Here," he said, "we have lived well and happily throughout the winter, we have enjoyed everything, all was for the best, all were friendly, there were no quarrels—but perhaps we have not helped our neighbors very much." He added, "We should be glad to share with others sometimes, but we don't know with whom, we don't know whom to help."

Everyone began to stir, breathing more freely, then set off for home.

From my diary for March 15, 1937:

"A few days ago at a dinner in a club where I was to lecture, an American asked me if I had gone to the Paris Exposition. No, I replied, I had not.

" 'Oh, that's too bad, why not? You should have seen it, it was most interesting. And I recommend something else: go to Arizona, take a plane.'

"I tried not to listen to why I should go to Arizona. If I had three hundred dollars, I thought, I would go to Rome and say goodbye to my sister—perhaps for the last time. Melancholy thoughts. I had recently read Rousseau's *Confessions*. People had invited him to dinner, to be their guest, to be sheltered, he was surrounded by the wealthy, but not one of them showed him an escape from poverty, a real escape, not humiliating. How could I hope, I thought, for any way out for me? One had to learn, like the pilgrims of old on being given a copper coin, to cross oneself and say, 'May Christ bless you,' not to scorn the giver in his pride."

When the fourth and last Sunday sermon was over, we again had to earn money and find ourselves some shelter. We returned to Palm Beach. Perhaps we could find employment there among the rich. We rented two rooms over a garage in West Palm Beach for thirty-five dollars a month, and went out to look for work.

Palm Beach is a magnificent place with its alleys of palms, its palatial residences, its flowery gardens. Its beach is superb, but it is entirely private. In Palm Beach, it is said, the rich spend money; in West Palm Beach they try to earn it.

When you do your own heavy work on a farm, you are your own master. It is another matter when you hire yourself out.

"Your name? How much do you weigh? What recommendations have you? Intellectual work? No, no, we have no such requests. Would you like to help with housework?"

Americans don't say "servant," they say, "helper."

"But is knowledge of languages and literature of no use? Perhaps to teach children, to translate, perhaps someone needs a governess or a companion?"

Nothing resulted. Our money was disappearing. Then, unexpectedly, fortune smiled on us. We came to know a very rich Russian woman. She was bored and proposed that Olga give her Italian lessons. I was again asked to give some talks for a very low fee.

There in West Palm Beach we met the brother of our dear friend, Sam Yarrow, and his wife. They were as poor as we were. Jim Yarrow was selling some kind of little magazine and was very happy when I offered him a quarter of what I received for any appearance he could arrange for me. But this was quite a new sort of endeavor for him, and so there were scant opportunities. I had to speak for very small fees, twenty-five to thirty dollars, but I was glad of even that amount.

From West Palm Beach I used to visit the neighboring towns. I was invited to give a lecture in Miami, in a large hotel on the shore. Olga and Vesta, our constant companion, went with me.

First there was a gala dinner. When we reached the hall, we saw it was full. Next to me was the owner of the hotel. The director of the local Chamber of Commerce introduced me. I began with a discussion of Tolstoy and the Russian Revolution, speaking over a microphone. The hall was not only crowded, but the ceilings were low and instead of windows there were portholes, as on a ship. I had just come to the point of accusing the Bolsheviks when a mad concert of yowling cats broke out just outside. The audience could not hear them, but it was very hard for me to compete with the racket. So as to attract the chairman's attention to the noise, speaking on about the Bolsheviks' executing Lenin's old comrades (Zinoviev, Kamenev, Rykov, and the others), I added, "Unfortunately, you can't hear it, but right now below these windows outside our Bolshevik comrades are conducting a wake for their victims by a cats' concert."

Either the chairman was deaf or he failed to grasp my meaning. Later I asked, "Why didn't you send someone to quiet down those Bolsheviks under the windows?"

"What Bolsheviks? Those were just cats."

Just then a secretary came up with a piece of paper—a typical, insolent Communist leaflet. I went home in a car with police standing on the running boards.

It seemed that the lecture was a success. Jim Yarrow triumphantly informed me that I had been asked to speak at the University of Miami and two other places. We were invited to stay with Mrs. M., our Washington friend. She was a young, attractive Russian whose husband was an influential American, old and rich, with a bad heart. Since Mrs. M. knew that I loved fishing, she arranged a trip to Key West. But then all our plans were upset. I fell ill again with those terrible stomach pains. We soon had to head back north because three lectures were scheduled in North Carolina.

After North Carolina I planned to go to Washington, where I was to stay with Mrs. M. again, but she wrote she could not take me in for reasons she could explain only in person. Some weeks later I called on her.

"Forgive me," she said, "that I couldn't receive you. You remember you were going to be with us in Miami, but you fell ill and did not come. Before your expected arrival the newspapers in Miami were full of accounts of your scheduled lecture.

"That night when you were to stay with us but became ill and did not come, I was awakened by the smell of gas. I had a headache. Looking out of my window, I saw a light shining in the yard, and the shadows of two men were moving. Should I rouse my husband? He has a bad heart. What if he should die from an attack? I sat there trembling. Finally the light went out and the shadows disappeared. I had not a wink of sleep all night. In the morning my husband told me we had had thieves and that they had removed the screen on one of the windows in the guest room where you were to have spent the night. There was the screen, standing against the wall. They had stolen nothing, though we had a lot of valuable things, silver and so on. It was obvious why they came. First they would have tried to stupefy you by turning on the gas—they knew you had a dog that would bark—and then they would have killed you.

"Several days later I went out to go to the hairdresser. It was already dark, and, you know, the beach there is pretty empty. Two men came up to me. 'Just you try to arrange a lecture for Miss Tolstoy, and you'll see what will happen to you!' said one. I was terribly frightened, but said something about informing the police. 'The police!' exclaimed the man, 'take a look!' He turned back his lapel, showing me some kind of a badge. Obviously he was a Communist agent. If the FBI or the local police had wanted to see me, they would have come openly to our Miami house. So, you will forgive me, but I can't ask you to stay with us."

I have given her account exactly as she gave it to me.

What did all that mean? Were such things facts? Or was I exaggerating from a sense of persecution? I have often asked myself that question. Might it all have been just my imagination?

Once, in Los Angeles after a lecture, I was taken to a hotel where I was expected to spend the night, then travel on the next day. I took a shower, put on my nightgown, and was about to go to bed when I heard a strange noise. Was someone trying to open the door? No, it was not my imagination. Someone was tampering with the lock. Standing there, I thought, what am I to do? On the table I saw a quart bottle of ginger ale. If that person gets in, I thought, I will hit him on the head with it. The door handle was moving. Petrified, I waited. The door knob moved. Slowly the door began to open. Involuntarily, I shoved the door with all my weight. A roar of pain in a man's voice. Minutes passed—or seconds. I stood there shaking. Silence. I went out into the corridor. A man ran up. "Lady, what happened? I'm from the police, assigned to protect you. What was that noise?"

Blessed relief. I told him what had occurred. He rushed off after the invader, then other police arrived. They searched everywhere, they questioned the staff, but found no one. "The nefarious wretch," as the Communists called me, was unharmed. But even now, when I remember that night, I shudder.

CHAPTER NINETEEN

The Birth of an Idea

In 1937 I was still ashamed, I could not understand how the Soviet tyranny continued. I could not understand the passivity of the Russian people, who did not rise up and rebel. The complacency of foreign governments, who watched the horrors continuing in the Russian land and at the same time discussed international peace in the League of Nations with Soviet representatives like Litvinov—that was beyond my comprehension.

In my own heart I was deeply unhappy and confused because I had no idea how to direct my personal efforts. On returning from Florida we did not go directly to the Connecticut farm. We still thought we should try to find work in New York. We asked Marta Knudsen to locate an apartment for us, so we lived on East 120th Street for a short time. I could not adapt to the bustle and filth of city life, however, and yearned for the country once more. I said to myself, only a hundred chickens and a small garden, my own vegetables, that will make me happy—I will go back to the farm and make a living somehow. Olga found work in a place near New York, but Marta and I took Vesta, who was equally glad to go, and returned to the farm.

In the year 1938 I was physically tired and mentally depressed. The work was as hard as ever, cleaning hen manure, feeding and watering a thousand hens and some two thousand chicks, hauling away the manure of the two cows. I had never really learned how to milk a cow; the exercise hurt my hands.

Still, there was joy. Despite the heavy labor and material discomforts, the cramped quarters, the lack of a bath, the miserable clothing, I loved my farm and the two new, beautiful Belgian police dogs we had acquired. They were big, black, without markings; their ears stood straight up, and their great, dark eyes watched us wisely, waiting for orders. They had been trained not to attack. They did not even touch the pheasants.

I don't know where that pair of pheasants came from. Most of the time they sat on the roof, wandering now and then in the meadow. In the spring the young pheasants emerged. It was comical to watch how the babies, little as sparrows, would hide somewhere, or climb up on Vesta and the police dogs, walking boldly along their backs. The dogs merely gazed at us in mild protest.

The strawberries were now ripening, and I went out to gather some. Just then the mother pheasant, whom I had frightened, started up with her chicks behind her. When the berries ripened, the pheasants pecked them all.

Suddenly I received a cable from Europe that brought a radical change in my life. It informed me of the arrival of Tatiana Alexeevna Schaufuss, whom I had not seen for eighteen years. Our last meeting had been in 1922, when we were both arrested by the Bolsheviks.

I met her at the little station at Meriden, fifteen miles from our farm. When she saw my worn-out clothes and my stockings that did not match, she was very unhappy. In the summer I wore no stockings at all at the farm.

Tatiana and I had known each other in Moscow. She and her friend Ksenia Andreevna Rodzyanko (they were both Red Cross nurses) often visited me in Merzlyakovsky Lane at the headquarters of the Society for the Study of the Works of Leo Tolstoy, then preparing the first complete ninety-two volume edition of my father's writings, which appeared in 1929. I lived next to the editorial office, where—a most unusual advantage at the time—I had hot water and a bath in my apartment. The nurses came partly for the sake of a bath. Sometimes my niece Annochka Tolstoy and I would sing Russian songs and gypsy airs to the accompaniment of my guitar.

Subsequently I lost track of the two nurses. In time I learned that both had been arrested for their Orthodox convictions and were in prison, at first in the notorious Moscow prison, the Lubyanka, then they were transferred to the Ivanovsky concentration camp. From there they were exiled to Siberia until the end of the civil war. During a scarlet fever epidemic which broke out there, they worked in the villages, nursing. The peasants paid them for their services with food—chickens, eggs, milk, and butter. The camp was near the rich forests of Krasnoyarsk along the upper banks of the Yenisei River. There they gathered berries and mushrooms; so all in all they were not badly off.

Now, eighteen years later, Tatiana had come to visit me on my American farm, where I was living with Marta. The American Red Cross had invited her to come from Czechoslovakia, where she and Ksenia had been working with the Committee for Aid to Refugees under the direction of Alice Masaryk, daughter of Thomas Garrigue Masaryk, the first president of Czechoslovakia.

When Tatiana saw my farm, she exclaimed, "What are you doing in this hole, cleaning manure out of the hen roosts?"

"Yes," I answered, "I feed the chickens, I milk the cows, though not very well; in my spare time I do some writing, also not very well. But on the whole it's not a bad life."

Here on the farm, after endless discussions, my friend Tatiana and I developed the idea of forming a committee for the relief of refugees. We would help those coming mainly from Czechoslovakia and France, where Russians were having a desperate time trying to earn a living. We were determined to act on this idea. But how to do this? Who would help? Where could we find the funds? Neither Tatiana nor I had any money at all.

I sold the farm and moved to a small apartment on Riverside Drive in New York City.

CHAPTER TWENTY

Creation of the Tolstoy Foundation

By chance we met a lady named Elizaveta Vitalievna Alekseev, who was a representative of a children's aid society. She at once supported the idea of a committee to aid not only certain Russians, such as children, high school graduates, graduates of institutes, lawyers, doctors, engineers, invalids—but all Russians deserving help. She suggested that our new organization become a subdivision of the children's aid society.

Early in the spring of 1939, in the New York apartment of Boris Alexandrovich Bakhmetev, who had been the last non-Soviet ambassador to the United States (appointed by Kerensky), we held a first organizational meeting. Besides the ambassador there were present the renowned aviator Boris V. Sergievsky; the musician Sergei Rachmaninov; Countess Sophie V. Panin; Dr. Ethan Colton, an American who had been a close friend and collaborator of former President Herbert Hoover, who was known for his relief work in Russia during the famine years; the historian Mikhail I. Rostovtsev; a lawyer; Tatiana Schaufuss; and myself. At this meeting we decided that, despite our admiration for the children's aid society, we would decline Alekseev's offer. Our aims and undertakings would have a far wider objective.

The new organization, it was decided, would be called the Tolstoy Foundation, in memory of my father, and it was thus registered in New York State on April 15, 1939. The founders named above were joined by Igor Sikorsky, and Alexis Wiren. President Hoover became the honorary chairman. The purpose of the Foundation was and is to assist victims of oppression by rehabilitating them within the free world, by promoting their immigration to countries willing to offer asylum, and by aiding them to integrate in their new communities without the sacrifice of their ethnic traditions.

The guiding principle of the Foundation was and is that its assistance should recognize human dignity and the desire for independence in every individual and his right to freedom of choice of a country in which to live. It aims to assist the newcomer in becoming an asset to his new environment, contributing to it culturally and economically.

CHAPTER TWENTY-ONE

The Beginning

Our first donors were Ambassador Bakhmetev and Boris Sergievsky, who at once contributed his first check for twenty-five dollars for office expenses. At that time Tatiana was attached to the American Christian Committee, but later, as the activities of the Tolstoy Foundation expanded, she withdrew from that organization to give all her time to our work, devoted to any and all Russian refugees.

We had no funds at all. We knew nothing of social work as practiced in the United States. Only the dire need for such aid and our faith gave us the strength to raise the needed money. The Episcopalian Committee gave me a desk in its office on Fourth Avenue in New York, where later the Tolstoy Foundation was able to rent a room. Twice a week we had a stenographer, whom we paid five dollars a day.

What should our first steps be? Clearly, to get funds. But how? Through letters? But how to dictate in English? I had never dictated anything in my life. Our unsmiling, tight-lipped secretary, her red-painted fingernails ready with a pencil, waited for me to begin. Silent and scornful, she endured the long pauses while this new officer of the Tolstoy Foundation sought the appropriate words.

Finally, the first appeal was sent out. The first response came from a Mr. Avinov, the head of a Pittsburgh museum—three dollars. Gradually, our work picked up. More donations came. The Tolstoy Foundation at last began to send aid to refugees in France and Czechoslovakia.

On November 30, 1939, the USSR declared war on Finland. It would seem that a powerful giant like the Soviet Union might easily have crushed tiny Finland. Yet the Soviets suffered defeat, unheard of, shameful. Their huge armed forces showed the world first-hand evidence of Bolshevik cruelty, inhumanity, and total disorganization. The heroic Finns, though outnumbered, successfully defended their nation. The Red Army, shod in rags, hungry, frozen, driven from the rear by machine guns, marched they knew not where. They died from exhaustion and cold in the forty degrees below zero temperatures of the Finnish forest. About 50,000 prisoners were taken by the Finns. And how many were killed, how many frozen to death? No one will ever know the exact figures. Not without reason did the Finnish minister, Prokope, call this war, "a black march backward into the Middle Ages."

One Finnish soldier in a letter to his uncle in January 1940 described the Soviet soldiers thus:

"One rarely sees Red soldiers wearing shoes. Rough scraps of cloth are wrapped round their feet. They are dirty and flea-ridden. Their commanding officer often fires into his troops from behind, forcing them into battle. Many Soviet planes voluntarily landed on our side to avoid the fighting."

The Soviet government's cruel and inhuman attitude to the Russian citizens was also evident in the Bolsheviks' refusal to sign the International Geneva Convention on the care and help of prisoners of war. All other countries signed the Convention and were expected to make regular payments for their own prisoners of war. The Soviet Union was the only exception. Tiny, war-torn Finland could not feed, clothe, and provide shoes for the 50,000 Russian soldiers in that land.

Meanwhile the sympathies of America and the entire free world stood on the side of Finland, the nation that had suffered so much at the hands of the Soviet barbarians. The Americans mistakenly blamed not the Soviet government but the Russian people, not comprehending that the Russian people had suffered more from this savage, mindless war than had any other nation. Tens of thousands of persons had perished. Only the International Red Cross sent food parcels to the Russian prisoners of war in Finland.

The Tolstoy Foundation immediately declared a campaign for funds and began aiding the prisoners of war through the International Red Cross. This was the first significant step of the Foundation. Prince Paul Chavchavadze* took an ardent part in this work. Thirty-four thousand dollars worth of food parcels were mailed. However, the Russian soldiers never found out that not only the American Red Cross but also Russian émigrés, working through the Tolstoy Foundation, had responded to their suffering. Letters of thanks were addressed only to the Red Cross, though the packages were sent by their fellow countrymen.

How touching those letters were! The Red Cross allowed Tatiana Schaufuss and me to read them. How much warmth, how much longing and suffering they conveyed! And how much gratitude to those on the other side who had not forsaken them! It was hard to read these letters without crying. What a deep faith was theirs—some asked for rosaries with a crucifix, while others asked

---

* Prince Paul Chavchavadze (1899–1971) was a distinguished Georgian of an ancient family with a large estate in the Caucasus, Tsinandali. He married Nina Romanov, and was thus related to both Russian and Georgian royalty. He emigrated to the U.S., became an American citizen, and served during World War II as a liaison officer between Allied and Soviet forces. He lived in Wellfleet, Cape Cod, for many years. His charming autobiography, *Family Album* (1949) describes pre-Revolutionary scenes in St. Petersburg and Georgia.

for Bibles. Their wishes were answered: the Tolstoy Foundation sent the prisoners of war, through the Bible Society, 5,000 crucifixes on chains and 10,000 Bibles.

Nevertheless, despite our aid and that of the Red Cross, the Finns still had difficulty feeding the prisoners of war. As the war ended, therefore, the Red Army soldiers were sent back to the USSR. But then another frightful crime was added to the heinous record of the Soviet dictatorship: we heard that 36,000 of the Red Army's surviving prisoners of war forcibly returned to the USSR had been shot.*

CHAPTER TWENTY-TWO

Reed Farm

When Tatiana Schaufuss and I were asked, "How does the Tolstoy Foundation manage to exist?" we used to respond, "By a miracle of God." Early in the spring of 1941 such an event seemingly did take place. We had long formed the idea of building a refuge for Russian émigrés, where the homeless might find shelter and occupation on a farm.

Ambassador Bakhmetev supported this idea. "If you both plan to manage a farm, then I shall contribute the first $5,000 toward this goal," he told us. Despite the fact that land was much cheaper in those days, to acquire the feasible acreage and build-

---

*The Yalta Conference agreement, signed in 1945 by Churchill, Roosevelt, and Stalin, called for the repatriation of all prisoners. In effect, however, thousands of Russian nationals were forcibly repatriated, even though many of them wanted to remain out of their homeland. Many chose suicide instead. The Tolstoy Foundation aimed at their rescue first of all whenever possible. When their numbers slacked off other nationals were included. For further reading, see Nikolai Tolstoy, *Victims of Yalta* (London: Hodder and Stoughton, 1977; Corgi paperback, 1979), especially pp. 117–23.

ings for such a low price was impossible. Nevertheless, we began looking for just the right spot.

Tatiana Schaufuss was then still working in the office for aid to Christian refugees, so my close friend Marta Knudsen and I drove around looking at farms suggested by a real estate office. Unfortunately, all those we viewed were either too expensive or just not good enough. Then an agent suggested that we take a look at what he assured us was a nice farm some thirty miles from New York, priced at $15,000. We liked the sound of it very much, and so one Sunday when Tatiana was free the three of us went to look it over, together with the agent. He said that it belonged to Mrs. Mary Stillman Harkness, who had created the foundation of that name, which had funded hospital and university building. At one time there had been at Reed Farm a sanatorium for children with heart diseases, but as the house had three stories and the children could not use the stairs, the sanatorium was closed.

The road from New York ran along the Hudson River through beautiful, wooded country. Here and there were little white cottages and now and then a large, deep lake. The seventy-acre farm included two houses, many other buildings, all in good shape, and an artesian well. The price was $15,000, but all we had was the $5,000 promised us by Ambassador Bakhmetev. Could we perhaps get a loan from the bank? What to do?

One day Tatiana was in her office when an American woman, a good friend of hers, dropped by on business. "What's wrong with you today?" she asked, "you seem worried about something."

"True enough, and I don't know what to do," answered Tatiana. "Alexandra Tolstoy has got it into her head that we must buy a farm to solve the resettlement problem of the refugees. We have found just the right place, but we have only a third of the price asked."

"Who owns the farm?"

"A Mrs. Harkness."

"Oh, that is the same one who created the Harkness Commonwealth Fund, which built the Medical Center at Presbyterian

Hospital and other buildings at Yale and Harvard Universities. My husband knows her very well. He will speak to her."

A few days passed. I was at work in my office when the telephone rang. The manager of the Harkness Fund was on the line. He asked me several questions, mainly concerning the percentage devoted to the organizational expenses of the Tolstoy Foundation. I myself was at a loss, but my severe secretary quickly figured out how much we were spending for that purpose—our overhead, in other words. It proved to be three percent, and we responded with this answer within forty-eight hours.

A few days later the telephone brought us the news that Mrs. Harkness had decided to donate Reed Farm with its buildings to the Tolstoy Foundation. I nearly toppled from my chair: a miracle! The Tolstoy Foundation had just been given a large and valuable piece of property.

Early in June 1941 we held the solemn blessing of our farm and the first children's camp was set up. In front of the main house under the old shade trees, Metropolitan Feofil held a service blessing the estate. Many persons from New York and its environs had gathered there. During the ceremony a hydroplane suddenly appeared overhead circling the farm—our friend Sergievsky! He landed nearby at Rockland Lake and was driven to the farm.

During lunch, while the guests were eating and drinking and merry-making, I noticed an old Russian woman sitting alone in a corner of the yard. She was weeping bitterly, and so I approached her. "What is your trouble?" I asked.

"I've just buried my daughter," she said sobbing. "Why am I alive? I don't know, I'm lame and old and all alone, who needs me?"

"We need you," I said, pitying her. "We need you. Come live with us, we'll try to be your family, at least in part."

"Could I really?"

"Of course. This house exists for lonely people like you." And thus Maria Aleksandrovna joined our family.

She was often witty and gay, yet demanding of herself and others. She helped everyone in every possible way. She sang in the choir, she sewed, she embroidered the priests' vestments. When the cheap second-hand boards we had bought for a henhouse arrived, with nails still in them, everybody, even the older children, began pulling them out, and so did she, to our amazement, despite her lame leg, entertaining us all with her witticisms and her energy.

When I recall those days, I ask myself, how was it there was such an upsurge of spirit then? People toiled for the sake of an idea, they counted neither the labor, nor the hours, nor the pay. How happy we were, how contented, and what friends! We sang as we worked. Maria Aleksandrovna had a pure, sweet soprano. I sang along with her, and the others chimed in.

In the garden, under cover, grew a little raspberry. . .

It was truly a great event, our acquisition of that farm, crucial to our subsequent activities. We started from virtually nothing. The buildings had been emptied: not a chair, not a table, not a tool was to be found. No one had lived on the property but an old watchman and his wife, who occupied one of the cottages. In order to function at all we had to start from scratch. We had one ancient Ford and it, like its owners, knew no rest. Tatiana, Marta, and I commuted to the farm from New York. Tatiana drove again and again to the junkyard, to auctions, to acquire essential furniture. She bought some chairs at an auction for fifty cents each; they serve us to this day.

Ambassador Bakhmetev's $5,000 went for equipment. A group of Quakers donated beds; a wealthy American woman provided two large thoroughbred cows; another gave us a pig, the forebear of many generations bred on the farm in subsequent years.

I labored in the garden along with two young boys, sons of Emelyan, our only paid worker. His wife, the good serene Anna, worked in the kitchen. Later we acquired a tractor, which was invaluable in the garden for mowing and haying. Marta busied herself with the household; when our activities broadened, she took on raising our chickens. Later she became director of the children's camp, the kind of work she loved best, where she ruled for several years.

Once during the summer, when work on the farm was at its peak, a troop of boy scouts appeared with their scoutmaster, Colonel Vladimir Petrovich Petrov, who was an active member of the Federation of Russian Orthodox Clubs. At once he took an active interest in the Tolstoy Foundation and enlisted in our cause several club members who soon became invaluable. These young people took on every sort of work; washing, cleaning, hauling, installing furniture, and—most important—they did everything happily and with good will, thus spreading their own cheer among the farm's organizers.

Year by year the farm was built up, both in equipment and activities. Workers for the Tolstoy Foundation never needed a cause—causes came to us, seeking aid, and we met them halfway. For example, Tatiana Schaufuss somehow learned that a Russian brother and sister were in a New York orphanage. She was horrified by their living conditions. Locked up in stuffy, dim rooms, without any amusements or occupations, the place was like a prison. The parents were in a mental hospital. No one else had any responsibility for them. She succeeded in getting them out and brought them to the farm. Thus our Children's Home came into being. Very soon it was filled. We could shelter from twelve to fifteen such orphans and semi-orphans. The children benefited from a religious upbringing, studied the Russian language, and learned about Russian culture, agriculture, and sports.

From the very beginning we thought of holding church services. The only feasible place was in the largest room on the second floor of the main house. We gathered ikons, the priest blessed our little temple, and a choir formed. We had no ikonostasis, but we held services just the same.

Our first regular priest was Bishop Savva, a refugee from Poland. He especially loved the children; he taught them God's law, worked alongside them in our garden, and even went swimming with them in our lake. Then came Reverend Mikhail Yelenevsky, who served from 1947 to 1970.

How many children came and went! And how many persons

gave their time and energy to the development of our farm! They worked endlessly, day and night, happy for their sacrifice, for any cause bears fruit if people devote themselves to it wholly and unselfishly. The more they gave, the more their efforts produced, and thus the greater their love and energy.

CHAPTER TWENTY-THREE

Kind People

C an anyone forget "Martochka," as we called Marta? It was said that when she was made the mold was broken. Usually, and very naturally, people give their time and energy to their own families, or to work that brings them some material happiness, some money. Few persons give themselves wholly and unselfishly to social work, but Marta Andreevna Knudsen was one such person. With her, all selfish interests were pushed into the background. Money? It did not concern her in the least. Whatever she received, she gave away. Clothes did not interest her either. She wore black or gray, always very clean, with high-collared blouses. She had a gentle, slightly crooked smile and kind, gray eyes. Her smooth, fair hair, which had never known a permanent, harmonized with her intelligent gaze. As for health and energy, all she needed was enough for the duties in which she believed.

Soon, Tatiana, Marta, and I all moved to Reed Farm from the city, for our work had begun to pile up. Marta knew how to do everything. She sewed, she was a wonderful cook, she learned how to raise chickens, she typed—but her chief vocation lay with the children. She did everything without haste, slowly, every step considered, fulfilling each project to the last detail.

I remember the day that new chicks were delivered to the

newly-built henhouse. The heaters had just been installed, and we were expected to watch the temperature gauge, making sure that the tiny chicks neither froze nor were overheated. Marta was so worried that something might happen to them in the night that she brought her cot into the henhouse and spent the night, to make sure that the temperatures remained correct. She did this for about a week.

When there was no one free to cook, she would don an apron and take her place at the stove to prepare lunch or supper. When there was no one to clean the house or wash the floors, Marta kilted up her skirt and went to work.

In 1947–48 we would sometimes receive from fifty to seventy displaced persons at the farm, often as late as two or three o'clock in the morning. Marta, having sent the cook home, would herself feed them, always with a kind word whether in German, Austrian, Italian, or whatever. She took pains to ensure that all the bunk beds (which saved space) were properly made, with clean linen and towels. Children's beds were provided for them. She never complained of being tired, but sometimes her pale face seemed even paler and her long nose even longer.

When we were able to set up a home for orphaned or semi-orphaned children, Marta became the director. Here she found her element. Only rarely did she ever punish the children; her tears of distress and her apparent sorrow when the children did something bad worked on them more effectively than any other punishment. "Don't be angry, Marta Andreevna, I won't do it again." Not only the children but everyone else loved her.

Another devoted worker—unforgettable—who helped to put the Foundation on its feet was Leonidych. He had a gentle, half-shy smile and was devoted to our church, where he sang in the choir in his soft baritone. He came to the farm in order to work in the Russian carpenters' artel. His hands were always rough and callused. For some reason these carpenters worked only at night, and during the day they would get drunk, then sleep it off. Leonidych did the same, but when work ended and the carpenters went home, Leonidych stayed on at the farm. Over the years he became indispensable.

He did everything. He recited prayers, he sang in the choir, he built an ikonostasis, he performed a joiner's tasks, he painted, installed electric wiring, and repaired our cars. Yet on high holidays and on our name days Leonidych invariably got drunk. Then only Tatiana could handle him and talk him into getting some sleep. He adored her and would take orders from no one else.

Anna Ilinichna*, widow of the writer, lived on our farm for several years. She was jolly, full of life, and she loved jokes. Often she good-naturedly played tricks on our farm residents, and this livened the general atmosphere. She worked in the egg department, sorting and washing the eggs, then setting them out for sale. Whenever she spoke of her deceased husband, her big hazel eyes shone and her expression became young and vivid.

The supervisor of the egg stand was old Evgeniya Nikolaevna Navrotsky, who worked with a quick energy, not out of anxiety but because she was conscientious. Where did this educated woman, the wife of a public figure of Odessa, learn such diligence? She took on any job that would bring in more money to the Tolstoy Foundation.

"Evgeniya Nikolaevna, you've put a small egg in the box for large ones. You mustn't do that!"

"Never mind, no one will ever notice it. The larger eggs cost the more, so we'll get a bit more money this way."

Once, I was told, when a cat carried off a young chicken and ate one of its wings, Evgeniya Nikolaevna gave the bird a good cleaning and sold it anyway. Her customers all loved her, and, though she did not speak English, she could talk with them in French or German. As most of them were Jewish, they had no trouble understanding her.

It is hard now to say how the residents of the farm turned up there in the first place. At the request of Chaliapin's** widow, we

---

* She was presumably the second wife of Leonid Nikolayevich Andreyev (1871–1919), author of *He Who Gets Slapped* and numerous other plays and stories. She is known to have lived at Reed Farm in the 1940s.

** Feodor Ivanovich Chaliapin (1873–1938) was a Russian operatic bass, one of the greatest performers in the history of opera. After the Revolution he was lauded as an "artist of the invited his former manager to come to us. His name was Mark Michurin, and he had come from Czechoslovakia in great need of rest. He didn't take it easy for long however; he quickly joined in our common cause. Panting and soaked with sweat, that big, corpulent man did physical labor for the first time in his life. He mowed the lawn, he hauled stones that a volunteer group of Cossacks were using for the foundation of the henhouse. He simply could not bring himself to sit around relaxing in an armchair while everyone else was toiling away. So he became the object of some innocent chaffing.

Now there are few left who remember the pleasures of those first years on the farm. When the tomato crop was ripe, we set out tables under the trees, cleaned and sorted the fruit, and packed them in baskets. Everyone came to the "tomato club," where we told all the latest news as we worked. We often discussed plans for the future. Sometimes we sang songs and reminisced about our past lives.

Sorting the tomatoes demanded a bit of skill. We did it according to size, then we lined the bottom rows with the smaller, less ripe ones and the top rows with the big ones ready for the table. When the baskets were filled and weighed (a certain number of pounds had to be met), we loaded them into the car. At one o'clock in the morning Tatiana and Leonidych would set off for the market in New York. When we had sold the load, we filled our little truck with crates of fruit, which were sold for next to nothing on the eve of holidays.

Next time the "club" met, it would be an apricot or peach club. Again we sorted the fruit and preserved hundreds of jars for the winter. These fruit clubs were vastly enjoyed, for all could eat their fill.

Anyone desiring to do so sang at our church services. Our choir director was named Slutsky, a pupil of the well-known choir director Koshevsky, who in the past had worked with the biggest church choirs in Kiev. Now, however, he had only a few un-

---

people," but disagreement with the Soviet government caused him to remain outside Russia after 1921. He later sang with the Metropolitan Opera in New York.

trained farm workers to deal with. Our best baritone and reciter of church prayers was Leonidych, while our oldest choir member, M. A. Mikhailov, delighted us with her rich and youthful soprano.

Unhappily, our wonderful director and kind friend Slutsky died. Then Count Lamsford drove up from New York each Sunday to direct the choir. In 1946 Bishop Savva left for England, and Father Mikhail Elenevsky along with his wife and two young sons arrived from France. Sasha, the youngest, was still in the cradle. His three-year-old brother charmed us all. He was a calm and serious child who rarely cried. He looked at us and the world with a gentle, kind heart. His clear blue eyes reflected his good nature, and his blonde curls enhanced his intelligent little face.

Life on the farm continued in its usual friendly fashion. No one suspected that the Tolstoy Foundation farm would play the significant role it did after World War II in the immense task of resettling European refugees. Our activities were greatly expanded then; we were destined to give refuge or at least temporary shelter to many thousands of Russians, and later would ease the burden of hundreds of the ill and aged.

Alexandra Tolstoy became an American citizen in 1941. She continued to live at the Tolstoy Foundation in Valley Cottage, New York, and was active as its president and as a lecturer and writer. In 1978 she suffered a heart attack, and thereafter was bedridden. She died at the Tolstoy Foundation Nursing Home on September 26, 1979, at the age of ninety-five.

APPENDIX

The Tolstoy Foundation

The Tolstoy Foundation is an American, nonprofit, nonsectarian, nonpolitical voluntary agency for foreign service, founded by Alexandra Tolstoy and Tatiana Schaufuss. It was incorporated in April 1939 with the purpose of helping Russian refugees and displaced persons emigrate to countries offering asylum, and to facilitate their subsequent integration and assimilation into local communities. During the Hungarian crisis in 1956, the Foundation initiated a policy to extend assistance to refugees of nationalities other than Russian. The Tolstoy Foundation is a public charity and must depend on private contributions for much of its activity. In addition to refugee work, the Foundation tries to further its goal "to preserve, foster, and advance the finest tradition of Russian art, history, and in general the best humanitarian ideals of Russian culture."

The refugee program derives partial support from the Department of State and from the United Nations High Commissioner for Refugees. As part of its resettlement effort the Foundation has given special attention to the needs of families and the elderly, and has been aided in its efforts on their behalf by the governments of several host countries. The central office of the Tolstoy Foundation is in New York City; branch offices are maintained in Europe, South America, and Canada.

In 1941, the position of the Tolstoy Foundation in the United States was stabilized by a generous gift through the Commonwealth Fund. This was Reed Farm—seventy acres of land which became the Tolstoy Foundation Center in Valley Cottage, five miles north of Nyack, in Rockland County, New York.

During the nineteen-forties and fifties the existing buildings on the property were renovated and further structures built. Farming of all types was continued, primarily as a form of therapy for the refugees who came to stay for varied lengths of time. In its early years, the farm served as an initial haven and resettlement center for over 6,500 displaced persons of World War II—out of some 35,000 people brought to the United States and directly sponsored by the Tolstoy Foundation under special congressional legislation on behalf of refugees scattered all over the world after World War II.

Cultural activities in Russian and English were organized at the Center, lectures were given, and a summer camp, active until 1968, was established for some eighty needy children. Religion has played a prominent part in the Russian emigration and to meet the needs of the refugees and long-term residents of the Center a permanent church—built in the classic Pskov-Novgorod style and dedicated to St. Sergius of Radonezh—was erected in 1957.

In 1952 a special appeal for a home for the aged at the Tolstoy Foundation Center was launched by Alexandra Tolstoy and Tatiana Schaufuss. The home was established with the extensive financial help of new immigrants to America and functions under the regulations of the New York State and Rockland County departments of social services, serving fifty residents. In addition, a nursing home of ninety-six beds was built on land provided for the Tolstoy Foundation Nursing Home, Inc., in 1970. It continues to operate at full capacity at the Center in Valley Cottage.

The major work of the Tolstoy Foundation began with the advent of World War II in assistance to Russian prisoners of war in Finland and refugees. In the war's aftermath, thousands of Russian and other refugees throughout Western Europe and the Middle East were interviewed and either processed for emigration or placed in homes for the aged in France. In the fifties, further homes for the aged were established in France and Germany.

In 1953 the Foundation opened an office in Brazil, soon followed by similar offices in Argentina and Chile. All three offices assisted emigration to these countries, distributed food and clothing, and tendered legal assistance. A home for mentally handicapped Russian and East European refugees, constructed in Itaquera, Brazil, with the help of the United Nations High Commissioner for Refugees, was dedicated in 1976.

Among the many ethnic and religious groups assisted by the Tolstoy Foundation over the years are North Caucasians, Russian Old Believers, Kalmuks, Tibetans, Ugandans, and Hungarians. And, more recently, refugees from the eastern bloc countries and the USSR, including Rumanians and Armenians, have been helped.

Since the fall of Vietnam, Cambodia, and Laos in 1975, the Tolstoy Foundation has resettled some 10,000 Indochinese refugees in the United States.

In 1980, under the leadership of Teymuraz K. Bagration, who succeeded Tatiana Schaufuss as Executive Director, a Canadian Tolstoy Foundation office was opened in Montreal, Quebec, in memory of Alexandra Tolstoy. Similarly, a Russian Summer School and an Alexandra Tolstoy Memorial Library at the Foundation were opened in the summer of 1981.

Many distinguished Russian émigrés have warmly endorsed, in a published statement, the work of the Tolstoy Foundation. They include Joseph Brodsky, Alexander Galitch, Naum Korzhavin, Vladimir Maximov, Victor Nekrasov, Mstislav Rostropovich, Andrei Sinyavsky, Galina Vishnevskaya, and Alexander Solzhenitsyn.

Publications of Alexandra Tolstoy

EDITORIAL WORK

1911   *Posmertnye khudozhestvennye proizvedeniya Lva Tolstogo*
        (Posthumous works of fiction of Leo Tolstoy). 2 vols. V.
        Chertkov, ed. Published by Alexandra Tolstoy. Moscow,
        1911. Facsimiles.

1912   L. N. Tolstoy. *Polnoe sobranie sochinenii* (Collected works
        of Leo Tolstoy). 3 vols. V. Chertkov, ed. Moscow, 1912.

1929–1938   *Polnoe sobranie sochinenii Lva Tolstogo* (Collected works
        of Leo Tolstoy). 90 vols. Moscow: 1929–38. (Definitive
        edition. Alexandra Tolstoy is cited as co-editor in vols. 1–
        11, 17–19, 25–27, 32–33, 36, 38, 43–44, 47, 55–56, 58–59,
        63, 72, 82, 85–87.)

BOOKS

1916   *Léon Tolstoi, mon père* (Leo Tolstoy, my father). Edmond
        Cary, trans. Paris: Amiot-Dumont, 1916. 496 pp., portrait
        on cover, no notes or bibliography.

1925–193(?)   *Tolstoys Fluchte und Tod* (Tolstoy's flight and death).
        René Fülop-Miller and Friedrich Eckstein, eds. Vera Mi-
        trofanoff-Demelič, trans. Berlin: B. Cassirer, 1925. 250
        pp., illustrations, portrait, with letters and diaries of fam-
        ily and friends.

—   *Tolstojs flugte og død* (Tolstoy's flight and death). L. Nathanson, trans. Copenhagen: Hagerup, 1927.

—   *Ob ukhode i smerti L. N. Tolstogo* (On the departure and death of L. N. Tolstoy). Moscow: Yasnaya Polyana Museum, 1928. 62 pp.

—   *Tolsztoj futása és halála* (Tolstoy's flight and death). Bonkoló Sándor, trans. Budapest: Revai Kiadas (?), 193?. 251 pp., frontispiece, plates, portrait.

1930–1933   *Torusutoi no omoide* (Recollections of Tolstoy). Sadatoshi Yasugi and Naoyuki Fukami, trans. Tokyo: Iwanami, 1930. 636 pp., 13 plates.

—   *The Tragedy of Tolstoy*. Elena Varneck, trans. New Haven: Yale University Press, 1933. 249 pp., frontispiece, plates, portraits. London: Oxford University Press, 1933.

—   *Ma vie avec mon père* (My life with my father). André Pierre, trans. Paris: Rieder, 1933. 382 pp.

—   *La mia vita col padre* (My life with my father). Nina Kessler, trans. Milan: Casa Editrice A. Corticelli, 1933. 446 pp. (Authorized translation.)

1934–1965   *I Worked for the Soviet*. Alexandra Tolstoy with Roberta Yerkes, trans. New Haven: Yale University Press, 1934. 254 pp. London: Allen & Unwin, 1935.

—   *Probleski vo tme* (Rays of light in the darkness; original Russian version of *I Worked for the Soviet*). Washington: Literturno-Khudozhestvennyi Kruzhok v Kalifornii, 1965. 244 pp.

1953–1976   *Tolstoy. A Life of My Father*. Elizabeth Reynolds Hapgood, trans. New York: Harper & Bros., 1953. 543 pp., portraits, plates. London: Gollancz, 1954(?). 545 pp. Reprinted Belmont, Mass.: Nordland Publishing Co., 1975; New York: Octagon Books, 1976.

—   *Otets. Zhizn Lva Tolstogo* (My father. The life of Leo Tolstoy). 2 vols. New York: Chekhov Publishing House, 1953. 823 pp., notes, bibliography.

—   *Hayey avi* (A life of my father). A. Aviram, trans. Jerusalem: Karni, 1954. 464 pp.

—— *Tolstoi, Min Feders Liv* (Tolstoy, my father's life). Ramus Fischer, trans. Odensee, Sweden: Skandinavisk Bogforlag, 1956(?). 384 pp., illustrations.

—— *Una vida de mi padre* (A life of my father). Pedro Lecuena, trans. Buenos Aires, Argentina: Sudamericana, 1958. 567 pp., illustrations. Reprinted 1964(?).

1979 *Doch* (Daughter). London, Ontario: Zaria Publishing Co., 1979. 501 pp.

1981 *Out of the Past.* Katharine Strelsky and Catherine Wolkonsky, eds. New York: Columbia University Press, 1981. 430 pp., illustrations.

ARTICLES AND STORIES

1920–1942 "Otryvki vospominanii" (Passages from reminiscences). *Sovremennyya zapiski* (Paris), 1934–1936. Nos. 56–57, 59–60, 62.

—— "Iz vospominanii" (From reminiscences). *Sovremennyya zapiski* (Paris), 1931–1933. Nos. 45–52.

—— "Predrazsvetnzi tuman" (The early morning mist). *Novyi Zhurnal* (New York), 1942. 1:28–48; 2:38–58; 3:20–39.

1955 "Nikolka" (Nicholas). *Opyty* (New York), 1955. 4:38–44.

1978 "The Tolstoyans." *The Yale Review,* Winter 1978, pp. 161–66.

CHAPTERS IN BOOKS

1926 "Home Leaving and Death." In Aylmer Maude, *Family Views of Tolstoy.* London: Allen & Unwin, 1926.

1957 "Comment mon père écrivit *Guerre et Paix*" (How my father wrote *War and Peace*). In *Guerre et Paix*, Paris, 1957. Chapter 27.

1959 "Léon Tolstoi, mon père, à l'époque où il écrivit *Résurrection*" (Leo Tolstoy, my father, when he wrote *Resurrection*). In *Résurrection*. Paris, 1959.

PAMPHLETS

1949   *Short, Short True Stories*. New York: Tolstoy Foundation, 1949. 11 pp., illustrations. (On refugee work.)
1. "A Letter to Our Lord, Our Savior"
2. "Tchaikovsky's Autumn Song"
3. "A Letter from a Displaced Person"
4. "Why?"

1959   *Obrashchenie svobodnykh rossiyan iz svobodnogo mira, pervogo maya, 1959 goda* (Appeal of the Free Russians from the Free World, May 1, 1959). New York: no publisher listed, 1959. 19 pp., illustrations.

1968–1969   *The Real Tolstoy*. Morristown, N.J.: H. S. Evans, 1968. (Critique of Henri Troyat's book, *Tolstoy*.)

——   *A propos du "Tolstoi" d'Henri Troyat* (On the subject of Henri Troyat's *Tolstoy*). Saint-Etienne, France: Imprimerie Generale du Centre, 1969. 16 pp.

The sources of this bibliography are: *National Union Catalog*, Library of Congress, Washington, D.C., 1952–55, 1955–57, 1958–62; *Bibliografia Nazionale Italiana*, Florence, Italy, vol. 36; *Dictionary Catalog of the Slavonic Collection*, The New York Public Library, 2d ed., vol. 39, 1974; *Index Translationum*, Paris: UNESCO, vols. 1–28 (1949–79); Card Catalog of the Harvard College Library; Union Catalog of Harvard University; *General Catalogue of Printed Books to 1955 of the British Museum*, London, 1964; *Catalogue Général des Livres Imprimés de la Bibliothèque Nationale*, Paris, tome 191, 1965; The Library of the Tolstoy Foundation at Valley Cottage, New York; Tokyo University Library reference desk, Tokyo, Japan; and *The Literatures of the World in English Translation* (New York: New York Public Library, 1967), vol. 2, *The Slavic Literatures*.

Index